2020 edition

Economics

FOR THE IB DIPLOMA

Constantine Ziogas
Marily Apostolakou

OXFORD
UNIVERSITY PRESS

OXFORD
UNIVERSITY PRESS

Great Clarendon Street, Oxford, OX2 6DP, United Kingdom

Oxford University Press is a department of the University of Oxford. It furthers the University's objective of excellence in research, scholarship, and education by publishing worldwide. Oxford is a registered trade mark of Oxford University Press in the UK and in certain other countries

British Library Cataloguing in Publication Data
Data available

978 1 38 200942 3

1 3 5 7 9 10 8 6 4 2

Paper used in the production of this book is a natural, recyclable product made from wood grown in sustainable forests. The manufacturing process conforms to the environmental regulations of the country of origin.

Printed in China

Acknowledgements

The publisher and authors would like to thank the following for permission to use photographs and other copyright material:

Cover: Johan Siebke/Alamy Stock Photo.

Artwork by Aptara.

Every effort has been made to contact copyright holders of material reproduced in this book. Any omissions will be rectified in subsequent printings if notice is given to the publisher.

Contents

Glossary of key terms:
www.oxfordsecondary.com/9781382009423

1.1 What is economics?

Economics as a social science

The social nature of economics

Social sciences are academic disciplines that systematically study human behaviour from different perspectives and include psychology, anthropology, political science and others. Economics is one of the social sciences as it is concerned with human actions and social relationships while deploying the social scientific method, which refers to the collection and analysis of data and the formulation of testable and falsifiable hypotheses about social phenomena.

Microeconomics and macroeconomics

Economics is divided into two main branches microeconomics and macroeconomics –"micro" and "macro" are Greek words meaning small and large respectively.

- **Microeconomics** is concerned with the individual parts of the economy; it deals with individual units within the economy such as firms, consumers or markets.

- **Macroeconomics** is concerned with the economy as a whole; it deals with aggregates such as the overall level of unemployment, total output of an economy and its growth through time and the average price level.

The nine central concepts

The nine key concepts that are central to economics and that we will be discussing throughout this book are as follows.

Scarcity

Scarcity is fundamental to economics, as it is the problem all societies face. It refers to the excess of human wants over what can actually be produced to fulfill these wants. Human wants are unlimited. In contrast, the resources available to fulfill these wants are limited.

Choice

Since resources are scarce, not all wants can be satisfied. Choices must therefore be made. Societies have to choose between which goods or services to produce and how much of each they want. Economics is thus also concerned with choices over competing alternatives together with their current and future consequences.

Efficiency

Scarce resources must be used in the best possible way to produce the combinations of goods and services that are optimum for society. This is known as allocative efficiency. At the same time, it is important to use resources in a way that ensures minimum waste. This is known as technical efficiency.

Equity

Equity refers to the idea of fairness. Fairness is an elusive concept, as it means different things to different people. In economics, inequity is often interpreted to refer to inequality, which may apply to how income or wealth is distributed in a society. Promoting equity is a significant issue for societies. The extent to which markets or governments should, or are able to, create greater equity or less inequality in an economy is an area of much debate.

Economic well-being

Economic well-being relates to the living standards enjoyed by the members of an economy and includes the dimensions:

- security in terms of income, wealth, employment and shelter

- the ability to meet basic needs (food, housing, health care, transportation, education, childcare, clothing)

- the ability to make economic choices and feel a sense of security and personal fulfillment with personal finances and employment

- the ability to maintain all the above over time.

Sustainability

Sustainability refers to the ability of the present generation to meet its needs without compromising the ability of future generations to meet their own needs. It relates to the idea that current generations should be good stewards of the environment.

Change

The economic world is not static; it continuously changes. In terms of economic theory, economics focuses not on the level of a certain economic variable but on the change in that variable from one situation to another. With respect to the study of real-world phenomena, it is always subject to continuous change at institutional, structural, technological, economic and social levels.

Interdependence

Economic agents such as consumers, producers, governments and nations interact with each other. Any action of any economic agent will impact other agents, indicating that all economic agents are interdependent. The intended and unintended consequences of these interdependencies must therefore be considered.

Intervention

Intervention refers to government involvement in the workings of markets despite markets being considered as the best mechanism to organize economic activity. Markets often do fail, creating room for government intervention. Note that not only is the extent of government intervention a contentious subject of debate but also there is no guarantee that the outcome of any intervention will improve market outcomes.

The problem of scarcity and choice

Scarcity

Scarcity is the fundamental problem that all societies face. It refers to the excess of human wants over what can actually be produced to fulfill these wants. Human wants are unlimited, as individuals typically prefer to have more and better goods and more services. Yet, it is not possible to produce all of the goods and services to satisfy all wants. This is due to the fact that resources are limited.

Resources (factors of production)

Resources refer to whatever is used to produce goods and services and are also known as factors of production. There are four factors of production, as defined below.

- **Land and raw materials** are inputs into production provided by nature, for example agricultural and non-agricultural land, forests, pastures, mineral deposits, oil, natural gas, lakes and rivers. The world's land area and raw materials are limited. Some resources, such as oil and coal deposits, are non-renewable: if they are used now, they will not be available in the future. Other resources, for example forests (timber) and the stock of fish, are renewable.

- **Labour** is the human input, both physical and mental, into production. The labour force is, at any point in time, limited both in number and in skills. The total number of people available for work is referred to as the labour force or working population.

- **Capital** includes manufactured resources; in other words, produced means of production. The world has a limited stock of capital (a limited supply of factories, machines, tools and other equipment). Note that the meaning of capital in economics is different from that used in ordinary speech where people refer to capital as money.

- **Entrepreneurship** is the willingness and ability that some individuals have to take risks and to manage the other three factors of production. Entrepreneurship is related but not identical to management. When a new venture is being considered, risks exist. They involve the unknown future. Someone must assess these risks and make judgments about whether or not to undertake them. The people who do so are called entrepreneurs.

Choice

Scarcity has an important consequence. Scarcity necessitates choice. Societies must choose between which goods or services to produce and how much of each they want given the available resources. For example, society cannot enjoy all the books and all the tables it wants because the number of trees required to produce these two goods is limited. It somehow has to decide how many books and how many tables it wants to produce. If there were no scarcity, no choices would have to be made.

The problem of scarcity has a second important consequence. Since resources are scarce, it is important to produce the combination of goods and services that society values the most and also to avoid wasting any scarce resources.

Scarcity and sustainability

The concept of sustainability is closely related to the environmental effects of current patterns of production and resource allocation. The fact that virgin forests are disappearing (being cut down for timber or firewood) or that fish stocks in many parts of the world are severely depleted or that the atmosphere is becoming so polluted demonstrates the current impact of human activities on the environment. Such activities pose a threat to sustainability, as resources will not be available for others to use in the future. Given that resources are also scarce it is of great importance to use them in a sustainable manner. The goal should be preserving and even increasing or improving the available stock of natural resources.

Opportunity cost

The cost of choice

Every choice involves sacrifice. For example, choosing to produce corn using the available land implies that some other agricultural product, for example wheat, has been sacrificed. This alternative foregone is the opportunity cost of that choice. The opportunity cost of choosing any activity is thus the value of the next best alternative sacrificed. If resources were unlimited, no sacrifices would be necessary, and the opportunity cost of producing any good or service would be zero.

Economic goods versus free goods

Economic goods are goods and services that require scarce resources to be sacrificed in order for them to be produced. In contrast to economic goods, free goods have a zero opportunity cost of production, as there were no scarce resources sacrificed in their production. There are very few real-world examples, perhaps seawater and air. Note that goods available at a zero price are not free in the economist's sense if scarce resources have been used up to produce them.

The basic economic questions

Scarcity forces every economy to answer three fundamental questions, independently of their level of economic development or the economic system adopted.

1. **What to produce?** Choices must be made in all economies about which goods will be produced and in what quantities.

2. **How to produce?** All economies must make choices on how to use their resources in order to produce goods and services. Should a good be produced using more labour and less capital (machines) or perhaps rely more on capital and less on labour?

3. **For whom?** All economies must make choices about how the goods and services produced are to be distributed among the population. Should all enjoy education and health services? Should all enjoy the same amount of all goods?

Means of answering the economic questions

Markets versus government intervention

A market should be thought of as a mechanism that can provide answers to the three fundamental questions. For example, the market can determine:

- whether this good or that good will be produced and in what quantities

- which production technology a firm should use to produce a good or a service
- how much income the owner of each factor of production will earn.

Yet, there is no guarantee that the market outcome is the best outcome from society's point of view. Sometimes the market as a mechanism succeeds and results in the best possible answers for society to these questions. Many other times, the market as a mechanism fails. For example, markets may lead to too much pollution, or not enough libraries; they may lead to unacceptably high rates of unemployment, or to inadequate health care for lower income households; they may lead to excessively risky lending practices by financial institutions, or to not enough basic scientific research. When the market fails it automatically creates a role for the government to step in and attempt to correct the market failure. The purpose of government intervention is thus to help markets function better. However, there is no *a priori* guarantee that the answers governments provide are necessarily better, as government failure is also possible.

Economic systems: free market economy, command economy, mixed economy

The market mechanism and government intervention explained above are two ways through which the basic economic questions can be answered. We can in turn distinguish between the types of organization of each economy. There are two extreme cases: the free-market economy and the command economy.

In the **free-market economy**, markets through the interaction of households and firms answer the three fundamental questions. Households decide what goods to consume. Firms decide what goods to produce and what resources to use. Then markets ensure that these decisions are coordinated.

In the **command economy**, the state owns all capital and land. This means that the state answers the three fundamental questions.

Between these extremes are mixed economies. In a mixed economy the answers to the three fundamental questions are given partly by the market and partly by the state. In practice all economies are mixed; yet, the roles and importance of the state and of markets can differ substantially.

The production possibilities curve (PPC) model

The production possibilities curve (PPC), also referred to as the production possibilities frontier (PPF), is the first economic model we will study.

Assumptions of the model

The production possibilities curve (PPC) provides a visual account of an economy at a point in time. It refers to a country with a fixed amount of resources and some level of technology producing only two goods or services. It is unrealistic but still, as you will see, powerful enough to illustrate a number of key concepts.

Figure 1.1.1 will help you to visualize a PPC. Assume that an economy devotes all of its resources to the production of two goods: X and Y (X and Y can be any goods or services such as wheat and cotton, or health care and national defence).

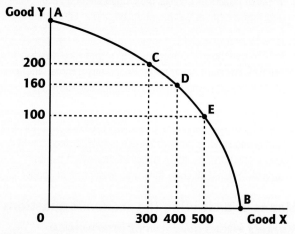

Figure 1.1.1 The PPC

The PPC shows for each amount of one good produced, the maximum amount of the other good that can be produced given its resources and its technology. For instance, if 300 units of good X are produced then this economy can produce at the most 200 units of good X if it fully uses all of its resources with its technology.

Choice, opportunity cost and scarcity

The PPC also illustrates choice and opportunity cost. As Figure 1.1.1 shows, if the economy chooses to produce more of good X it will have to sacrifice the production of some of good Y. This is shown by *moving along* the PPC from point C to point D. This sacrifice of good Y is the opportunity cost of producing the additional amount of X. Specifically, we realize that the opportunity cost of producing an additional 100 units of good X (400 units instead of 300 units) is the 40 units of good Y (160 instead of 200) that must be foregone.

It is because of scarcity that the PPC is negatively sloped: to produce more of X, less of Y can be produced as scarce resources will need to be diverted from the production of Y to the production of X. If scarcity were not the case, then the idea of a PPC would make no sense as any combination of the two goods could be produced.

Increasing opportunity costs

The PPC also illustrates the phenomenon of increasing opportunity costs. The opportunity cost of producing more and more units of good X is ever-increasing quantities of good Y sacrificed. As already mentioned, when moving from point C to point D the opportunity cost of producing an additional 100 units of good X is the 40 units of good Y that must be foregone. Now consider moving from point D to point E. The opportunity cost of producing an additional 100 units of good X (500 units instead of 400 units) is the 60 units of good Y (100 instead of 160) that are sacrificed. Producing these additional 100 units of good X is now costlier as 60 units instead of 40 units of good Y have been sacrificed. This means that an economy producing more and more of one good is forced to sacrifice *increasing* amounts of the other good.

The reason for this is that resources tend to be specialized. As the economy concentrates more and more of its production on one good, it must start using resources that are less and less suitable for its production (that is, resources that would have been more appropriate to produce the other good). The PPC is concave (bowed-in towards the origin) rather than being a negatively sloped straight line exactly because opportunity cost increases as more and more of X is produced.

Actual growth

What if the economy is operating inside the PPC producing a combination like point A shown in Figure 1.1.2? Then the available resources are not being fully utilized; for example there is unemployment. Point A is therefore an inefficient production combination. Lower unemployment in the country and, more generally, more efficient use of existing resources will allow the economy to move to another combination towards the northeast, closer to the curve itself.

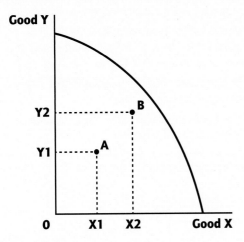

Figure 1.1.2 Actual growth

The movement from point A to point B depicts economic growth as this movement illustrates an increase in the economy's actual output. Point B reflects production of more of good X and more of good Y compared to point A (as X2 > X1 and Y2 > Y1). This increase in actual output represents economic growth.

Potential growth

Economic growth can also be illustrated through an outward shift of the PPC, as shown in Figure 1.1.3.

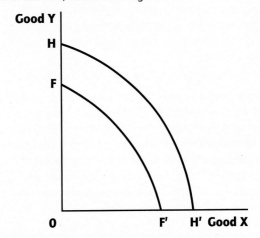

Figure 1.1.3 Potential growth

The production possibilities of this economy have expanded and the PPC has shifted from FF' to HH'. Given that each point represents a specific combination of output, it should be clear that this economy is now in a position to produce and enjoy combinations of good X and of good Y that were previously unattainable. Such a shift is possible if the quantity or quality of available resources increases or improves and/or if the available technology advances.

Modelling the economy

The circular flow of income model

The circular flow model is a simplified representation of how the basic decision-making units of an economy (households, firms, the government and, in an open economy, the foreign sector) interact.

At first, consider an economy with only households and firms. Households own all factors of production, which they offer to firms. In exchange for the factors of production, firms make payments to households in the form of rents (for land), wages (for labour), interest (for capital) and profits (for entrepreneurship). The sum of these payments makes up national income. Firms use the factors of production to produce goods and services, which they offer to households, and so households make expenditures on the goods and services produced by firms.

In this basic view of the economy there are transactions that take place by two kinds of flows: real flows of factors of production and goods or services in one direction, and monetary flows of factor payments (income) and spending on goods or services in the opposite direction. The real flows are shown in grey and the monetary flows in blue in Figure 1.1.4.

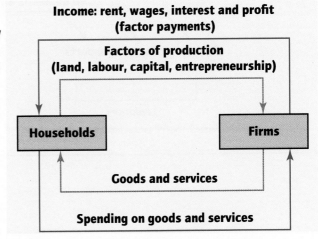

Figure 1.1.4 Transactions: real flows and monetary flows

The monetary flows described above must be equal as it is initially assumed that there is no "tomorrow" so all income generated must be spent. The income that flows from firms to households, as payments made for the use of the factors of production, must be equal to the spending by households that flows back to firms as payment for the goods and services produced. This is the circular flow of income.

If there is a "next period" then part of the income generated may be saved—a leakage from this circular flow—while it is not only households that spend on domestic output but also firms that spend on capital goods (that is, investment spending occurs). This latter expenditure is an injection to the circular flow. Where did this injection come from? The answer is that banks or financial intermediaries attract savings and then lend firms the funds they need to finance their investments.

It follows that the flow in this system will neither increase nor decrease if injections are equal to leakages. In this simplified version of an economy, without government and without a foreign sector, the equilibrium condition for national income (Y) is:

$$I = S$$

If a government is added then part of the income generated in this economy may not be spent because it leaks out of the circular flow of income in the form of taxes (T). On the other hand, injections into the circular flow will also include government expenditures (G) on domestically produced output. Domestic output in this model can be bought by households and firms as well as the government. The equilibrium condition therefore becomes:

$$(I + G) = (S + T)$$

Lastly, if we make this model more realistic and add a foreign sector then we have one more source of expenditures on domestic output, namely the expenditures foreigners make on it. Now, not only do domestic households, firms and the government spend on domestic output but also foreigners. These expenditures foreigners make on domestic output constitute the export revenues (X) of the economy and they are an injection to its circular flow. On the other hand, part of the income generated in this economy may now be spent on foreign output. This spending represents our imports (M) and is a leakage to the circular flow. The equilibrium condition becomes:

$$(I + G + X) = (S + T + M)$$

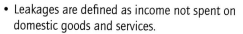

Recap
Leakages and injections

- Leakages are defined as income not spent on domestic goods and services.
- Injections can be thought of as expenditures on domestic goods and services not originating from households.
- If injections into the circular flow are equal to leakages from the circular flow then the level of national income will not change.
- If injections are larger than leakages then national income will tend to increase.
- If injections are smaller than leakages national income will tend to decrease.

A simplified representation of the circular flow is shown in Figure 1.1.5.

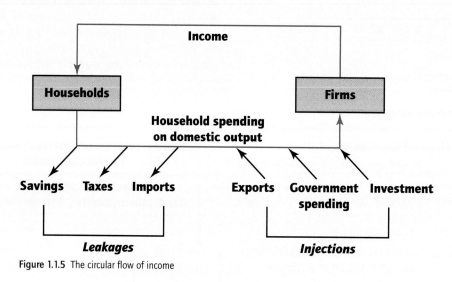

Figure 1.1.5 The circular flow of income

1.2 How do economists approach the world?

Economic methodology

Economists frequently distinguish between "positive" and "normative" economics.

The role of positive economics

Positive economics is concerned with the development and testing of positive statements about the world that are objective and verifiable. A positive statement is a statement of fact. It can be proven right or wrong. "Unemployment is rising" and "Inflation will be over 6% by next year" are examples of positive statements.

- **The use of logic:** positive economic thinking relies on the use of logic. Economists use careful reasoning in order to draw out potential implications for economic behaviour. Very often, economic reasoning is expressed through mathematical models.

- **The use of hypotheses:** economists make general hypotheses about the causes of economic phenomena—for example, that consumer demand will rise when consumer incomes rise. These hypotheses are typically based on observations.

- **Empirical evidence:** once a hypothesis has been formulated it can then be tested against empirical evidence. Empirical evidence refers to the collection of real-world observations and numerical data.

Consider the following example of how the above can be applied to an economic issue.

- We have the following information about the world: supermarkets are selling more organic apples than before—and we want to know why this is the case.

- Next we state a hypothesis: the volume of organic apples that a supermarket will sell rises if the price at which they are sold is reduced.

- Then we test our hypothesis by looking for evidence to support the link between volume of sales at different prices in different countries and for different time periods.

- If the evidence supports the hypothesis we accept it, and move on to more refined hypotheses, such as those relating to how big the response by consumers is to price changes.

- If the evidence does not support the hypothesis, we reject it and then modify it.

This process of trial and error gradually leads to a theory that fits well with experience.

- **The use of theories:** economists formulate theories to explain how the economic world works. A theory is a well-substantiated explanation of an aspect of the economic world that can incorporate hypotheses and evidence. It should be noted that a theory can never be as complex and rich as the reality it seeks to explain, so theory is about simplification.

- **The use of models:** theories give rise to models, which are analytical tools used to illustrate theories and to show simplified relationships between various economic variables. Most models can be described, but they can also be represented with diagrams and with simple or advanced mathematics. The aim is to draw conclusions from the constructed models.

- **The ceteris paribus assumption:** an important part of many models is the assumption of ceteris paribus, a Latin phrase that means "other things equal" or "all else constant". In order to focus on the possible relationship between two economic variables, in economics it is often assumed that no other variables change. Of course, in the real world, many things are usually changing at the same time.

- **Refutation:** theories and models can be judged according to how successful they are in explaining and predicting. If the data and the empirical evidence do not support a hypothesis then it must be rejected or modified. This process is referred to as refutation.

The role of normative economics

Normative economics relate to opinions or points of view. A normative statement is a value judgment: a statement about what ought to be, about whether something is good or bad, desirable or undesirable. "It is right to tax the rich more than the poor" and "The government ought to reduce inflation" are examples of normative statements. They cannot be accepted or rejected by a simple appeal to the facts as positive economic statements and theories can. If a statement or a theory cannot be tested and refuted or accepted then it is a normative statement or theory.

- **Value judgments in policy-making:** it is important to realize that economists practising positive economics do, however, make value judgments. Any analysis involves an element of subjectivity. First, even what to analyse and how to analyse it often depend upon the subjective views of the analyst regarding what is, and what is not, important. In addition, economists can contribute to questions of policy based on their value judgments; that is, they can advise policymakers of which policies to pursue depending on the issues faced. For example, economists may suggest that a policy of increasing government expenditure will reduce unemployment.

- **The meaning of equity and equality:** equitable does not mean equal. It means fair—but fairness means different things to different people. Equity is therefore a normative concept. The ideas of equality and equity often arise in relation to the distribution of income. Equality in the distribution of income is where each individual in the economy receives the same share of income. Equity is where income is distributed in a way that is considered to be fair or just. The problem with this, however, is that people have different notions of fairness. For example, a rich person may well favour a much higher degree of inequality than a poor person. As a result, both terms are often being used interchangeably, and equity in the distribution of income is often interpreted as less inequality in the share of income received by members of society.

Economic thought

Economic ideas have originated way back in time, and are known to have been important topics in ancient Greece and the Middle East. In fact, the word *economy* can be traced back to the Greek word *oikonomia* (= οικονομία), which in turn is composed of two words: *oikos*, which is usually translated as *household*; and *nemein*, which is best translated as *management and dispensation*. Thus, the cursory story usually goes, the term *oikonomia* referred to *household management* and while this was in some loose way linked to the idea of budgeting, it has little or no relevance to contemporary economics.

Still, scholars in the Antiquity and the Middle Ages thought a great deal about trade, money, prices and interest rates, but an autonomous discipline only developed toward the late 17th to early 18th centuries. Despite the interest of the early literature, a detailed account of it would be beyond the scope of this section. Instead the review of economic thought will start from the late 18th century. Focus will be on **Adam Smith (1723-1790)**, who is widely regarded as one founder of the discipline; the remainder of this section will outline the development of economic thought in the 19th, 20th and into the 21st centuries.

18th century

In his 1776 *Wealth of Nations*, Adam Smith laid the foundations of what would become basic principles of economists' understanding of individual behaviour, the market mechanism and the role of markets in relation to governments.

Smith was the first to characterize individual economic behaviour explicitly as self-interested behaviour, admitting that it is people's desire for a gain that explains work, production and ultimately the existence of an economic system: "It is not from the benevolence of the butcher, the brewer, or the baker that we expect our dinner, but from their regard to their own interest".

His work also contributed to shaping economists' view of the market as a mechanism that ensures that individual decisions are consistent with one another and lead to an orderly result. Adam Smith's "invisible hand" has often been recognized as an effective representation of this mechanism. This is also known as the laissez-faire approach that relates to the idea that markets should be allowed to operate freely. While acknowledging the merits of the market, Smith did not deny the need for a solid government. In particular, he insisted that governments should ensure the basic conditions that allow markets to function properly.

19th century

Adam Smith's work stimulated much reflection that shaped economic thinking of the 19th century. Economists of this time period are often referred to as "classical" economists.

Early 19th century classical economists were mainly interested in production and supply as well as in the relationship between wages and profits, while they placed relatively less emphasis on consumption and demand. From the second half of the 19th century onwards, however, increased emphasis was put on consumption rather than production only, with the introduction of the concept of utility as a measure of individual satisfaction from the consumption of goods or services. Below is an outline of a few of the main contributors of the Classical school.

Alfred Marshall (1842-1924) is renowned for developing the framework of demand and supply. Marshall focused on the study of a competitive market and illustrated with the help of price-quantity diagrams that the intersection of supply and demand identifies equilibrium where the market clears. The equilibrium approach is known as the "scissors" analysis where demand and supply resemble the two blades of a pair of scissors.

William Stanley Jevons (1835-1882) advanced the so-called marginal revolution. He distinguished between total utility and marginal utility—namely, the change in the level of utility that results from a given increase in the quantity of the good. Marginal utility was thought to diminish with the quantity consumed. The importance of thinking in terms of marginal changes rather than total proved so useful to account for utility and demand that it was subsequently extended to supply with the concepts of marginal productivity and marginal cost of production.

Jean-Baptiste Say (1767-1832) is best known for Say's Law that in its simplest formulation states that supply creates its own demand. There are several interpretations of this law. Nevertheless, Say wrote: "it is production which opens a demand for products ... . Thus the mere circumstance of the creation of one product immediately opens a vent for other products". In other words, Say claimed that production is the source of demand. One's ability to demand goods and services derives from the income generated by one's own acts of production. Wealth is created by production not by consumption.

The Marxist critique was influenced by classical authors but at the same time critical of them, **Karl Marx (1818-1883)** highlighted the conflict between labour and capital, and the historical tendencies that brought about the modern economic system but that would also generate tensions that eventually would bring about its collapse. His work was the most widely adhered-to critique of market economics during much of the 19th and 20th centuries. Marx's *Das Kapital* (also known as *Capital*), published in 1867, attracted many followers in economics and also inspired political action directed at radical social, economic and political change.

20th century

In the aftermath of the Great Depression, macroeconomics also entered the scene bringing along the Keynesian "revolution". **John Maynard Keynes (1883-1946)** is perhaps the most influential economist of the 20th century. He changed the relationship between government and the economy and stressed the need for government intervention and stabilization policies. Keynes "General Theory" was published in 1936. In the Keynesian framework no endogenous forces exist that restore full employment. Instead of believing in "supply creating its own demand" (Say's law), Keynes turned things inside out, postulating that it is effective demand that determines the equilibrium level of real output in an economy. If, for whatever reason, aggregate demand proves insufficient to establish full employment then a market economy will suffer a system-wide failure, as it will be unable on its own to restore full employment conditions. As such, there is an active role for the government. Through fiscal policy the government can stabilize the economy and achieve full employment. Keynesian interventionist ideas reigned until the mid 1970s but for many they have been resurrected in the 2008–09 global financial crisis and again in 2020 in the Covid-19 crisis.

In the 1970s, monetarism and the monetarist counter-revolution emerged at the University of Chicago with Nobel Prize Laureate **Milton Friedman (1912–2006)** being the most widely known advocate of monetarist ideas. Friedman strongly opposed many of the policy proposals by the Keynesian economists. He argued for deregulation in most areas of the economy, calling for a return to the free market. The idea behind this view is that the government creates more problems than it solves. Monetarism spread widely in the early 1980s and had a strong influence on policy-making. Keynesian ideas did not completely vacate the scene, though: many became convinced that government policies can still have a temporary effect and that the Keynesian framework of analysis applies in the short run, while the monetarist framework applies in the long run.

21st century

One branch of economics that has seen considerable growth in recent years is **behavioural economics**. Behavioural economists have challenged the conventional rational decision-making approach and have studied the effects of psychological, cognitive, emotional, cultural and social factors on the economic decisions of individuals and businesses. Behavioural economic analysis extends the traditional model in an attempt to provide a better, more realistic explanation of human decision-making. Some researchers, for example, have focused on how happiness and individual satisfaction, as well as prosocial and cooperative attitudes, may be important determinants of individual behaviour that were not fully accounted for in the standard economic model.

In addition, over recent years sustainability has emerged as an important concept due to the growing awareness regarding the interdependencies that exist between the economy, society and the environment. In fact, sustainable development requires a balance between the economic, social and environmental dimensions. For this reason the idea of moving towards a **circular economy** has emerged. In a circular economy goods and services are designed in a way that allows them to be reused, either in the biological or technical cycles. Products are manufactured in a way so they can be disassembled and materials can either be broken down by nature or returned to production. The goal is to throw nothing away and to reduce the need for purchasing new commodities, while production and transportation should be best achieved with renewable energy.

2.1 Markets—demand

The interaction of consumers and producers determines the market price of each product. Markets are institutions that permit the interaction between buyers and sellers. They determine which goods and services will be produced in an economy and so how scarce resources will be allocated. Changes in market conditions therefore result in changes in market prices. These changes set off a chain of events leading to more or less of the good being produced and consequently to a new allocation of scarce resources. To analyse how product markets function we need to examine first the behaviour of consumers and then the behaviour of producers.

Definition of demand

The demand for a good is an analytical way of summarizing the behaviour of buyers in a market. Specifically, demand can be defined as the relationship between various possible prices of a good and the corresponding quantities that consumers are willing and able to purchase per time period, ceteris paribus.

The law of demand

The relationship between price and quantity per period of time is inverse (negative), meaning that if the price increases then quantity demanded will decrease as consumers will be willing and able to buy less per period. This inverse relationship between price and quantity demanded is referred to as the law of demand. The law of demand states that if the price of a good rises then quantity demanded per period will fall, ceteris paribus.

HL

Behind the law of demand
The substitution and income effects

The law of demand holds because of the substitution and income effect.

- **The substitution effect:** if the price of a good rises, the good will now cost more than alternative or substitute goods. That is to say, all other goods automatically become relatively cheaper and so people will tend to switch to these substitutes. This explains why following an increase in price, quantity demanded decreases.

- **The income effect:** if the price of a good rises, consumers feel poorer; they will not be able to afford to buy so much of the good with their income. That is to say, the purchasing power of their income (their "real income") falls and so people will tend to buy less of that good. Again, this explains why following an increase in price, quantity demanded decreases.

The law of diminishing marginal utility

Another explanation behind the law of demand rests on the law of diminishing marginal utility.

Utility refers to the satisfaction one gains by consuming a good or a service. The typical consumer has a fixed amount of income and he or she faces a fixed set of prices. We assume that consumers allocate their expenditures among all the goods and services that they might buy so as to gain the greatest possible utility. This means that the goal of typical consumers is to maximize their utility subject to their budget constraint (that is, income).

We will now examine the relationship between utility and the quantity consumed for an individual consumer. Marginal utility is defined as the additional satisfaction derived from consuming an additional unit of a good. The idea is simple. As one consumes additional units of a good per period (that is, per hour, per day, per week and so on), the *additional* satisfaction enjoyed decreases. If this is the case, then individuals will be willing to pay less and less to buy more and more units of a good per period of time.

The demand curve

The demand curve illustrates the relationship between the price of a good and the quantity of the good demanded over a time period. Price is measured on the vertical axis; quantity demanded is measured on the horizontal axis. Given that the relationship between price and quantity demanded is inverse (law of demand) the demand curve is downward sloping from left to right: it has a negative slope.

A demand curve can be for an individual consumer or more usually for the whole market. The market demand derives from adding up at each price the quantities demanded by all consumers in a market. For example, at the price of $2.00, consumer A is willing and able to buy three cappuccinos per week while consumer B is willing and able to buy five cappuccinos per week. If the market consists of these two consumers then at the price of $2.00, market demand is eight cappuccinos per week. Diagrammatically the market demand curve is derived by the horizontal summation of the individual demand curves.

In Figure 2.1.1, if the price per unit is P1 then consumers will be willing and able to buy Q1 units per period, ceteris paribus. If the price increases to P2 then consumers will be willing and able to buy Q2 units per period, ceteris paribus.

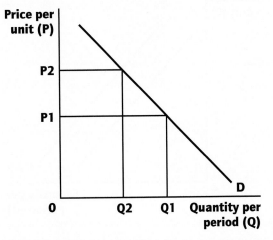

Figure 2.1.1 A typical market demand curve

Non-price determinants of demand ("shift" factors)

The non-price determinants of demand are the factors other than the good's own price that can affect demand. They are the factors that are assumed to be constant under the ceteris paribus assumption. If any of the non-price determinants of demand changes, the demand curve shifts. Particularly, if a change in one of the determinants of demand causes demand to increase then the demand curve shifts to the right. This means that at each price more quantity of the good (or service) is demanded. Or, if a change in one of the determinants of demand causes demand to decrease then the demand curve shifts to the left. This implies that at each price less quantity of the good (or service) is demanded.

The non-price determinants of demand include the following.

Income

Changes in consumers' income may affect demand.

As income rises, demand for most goods will rise. Such goods are called normal goods. Therefore, an increase in income will lead to an increase in the demand for a normal good and the demand curve will shift to the right from D1 to D2 as shown in Figure 2.1.2a.

For some goods, typically lower quality goods, an increase in income will lead to a decrease in demand and a shift of the demand curve to the left as consumers may switch to other, higher quality products. This is the case of inferior goods. The demand for inferior goods decreases when incomes increase and the demand curve shifts to the left from D1 to D2, as shown in Figure 2.1.2b.

The same good may behave as a normal good in one society or market and as an inferior good in another. For example, in a country with a generally low-income population, an increase in income may lead to an increase in the demand for used cars, whereas in another country where people have higher incomes, a further increase in income levels may lead to a decrease in the demand for used cars.

Price of related goods

Substitute goods: two goods are considered substitutes if they are in competitive consumption and consumers typically buy one or the other as the goods satisfy the same need or want. Examples include Pepsi and Coca-Cola, coffee and tea, pizza and burgers. For instance, the demand for Coca-Cola is

(a) Normal good

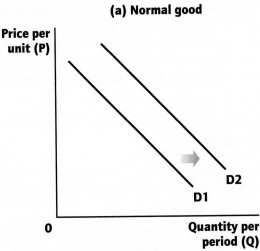

(b) Inferior good

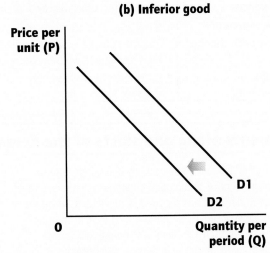

Figure 2.1.2 The effect of an increase in income on the demand for a normal and an inferior good

expected to increase if a supermarket increases the price of Pepsi. More generally, if good X and good Y are considered as substitutes then an increase in the price of good Y will lead to an increase in the demand for X. Demand for X will shift to the right from D1 to D2, as shown in Figure 2.1.3.

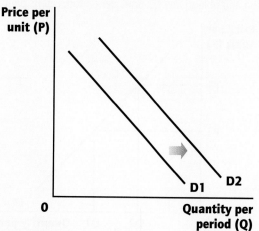

Figure 2.1.3 The effect of an increase in the price of a substitute

Complement goods: two goods are considered complements if they are consumed together ("jointly consumed"), such as peanut butter and jelly or coffee and sugar. For instance, if the price of coffee increases then the demand for sugar may decrease. More generally, if goods X and Y are considered as complements then an increase in the price of good Y will lead to a decrease in the demand for good X. Demand for X will shift to the left from D1 to D2, as shown in Figure 2.1.4.

Tastes and preferences

The more desirable people find a good, the more they will demand it. Tastes are affected by advertising, by fashion, by observing other consumers, or by considerations of health.

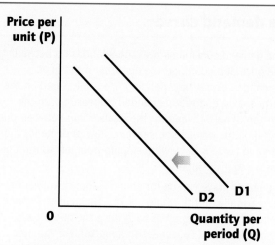

Figure 2.1.4 The effect of an increase in the price of a complement

For example, the heavy promotion of adopting a healthy eating behaviour has increased the popularity of certain products such as kale and quinoa that are deemed to be of high nutritional value. The demand for such products will increase and the demand curve will shift to the right.

Expectations of future price changes

If people expect that the price of a good is going to rise in the future, they are likely to buy more now before its price goes up. This will lead to an increase in demand and a rightward shift of the demand curve. In the same way, if consumers anticipate that the price of a product will fall in the future, they are likely to withhold their purchases now to take advantage of the lower future price. Thus, the demand for the product will now decrease and the demand curve will shift to the left.

Number of consumers

As the number of consumers in a market (or the size of a market) increases, demand for most products will tend to rise and vice versa.

Recap

Non-price determinants of demand (shift factors)	
Income	• An increase in consumers' income will lead to an increase in demand for a **normal good** and to a rightward shift of the demand curve. However, an increase in consumers' income will lead to a decrease in demand for an **inferior good** and to a leftward shift of the demand curve.
Prices of related goods	• If goods X and Y are substitutes, an increase in the price of good Y will lead to an increase in demand for X and the demand curve will shift to the right.
	• If goods X and Y are complements, an increase in the price of Y will lead to a decrease in demand for X and the demand curve will shift to the left.
Tastes and preferences	• If a good appears more attractive to consumers as a result of advertising, fashion, trends or health considerations, then demand for that good will increase and the demand curve will shift to the right.
Expectations of future price changes	• If the price of a product is expected to rise in the future, then its demand will now increase and the demand curve will shift to the right. Or, if the price is expected to fall in the future, then its demand will now decrease and the demand curve will shift to the left.
Number of consumers	• If the number of consumers in a market increases, demand will increase and the demand curve will shift to the right, and vice versa.

Movements along and shifts of the demand curve

A shift in the demand curve occurs when a determinant other than the price of the good changes; we then say that a change in demand has occurred. A movement along the demand curve occurs when there is a change in the price of the good; we then say there is a change in quantity demanded. Given an increase in price, the decrease in quantity demanded is also known as a "contraction" in demand whereas the rise in quantity demanded that follows a price decrease is also known as an "extension" of demand.

Movement along the demand curve: when the price of the good changes

Shift of the demand curve: when any of the non-price determinants of demand changes

2.2 Markets—supply

Definition of supply

The concept of supply is merely a way to summarize analytically the behaviour of firms. It is defined as the relationship between various possible prices and the corresponding quantities that firms are willing to offer per time period, ceteris paribus.

The law of supply

The relationship between price and quantity supplied per period is direct (positive), meaning that if the price increases then quantity supplied will also increase, as producers will be willing to offer more per period. This positive relationship between price and quantity supplied is referred to as the law of supply. The law of supply states that if the price rises then the quantity of a good supplied per period will increase, ceteris paribus.

HL

Behind the law of supply

The producer is assumed to seek to maximize profits. Assuming that a firm has fixed productive capacity, producing ever-increasing quantities of a good becomes more and more difficult (that is, more and more costly). This is the result of the law of diminishing marginal returns and increasing marginal costs.

More specifically, the law of diminishing marginal returns states that as more and more units of a variable factor (usually labour) are used with a fixed factor (usually capital), there is a point beyond which total product will continue to rise, but at a decreasing rate, or equivalently, that marginal product will start to decline. Marginal cost is the extra (additional) cost resulting from an increase in output; it is thus the change

in costs because of a change in output. Due to diminishing returns, the marginal cost may fall initially as there are increasing marginal returns but eventually, when diminishing returns set in, the costs will start to rise. If an additional unit of labour leads to less and less additional output, then to achieve equal additional units of output, more and more units of labour will be required. It follows that the additional cost (the marginal cost) of additional units will be increasing.

It should now be clear that if the additional cost of producing more and more units is increasing, then a firm will be willing to offer more and more units only at a higher and higher price. Thus more units will be offered per period only at a higher price, which reflects the direct relationship of the law of supply.

The supply curve

The supply curve is a graph that shows the relationship between the price of a good and the quantity of the good supplied over a given period of time. The price is measured on the vertical axis; quantity supplied is measured on the horizontal axis. Given the direct relationship between price and quantity supplied (the law of supply), the supply curve is upward sloping: it has a positive slope and can be drawn as shown in Figure 2.2.1.

A supply curve may be an individual firm's supply curve or a market supply curve (that is, the supply curve of the whole industry). As with the market demand, the market supply derives from adding up the quantities supplied at each price by all producers. So, if a market consists of 100 identical firms and each is willing to offer 200 units per month at the price of $5.00, then the market supply will be 20,000 units per month priced at $5.00 per unit.

In Figure 2.2.1, if the price is P1 then producers will be willing to offer Q1 units per period, whereas if the price

increased to P2 per unit then producers will be willing to offer Q2 units per period.

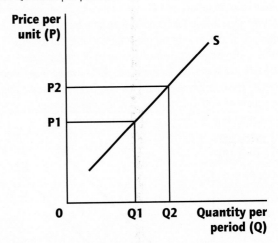

Figure 2.2.1 A typical market supply curve

Non-price determinants of supply ("shift" factors)

The non-price determinants of supply are the factors other than the good's own price that can affect supply. They are the factors that are assumed to be constant under the ceteris paribus assumption. If any of the non-price determinants of supply changes, the supply curve shifts. Particularly, if a change in one of the determinants of supply causes supply to increase then the

supply curve shifts to the right. This means that at each price more quantity of the good (or service) is supplied. Or, if a change in one of the determinants of supply causes supply to decrease then the supply curve shifts to the left. This implies that at each price less quantity of the good (or service) is supplied.

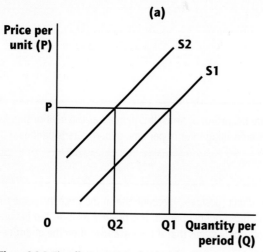

(a)

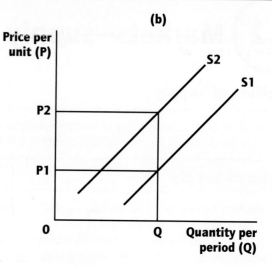

(b)

Figure 2.2.2 The effect on supply of an increase in wages paid

The non-price determinants of supply include the following.

Changes in costs of factors of production

If input prices increase (for example, if the wages paid to labour increase or the price of a raw material used in the production of the good increases) then, ceteris paribus, supply is expected to decrease. So, the supply curve is expected to shift to the left. At each price, firms will be willing to offer less, or they will be willing to offer each unit at a higher price than before.

Figure 2.2.2 shows the effect of an increase in the wages paid. Assume that the original supply curve is S1. Look at Figure 2.2.2a—before an increase in wages paid, firms were willing to offer Q1 units per period at price P. If wages paid increase then production costs will rise, so firms will be willing to offer only Q2 units per period at price P. The same holds at each price so supply decreases, shifting to the left to S2. Now refer to Figure 2.2.2b—before an increase in wages, firms were willing to offer Q units at price P1. After wages increase, firms will be willing to offer Q units only at the higher price P2. The same holds for all units so supply decreases, shifting left to S2.

Prices of related goods

Goods in joint supply: sometimes when one good is produced, another good is also produced at the same time. These are said to be goods in joint supply. A farm that is producing lambs is also producing wool. If the price of lamb meat increases in the market, lamb farmers will have an incentive to increase the quantity supplied of lambs, but at the same time the supply of wool will increase and its supply curve will shift to the right from S1 to S2, as shown in Figure 2.2.3.

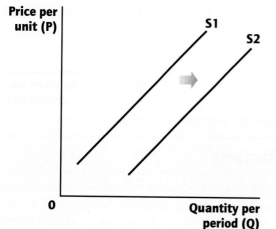

Figure 2.2.3 The effect of an increase in the price of a jointly supplied good

Goods in competitive supply: a change in the price of a good in competitive supply will also have an effect. Other goods are likely to become more profitable if their prices rise. For example, consider a farmer with a fixed amount of land using it to produce carrots and potatoes. If the price of carrots goes up, farmers may decide to reduce potato production in order to produce more carrots. The supply of potatoes will decrease and the supply curve will shift to the left from S1 to S2, as shown in Figure 2.2.4.

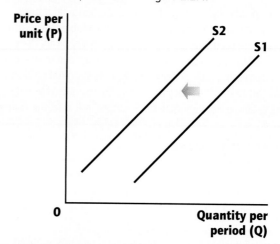

Figure 2.2.4 The effect of an increase in the price of a good in competitive supply

Indirect taxes and subsidies

Changes in government policy, such as indirect taxes and subsidies, affect costs of production. Indirect taxes and subsidies affect the cost of producing an extra unit of a good. An indirect tax is a payment to the government by firms per unit of output produced, whereas a subsidy is a payment to firms by the government per unit of output produced. An indirect tax will increase production costs and lead to a decrease in supply and a shift of the supply curve to the left, whereas a subsidy will decrease production costs and lead to an increase in supply and a shift of the supply curve to the right.

Expectations of future price changes

If the price of the product is expected to rise, producers may temporarily reduce supply now. They are likely to build up their stocks and only release them on to the market when the price rises in the future. At the same time they may install new machines or take on more labour, so that they can be ready to supply more when the price has risen.

Changes in technology

Improved technology allows firms to offer more units of the good at the same price, increasing supply and shifting the supply curve to the right. Improved technology decreases the cost of producing each additional unit of the good.

Number of firms

Changes in the size of the market (the number of firms) affect supply. As more firms join a market, for example, supply will tend to increase, shifting the supply curve to the right, since at each price more units will be offered.

Recap

Non-price determinants of supply (shift factors)	
Changes in costs of factors of production	• An increase in the costs of factors of production (such as wages, raw material prices) will lead to a decrease in supply and to leftward shift of the supply curve.
Prices of related goods	• If goods X and Y are in joint supply, an increase in the price of good Y will lead to an increase in the supply of good X and to a rightward shift of the supply curve. • If goods X and Y are in competitive supply, an increase in the price of good Y will lead to a decrease in the supply of good X and to a leftward shift of the supply curve.
Indirect taxes and subsidies	• An indirect tax will increase costs of production, leading to a decrease in supply and to a leftward shift of the supply curve. • A subsidy will decrease costs of production, leading to an increase in supply and to rightward shift of the supply curve.
Expectations of future price changes	• If the price of the product is expected to rise, producers may reduce supply now and the supply curve will shift to the left.
Changes in technology	• Improved technology will lead to an increase in supply, shifting the supply curve to the right.
Number of firms	• If more firms enter a market, supply will increase, shifting the supply curve to the right.

Movements along and shifts of the supply curve

The principle here is the same with demand curves. The effect of a change in price is illustrated by a movement along the supply curve. If any other determinant of supply changes (such as costs of production, number of producers) the whole supply curve will shift. A rightward shift illustrates an increase in supply. A leftward shift illustrates a decrease in supply.

Movement along the supply curve: when the price of the good changes

Shift of the supply curve: when any of the non-price determinants of supply changes

2.3 Competitive market equilibrium

Market equilibrium

The price at which a good will be sold in a competitive market will be determined by the interaction between consumers and producers (that is, by the interaction of demand and supply).

Consider the market demand and supply shown in Figure 2.3.1. What will be the price that will prevail in the market?

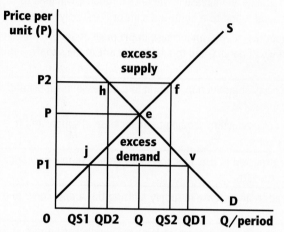

Figure 2.3.1 The determination of equilibrium price in a competitive market

If the price per unit is at P1, then quantity demanded per period exceeds quantity supplied as QD1 > QS1. In other words, at P1 consumers are willing and able to purchase a greater quantity of the good compared to the quantity producers are willing and able to offer. There is **excess demand** or, a **shortage** equal to line distance (jv). If at P1 more quantity is demanded than is supplied then the price cannot remain at that level; it will tend to increase. The effect of excess demand (or, of a shortage) is to create a tendency for the price to increase (that is, to drive the price upwards). Since there is a tendency for the price to change, P1 *cannot* be the price that will prevail in the market.

Symmetrically, if the price per unit is at P2, then quantity supplied exceeds quantity demanded as QS2 > QD2. In

other words, at P2 producers are willing and able to offer a greater quantity of the good compared to the quantity consumers are willing and able to buy. There is **excess supply** or, a **surplus** equal to line distance (hf). If at P2 more quantity is supplied than is demanded then the price cannot remain at that level; it will tend to decrease. The effect of excess supply (or, of a surplus) is to create a tendency for the price to decrease (that is, to drive the price downwards). Again, since there is a tendency for the price to change, P2 *cannot* be the price that will prevail in the market.

In fact, there is *only one* price from which there is no tendency to move away—the price where quantity demanded per period equals quantity supplied, namely P. At P there is neither excess demand nor excess supply so the market "clears". Thus, P is the price that will prevail in the market and it is called the **equilibrium price**. The corresponding quantity Q is called the **equilibrium quantity**. The equilibrium price and quantity are found at the point where the demand curve intersects the supply curve—at point e, which is the **market equilibrium**.

> If Qd > Qs there is excess demand →
> the price rises → not equilibrium
>
> If Qs > Qd there is excess supply →
> the price falls → not equilibrium
>
> If Qd = Qs the market clears → no tendency
> for the price to change → equilibrium

Info

When a market is in equilibrium, quantity demanded equals quantity supplied, and there is no tendency for the price to change. Market equilibrium is determined at the intersection of the demand and the supply curve. The price in market equilibrium is the equilibrium price, and the quantity is the equilibrium quantity.

Changes in market equilibrium

Market equilibrium will remain unchanged only so long as the demand and supply remain unchanged. If either demand or supply changes, a new equilibrium will be formed.

A change in demand

If one of the determinants of demand changes, then demand will either increase or decrease and in turn the demand curve will shift either to the right or to the left.

Figure 2.3.2a shows the case where demand for chocolate bars has increased. Initially, the market is at equilibrium point h where the equilibrium price is P1 and equilibrium quantity is Q1. A rise in consumer incomes leads to an

increase in the demand for chocolate bars, assuming that chocolate bars are a normal good. The demand curve shifts to the right from D1 to D2. At the original equilibrium price P1, there is excess demand equal to line distance (hk), as quantity demanded exceeds quantity supplied. This exerts an upward pressure on the price. As the price increases, there is a movement along the supply curve from h to g, and along the new demand curve (D2) from k to g. At g, the excess demand has been eliminated and the new equilibrium is established at a higher price P2 and a higher quantity Q2 (given by the intersection of D2 with S).

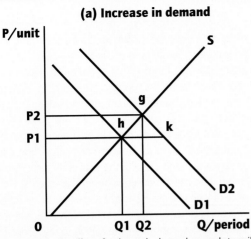

(a) Increase in demand

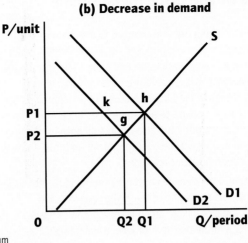

(b) Decrease in demand

Figure 2.3.2 The effect of a change in demand on market equilibrium

Figure 2.3.2b shows the case where demand for chocolate bars has decreased. Initially, the market is at equilibrium point h where the equilibrium price is P1 and equilibrium quantity is Q1. A decrease in the price of a substitute good, such as cereal bars, has decreased demand for chocolate bars. There is a leftward shift in the demand curve from D1 to D2. At the original equilibrium price P1, there is excess supply equal to line distance (hk), as quantity supplied exceeds quantity demanded. This exerts a downward pressure on price. As the price falls, there is a movement along the supply curve from h to g, and along the new demand curve (D2) from k to g. At g, the excess supply has been eliminated and the new equilibrium is established at a lower price P2, and a lower quantity Q2 (given by the intersection of D2 with S).

A change in supply

Similarly, if one of the non-price determinants of supply changes, then supply will either increase or decrease and in turn the supply curve will shift either to the right or to the left.

In Figure 2.3.3a the initial equilibrium for wheat is at j where equilibrium price and quantity are P1 and Q1. An increase in supply, say, due to an improvement in agricultural technology, shifts the supply curve from S1 to S2. At the original equilibrium price P1, there is excess supply equal to line distance (jk), since quantity supplied exceeds quantity demanded. Therefore, price begins to fall, and there results a movement along the demand curve from j to h and along the new supply curve (S2) from k to h. At h, excess supply has been eliminated and there is a lower equilibrium price, P2, but a higher equilibrium quantity, Q2 (given by the intersection of S2 and D).

A decrease in supply is shown in Figure 2.3.3b say, due to an elimination of farm subsidies. The initial equilibrium is at point j where equilibrium price and quantity are P1 and Q1. The decrease in supply is shown by a leftward shift of the supply curve from S1 to S2. At the initial price P1, there is excess demand, equal to line distance (kj). This causes an upward pressure on price, which begins to increase, causing a movement along the demand curve from j to h and along the new supply curve (S2) from k to h. Equilibrium is reached at h, where the excess demand has been eliminated, and there is a higher equilibrium price P2 and lower quantity Q2.

> A shift in one curve leads to a movement along the other curve to the new intersection point.
> - A shift in the demand curve leads to a movement along the supply curve to the new intersection point.
> - A shift in the supply curve leads to a movement along the demand curve to the new intersection point.

Both demand and supply change

Sometimes a number of determinants might change, causing both demand and supply to change. This might lead to a shift in both curves. When this happens, equilibrium simply moves from the point where the old curves intersected to the point where the new ones intersect. In such cases, the effect on equilibrium price and equilibrium quantity depends on how much demand and how much supply have changed. This can be determined diagrammatically according to which of the two shifts is larger.

(a) Increase in supply

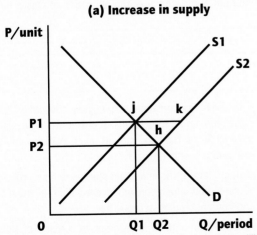

(b) Decrease in supply

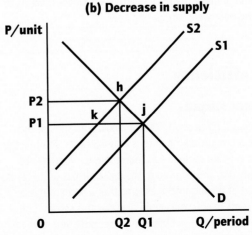

Figure 2.3.3 The effect of a change in supply on market equilibrium

The role of the price mechanism

The operation of the price mechanism, also known as the invisible hand (a phrase introduced by Adam Smith), allows markets to reach equilibrium automatically. More specifically, in a competitive market, where there are very many firms producing the same product, a change in the demand or the supply of a product leads to a change in its price. This change in price acts as a **signal** and also creates **incentives**, leading to either more or less of the good produced and thus a change in the allocation of scarce resources.

Consider the case where demand for a product has increased. For example, the spreading of the health benefits and nutritional value of kale (a green leafy vegetable) has led to an increase in the demand for kale in the market. This is shown in Figure 2.3.4.

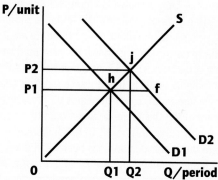

Figure 2.3.4 Increase in demand: the market for kale

Initially the market is in equilibrium at h whereby the price of kale is at P1 per unit and quantity is at Q1 per time period with some scarce resources of land, labour and capital allocated to the production of the good. The increase in demand for kale is illustrated by a rightward shift of the demand curve from D1 to D2. At P1, there is now excess demand for kale equal to the line distance (hf) that puts an upward pressure on the price of kale. The increase in the price of kale emits information and thus acts as a signal to producers of kale that

demand for kale has increased. It also creates the incentive for producers to offer more kale to the market, as it is now more profitable for them. So, as the price increases, there is an "extension" along the supply curve–from h to f. At the same time, some consumers will be cutting back on their purchases of kale or even dropping out of the market. The increase in price also leads to a decrease in quantity demanded. There is a "contraction" along the new demand curve–from f to j. As long as excess demand exists in the market for kale, its price will continue to rise. A new equilibrium is reached at j when the price of kale reaches P2 and the equilibrium quantity Q2. What effectively is happening is that the higher price of the good is signalling that consumers are willing to see resources diverted from other uses. This is just what producers do: they divert resources (such as land, labour and capital) from uses and allocate them in the production of kale. A resource reallocation takes place only as a result of the change in the price of kale.

More generally, a rise in the demand for a good raises its price and profitability. Firms respond by increasing the amount of the good offered. To do so, they divert resources from goods with lower prices to goods that have become more profitable. Therefore, society's scarce resources are reallocated. Symmetrically, a fall in demand is signalled by a fall in price. This then acts as an incentive for producers to decrease the amount of the good they offer to the market. The goods are now less profitable to produce. Resources will again be reallocated.

As such, producers and consumers acting in their own self-interest and responding only to changes in relative prices adjust their behaviour and are responsible for the new outcome. It is as if an invisible hand guides their behaviour.

We have seen that prices have a signalling and incentive role in a market. They also have a **rationing function**. If a market is free, meaning that there is no government intervention, then whoever is willing and able to pay the market-determined price will end up with the good.

Recap

The functions of the price mechanism	
The **signalling** function	Changes in price act as signals, communicating information to market participants.
The **incentive** function	Changes in price create incentives, motivating market participants to respond to the information.
The **rationing** function	The market-determined price will guarantee that the buyers who are willing and able to pay that price are the ones who will end up with the good.
The operation of the price mechanism moves markets to equilibrium and determines the allocation of scarce resources between competing uses.	

Market efficiency

Consumer surplus

You may be willing to pay $1.00 for a cold soft drink at the beach but you find that the price is only 75 cents. You buy the drink (as it is worth more to you than the price you have to pay). We say that you enjoyed a consumer surplus of 25 cents. For the sake of the argument, assume that a second unit is worth 90 cents to you. You would also buy this second unit as it is worth more to you than the market price you have to pay. The consumer surplus you enjoyed from the second unit

is 15 cents. The consumer surplus from consuming both units is therefore equal to 40 cents. You were willing to pay at the most $1.90 for the two units (as much as they were worth to you) and you ended up paying only $1.50.

More generally, the consumer surplus refers to the difference between how much consumers are willing at the most to pay and how much they actually pay.

For each Q in a demand diagram, the vertical distance to the curve illustrates how much that specific unit is worth, at the most, to consumers. Unit Q in Figure 2.3.5 is worth P dollars (or distance QH) to consumers as they would be willing to pay P dollars at the most to buy it, not a cent more. If the price was even slightly higher (say, at the level of the grey dotted line), then they would not have been willing to buy that last unit Q. Equivalently, unit Q' is worth P' to consumers (or distance Q'F) as that is the most they would be willing to pay to acquire it. The vertical distance to a demand curve measures the marginal benefit (MB) enjoyed from that unit.

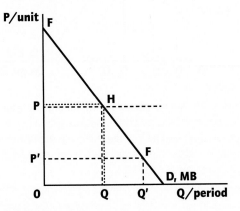

Figure 2.3.5 Consumer surplus

If it happens that the price in the market is P dollars then consumers will buy all units up until (at the limit) unit Q, as each of these units is worth more to them than the market price would require them to pay. They would not buy any units past unit Q. For example, they would not buy unit Q' as it is worth P' dollars (or distance Q'F) to them (this is as much as they would be willing to pay for it at the most) and the price (what they would be forced to pay) is higher, at P dollars. It follows that Q units are worth area (0QHF) to consumers as that is the amount they would have been willing to pay to enjoy all these units, which is the sum of all vertical distances up until unit Q. Given a market price of P dollars, they will end up paying area (0QHP) to enjoy Q units, or the price per unit times the quantity consumed. Consumer surplus is therefore area (PHF), the difference between area (0QHF) and area (0QHP).

> On a diagram, consumer surplus is the area below the demand curve and above the price line for the units of the good consumed.

Producer surplus

A firm may be willing to offer a unit of a good for $2.00. If the market price is $3.00 then the firm will certainly decide to offer that unit. We say that the firm enjoys a producer surplus equal to $1.00. Assume that the firm would have been willing to offer the next unit if the price was at least $2.20. Since the market price is $3.00 the firm would also offer this unit, enjoying from it a producer surplus of 80 cents. The producer surplus it enjoyed from offering both these units is $1.80. It required at least $4.20 to be willing to offer these units but it earned $6.00.

More generally, the producer surplus refers to the difference between the minimum producers (firms) would be willing to receive to offer some amount of the good and what they actually receive from offering this amount.

For each Q in a supply diagram, the vertical distance to the curve illustrates the minimum a firm requires to be willing to offer that specific unit. This would be nothing but the

additional cost of producing that extra unit. A firm would never accept anything less to be willing to offer an extra unit. The minimum it would accept is the cost of producing it. Later you will realize that the supply curve is nothing but the marginal cost (MC) curve of the firm.

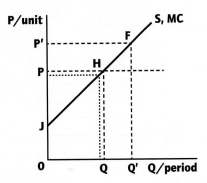

Figure 2.3.6 Producer surplus

So, for a firm to be willing to offer unit Q in Figure 2.3.6, the lowest price required is P dollars (or distance QH), not a cent less. If the price was even slightly less (say at the level of the grey dotted line), then the firm would not have been willing to offer that last unit Q. It would be willing to offer fewer units per period but not unit Q. Equivalently, for the firm to be willing to offer unit Q' the least payment required is P' (or distance Q'F).

If it so happens that the market price is P dollars per unit, then firms will be willing to offer per period all units up until and including unit Q. They would not be willing to offer unit Q' as they would require more (P' or distance Q'F) than they would get from the market. It follows that the minimum firms would require to be willing to offer Q units is area (0QHJ), which is the sum of all vertical distances up until unit Q. Given a market price of P dollars per unit, firms will actually earn area (0QHP) by selling Q units or the price per unit (P) times the quantity offered (Q). So, producer surplus is area (JHP), the difference between area (0QHP) and area (0QHJ).

> On a diagram, producer surplus is the area above the supply curve and below the price line for the units of the good produced and sold.

Social or community surplus

Social or community surplus is defined as the sum of the consumer surplus and the producer surplus. It is a measure of welfare.

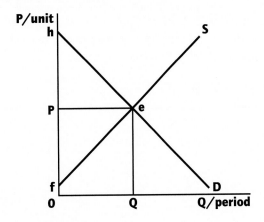

Figure 2.3.7 Social surplus

In Figure 2.3.7, given a market price P and an equilibrium quantity Q, consumer surplus is equal to area (heP) while producer surplus is area (Pef). Given the definition of social surplus it follows that it is equal to area (feh).

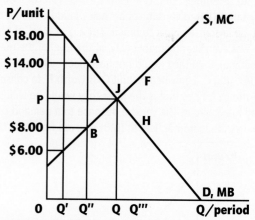

Figure 2.3.8 Allocative efficiency

Recap

Consumer surplus:	the difference between how much consumers are willing at the most to pay and how much they actually pay
Producer surplus:	the difference between the minimum producers (firms) would be willing to receive to offer some amount of the good and what they actually receive from offering this amount
Social surplus:	the sum of consumer and producer surplus

Allocative efficiency

Assume two goods: apples and oranges, and one resource, land. Determine some allocation of land, which, in turn, determines some amount of apples and some amount of oranges being produced. The question that arises is: should one more unit (a kilogram, a ton) of apples be produced? Consequently, should more land go to the production of apples? The answer will be yes if the following applies. The one more unit of apples is valued more by society (measured by how much society would be willing to pay, the vertical distance up from that quantity (Q) towards the demand curve) than what it costs society to produce it; that is, more than the value of sacrificed oranges (measured by the vertical distance up from that Q towards the supply curve).

Thus, more should be produced as long as the extra benefit to society from the increased production exceeds the extra cost it entails that reflects the value of the alternatives sacrificed. Output is optimal from society's point of view when *for the last unit*, price (= MB) is equal to marginal cost. Note that in a free competitive market, market forces themselves will lead to the optimal amount of each good being produced and consumed and thus to an optimal resource allocation from society's point of view. Social surplus (the sum of the consumer and producer surplus) is maximized. Allocative efficiency is achieved.

In Figure 2.3.8, the optimal amount of the good from society's point of view is Q units. Society would like to enjoy all units up until and including unit Q. For the last unit Q produced, P = MC, or, more generally, marginal benefit (MB) is equal to marginal cost (MC).

It is easy to understand why. Referring to Figure 2.3.8, society would want unit Q' to be produced as it is worth $18.00 to consumers, which is more than the $6.00 it would cost firms to produce. We could say that if the market did indeed produce that unit, society would gain a surplus of $12.00 from unit Q'. Similarly for unit Q", as it is worth more ($14.00) than it would cost to produce ($8.00); society would gain a surplus of $6.00 from unit Q". The same argument holds up until and including unit Q which is worth to consumers as much as it would cost to produce it; that is, P (= MB) = MC.

What about unit Q'''? Society would not want that unit produced as this would mean that scarce resources would not be properly used. Why? It is because that unit is worth to consumers less than it would cost to produce it. If unit Q''' were produced, society would have lost surplus from its production equal to FH. It would have lost surplus equal to area (JHF) from the production of all units QQ'''.

What if only Q" units were produced and for some reason units Q"Q were not produced and enjoyed by society? Then society would have lost the surplus represented by the area (ABJ) as all units up until unit Q are worth more than they would have cost to produce. If, by producing either less or more than Q units, a portion of social surplus is lost, it follows that by producing exactly Q units per period, social surplus is maximized.

> If, for the last unit produced, P (= MB) = MC, then allocative efficiency is achieved and social surplus is maximized.

Calculating consumer and producer surplus

You may be asked to calculate the consumer and producer surplus from a diagram. The following exercise will take you through the process.

Consider Figure 2.3.9, which depicts the market for quinoa in Peru.

The price per kilo of quinoa is in sol (the Peruvian currency) and the quantity is in thousands of kilos.

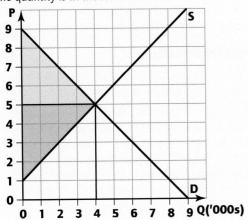

Figure 2.3.9 The market for quinoa in Peru

Identify the equilibrium price and quantity

In this case the equilibrium price is sol 5 and the equilibrium quantity is 4,000 kilos.

Calculate the consumer surplus

The consumer surplus is the area of the triangle below the demand curve and above the price line. The area of a triangle is $\frac{\text{base} \times \text{height}}{2}$. In this case the base is 4,000 kilos and the height is sol 4. Thus:

$$\frac{4,000 \times 4}{2} = \text{sol } 8,000$$

Calculate the producer surplus

The producer surplus is the area of the triangle above the supply curve and below the price line. The area of a triangle is $\frac{\text{base} \times \text{height}}{2}$. In this case the base is 4,000 kilos and the height is sol 4. Thus:

$$\frac{4,000 \times 4}{2} = \text{sol } 8,000$$

In this case consumer and producer surplus are the same amount, but this may not necessarily be the case.

2.4 Critique of the maximizing behaviour of consumers and producers (HL)

Rational consumer choice

When analysing consumer behaviour, economists work with a model of rational consumer choice. The assumptions underlying rational consumer choice are explained here.

Consumers decide upon the purchase of different baskets of goods and services based on their preferences.

- Preferences are considered complete: that is, the consumer is able to rank any two baskets of goods and services. For example, the consumer can state whether he or she prefers basket A to basket B or prefers basket B to basket A.
- Preferences are transitive, meaning that the consumer makes choices that are consistent with each other. For instance, if a consumer prefers basket A to basket B and basket B to basket E, then it is expected that the consumer prefers basket A to basket E.
- More is better; having more of a good is better for the consumer.

Utility maximization

The goal of the rational consumer is to maximize utility while satisfying the budget constraint. That is, each consumer will choose the basket of goods and services that allows him or her to reach the highest utility (satisfaction) while being on their budget (income). This is the consumer's optimal choice.

Perfect information

Consumers have perfect information. That is to say there is full awareness by consumers about alternative products and prices, which reduces uncertainty surrounding choices.

According to standard economic theory, rational consumers, based on their preferences and while using all available information, will reach a consumption choice that maximizes utility while allowing them to live within their budget constraints. This choice is the optimal choice and this behaviour has been a result of pure self-interest.

Behavioural economics

Prominent behavioural economist Richard Thaler has defined behavioural economics as "economics with strong injections of good psychology and other social sciences" (Thaler 2015). Behavioural economics argues that people are not the rational decision-makers assumed by standard economic theory. There are many deviations from the predictions of the standard model, indicating that consumer behaviour is much more complex than the model supposes.

Biases

Behavioural economics using psychological experimentation has identified a range of biases that affect individuals' decision-making, leading to choices that are not optimal. Some of the more common biases include the rules of thumb, anchoring, framing and availability.

- **The rules of thumb** (also known as heuristics) refer to decision-making shortcuts, which enable individuals to make quick decisions. Rules of thumb are usually a result of common sense, practice and experience. For example, a rule of thumb—often used automatically—is recognition. Recognition of a hotel brand involves choosing the hotel with the most recognizable name. Applying such rules helps to simplify economic decision-making. Nevertheless, they can also result in poor decisions, which could have been improved if more effort had been devoted to considering the alternatives available.
- **Anchoring** takes place when people rely on a piece of information that is not necessarily relevant as a reference point when making a decision. For instance, in one experiment participants were asked to write down the last three digits of their phone number multiplied by one thousand (for example, 576 = 576,000). They were then asked to estimate the prices of different houses. Results

showed that participants with higher-ending telephone digits valued all the houses more highly. Anchoring works similarly in practice. For example, the first house shown to an individual by a real estate agent serves as an anchor and influences perceptions of houses presented next (as relatively cheap or expensive). This of course is known and exploited by businesses.

- **Framing** refers to how options and opportunities are presented to people, which can significantly influence their choices. Of particular importance is whether people are presented with a negative or positive frame. Consider the following two options: (a) "If you get the flu vaccine, you will be less likely to get the flu" and (b) "If you do not get the flu vaccine, you are more likely to get the flu". Both statements contain the same information but they have been framed differently. People are most likely to prefer the option that is presented in a positive way. As another example, think of two fast food chains presenting their new burger. One uses the label "91% fat free" and the other uses the label "9% fat". Individuals will tend to prefer the first as it frames the burger as healthier despite the fact that both burgers contain the same amount of fat.
- **Availability** relates information that is most recently available and on which people place most importance. For instance, people make judgments about the likelihood of an event based on how easily an example, instance or case comes to mind, which can then lead to erroneous decisions. It has been found that there is an increased purchase of earthquake insurance immediately after a major earthquake, despite the fact that the likelihood of recurrence in the near future is low. Similarly, individuals with a greater ability to recall antidepressant advertising were found to consider that depression is more prevalent compared to individuals with a

lower recall. Or, for example, investors may judge the quality of an investment based on information that was recently in the news, ignoring other relevant facts.

Besides biases that influence consumers' decision-making, behavioural economists have also challenged the rational consumer choice on other grounds, as outlined below.

Bounded rationality

Herbert Simon pioneered the idea of bounded rationality to highlight the barriers to optimal consumer decision-making. More specifically, bounded rationality refers to the idea that people make choices with the restricted information, time constraints and cognitive limitations that they face. Cognitive limitation does not mean that individuals are somehow inferior, but that even the "smartest" cannot necessarily make fast and accurate assessments of the costs and benefits of all individual decisions. Instead of considering all possible options, people limit their attention to a more-or-less subjective subset of possibilities. As a result, people may not make the optimal choice but they at least make a choice that will move them towards their goal.

Bounded self-control

Sometimes individuals make choices that do not maximize their utility due to lack of self-control. If people prefer not to smoke but they smoke, if they prefer not to eat junk food but they eat junk food, if they prefer not to spend too much time on their smartphone but they spend too much time on their smartphone then they are showing signs of bounded self-control. This can result in making choices that they prefer not to make or decisions that they soon regret.

Bounded selfishness

As mentioned above, the rational consumer is a maximizer driven by self-interest. The rational consumer therefore behaves selfishly. However, many people in many circumstances engage in non-selfish behaviour to contribute to the public even if their personal welfare is reduced.

Imperfect information

Rational consumer choice is based on the assumption that consumers have perfect information. Yet, in practice consumers cannot have access to full and perfect information—so their choices are not fully informed and therefore cannot be optimal.

Overall, behavioural economists do not deny that rational consumer choice plays a part in people's decision-making, but they believe that the standard model provides an incomplete picture of the factors that influence the choices people make. Behavioural economic analysis extends the traditional model in an attempt to provide a better, more realistic explanation of human decision-making.

Behavioural economics in action

`HL`

People's choices often end up being inconsistent with their preferences. Too often, individuals are unable to appreciate what is in their own best interest. This provides the opportunity for positive intervention in the decision-making process to motivate people to make choices in the individual's best interest. Specific aspects of this are explored below.

Choice architecture

How a particular choice is presented—the choice architecture—can have a significant effect on the choice made. The choice architect is the individual or organization that is responsible for organizing the context in which people make decisions and that necessarily knows more about what is the consumer's best interest. Choice architecture can offer three types of choices.

- **Default choice:** this is the option that a consumer "selects" if he or she does nothing. Default choices are therefore made automatically. The nature of the default option strongly affects consumer behaviour. To encourage a particular behaviour that is welfare improving, the choice architect can set the desired outcome as the default choice. For example, if society would benefit from higher rates of organ donation, then the default choice can be set to everybody's organs being donated upon death. An individual may still choose to opt out of organ donation but that would not be the default. Similarly, to encourage pension scheme enrollment, workers are automatically signed up for pensions. This is the default choice. A worker can still opt out but that would not be the default.

- **Restricted choice:** the way in which the options are categorized and presented to the decision-maker can also be used by the choice architect to influence people's choices. Consumers can find it increasingly difficult to make decisions when the number of options is large. Therefore, restricting the number of available choices may be more likely to cause consumers to make a decision resulting in a better outcome. For example, in the case of pensions, offering people a vast number of options can result in a low take-up rate and inappropriate decisions being made. Restricted choice may therefore be better.

- **Mandated choice:** this is a variation of default choice; it is where people are required by law to make a decision. For example, when people apply for important national documents, such as a passport or driving licence, they could be required to choose whether or not they are willing to donate their organs when they die.

Nudge theory

Another way to influence people's choices is through nudges. A nudge helps people make better choices for themselves without restricting their freedom of choice. An expert can nudge people's choices in the direction the expert considers to be correct. According to Richard Thaler, "small and apparently insignificant details can have major impacts on people's behaviour" (Thaler 2015).

Nudging can be used to tackle the growing obesity problem. For example, sellers of goods and services can be nudged to display products or lists of products (for example, on a menu) in a manner that induces people to buy healthier foods. This could simply be putting fruit and vegetables in grocery stories at eye level. Nudging can also be used to induce environmentally friendlier behaviour. For instance, in some places bins provided for recycled material are twice or even three times bigger than bins for other waste. Having less room for general waste nudges people to recycle more. Similarly, nudging can be used to reduce food waste. An experiment carried out by Green Nudge—a social enterprise with an environmental focus—showed that by reducing plate sizes in hotel restaurants by 2 inches, they were able to reduce food waste by as much as 22% while guest satisfaction stayed the same. Lastly, nudging was used

in the UK to aid with tax collection. Letters that included phrases such as "9 out of 10 people in your area are up to date with tax payments" were sent to those in arrears on their taxes. Tax payments from people that received the letters went up 15%.

Critics of the use of choice architecture and nudges claim that they interfere with an individual's freedom to choose. However, if people are always influenced by the context in which decisions are made, complete freedom of choice is not really feasible. Perhaps to prevent people from being misled some intervention is required. With proper regulations it is more likely, but not necessary, that the choices people make are better choices.

Business objectives

Standard economic theory assumes that the goal of a rational producer is to maximize profits: that is, to produce that level of output that maximizes the difference between its total revenue and total cost (see section 2.11). However, a firm may choose to pursue a range of other goals instead of maximizing its profits. These include the following.

Corporate social responsibility

Firms may depart from a strict free-market, profit-maximizing mode of operation and may pursue objectives that are in line with the interests of the wider community in which they operate, both the local and global communities. This involves avoidance of activities such as pollution, the use of child labour or dangerous working conditions, all of which may create a negative image with consumers. Overall, corporate social responsibility involves ethical ways of doing business and a sense of obligation to satisfy long-term goals that include goals encompassing positive impact on the lives of the workforce and their families as well as of society at large.

Market share

Market share is the percentage of total sales (by value) or total output that a business has in a specified market. Firms often seek to increase their market share. This occurs since increased market share can increase market power and may

enable the firm to raise prices and enjoy more profit in the long term. Also, increasing market share may force rivals out of business, which reduces competition and increases dominance in the market.

Satisficing

The term *satisficing* was introduced by Herbert Simon and derives from "satisfy" and "suffice". It describes when, because of conflicting objectives of the various stakeholders within a firm as well as informational limitations, a firm does not aim at maximizing profits or revenues. Instead it only strives to achieve at least some pre-determined minimum level of profits or revenues. This means that firms aim to achieve a satisfactory outcome.

Growth

Firms may also wish to maximize growth (that is, the volume of output sold subject to non-negative profits). By maximizing growth the firm may be able to lower unit costs. A larger firm is also in a better position to diversify into different markets as well as into different products. The consequence of such diversification is an overall lowering of associated risks. The condition to maximize the volume of output without incurring losses is that at the chosen level of output the average revenue earned should equal the average costs incurred (see section 2.11).

2.5 Elasticities of demand

Price elasticity of demand (PED)

Price elasticity of demand (PED) measures the responsiveness of quantity demanded to a change in price.

The following formula is used to calculate PED:

$$PED = \frac{\%\Delta Qd}{\%\Delta P} = \frac{\dfrac{Q2 - Q1}{Q1}}{\dfrac{P2 - P1}{P1}} = \frac{Q2 - Q1}{P2 - P1} \times \frac{P1}{Q1}$$

Price and quantity demanded have an inverse relationship that reflects the law of demand. Therefore, since PED is the ratio of change of two variables—price and quantity demanded, that move in opposite directions—PED is always a negative number. However, the minus sign can be ignored and PED is usually treated as a positive number. Note though that the minus sign should not be ignored in calculations.

Degrees of PED

A. Demand is **price elastic** if PED > 1; that is, the percentage change in quantity demanded is larger than the percentage change in price.

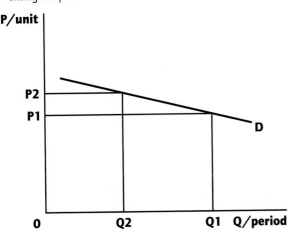

Figure 2.5.1 Price elastic demand

As shown in Figure 2.5.1, when demand is price elastic, a change in price (from P1 to P2) leads to a **proportionately** greater change in quantity demanded (from Q1 to Q2). This means that demand in this range is relatively responsive to price changes.

> Tip: to draw a price elastic demand curve make sure you draw the demand curve quite flat and also far from the origin.

B. Demand is **price inelastic** if 0 < PED < 1: that is, the percentage change in quantity demanded is smaller than the percentage change in price.

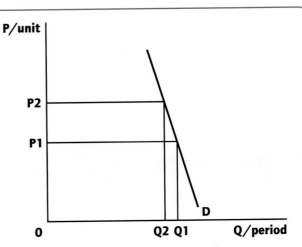

Figure 2.5.2 Price inelastic demand

As shown in Figure 2.5.2, when demand is price inelastic, a change in price (from P1 to P2) leads to a **proportionately** smaller change in quantity demanded (from Q1 to Q2). This means that demand in this range is relatively unresponsive to price changes.

> Tip: to draw a price inelastic demand curve make sure you draw the demand curve quite steep and also far from the origin.

> Note that even along a linear (that is, a constant slope) demand curve, PED is **not constant**, but continuously changes. (See the HL section on page 26.)

C. Demand is **unit elastic** if PED = 1; that is, the percentage change in quantity demanded is equal to the percentage change in price.

D. Demand is **perfectly elastic** if PED → ∞; that is, a small change in price leads to an infinitely large change in quantity demanded.

E. Demand is **perfectly inelastic** if PED = 0; that is, a change in price has no effect on quantity demanded.

The following is shown in Figure 2.5.3.

- A demand curve of zero elasticity is a straight vertical line.
- A demand curve of infinite elasticity is a straight horizontal line.
- A demand curve of unitary elasticity is a rectangular hyperbola, so that the demand curve does not touch the axes.

> Note that the three cases above are **exceptions** and PED is constant throughout the length of the curve.

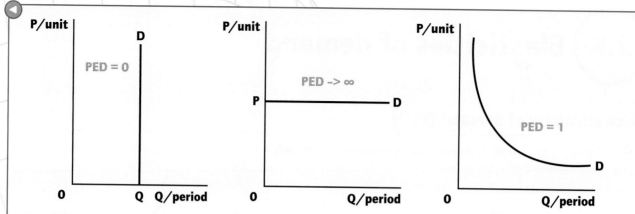

Figure 2.5.3 Constant PED throughout the length of the curve

Recap

Price elasticity of demand (PED)			
If, PED > 1	demand is price elastic	so, $\%\Delta Q_d > \%\Delta P$	Draw the curve flat but far from the origin
If, 0 < PED < 1	demand is price inelastic	so, $\%\Delta Q_d < \%\Delta P$	Draw the curve steep but far from the origin
If, PED = 1	demand is unit elastic	so, $\%\Delta Q_d = \%\Delta P$	Draw a curve that never touches either axis
If, PED → ∞	demand is perfectly elastic	so, consumers will buy any amount at some price	Draw parallel to the Q-axis
If, PED = 0	demand is perfectly inelastic	so, when P changes, Qd doesn't	Draw vertical to the Q-axis

Changing PED along a straight-line downward sloping demand curve

Along any straight-line demand curve, PED continuously varies. PED can be calculated as:

$$\frac{\Delta Q}{\Delta P} \times \frac{P1}{Q1}$$

It follows that PED is the product of the slope of the demand function Q = f(P) or the inverse of the slope of the demand curve $\left(\frac{\Delta Q}{\Delta P}\right)$ multiplied by the original price over quantity ratio $\left(\frac{P1}{Q1}\right)$.

The slope of a straight-line demand curve is constant but the ratio $\left(\frac{P1}{Q1}\right)$ continuously varies as we move along the demand curve.

Hence, **PED is not represented by the slope of the demand curve**. Whereas the slope is constant for a linear demand curve, PED varies throughout its range.

Demand is price elastic at high prices and low quantities, and price inelastic at low prices and large quantities. This is because as a result of the law of demand, when price increases, quantity demanded decreases so the ratio $\left(\frac{P1}{Q1}\right)$ is greater at higher prices and so is PED.

From a less technical viewpoint, demand is price elastic at high prices and price inelastic at low prices because consumers will be more responsive to any price change when the price is already high than when it is low. For instance, if

a good is already quite expensive then a relatively greater response will be caused if it becomes more expensive or slightly cheaper. In contrast, if a good is already cheap then a relatively smaller responsiveness will be induced if it becomes a bit more expensive or a bit cheaper.

Figure 2.5.4 shows how PED varies from infinity to zero along a negatively sloped demand curve.

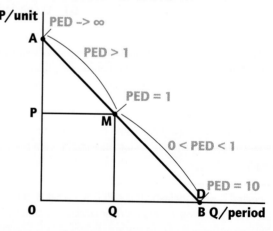

Figure 2.5.4 The range of PED values

Refer to Figure 2.5.4.

- As point A is approached, PED tends to infinity, while at point B we see that PED is zero.
- At the midpoint M of a linear demand curve, PED is equal to 1.

26

- Within line segment AM, corresponding to prices higher than P within the segment AP, demand is price elastic (PED > 1).
- Within line segment MB, corresponding to prices lower than P within the segment PB, demand is price inelastic (0 < PED < 1).

Since PED varies along a demand curve how is it that we can draw a price elastic or a price inelastic demand curve? Hint: think of why in the tips above it is advised that to do so one must draw the curves far from the origin.

Determinants of PED

The number and closeness of available substitutes

The more substitutes there are for a good, and the closer they are, the more price elastic demand is expected to be. If the price of a good with many and close substitutes rises, people will easily switch to these alternatives and so there will be a relatively large drop in quantity demanded. On the contrary, if a good has few if any close substitutes, then an increase in price will bring about a relatively small drop in quantity demanded. Note that this also depends on how *broadly or narrowly* the good is defined (for example "soft drinks" versus "Fanta"). The broader the definition, the fewer the available substitutes and so the more price inelastic demand is expected to be. Beer is not a close substitute for soft drinks whereas Sprite is a much closer substitute for Fanta.

The nature of the good

- If a good is a **necessity**, quantity demanded is less responsive to a change in its price and demand is expected to be more price inelastic. Food products can be considered necessities; as such quantity demanded is not very responsive to price changes.
- If a good is **addictive**, such as cigarettes and alcoholic drinks, it is more difficult to reduce consumption following an increase in price. Therefore, demand is expected to be more price inelastic.

The proportion of income spent on the good

If a small proportion of income is spent on a good then a change in price will not affect consumers' spending behaviour. If, for example, the price of lettuce increases by 10% the typical consumer will decrease quantity demanded by much less than 10%. This is because the person's monthly expenditure on lettuce is a small proportion of his or her income. On the contrary, the higher the proportion of income that is spent on a good, the more price elastic demand is expected to be. For example, demand for laptops or cars for the typical consumer is more price elastic. In contrast, demand for fresh milk for an unemployed mother or a pensioner will be more price elastic because their monthly expenditure on fresh milk represents a greater proportion of their low monthly income.

The time period involved

It is difficult for consumers to change patterns of consumption immediately. It takes time to find suitable substitutes and to cut back consumption of a good following an increase in price. Over a short period of time demand is more price inelastic but it becomes more price elastic as time goes on, as consumers are able to make adjustments and find substitutes, reducing consumption further. The longer the time period after a price change, the more price elastic demand is likely to be. For instance, if the price of fuel oil rises, it may be difficult to use substitute fuels, such as coal or cooking gas. Given sufficient time, though, people will make adjustments and use coal or cooking gas instead of the fuel oil with its higher price.

> **Recap**
>
> ### Determinants of PED
>
> The determinants of PED are:
> - the number and closeness of available substitutes
> - the nature of the good: for example, whether the good is a necessity or addictive
> - the proportion of income spent on the good
> - the time period involved.

PED and total revenue

Total revenue (TR) is the product of price times quantity bought.

$$TR\ (Q) = P \times Q$$

Revenues are not the same as profits, which are defined as the difference between the revenues collected and the costs of production. Knowledge of the PED for a product allows a firm to predict the effect that a price change will have on its revenues.

Case 1: The price increases

When the price of a good increases, quantity demanded is expected to decrease because of the law of demand. What will happen to a firm's revenues following the increase in price? The answer depends on PED.

- If demand is price elastic (PED > 1), a 10% increase in price results in a **larger** than 10% decrease in quantity demanded. The effect on total revenue of the decrease in quantity demanded is larger than the effect of the increase in price; therefore, total revenue falls.
- If demand is price inelastic (0 < PED < 1), a 10% price increase leads to a **smaller** than 10% decrease in quantity demanded. The effect on total revenue of the increase in price is larger than the effect of the decrease in quantity demanded; therefore, total revenue rises.
- If demand is unit elastic (PED = 1), a 10% increase in price produces a 10% decrease in quantity demanded. The effect on total revenue of the increase in price is matched by the decrease in quantity demanded; therefore, total revenue remains unchanged.

Case 2: The price decreases

When the price of a good decreases, quantity demanded is expected to increase because of the law of demand. The effect of the price decrease on a firm's revenue again depends on PED.

- If demand is price elastic (PED > 1), a 10% price fall results in a **larger** than 10% increase in quantity demanded. The effect on total revenue of the increase in quantity demanded is larger than the effect of the decrease in price; therefore, total revenue increases.

- If demand is price inelastic (0 < PED < 1), a 10% price fall results in a **smaller** than 10% increase in quantity demanded. The effect on total revenue of the decrease in price is larger than the effect of the increase in quantity demanded; therefore, total revenue falls.

- If demand is unit elastic (PED = 1), a 10% increase in price produces a 10% decrease in quantity demanded. The effect on total revenue of the decrease in price is matched by the increase in quantity demanded; therefore, total revenue remains unchanged.

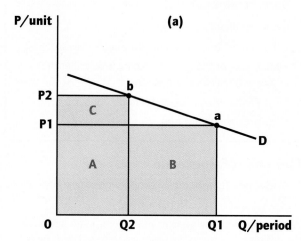

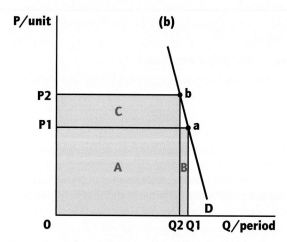

Figure 2.5.5 PED and total revenue between two points

Figure 2.5.5 shows the effect of an increase in price on total revenue. Total revenue is given by the area derived by multiplying price times quantity. In Figure 2.5.5a demand is price elastic between the two points.
At the original price and quantity, P1 and Q1, total revenue is given by the sum of areas A and B. When price increases to P2 and quantity decreases to Q2, total revenue is given by the sum of areas A and C. Area B is lost while area C is gained. Since the revenue lost (B) is larger than the revenue gained (C), total revenue falls. In Figure 2.5.5b, demand is price inelastic between the two points. Following the price increase, the revenue gained (area C) is larger than the revenue lost (area B) and so total revenue increases.

Recap

If price changes and PED > 1

When demand is price elastic, quantity demanded changes **proportionately** more than price and total revenue changes in the same direction as quantity demanded.

- If P rises, Q falls proportionately more; therefore TR falls.
- If P falls, Q rises proportionately more; therefore TR rises.

If price changes and 0 < PED < 1

When demand is price inelastic, quantity demanded changes **proportionately** less than price. Thus, the change in price has a bigger effect on total revenue than does the change in quantity demanded and total revenue changes in the same direction as price.

- If P rises, Q falls proportionately less; therefore TR rises.
- If P falls, Q rises proportionately less; therefore TR falls.

The overall relationship between PED and total revenue is also shown in Figure 2.5.6, which shows the typical, linear, negatively sloped demand curve. At zero quantity (point at the origin), TR is zero and at a zero price (H) TR is also zero. As price decreases (thinking of walking down the price axis) from F to P, quantity demanded increases from 0 to Q. Since demand for that price range is price elastic, the resulting increase in quantity demanded is proportionately greater, so TR rises. Skipping the midpoint price P, if price continues to decrease past P all the way down to zero, quantity demanded increases from Q to H. Since demand is now price inelastic, the resulting increase in quantity demanded is proportionately smaller, so TR decreases. Having established that TR rises all the way to midpoint Q and then, right after Q, TR decreases, it necessarily follows that at Q it is at a maximum. So, right below the midpoint of the linear demand curve where PED = 1, TR is maximized.

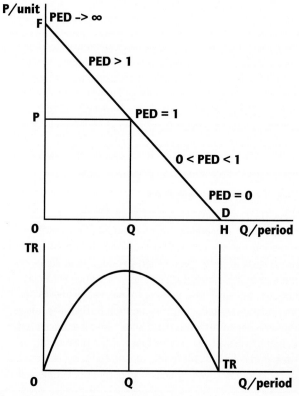

Figure 2.5.6 PED and the shape of the TR curve

Importance of PED for firms and government decision-making
Importance of PED for firms

- PED permits a firm to predict the direction of change in its revenues given a price change. For example, a firm wishing to increase its revenues will lower the price of a good if demand for it is thought to be price elastic and it will increase the price if its demand is price inelastic. Consider the case of a hairdresser. If she is thinking of increasing the price she charges for a haircut, her revenues will increase if the demand for her services is price inelastic. Her clients must consider her services desirable and different from other hairdressers in the area. Quantity of haircuts demanded will then decrease (because of the law of demand) but will decrease proportionately less so that her weekly revenues will rise. If her services are considered very similar to those offered by other hairdressers in the neighbourhood then demand for her services will be price elastic. If she increases the price she charges for a haircut demand will fall proportionately more as many of her clients will switch to competitors and her weekly revenues will decrease.

- PED also helps firms determine the extent to which they can shift an indirect tax (a tax on goods and services) on to the consumer. Ceteris paribus, the more price inelastic the demand faced is, the greater the proportion of the tax that can be shifted on to the consumer in the form of a higher price. The idea is intuitively simple. If demand is price inelastic it implies that consumers have few if any close substitutes to switch to so the increase in price will have a relatively small impact on quantity demanded.

Importance of PED for governments

- Governments looking into raising tax revenues must consider the PED of the goods to be taxed. Tax revenues collected equal the tax imposed per unit times the level of consumption following the tax. The lower the PED, the greater the tax revenues to be collected. This is because the higher price resulting from the tax produces a smaller decrease in quantity demanded when demand is price inelastic than when demand is price elastic. Tax revenues collected will be greater. This explains why governments seeking to maximize tax revenue collection impose indirect taxation on, for example, fuel.

- Governments interested in curtailing the consumption of certain goods often referred to as demerit goods, such as tobacco and alcohol, also need to have knowledge of PED. Tobacco is addictive so demand is quite price inelastic. This means that if the goal is to decrease smoking, a very high tax will be needed so that the monthly expenditure on cigarettes becomes a prohibitively large proportion of the typical consumer's monthly income. PED will help in determining how high the indirect tax needs to be to curtail consumption by some specific target percentage.

Recap
Importance of PED

PED is important for **firms** because:
- it allows them to predict the direction of change of their revenues given a price change
- it helps them to determine the extent to which they can shift an indirect tax on to the consumer.

PED is important for **governments** because:
- it helps governments interested in increasing their tax revenues to decide on which goods to impose an indirect tax
- it allows governments to estimate the size of the necessary tax required to decrease consumption of demerit goods, such as cigarettes or alcoholic drinks.

HL

PED for primary commodities versus manufactured products

Primary commodities are goods derived directly from the use of the factor of production land and include both agricultural and non-agricultural products. Agricultural products include food (corn, wheat, potatoes) as well as other, non-food commodities such as cotton. Non-agricultural commodities include products of extraction such as minerals (copper, tin, cerium), oil and coal. The PED for primary products is typically lower than the PED for manufactured goods. For instance, the demand for most food products is price inelastic because they are necessities and do not have close substitutes. The same is true for the majority of primary commodities. Consider lanthanum, a rare earth mineral necessary in the production of the batteries needed for hybrid cars. Given the lack of substitutes, even if the price of lanthanum increases, manufacturers of batteries for hybrid cars will not have much of a choice and so they will be less responsive to the price increase. By contrast, the demand for manufactured products tends to be more price elastic, because these products usually do have substitutes as a result of the extensive product differentiation. If someone is considering a BMW she may also consider a Mercedes. If someone is planning on buying a new Dell laptop he will probably also consider an HP or a Mac. Expenditures on manufactured goods are often a big proportion of income for many consumers, though. That may also explain why their demand is typically more price elastic.

Therefore, given a price change, quantity demanded is generally more responsive in the case of manufactured products than for primary commodities.

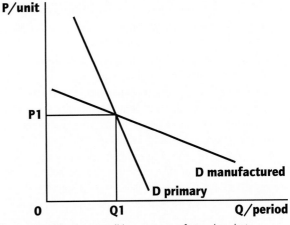

Figure 2.5.7 Primary commodities versus manufactured products

For small changes around P1, demand for manufactured products is more price elastic compared to demand for primary products.

Calculating PED

1. Assume that price falls by 6% leading to an increase in quantity demanded of 9%. What is the PED?

To calculate PED enter the percentage changes into the formula with their sign:

$$PED = \frac{\%\Delta Qd}{\%\Delta P}$$

$$PED = \frac{9\%}{-6\%} \Rightarrow PED = \mathbf{-1.5} \text{ (or, 1.5)}.$$

Demand is therefore price elastic.

2. Assume that the price increases from $3 to $9, causing quantity demanded to fall from 12,000 units to 4,000 units. What is the PED?

To calculate PED enter the above values into the formula:

$$PED = \frac{\%\Delta Qd}{\%\Delta P} = \frac{\dfrac{Q2 - Q1}{Q1}}{\dfrac{P2 - P1}{P1}} = \frac{Q2 - Q1}{P2 - P1} \times \frac{P1}{Q1}$$

$$PED = \frac{\dfrac{4{,}000 - 12{,}000}{12{,}000}}{\dfrac{9 - 3}{3}} = \text{(if GDC is allowed then EXE)}$$

$$\frac{-8{,}000}{6} \times \frac{3}{12{,}000} \Rightarrow PED = \mathbf{-0.33} \text{ (or, 0.33)}.$$

Demand is therefore price inelastic.

3. Assume that PED is −0.74 and price increases by 12%. Calculate the change in quantity demanded.

Again, the PED formula can be used to calculate the change in quantity demanded:

$$PED = \frac{\%\Delta Qd}{\%\Delta P}$$

$$-0.74 = \frac{\Delta Q\%}{12\%} \Rightarrow \%\Delta Q = -0.74 \times 12\% = \mathbf{-8.88\%}$$

Remember the minus sign for PED in this case. Since the price has increased it follows that quantity demanded will change in the opposite direction because of the law of demand.

Income elasticity of demand (YED)

Income elasticity of demand (YED) measures the responsiveness of demand to a change in income. YED provides information on the direction of change of demand given a change in income and on the size of demand curve shifts.

The formula used to calculate YED is the following:

$$YED = \frac{\%\Delta Qd}{\%\Delta Y} = \frac{\dfrac{\Delta Q}{Q1}}{\dfrac{\Delta Y}{Y1}} = \frac{\Delta Q}{\Delta Y} \times \frac{Y1}{Q1} = \frac{Q2 - Q1}{Y2 - Y1} \times \frac{Y1}{Q1}$$

Since YED is the ratio of the percentage changes in demand and income levels, it follows that if both changes are positive (plus sign) or if both are negative (minus sign) then YED is a positive number. For example, if an increase in income leads to more of a good being demanded or a drop in income leads to less being demanded, then YED is a positive number. If one change is positive (plus sign) and the other is negative (minus sign), then YED is a negative number. For example, if an increase in income leads to a decrease in quantity demanded, or a decrease in income leads to an increase in quantity demanded, then YED is a negative number.

We can distinguish between normal and inferior goods based on whether YED is positive or negative.

- If YED > 0 the good is a normal good since demand increases (decreases) as consumer income increases (decreases): both income and demand change in the same direction.
- If YED < 0 the good is an inferior good since demand decreases (increases) as consumer income increases (decreases): income and demand change in opposite directions.

Focusing on normal goods, we can state the following.

- If YED > 1 then the percentage change in quantity demanded is greater than the percentage change in income. We say that demand is income elastic, as a rise in income leads to a faster rise (a proportionately greater increase) in demand. Luxury goods, as well as most services, are usually considered income elastic. For example, demand for plastic surgery, spa therapy or haute couture clothing is income elastic in many markets.
- If 0 < YED < 1 then the percentage change in quantity demanded is smaller than the percentage change in income. We say that demand is income inelastic as a rise in income leads to a slower rise (a proportionately smaller increase) in demand. Basic goods (everyday goods or

staple goods) are usually income inelastic. For example, demand for many food products is income inelastic. Demand for milk or rice or chocolate will not increase much following an increase in income in a market where consumers earn at least an average level of income.

- If YED = 0 then demand for the good is not affected by a change in income. Income may increase or decrease but demand for the good remains the same.
- If YED = 1 then the percentage change in income is equal to the percentage change in quantity demanded: a 5% increase in income leads to a 5% increase in quantity demanded, for example.

YED values can be graphically represented by an Engel curve, which is just a graph with income on the vertical axis and quantity demanded on the horizontal axis. If the curve is positively sloped then YED is positive and the good is normal. If the slope is negative then YED is negative and the good is inferior. If the curve is vertical then YED is zero. All three cases are shown in Figure 2.5.8.

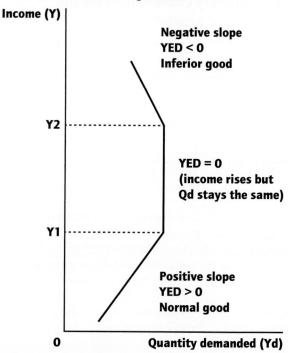

Figure 2.5.8 YED represented by an Engel curve

Consider Jane and her demand for white bread. If her income is initially very low and then it increases up to Y1, the quantity demanded of white bread by Jane will increase. YED is thus positive up to income Y1. As her income increases more and up until income level Y2, she will not consume more white bread as she already consumes a sufficient amount per week. If her income now rises past Y2, then she may consider switching away from white bread and start consuming more nutritious and expensive whole wheat bread. Past Y2, YED is thus negative and white bread becomes for Jane an inferior product.

It is possible to illustrate the cases of products with income elastic and income inelastic demand as well as the case where YED = 1. To illustrate a product with:

- income elastic demand, draw a straight line Engel curve that cuts the vertical axis
- income inelastic demand, draw a straight line Engel curve that cuts the horizontal axis

- YED equal to 1, draw any straight line Engel curve that goes through the origin.

The proof requires manipulating the formula using simple algebra, which is beyond our scope here. These cases are shown in Figure 2.5.9.

Normal goods (YED > 0)	
0 < YED < 1	YED > 1
Income inelastic demand	*Income elastic demand*
Typically:	Typically:
farm products; food;	most services; expensive (luxury) goods
basic day-to-day goods; necessities	(nail salons, cruises, plastic surgery cars, dishwashers, iPhones, sail boats)
(rice, spaghetti sauce, canned tuna, pencils, erasers, haircuts, napkins)	
Inferior goods (YED < 0)	
Typically: used cars, lower quality clothing, lower quality food	

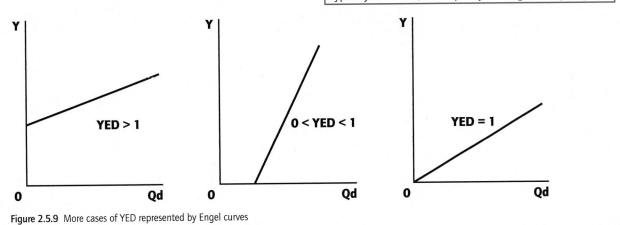

Figure 2.5.9 More cases of YED represented by Engel curves

Importance of YED

Importance of YED for firms

Firms would like to know whether demand for their product is highly income elastic or moderately income inelastic to help them better plan their investments. In periods of economic growth, incomes in the country increase. As incomes increase, markets for goods with high YED will expand more compared to markets for goods with low YED. Hence, if an economy is growing and incomes are increasing fast, then firms producing highly income elastic products may have to invest now in expanding their capacity to be able to meet the increased demand.

Conversely, farmers growing, say, potatoes (that have a low YED), may think of switching to kiwi fruit or to agro-tourism, which have a higher YED. Over the long term, farmers producing agricultural products with a low YED will witness a slower increase of their income relative to the rest of the population, widening income inequality.

Now consider what happens if an economy is in a recession. Incomes will decline. As a result, goods and services with high YED will face a large drop in their sales, products with low YED can avoid large declines in their sales, while inferior goods will experience increases in sales. For example, as a result of the 2009 eurozone crisis incomes decreased, with different effects on firms in various markets. Firms offering

goods with income inelastic demand such as food and fuel faced a smaller decline in their sales compared to furniture retailers, foreign travel agencies or high-end restaurants.

Importance of YED for the economy

Economies have three sectors: the primary sector, the manufacturing sector and the services sector. As an economy grows and incomes rise over the long term, the relative size of the three sectors can change. Many agricultural products have a low YED once a certain threshold level of income is reached. Any further increases in income are mostly spent on products from the manufacturing sector, for example cars, appliances and furniture, which carry a higher YED. Luxury items and services are considered to have an even higher YED so once households have attained a certain standard of living, further increases in discretionary income are spent mostly on vacations, spa treatments, expensive clothing and expensive cars. In this way the relative size of the primary sector and later of manufacturing shrinks while that of services expands. In the UK both the agricultural and the manufacturing sectors have been in relative decline since the 1960s. According to the UK Office for National Statistics (ONS), currently the services sector is the largest sector in the UK, accounting for more than 75% of GDP. Manufacturing and production contribute less than 21% of GDP, and agriculture contributes less than 0.60%.

HL

Calculating YED

1. Suppose that an increase in national income of 2.4% leads to a 4.75% fall in bus journeys. Calculate the YED for bus journeys.

$$YED = \frac{\%\Delta Qd}{\%\Delta Y}$$

Enter the percentage changes into the formula remembering the signs:

$$YED = \frac{-4.75\%}{+2.4\%} \Rightarrow YED = -1.98.$$

Note that here the negative sign **must** be kept. It informs us that bus journeys in this economy are inferior products.

2. Assume annual per capita income levels in Shanghai increase from Rmb 55,000 to Rmb 61,600 leading to an increase in the number of manicure appointments from 350,000 to 413,000. Calculate the YED for manicure treatments.

Enter the above values into the formula:

$$YED = \frac{\%\Delta Qd}{\%\Delta Y} = \frac{Q2 - Q1}{Y2 - Y1} \times \frac{Y1}{Q1}$$

$$YED = \frac{413{,}000 - 350{,}000}{61{,}600 - 55{,}000} \times \frac{55{,}000}{350{,}000} \Rightarrow YED = \mathbf{1.5}$$

Demand for this service in Shanghai is income elastic.

2.6 Elasticity of supply

Price elasticity of supply (PES)

Price elasticity of supply (PES) measures the responsiveness of quantity supplied to a change in price.

The following formula is used to calculate PES:

$$PES = \frac{\%\Delta Q_s}{\%\Delta P} = \frac{\frac{Q2 - Q1}{Q1}}{\frac{P2 - P1}{P1}} = \frac{Q2 - Q1}{P2 - P1} \times \frac{P1}{Q1}$$

Price and quantity supplied have a positive relationship that reflects the law of supply. If price increases then quantity supplied increases and vice versa. Therefore, since PES is the ratio of change of two variables—price and quantity supplied, that move in the same direction—PES is always a positive number.

Degrees of PES

PES ranges in value from zero to infinity.

A. Supply is **price elastic** if PES > 1; that is, the percentage change in quantity supplied is larger than the percentage change in price.

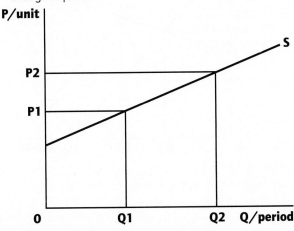

Figure 2.6.1 Price elastic supply

As shown in Figure 2.6.1, when supply is price elastic, a change in price (from P1 to P2) leads to a **proportionately** greater change in quantity supplied (from Q1 to Q2). This means that supply in this range is relatively responsive to price changes.

A price elastic supply curve must cut the vertical axis.

B. Supply is **price inelastic** if 0 < PES < 1; that is, the percentage change in quantity supplied is smaller than the percentage change in price.

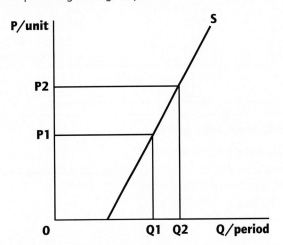

Figure 2.6.2 Price inelastic supply

As shown in Figure 2.6.2, when supply is price inelastic, a change in price (from P1 to P2) leads to a **proportionately** smaller change in quantity supplied (from Q1 to Q2). This means that supply in this range is relatively unresponsive to price changes.

A price inelastic supply curve must cut the horizontal axis.

C. Supply is **unit elastic** if PES = 1; that is, the percentage change in quantity supplied is equal to the percentage change in price.

D. Supply is **perfectly elastic** if PES -> ∞; that is, a small change in price leads to an infinitely large change in quantity supplied.

E. Supply is **perfectly inelastic** if PES = 0; that is, a change in price leads to no change in quantity supplied.

The following is shown in Figure 2.6.3.

- A supply curve of unitary elasticity passes through the origin.
- A supply curve of infinite elasticity is a straight horizontal line.
- A supply curve of zero elasticity is a straight vertical line.

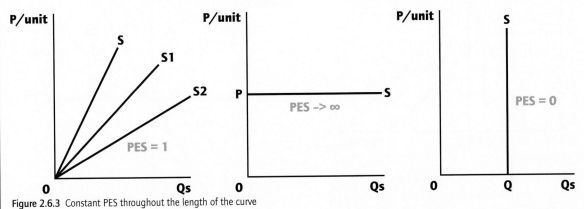

Figure 2.6.3 Constant PES throughout the length of the curve

Recap

Price elasticity of supply (PES)			
If, PES > 1	supply is price elastic	so, $\%\Delta Q_s > \%\Delta P$	The curve must "cut" the vertical axis
If, 0 < PES < 1	supply is price inelastic	so, $\%\Delta Q_s < \%\Delta P$	The curve must "cut" the horizontal axis
If, PES = 1	supply is unit elastic	so, $\%\Delta Q_s = \%\Delta P$	The curve must go through the origin (any slope)
If, PES → ∞	supply is perfectly elastic	so, a small change in price leads to an infinitely large change in quantity supplied. Effectively, it shows that the firm is willing to offer any amount at the current price.	Draw the curve parallel to the Q-axis
If, PES = 0	supply is perfectly inelastic	so, when price changes, quantity supplied does not.	Draw the curve vertical to the Q-axis

Determinants of PES

The time period involved

Time in economics is distinguished into the momentary run, the short run and the long run.

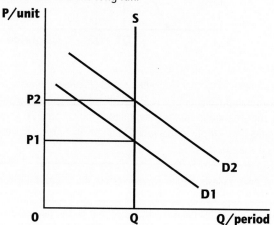

Figure 2.6.4 PES in the momentary run

In the **momentary run** (market period) all factors of production are considered fixed; firms can thus make no adjustments. As a result, supply is perfectly inelastic (PES = 0). Producers cannot respond to any change in price. If demand increases, quantity supplied remains the same and only price increases.

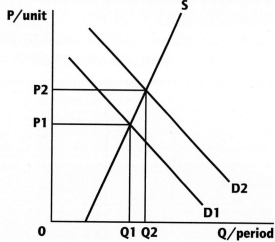

Figure 2.6.5 PES in the short run

In the **short run**, at least one factor of production is considered fixed. For example, the capital employed by the firm is fixed but it can change the number of workers or the hours they work. Thus, some adjustments are possible. As a result, supply is price

inelastic (0 < PES < 1). Producers can only marginally respond to changes in price. If demand increases there will be both an increase in quantity supplied and an increase in price, yet the effect on price will be proportionately greater.

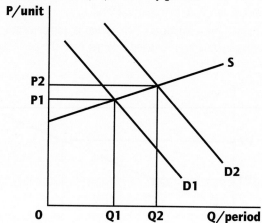

Figure 2.6.6 PES in the long run

In the **long run**, all factors of production are considered variable by the firm; all adjustments are possible. The firm can change both capital and labour (that is, it can change its scale of operations). As a result, supply is price elastic (PES > 1). Producers can fully respond to changes in price and the firm is able to increase in size. If demand increases there will be both an increase in quantity supplied and an increase in price, yet the effect on quantity supplied will be proportionately greater.

Therefore, over time, supply tends to become more price elastic as firms can make more and more adjustments.

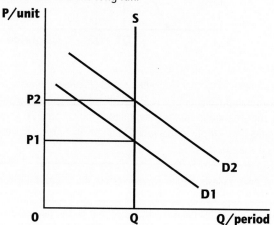

Figure 2.6.7 PES over time

The mobility of factors of production

The mobility of labour is relevant. If, for example, labour is occupationally or geographically immobile then it will be more difficult to meet an increase in the demand for a product than if labour is mobile between occupations or between regions.

The extent to which spare (excess) capacity exists

When a firm is operating at full capacity, it is very difficult to increase output. Supply is price inelastic. A firm is able though to increase output if it does have available spare capacity. For example, a factory that has machines that are idle will easily be able to increase output if there is an increase in price. The greater the extent of spare capacity available, the more responsive quantity supplied will be to an increase in price. Supply is more price elastic.

The need for skilled as opposed to unskilled labour

In an economy there are more unskilled than skilled workers. It is easier for firms that use unskilled labour to find and hire more workers in order to increase output. Supply of the product is more price elastic. When specialized labour is needed, a firm may not be able to find and employ more labour as quickly so supply is more price inelastic. For example, it will be easier for a food delivery firm to hire more workers than it will be for a mental institution to find more doctors; the former does not require specialized labour, in contrast to the latter.

The ability to store the product

Quantity supplied can easily be increased when the firm is able to hold stocks of the product. Goods can be released onto the market very quickly; therefore supply is more price elastic. For example, firms can maintain stocks of plastic flowers but not of fresh flowers.

The time lags that characterize the production process

The longer the time lags, the longer it takes for producers to respond to price increases. Primary sector products are usually characterized by long time lags. For instance, grapes and apples are agricultural products. It takes a long time for farmers to plant seedlings and for the crops to mature and be harvested. This means that an increase in price can only bring about a very insignificant output response. The same applies to the oil and the copper industries, which are extractive industries. It takes a long time to bring new copper mines into production and it takes a long time to find and bring a new oil field into production. Supply is therefore price inelastic.

The speed by which costs rise as output increases

The higher the additional (marginal) costs of producing additional output, the more difficult it will be for firms to increase output following an increase in price, so the more price inelastic supply will be. For example, heavy mining equipment used in the extraction industry is extremely expensive. For a mining company it is very difficult to expand output given the additional cost of acquiring such equipment.

Recap

Determinants of PES

PES is determined by:

- the time period
- the mobility of factors of production
- the extent to which spare (excess) capacity exists
- the need for skilled as opposed to unskilled labour
- the ability to store the product
- the time lags that characterize the production process
- the speed by which costs rise as output increases.

HL

PES for primary commodities versus manufactured products

Overall, primary commodities usually have a lower PES compared to manufactured products. This is due to the long time lags that characterize the production of primary products as opposed to manufactured goods. In the case of agriculture, farmers need at least a planting season to be able to respond to higher prices. In the case of other primary products, such as oil, natural gas and minerals, time is needed to make the necessary investments for extraction and to begin production.

Calculating PES

1. Calculate the PES for foot massage services in Singapore if the number of appointments offered per week increases from 2,140 to 2,568 when the market price increases from S$50 to S$55 per appointment.

Enter the values into the formula:

$$PES = \frac{\%\Delta Qs}{\%\Delta P} = \frac{\frac{Q2 - Q1}{Q1}}{\frac{P2 - P1}{P1}} = \frac{Q2 - Q1}{P2 - P1} \times \frac{P1}{Q1}$$

$$PES = \frac{2,568 - 2,140}{55 - 50} \times \frac{50}{2,140} \Rightarrow PES = 2$$

PES for foot massage services Singapore is 2, which means that supply is price elastic.

2. If PES for wax candles is estimated at 1.4 and there is an 8% increase in price, calculate the response in quantity supplied.

Enter the values into the formula:

$$PES = \frac{\%\Delta Qs}{\%\Delta P}$$

$$1.4 = \frac{\Delta Qs\%}{8\%} \Rightarrow \Delta Q = \mathbf{11.20\%}.$$

Quantity supplied for wax candles will increase by 11.20%.

2.7 Role of governments in microeconomics

Government intervention in markets

Governments intervene in markets for various reasons, which include to:

- support certain producers, usually farmers
- support low income households ensuring that basic goods and services services, such as food and housing, are affordable
- influence the level of output in a market
- influence the level of consumption of the good or service
- correct market failures (that is, cases where market forces fail to reach the socially efficient outcome)
- promote equity.

Indirect taxation

What are indirect taxes?

Indirect taxes are taxes on goods or services, or on expenditures. They are distinguished into unit (specific) taxes and ad valorem taxes. Unit taxes are a fixed "dollar" amount per unit of the good (for example, $4.00 per pack of cigarettes). Ad valorem taxes are a percentage on the price of a good (for example, the 15% GST in New Zealand).

Why do governments impose indirect taxes?

Indirect taxes are imposed to:

- collect tax revenues needed to finance government expenditures
- decrease the consumption of demerit goods such as tobacco, alcohol and sugar that harm not only the individual consumer but also society at large
- decrease production processes that generate pollution, or decrease the use of fossil fuels
- decrease imports in certain industries and thus help domestic producers and workers.

Analysing indirect taxes using a diagram

An indirect tax is considered an additional cost of production and, as a result, it decreases supply, shifting the supply curve left or, better yet, vertically upwards by the amount of the tax. If the tax is a specific tax the shift is parallel to the original supply curve. If the tax is an ad valorem tax, the new supply curve is steeper because the "dollar" amount of the tax, and so the vertical distance between the two supply curves, is bigger at higher prices.

Impact on market outcomes

In the market for sugar-sweetened beverages, shown in Figure 2.7.1, demand D and supply S lead to a market price P and an equilibrium quantity Q.

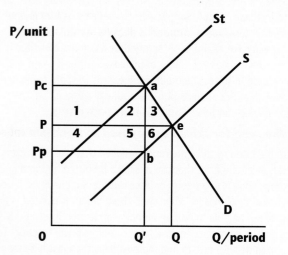

Figure 2.7.1 Impact of an indirect tax: market for sugar-sweetened beverages

The indirect tax will shift the supply curve vertically upwards by the amount of the tax to St. As a result, the market price consumers pay increases to Pc and the equilibrium quantity decreases to Q'. Producers now earn per beverage Pp, which is the price consumers pay minus the tax (ab).

The tax revenues the government collects are equal to the tax per unit (ab) times the new equilibrium quantity Q'. This is area (PpbaPc) or area (1 + 2 + 4 + 5).

The proportion of the tax paid by consumers is equal to $\left(\frac{PPc}{PcPp}\right)$.

It is referred to as the incidence of the tax to consumers.

It follows that the incidence of the tax to producers is $\left(\frac{PPp}{PcPp}\right)$.

Note that the above analysis is the same if the tax is an ad valorem tax (except that St is steeper than S).

Consequences for stakeholders

- Consumers are worse off as they pay a higher price (Pc > P) and enjoy less of the good (Q' < Q). Consumer surplus decreases by area (1 + 2 + 3). Of course, if the product taxed is a demerit good then, at least in the long term, the lower level of consumption and the resulting health benefits make them better off, despite the higher price. Note that indirect taxes are considered unfair as they are regressive with respect to consumers' income. If two individuals purchase the same good, the "dollar" amount of the tax is the same for both, but it represents a higher proportion of the income of the poorer individual. This explains why basic goods (basic food products or heating oil) in many countries are typically not subject to tax (see Chapter 3, section 3.4).

- Producers are worse off as they earn less per unit (Pp < P) and sell fewer units (Q' < Q). The revenues they collect decrease from area (0QeP) to area (0Q'bPp). Producer surplus decreases by area (4 + 5 + 6). Since less of the good will be produced and sold, workers may be laid off so they will be adversely affected. Also, if the good taxed is used as an input for the production of other goods then production costs will increase, forcing firms to raise price and suffer a decrease in their sales and in employment levels.

- The government collects tax revenues equal to area (1 + 2 + 4 + 5) that may be spent on infrastructure, education, health care services and so on, so this cannot be considered a loss to society.

- Consumers and producers together lose surplus equal to area (1 + 2 + 3 + 4 + 5 + 6) but since the government collects tax revenues equal to area (1 + 2 + 4 + 5), the resulting welfare loss is equal to area (3 + 6). This represents net value lost by society from units Q'Q not being produced as a result of the indirect tax, even though they should have been from society's point of view.

- Note though that there is no welfare loss if the indirect tax was imposed on demerit goods or on industries that generate pollution because a lower level of production and consumption in both cases is considered socially optimal.

What does the incidence of an indirect tax depend on?

An indirect tax typically burdens both consumers and producers. This may sound counterintuitive but often producers are forced to lower the pre-tax price charged in order to avoid a significant loss of sales as a result of the tax. In general, the incidence of an indirect tax depends on both PED and PES. If demand is more price inelastic than supply, then the incidence is greater on consumers as they pay a greater proportion of the tax. If supply is more price inelastic than demand, then the incidence on producers is greater. The following relationship applies, which is very helpful in determining tax incidence:

$$\frac{\% \text{ of tax incidence on consumers}}{\% \text{ of tax incidence on producers}} = \frac{PES}{PED}$$

The sum of the two percentages is of course 100% since if, for example, the incidence on consumers is 80%, then the incidence on producers must be 20%. Inspecting this relationship, it becomes clear that firms will be able to shift onto consumers 100% of an indirect tax if either demand is perfectly price inelastic (vertical) or supply is perfectly elastic (horizontal). If it happens that PES = PED then an indirect tax will be split 50%–50%. Carefully constructed diagrams will illustrate the above.

Subsidies

What are subsidies?

A subsidy is a payment by the government to firms that aims to decrease their production costs and so price and to increase production and consumption of the good. For example, in Malaysia since 1980, rice farmers receive a pre-determined amount of Malaysian ringgit for each ton of rice harvested. In 2018 governments around the world were paying an estimated US$35 billion in subsidies to their fishing fleets (mostly on fuel subsidies) to decrease their cost of inputs.

Why do government grant subsidies to firms?

- To increase revenues of particular producers: typically these are farmers, as demand for most farm products is income inelastic. As an economy grows and average incomes increase, farmers' incomes grow more slowly. By increasing farmers' income, rural–urban income inequality decreases and so does rural–urban migration. Agricultural subsidies are also considered to promote food self-sufficiency. In addition, they decrease the price of food, which is very important for low income households and improves nutrition among the poor.

- To decrease the price of certain goods or services so that they become more affordable to low income households. Beyond basic food products, gasoline, public transportation and rent are also sometimes subsidized.

- To help certain industries grow: for example, subsidies are granted to promote the adoption of green technologies (solar, wind, hydro and geothermal) by firms. Subsidies to the solar panel industry in the USA, China and other countries are responsible for its growth over the past years. Aircraft manufacturers, such as Airbus, have been accused of receiving government subsidies.

- To increase consumption of merit goods such as education and health care services: consumption of these services not only benefits the individual consumer but also society at large.

- To protect domestic firms from import penetration, or to assist them in increasing export competitiveness, governments may grant subsidies.

Analysing subsidies using a diagram

A subsidy decreases production costs of firms and, as a result, increases supply. This shifts the supply curve to the right or, better yet, vertically downwards by the amount of the subsidy. The shift is parallel to the original supply curve.

Impact on market outcomes

In the market for rice shown in Figure 2.7.2, demand D and supply S lead to a market price P and an equilibrium quantity Q.

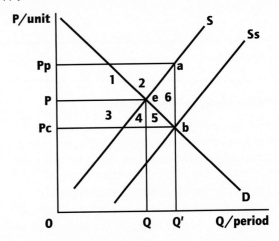

Figure 2.7.2 Impact of a subsidy: market for rice

The rice subsidy will shift the supply curve vertically downwards by the amount of the subsidy to Ss. As a result, the market price consumers pay for rice decreases to Pc and the equilibrium quantity produced and consumed increases to Q'. Rice producers now earn per unit of rice sold Pp which is the price buyers pay plus the subsidy (ab) paid by the government.

The cost of the subsidy to the government is equal to the subsidy paid per unit (ab) times the new equilibrium quantity Q'. This is area (PcbaPp) or area (1 + 2 + 3 + 4 + 5 + 6).

Consequences for stakeholders

- Consumers are better off as they pay a lower price (Pc < P) and enjoy more of the good (Q' > Q). Consumer surplus also increases by area (3 + 4 + 5).

- Producers are also better off as they earn more per unit (Pp > P) and sell more units (Q' > Q). Revenues collected increase from area (0QeP) to area (0Q'aPp). Producer surplus increases by area (1 + 2). Since more of the good is produced and sold, more workers will be employed. Also, if the subsidized product is used as an input for the production of other goods then production costs would decrease permitting producers also to lower price and increase output and employment levels.

- The government must finance the cost of this subsidy, which is equal to area (1 + 2 + 3 + 4 + 5 + 6), so it will have to tax more now, borrow more now and tax later or cut back now on another government programme. Financing a subsidy therefore involves an opportunity cost for society.

- Since a subsidy makes both consumers and producers better off and together they enjoy an increase in surplus equal to area (1 + 2 + 3 + 4 + 5) it seems that social welfare increases and so resource allocation improves. This is typically not the case. In addition, we have to consider the cost of the subsidy to the government, which is equal to area (1 + 2 + 3 + 4 + 5 + 6), and thus greater. A welfare loss equal to area (6) results, which represents net value lost by society from units QQ' now being produced even though, from society's point of view, they should not have been.

- Note though that there is no welfare loss involved if the subsidy was granted to increase consumption of merit goods or use of pollution-abating technologies. More generally, the welfare effects of a subsidy have to be judged by weighing the expected benefits for society of the policy subsidized against its cost (that is, the value of what society will have to sacrifice to finance it).

Recap

Impact of indirect taxes and subsidies on stakeholders

Impact of an indirect tax on stakeholders	Impact of a subsidy on stakeholders
• Consumers pay a higher price and enjoy less of the good.	• Consumers pay a lower price and enjoy more of the good.
• Consumer surplus decreases.	• Consumer surplus increases.
• Firms earn less per unit and sell fewer units so revenues collected decrease.	• Firms earn more per unit and sell more units so revenues collected increase.
• Producer surplus decreases.	• Producer surplus increases.
• Government collects tax revenues that may be spent on infrastructure, education, health care and so on.	• The government must finance the cost of the subsidy so it may have to increase taxation now, borrow now and tax later or cut back on another government programme.
• A welfare loss results unless the good taxed is a demerit good or its production generates pollution.	• A welfare loss results unless the subsidized good is a merit good or its production generates significant benefits for society.

Policymakers' perspective

Imposing indirect taxes is necessary for the reasons explained above but their regressive nature must always be recognized by policymakers. They may be easier to collect than income taxes but by disproportionately hurting the poor they may lead to increased income inequality.

Indirect taxes must definitely be considered as a tool to decrease polluting production processes as well as the consumption of tobacco, alcohol and even perhaps sugar-sweetened beverages. Governments, in the case of tobacco, alcohol and other goods that are addictive in nature and so rather price inelastic, must be prepared

to impose a high tax if the goal is truly to curtail consumption and not just to raise tax revenue. However, high taxation raises the possibility of smuggling and of parallel markets arising as there is room for making a profit. Whether such phenomena are observed is a function of the size of the penalties and the degree to which the laws are enforced. In the case of polluting activities such as driving, flying or production processes that use fossil fuels as energy, a government must be prepared to face popular resentment if it decides to impose indirect taxes to curb their use. Few want to pay more for driving or flying or for their monthly electricity bill.

Subsidies benefit both consumers and producers so are far easier for a government to grant instead of imposing taxes. There are several valid reasons, all based on sound economics, for the granting of a subsidy but subsidies are often also captured by special interest groups that represent powerful industries and confer benefits only to their members.

Whether a subsidy is granted or not should depend on weighing all the benefits and all the costs for society. Sometimes it is difficult for us to judge whether a subsidy is necessary because we may not have all the necessary information, especially if the benefits are mostly realized in the long term. For example, farm subsidies are typically considered wasteful and a result

of political pressure. However, if they manage to slow down rural–urban migration and permit the government to build in the meantime more schools, hospitals, roads and other infrastructure then society at large may benefit in ways not initially realized. On the other hand, if a government decides to subsidize the domestic fishing industry in order to feed its population and to ensure jobs for workers in coastal regions then, from a national perspective, these subsidies may perhaps be sensible. If the framework of analysis is global, though, fishing subsidies are harmful and should stop because they deplete world fisheries and the resulting global social costs exceed any national social benefits.

Often, governments consider the market-determined price of a product unsatisfactory: that is, either too high or too low. In these cases, the government intervenes and sets the price of the good either below or above the market price.

Price ceilings (maximum prices)

What are price ceilings (maximum prices)?

A price ceiling (maximum price) is a form of price control that a government can impose in a market if it considers the market-determined price is too high. Price ceilings act as the highest possible price that can be charged for a good and so they are set below the market equilibrium price. In this way the government restricts the price to the desired level and therefore protects consumers, especially low income households, against prohibitively high prices.

Why do governments impose price ceilings (maximum prices)?

Price ceilings can be imposed on basic goods, usually on food products, such as milk or bread, but also on gasoline and heating fuel. For instance, up until the late 1980s the French government had set a price ceiling in the market for the baguette, which did not allow bakeries to sell baguettes above the legal maximum price. In many cities around the world, authorities have also imposed rent controls in the rental housing market. Rent controls are examples of price ceilings that prevent landlords from renting their properties above the legal maximum rent. For example, in the USA in 2019 Oregon and California approved statewide rent controls, and New York strengthened its existing rent regulations. Price ceilings therefore aim to make certain basic goods and services cheaper and so more affordable to low income consumers.

Analysing the impact of rent controls using a diagram

In the rental housing market in Portland, Oregon, USA, shown in Figure 2.7.1, the equilibrium rental price is Pe and Qe is the equilibrium quantity. The rent control (P') is set below the market determined rental price (Pe) and acts as the maximum rental price landlords can legally charge. At P' the housing units now offered by landlords are fewer than the housing units tenants are willing and able to rent (that is, Qs < Qd). A shortage of housing units results, equal to the line distance (QsQd or ab).

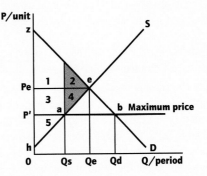

Figure 2.7.3 The impact of imposing a price ceiling: rent control

Consequences of rent controls

Rent controls render housing more affordable and may thus prevent the displacement of low income residents and decrease the prevalence of homelessness. However, the resulting shortage means that not all tenants who are willing and able to pay P' will find rental housing units. This creates further problems.

- **Non-price rationing mechanisms:** once a shortage arises the price is no longer able to perform its rationing function and alternative rationing mechanisms are developed.
  - Allocation may be on a "first come, first served" basis. This may lead to real estate agencies adopting waiting lists for tenants wanting to secure rented housing.
  - Landlords may decide, according to their own preferences, to whom they will rent their property (for example, to households without a pet or without young children). There is also a high risk of discrimination based on ethnic background or religion.

- **Emergence of parallel markets:** landlords may demand "under-the-table" payments in addition to the legal maximum rent, or demand high deposits paid in advance. The result is that higher income individuals will manage to get rented housing and not the poor, who are the people intended to benefit from rent controls.

- **In the long-term additional problems may arise.**
  - Quality of housing may worsen, as landlords who are now earning less will not have the incentive to restore or maintain their rental units properly.

○ The number of rental housing units available may further shrink, making shortages more severe, as landlords may switch the use of their properties. For example, landlords may switch to short-term rentals through Airbnb or other similar platforms.

Welfare effects: Who gains and who loses

Before the imposition of the rent control the consumer surplus is equal to area (1 + 2) and the producer surplus is equal to area (3 + 4 + 5). Social surplus is therefore equal to area (1 + 2 + 3 + 4 + 5). When the rent control, P', is imposed the quantity of rental units is now only Qs. The result is as follows.

- The consumer surplus is equal to area (1 + 3). Some tenants lucky enough to find housing at the lower rent are better off—but these are not necessarily the poorer households. Some tenants are worse off. These are tenants who would have been able to find housing if the market was free but now, as a result of the shortage, are unable to. Tenants who are discriminated against or who end up paying significantly more because of the shortage are also worse off.

- The producer surplus shrinks to area 5. Landlords are worse off, unless they rent at an illegal higher rate where of course they run the risk of being caught. Often, many are forced to leave the market (for example, by selling their property) or they may be forced to witness a long-term deterioration of the value of their property if they cannot afford maintenance.

- Social surplus after the rent control is equal to area (1 + 2 + 5). This means that social surplus decreased by area (4 + 5), which represents the welfare loss to society; now there is allocative inefficiency in the market for rented housing.

Policymakers' perspective

Rent controls have many negative side effects. However, the rising rents in many cities around the world may make it necessary to impose rent controls. A major factor responsible for the rising rents has been gentrification. Gentrification is a process of reviving deteriorated urban neighbourhoods, usually as a result of an influx of more, typically affluent, residents. Demand for housing then increases. House prices and rents surge and as this process continues, lower income households are often displaced. In fact, in many major cities there is an increase in homelessness. Homelessness is a phenomenon that not only impacts negatively on the destitute but also on society at large. Therefore, some form of perhaps temporary rent controls may feature in a policy package that aims to eradicate this phenomenon. However, care has to be taken to ensure that there are incentives for the supply of housing to increase in the long term. For example, perhaps the rent controls should not apply to newer housing units but only to units that are older.

Imposing a price ceiling in the market for a basic good

A price ceiling in the market for a basic food product or in the market for fuel can be analysed in the same way with rent controls. Using Figure 2.7.1, the price ceiling would be set at P', below the market determined price (Pe) and would be the maximum price sellers could legally charge. As a result, the quantity of the good demanded would exceed the quantity of the good supplied (Qd > Qs) and so a shortage of the good equal to line distance (QsQd or ab) would result. Similar consequences will apply.

Price ceilings on basic products, such as bread, make these staples cheaper and more affordable for low income groups. However, the price P' cannot perform its rationing function anymore since individuals may be willing and able to pay the price but it is not certain that they will end up with the good, as a shortage exists.

- Rationing can be on the basis of "first come, first served", which may lead to queues developing outside grocery stores, bakeries and gas stations as people rush to buy the good before there is none left.

- Firms may decide which customers should be allowed to buy goods; they may prefer to sell to regular customers, attractive customers or important customers.

- There may be random allocation of supplies by ballot.

- The government may adopt a system of rationing: people could be issued with a set number of coupons for each item. For example, this may take place in wartime.

- It is likely that illegal markets will develop where some sellers will sell at prices above the legal maximum, depending on the willingness to pay and, of course, the income of buyers.

- Quality may worsen as producers may use lower quality inputs in an attempt to increase their profit margin. For instance, bakers may use lower quality flour.

- If other non-price-controlled goods may be produced with the same inputs, then the quantity offered may further shrink, making shortages more severe. For example, bakers may choose to sell cookies instead of bread.

Price floors (minimum prices)
What are price floors (minimum prices)?

A price floor (minimum price) is a form of price control that a government can impose in a market if it considers the market determined price is too low. Price floors act as the lowest possible price that can be charged for a good and are set above the market equilibrium price. The government's goal is to protect certain groups of producers.

Why do governments impose price floors (minimum prices)?

Governments impose price floors in order to prevent the market price from falling below a certain level. Price floors are typically encountered in agricultural product markets. In India the government has set a price floor on several agricultural products including wheat, soybeans, paddy and cotton. The reasons behind agricultural price floors may include the following.

- Fluctuations of prices and so fluctuation in farmers' incomes can be a problem. The supply of agricultural products is affected by weather conditions; for instance, droughts or floods can reduce supply. Changes in supply result in price volatility that leads to unstable incomes for farmers.

- The agricultural sector's share of national income may be decreasing. As economies grow, the demand for agricultural products grows but more slowly, as the income elasticity of demand for most farm products is rather low. Therefore, over time, farmers' incomes decrease relatively to incomes earned in the manufacturing and service sectors.

- The government could be aiming to protect employment in rural areas. Price floors support agricultural production and this may prevent local farmers from moving into the cities (urbanization). With a price floor imposed, employment in rural areas will be preserved and cities will experience less pressure on their infrastructure (roads, sewage, transport systems, schools and so on).

Analysing the impact of a price floor using a diagram

In the market for soybeans in India, shown in Figure 2.7.2, the market determined price is Pe and respective quantity is Qe. The price floor (P') is set above the equilibrium price (Pe). At P', producers offer Qs units of the good while consumers are willing and able to purchase Qd units. A surplus equal to line distance QdQs or ab results. In order for the price floor to be maintained (not to collapse), the Indian government must buy the surplus at the promised price (that is, at P'). This artificially increases demand to D + government purchases.

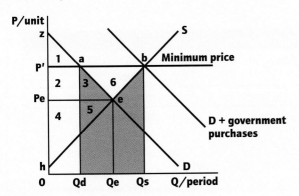

Figure 2.7.4 The impact of imposing a price floor

What does the government do with the surplus?

The government may:

- store the surplus and release the stock into the market in a subsequent period to avoid the price rising too much if there is a crop failure—but storage involves additional costs for the government

- destroy the surplus, which has been the case in many countries and which is simply a terrible waste

- sell the surplus abroad in other markets usually at a price below average cost (a practice known as dumping), which may disrupt trade relations, as local farmers will suffer from the lower price.

Impact on stakeholders: Who gains and who loses

- Producers and more specifically farmers are better off as their incomes are stabilized and increased. In fact, producers' revenue increases from area (PeQe0) to area (P'bQs0). The producer surplus increases from areas (4 + 5) to areas (2 + 3 + 4 + 5 + 6).

- Buyers pay more than they would otherwise and enjoy less of the good. Consumers are therefore worse off. The consumer surplus decreases from areas (1 + 2 + 3) to area (1). If the price-controlled product is used as an input in manufacturing, then production costs for these manufacturing firms will be higher. This may lead to higher prices in their goods. For example, a minimum price on corn in Mexico may lead to a higher price for tortillas.

- The government is forced to spend heavily to purchase the surplus. Specifically, the government must spend (P' × ab); that is, the product of the promised price floor times the amount of the surplus that is equal to area (QdabQs). This implies that there is an opportunity cost involved as financing this government expenditure will require imposing new taxes now, or borrowing more now and imposing higher taxes later or cutting back expenditures on some other government project (for example, not building some schools).

- The shaded area represents the welfare loss to society caused by the overproduction of the good and in turn the misallocation of resources; too much land is allocated to the production of one particular farm product. There is allocative inefficiency.

Policymakers' perspective

Despite the inefficiency, the waste and the additional government expenditures required by such a policy, it is not safe to argue that such policies should never be implemented. Policymakers must weigh the costs of a minimum price policy with the expected benefits. If the expected benefits for society are greater than the expected costs then such a policy should be adopted. For example, if by imposing a minimum price, farmers' incomes remain at an acceptable level and as a result a rural–urban wave of migration slows down then, at least temporarily, it may prove beneficial to society at large. Also, such support may be necessary as a means to alleviate rural poverty, which may also be important for maintaining a country's social fabric.

Imposing a price floor in the labour market

Price floors are also found in labour markets in the form of a minimum wage. In Luxembourg the minimum wage in 2020 is at 11.97€ per hour, in Greece at 3.94€ per hour and in Brazil at about $1.80 per hour. The reason for setting a minimum wage is to guarantee a socially acceptable level of income to unskilled workers. In Figure 2.7.3, the vertical axis measures the money wage rate (W) per worker and the horizontal axis depicts the number of workers (L).

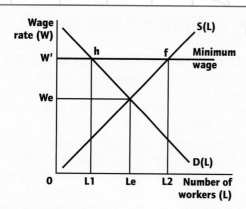

Figure 2.7.5 Minimum wage policy

Firms demand labour to produce the goods and services they produce. It is negatively sloped, as at higher wage rates firms will try to substitute capital for labour. Workers offer their labour services to the labour market. The supply of labour is upward sloping as at higher wage rates the opportunity cost of leisure increases (it becomes more expensive for someone to be outside the labour market) so more individuals will substitute work for leisure.

If the labour market is competitive then the equilibrium wage rate will be at We with Le individuals employed. If the government now considers that the market determined wage rate (We) is too low and decides to set a minimum wage at W', then firms at W' will want to hire fewer individuals than the number of individuals willing to offer their labour services. At the higher wage rate W' that the government sets, L2 individuals are looking for a job while firms will hire

only L1 workers. The excess supply (surplus) of labour L1L2 (or hf) represents unemployment.

A minimum wage policy will benefit some workers: those who will end up with a job at W' instead of We. It will typically, but not necessarily, create unemployment (L1L2) though, and will especially hurt the workers who would have had a job without this policy but are now left without one, namely individuals L1Le. It may not increase unemployment if firms are able to keep money wages below the competitive level.

Policymakers' perspective

If the minimum wage is not exorbitantly high then unemployment may not necessarily increase. Empirical evidence has shown that increases, modest at least, in the minimum wage have not resulted in higher unemployment. One reason for this outcome is that the increase in costs caused by the minimum wage is small relative to most firms' overall costs and only modest relative to the wages paid to low wage workers. On top, evidence suggests that employment increases faster when there is an increase in the minimum wage. Increased pay adds money to workers' income and allows them to buy more goods and services, creating higher demand, which in turn requires hiring more workers. Hence, the minimum wage may have little or no discernible effect on the employment prospects of low wage workers.

Recap

Price ceilings (maximum prices)		Price floors (minimum prices)	
Aim	to protect vulnerable consumers	Aim	to protect vulnerable producers, typically farmers
Price is set	below market-determined price	Price is set	above market-determined price
Results in	• a shortage • non-price rationing mechanisms • the emergence of parallel markets • worse quality and wider shortages in the long term	Results in	• a surplus • the government being forced to buy the resulting surplus • burdening taxpayers by the cost of the policy or in sacrifice of some other government project
Impact on consumers	some are better off, others are worse off	Impact on consumers	they are worse off
Impact on sellers	they are worse off	Impact on sellers	they are better off
Impact on welfare	inefficiency and welfare loss	Impact on welfare	inefficiency and welfare loss
Examples	rent controls, food price controls	Examples	agricultural price supports, minimum wage

2.8 Market failure—externalities and common pool or common access resources

Free markets: successes and failures

The fundamental economic problem that all societies face is scarcity: limited resources versus unlimited wants. This necessitates choices about which goods to produce and in what quantities. How will scarce resources be allocated? In a market economy, the answer is given by the market mechanism. The interaction of demand and supply, with consumers aiming to maximize utility and firms trying to maximize profits, determines how much of each good will be produced and consumed. If markets are free and competitive then the outcome is socially efficient. Allocative efficiency is achieved, as just the right amount of the good from society's point of view is produced and consumed, scarce resources are optimally allocated and social surplus is maximized.

In the real world however the necessary conditions to arrive at the socially efficient outcome are seldom present. Markets often do not work to the best interest of society and lead to either too much or too little of the good produced and consumed. When this happens, resources are misallocated, social surplus is not maximum and so the market fails. One such circumstance is the case of externalities.

Externalities

An externality is present if an economic activity (production or consumption) imposes costs on, or creates benefits for, third parties for which they do not get compensated, or do not pay for, respectively. Equivalently, an externality exists whenever there is a divergence between private and social costs of production or between private and social benefits of consumption. Externalities are also referred to as spillover effects.

An externality leads to a market failure as either more or less than the socially optimal amount is produced or consumed. Market forces alone fail to lead to an efficient resource allocation.

Externalities may arise in the production process, where they are known as production externalities, or in the consumption process, in which case they are known as consumption externalities. If they impose costs on third parties they are considered negative externalities. In contrast, if they generate benefits they are considered positive externalities.

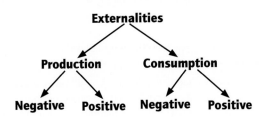

Relevant terms and definitions

Marginal private costs (MPC)

Marginal private costs are defined as the additional costs a firm incurs from producing an additional unit of a good. They include wages, costs of raw materials and other costs that a firm takes into consideration in its decision-making regarding production. It follows that the supply curve always reflects the MPC of a firm.

Marginal social costs (MSC)

These are defined as the costs of producing an additional unit of a good that are borne by society. They reflect the value of all resources that are sacrificed in the specific production process. This means that they include not just the labour and other resources that are sacrificed, the costs of which are taken into consideration by the firm, but also include any external costs that are not taken into consideration by firms in the form of, say, pollution. In this case the MSC of production exceed the MPC and should be drawn above the MPC (the supply) curve. This would be the case with a negative production externality. If, though, a production process creates benefits for a third party (say, another firm or the whole economy) then the MSC curve lies below the MPC (the supply) curve as there is an external production benefit involved in the process.

Marginal private benefits (MPB)

Marginal private benefits are defined as the additional benefits individuals enjoy from the consumption of an additional unit of a good. The willingness of consumers to pay for an additional unit is determined by the additional benefits enjoyed from consuming that additional unit. The demand curve always thus reflects the MPB enjoyed from consuming additional units of a good.

Marginal social benefits (MSB)

These are the benefits that society enjoys from each additional unit consumed. Marginal social benefits include the private benefits enjoyed by the individual consumers but in addition any benefits third parties may enjoy as a result (external benefits). It follows that the MSB curve lies above the MPB (the demand) curve. If, though, individuals' consumption imposes a cost on others then the MSC curve will lie below the MPB (the demand) curve, as there is an external cost of consumption generated by the process.

The Four Types of Externalities and Their Impact

A. Negative Production Externality

Heavy industry and power-plants in many countries use fossil fuels (coal, oil, natural gas) in their production process. But the burning of fossil fuels releases several greenhouse gases that contribute to global warming and climate change and lead to rising sea waters, extreme weather conditions (droughts and wildfires, floods, hurricanes), crop failures, health problems, the extinction of species and other costs. Demand, which always reflects the marginal private benefit of buyers, is identical to marginal social benefits as no external effects in consumption are assumed. Supply reflects the marginal private costs of such firms (that is, the costs they pay, such as for wages, energy and materials). Since the production process entails external costs in the form of pollution, it follows that society sacrifices more than such firms take into consideration. Society sacrifices environmental assets because of the pollution. The marginal social costs are therefore bigger than the marginal private costs by the amount of the external costs created given by the vertical distance (ab) in the figure below and so the MSC curve lies above the S, MPC curve.

> ### Tip
> There is no shift involved as the two curves, MPC and MSC, reflect different information.

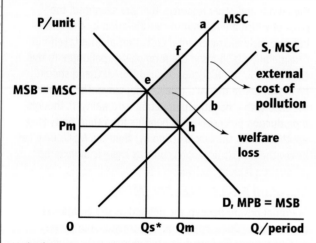

Market for steel: a case of negative production externality

Focusing on the figure above, the demand curve reflects both the MPB and the MSB since no externality is assumed in consumption. The market outcome is determined at the intersection of market demand and market supply leading to Qm units of steel produced at a market price of Pm.

The socially optimal level of output though is less at Qs*. Why at Qs*? Because for the last unit Qs*, the MSB is equal to the MSC. Note that for all units up to Qs*, the additional benefits society enjoys (MSB) from the steel produced exceed the additional costs society incurs (MSC), so all these units should be produced. On the other hand, past unit Qs*, the marginal costs incurred by society (MSC) are greater than the marginal benefits enjoyed by society (MSB). It follows that units Qs*Qm should not have been produced from society's point of view, but they are. There is overproduction of steel, which is the market failure in this case. The shaded area (efh) represents the welfare loss as a result of the market failure. This welfare loss reflects the net 'dollar' value lost by society from the production of units Qs*Qm. The market fails. Market forces lead to too much steel produced at too low of a price.

B. Negative Consumption Externality

When people consume alcohol there is always the risk of increased violence, of drunk driving, of lower productivity at work and other negative effects. These are all external costs of drinking. The supply of alcohol always reflects the MPC of liquor producers. The MPC are identical to the MSC as no external effects in the production process itself are assumed. Demand for alcohol reflects the MPB of those who consume the product. Since consumption of alcohol often creates external costs, it follows that the social benefits of alcohol consumption are lower than the private benefits that individuals enjoy when deciding whether to consume alcohol or not. The MSB of alcoholic beverages are therefore less by the amount of the external costs created given by the vertical distance (ab) in the figure below and so the MSB curve lies below the D, MPB curve.

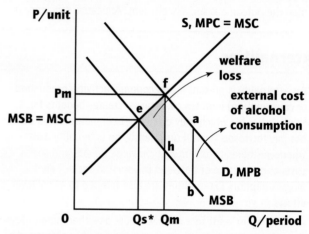

The market for alcoholic drinks: a case of negative consumption externality

Focusing on the figure above, the supply curve of alcohol reflects the MPC as well as the MSC of producing alcohol since no externality is assumed in the production of alcohol. The market equilibrium is determined at the intersection of the market demand and the market supply so Qm units of alcohol will be produced and consumed at a market determined price Pm.

The socially optimal level of alcohol consumption and production though is less at Qs*. Why at Qs*? Because for the last unit Qs*, the MSB is equal to the MSC. Note that for all units up to Qs*, the additional benefits society enjoys (MSB) from alcohol consumption exceed the additional costs society incurs (MSC), so all these units should be produced and consumed. On the other hand, past unit Qs*, the marginal costs incurred by society (MSC) are greater than the marginal benefits enjoyed by society (MSB). It follows that units Qs*Qm should not have been consumed from society's point of view, but they are. There is overconsumption and overprovision of alcohol, which is the market failure in this case. The shaded area (efh) represents the welfare loss as a result of the market failure. This welfare loss reflects the net 'dollar' value lost by society from the consumption of units Qs*Qm. The market fails. Market forces lead to too much alcohol consumed at too low a price.

Demerit goods

Demerit goods are a special class of goods that are defined as goods that governments would like to limit consumption of because individuals may not be aware of the costs arising from the consumption of such goods. This is a result of myopic behaviour and so the state takes a paternalistic role. Alternatively, demerit goods can be defined in terms of externalities generated. If the consumption of a good creates very significant negative externalities, then the product is referred to as a demerit good. Alcoholic drinks, tobacco products and even sugary drinks can all be considered good examples since individual consumers do not take into consideration the costs that arise from consuming such products while significant external costs arise. Analysis of demerit goods can thus be conducted within the negative consumption externality framework.

C. Positive Production Externality

The production of certain goods may generate positive externalities. The classic example of such a case was given by James Meade in his 1952 paper 'External Economies and Diseconomies in a Competitive Situation'. Imagine a region containing some apple orchards and some beekeeping. The beekeepers benefit from the apple farmers' trees as their bees feed on the apple blossom. But the apple farmers are not rewarded for the benefit they provide to the beekeepers. Demand, which always reflects the MPB is identical to MSB as no external effects in the consumption of apples are assumed. Supply of apples reflects the MPC of apple farmers. Yet, given the external benefits that arise from the production of apples, the social costs of apple growing are lower than the private costs. Thus, the MSC of apple production are less than the MPC incurred by apple farmers by the amount of the external benefit, illustrated by the vertical distance (ab) in the figure below. The MSC curve thus lies below the S, MPC curve.

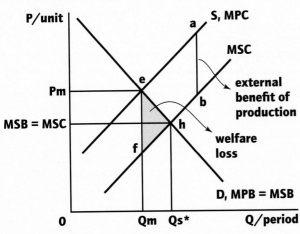

Market for apples: a case of positive production externality

Focusing on the figure above, the demand curve reflects both the MPB and the MSB since no externality is assumed in consumption. The market outcome is determined at the intersection of market demand and market supply so that Qm apples will be produced at a market price of Pm.

The socially optimal level of apple production though is more at Qs*. Why at Qs*? Because for the last unit Qs*, the MSB is equal to the MSC. For all units past unit Qm up until and including unit Qs*, the marginal benefits enjoyed by society exceed the marginal costs incurred by society, so units QmQs* should have been produced from society's point of view but they are not. The market leads to an underproduction of apples, which is the market failure in this case. The shaded area (efh) represents the welfare loss as a result of the market failure. This welfare loss reflects the net 'dollar' value lost by society from units Qm Qs* not being produced by the market even though they should have been from society's point of view. The market fails. Market forces lead to fewer apples being produced than the socially optimal.

A most significant example of positive production externalities relates to the production of infrastructure. Infrastructure investments, like the construction of a road network or of an airport, generate massive benefits not only for the users of the road network or the airport but for all society, as infrastructure permits faster growth. This explains why it is the state that typically finances such investments. Firms in the private sector would not be able to charge for all the benefits generated and thus less than the socially optimal level of infrastructure investment would result. The significance of infrastructure becomes painfully clear when examining many developing countries where it is either insufficient or crumbling. Another significant example of positive production externalities relates to R&D activities. When the outcome of a successful R&D project is such that it cannot be patented by a firm then the private sector will not be willing to get involved. Thus, R&D in basic science is also typically undertaken in state research agencies and universities or by government funded research institutions.

D. Positive Consumption Externality

If a student visits a doctor and gets vaccinated against the flu it is not only the student who benefits but also her classmates, teachers and others. Individuals wearing a mask during the covid-19 pandemic did not only protect themselves but also others. Focusing on vaccines, the supply of vaccines always reflects the MPC of producers of vaccines (pharmaceutical corporations). They are identical to MSC as no external effects in the production process of vaccines are assumed. Demand for vaccines reflects the MPB of those who are vaccinated. Since their vaccination creates external benefits to others in the form of a lower probability that those others will get sick, it follows that the social benefits of vaccine consumption are greater than the private benefits that individuals take into account in deciding whether to have a vaccination or not. The MSB of vaccines are therefore greater than the MPB by the amount of the external benefit created given by the vertical distance (ab) in the figure below and so the MSB curve lies above the D, MPB curve.

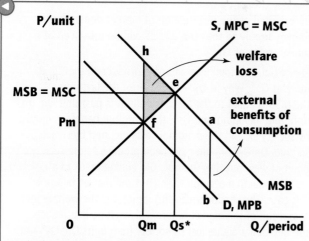

Market for vaccines: a case of positive consumption externality

Focusing on the figure above, the supply curve reflects the MPC as well as the MSC of producing vaccines since no externality is assumed in the production process. The market equilibrium is determined at the intersection of the market demand and the market supply so that Qm vaccines will be produced and consumed at a market price Pm.

The socially optimal level of consumption though is more at Qs*? Why at Qs*? Because for the last unit Qs*, the MSB is equal to the MSC. Units QmQs* should have been consumed from society's point of view but they are not. For all units past unit Qm up until and including unit Qs*, the marginal benefits enjoyed by society exceed the marginal costs incurred by society. The market therefore leads to an underconsumption of vaccines, which is the market failure in this case. The shaded area (efh) represents the welfare loss as a result of the market failure. This welfare loss reflects the net 'dollar' value lost by society from units Qm Qs* not being consumed even though they should have been from society's point of view. The market fails. Market forces lead to fewer vaccines being consumed than the socially optimal.

Merit goods

Merit goods are a special class of goods that are defined as goods that the government would like all members of society to consume in adequate quantities independently of their income or even their preferences. Individuals may not be aware of the benefits arising from the consumption of such goods because of myopic behaviour. This is why education is compulsory in many countries up to at least a certain level. Note the paternalistic role of the state in this case. Alternatively, merit goods can be defined in terms of externalities generated. If the consumption of a good creates very significant positive externalities then it is referred to as a merit good. Education and health care are prime examples. Analysis of merit goods can thus be conducted within the positive consumption externality framework.

Summary Table

Demand	Supply
Demand always reflects the MPB enjoyed by consumers: when drawing the demand curve instead of simply labelling it D, label it 'D, MPB'.	Supply always reflects the MPC paid by firms: when drawing the supply curve instead of simply labelling it S, label it 'S, MPC'.
If there is no externality in consumption then the benefits enjoyed by society are not any different from the benefits enjoyed by the individuals consuming the good, so label the demand curve 'D, MPB=MSB'.	If there is no externality in production then the costs imposed on society are not any different from the costs paid by the firms producing the good, so label the supply curve 'S, MPC=MSC'.
If, though, there is an externality in consumption then one of two cases applies: i. If there is an external cost in the consumption of the good then the MSB curve lies below the D, MPB curve (negative consumption externality). External costs arise in the market for alcoholic drinks, tobacco and sugar-sweetened beverages. ii. If there is an external benefit in the consumption of the good then the MSB curve lies above the D, MPB curve (positive consumption externality). External benefits arise in the market for flu vaccinations and more generally in health care and education services.	If, though, there is an externality in production then one of two cases applies: i. If there is an external cost in the production of a good then the MSC curve lies above the S, MPC curve (negative production externality). External costs arise in production processes that use fossil fuels and pollute. ii. If there is an external benefit in the production of a good then the MSC curve lies below the S, MPC curve (positive production externality). External benefits arise in the production of infrastructure and of basic science R&D.

Government intervention in response to externalities

Dealing with Negative Production Externalities

– Indirect (Pigovian) taxes

The pioneering work recommending government intervention in the case of polluting firms is attributed to Cambridge economist A.C. Pigou (1920) when he proposed the imposition of an indirect tax equal to the size of the external cost generated by the firm. The indirect tax would in principle internalize the externality in the sense that it would force the firm to take it into consideration. The tax would raise the firm's production costs (MPC) to the level of the social costs (MSC) associated with the production process. This would induce the firm to limit output to the socially optimal level. The principle underlying this solution is referred to as the 'polluter pays principle' and all taxes that force polluters to pay for the pollution they generate are referred to as Pigovian taxes. The figure below illustrates the effect of imposing a Pigovian tax on polluting firms in the steel industry.

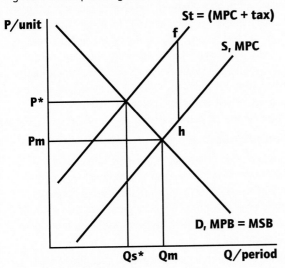

Market for steel: effect of a Pigovian tax

The government estimates the size of the pollution (external) costs that firms create and imposes an indirect tax equal to that amount which is given by the vertical distance (fh) in the figure above. Steel manufacturers now have to pay the tax in addition to their manufacturing costs. Thus, the new supply curve with the tax has shifted to the level of the MSC curve. The market will adjust to the Pigovian tax by moving to a new equilibrium, with a higher price of P* for steel and a lower quantity Qs*. The tax has resulted in the optimal level of steel production. In other words, steel is produced only to the point where the marginal social benefits are equal to the marginal social costs. Also, note that even though the tax was levied on producers, a portion of the tax is passed on to buyers in the form of a price increase for steel (from Pm to P*). This causes buyers to cut back their purchases from Qm to Qs*.

A gasoline tax is an example of a Pigovian tax. It raises the driver's cost to cover the negative externalities created by driving automobiles. In the United States, the federal gas tax was $0.183 per gallon in 2019. The average state gas tax was $0.2868 per gallon. The revenue goes into the federal Highway Trust Fund to pay for roadway maintenance. Other examples of Pigovian taxes on products include the tax often imposed on pesticides and on chemical fertilizers.

Nevertheless, determining the appropriate tax on every individual product that causes environmental damage can be a difficult task. Estimating the tax amount in monetary terms requires research and analysis. If the production of some goods causes relatively minimal environmental damages, then the small amount of taxes collected may not be worth the costs of estimating the correct amount of tax. Also, there are administrative costs involved in imposing and collecting the tax. If a product does not cause much environmental damage, then these costs might outweigh the revenues collected. In addition, even if the tax leads to the optimal rate of output Qs*, the size of the total level of pollution generated by the activity (which is equal to the area between the MSC and the MPC curves for output up to Qs*) is dependent on the PED for the good. If demand is very price inelastic, the total pollution generated may be still unacceptably high given all other pollution-generating activities in the economy. Moreover, the demand for any good reflects the preferences only of the present generation and ignores future generations, which will be hardest hit by polluting activities. Another issue is that the effects of polluting activities extend beyond national borders but Pigovian taxation does not.

Therefore, instead of imposing Pigovian taxes on final consumer products, economists generally recommend applying Pigovian taxes as far upstream in the production process as possible. An upstream tax is imposed at the level of raw production inputs. This is the case of carbon taxes analysed below.

– Carbon taxes

A carbon tax is a Pigovian tax levied on carbon-based fossil fuels in proportion to the amount of carbon dioxide emitted during production and use. Such a tax raises the price of carbon-based energy sources such as oil, coal and natural gas and so provides incentives to users to conserve energy as it would reduce their tax burden. At the same time, users thus are induced to switch to sources of energy that produce lower carbon emissions and are thus taxed at lower rates. As a result, the external costs of production decrease and the socially optimal level of output increases. The figure below illustrates the effect of the imposition of a carbon tax in the electricity industry.

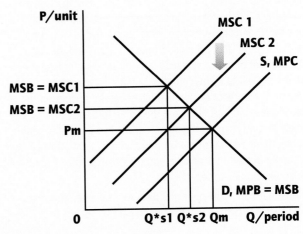

Market for electricity: effect of a carbon tax

The external costs of production decrease as a result of the lower use of carbon-based fuels and so the MSC curve shifts from MSC1 to MSC2. The fall in external costs allows the socially optimal level of output to increase from $Q*s1$ to $Q*s2$ which is closer to the market outcome Qm. The decreased vertical distance between MPC and MSC2 implies that the size of the required carbon tax on the cleaner (lower carbon content) fuel is lower.

A carbon tax has been in place since 2008 in British Columbia, Canada. The tax is equal to 30 Canadian dollars per ton of carbon dioxide and affects an estimated 77% of British Columbia's total greenhouse gas emissions. All revenue generated through this carbon tax programme is returned to British Columbians through rebates or cuts in other taxes. After four years in effect, British Columbia's per capita consumption of fuels subject to the tax was found to have declined by 19% compared to the rest of Canada.

Governments however may be reluctant to set carbon taxes high enough as they hurt businesses. In addition, in many cases the carbon tax placed on power-generating firms has led to higher energy bills for households which increase the cost of living and hurt even more lower income families.

Yet, in Canada to help protect low-income households from the resulting higher prices, the government through the Low Income Climate Action Tax Credit programme provides residents with lump sum tax credits. The carbon tax revenue collected is often divided equally among the whole population so lower income households receive rebates in excess of the carbon taxes they had paid. Also, governments can redirect the revenue from carbon taxes to lower other taxes. A carbon tax can be matched, for example, with a cut in income or social security taxes. In addition, the higher cost of energy may also create a powerful incentive for energy-saving technological innovations and stimulate new markets.

– Tradable pollution permits ('cap and trade' schemes)

Besides taxation another government response involves tradable pollution permits also known as cap and trade schemes, whereby each emitting firm is allocated a specific permissible level of greenhouse gas emissions. More specifically, the government sets the desired national goal of emissions and issues the permits accordingly. For example, if greenhouse gas emissions for a particular country are currently 40 million tons and the policy goal is to reduce this by 10 percent (4 million tons), then permits would be issued to emit only 36 million tons. The cap (and, hence, the number of permits) is reduced over time so that total emissions will fall. The permits can initially be allocated for free on the basis of past emissions or can be auctioned to the highest bidders. Firms are then able to trade permits freely among them in the open market. The price of a permit is determined through market demand and supply forces as a simple demand for permits and (vertical) supply of permits diagram can illustrate.

Firms that can lower their pollution and save permits at a cost that is less than what they can earn by selling their saved permits have an incentive to lower their level of pollution; on the other hand, firms that find it cheaper to buy additional permits in the open market than to lower their level of pollution have an incentive to buy permits. Thus, a new allocation of permits results but pollution will have decreased by those firms that can do it cost effectively i.e. with the least cost.

In 2005, the EU launched the European Union Emissions Trading Scheme (EU ETS), which operates in 31 countries and is the largest emissions trading system in the world. It limits emissions from more than 11,000 heavy energy-using installations (power stations and industrial plants) as well as airlines operating between these countries, and it covers around 45 percent of the EU's greenhouse gas emissions. Emissions in the EU were reduced by 22% between 1990 and 2015 and according to the European Environment Agency (EEA) the decrease was mostly driven by emissions reductions in power generation.

Although tradable permits in theory bring pollution down to the desired level, they may under certain circumstances actually lead to an increase in the level of emissions. If costs of reducing emissions fall drastically for some firms (those using newer technology), the permit price will fall, allowing plants with older technology to cheaply purchase more permits and actually increase emissions. Surprisingly, better pollution control technology can lead to more pollution by some firms. Nevertheless, this can be avoided by reducing the total number of permits issued.

– Direct regulation

Governments can also address the issue of negative production externalities by resorting to direct regulation. Governments can directly regulate the level of output of polluting firms, the prices they charge, where they may or may not locate as well as the type of machines, filters and fuel they can use.

For example, the International Maritime Organization (IMO) has recently decreased substantially the limit for sulphur in fuel oil on board ships. This regulation will result in a more than 75% decrease in sulphur oxide emissions from ships and will thus have major health and environmental benefits for the world, especially for people living close to ports and coasts.

Regulations are usually easier to design and implement compared to Pigovian taxation or tradable permits. In many cases they are considered a realistic, certain and cost-effective solution. Still, monitoring adherence by the authorities requires allocating a significant amount of resources that range from manpower to specialized instruments.

– Increasing awareness and education

This is a different set of solutions whereby the government attempts to change the preferences and practices of consumers and of firms by increasing their awareness of the external costs of certain activities they undertake. By making school children aware of the benefits of recycling today the government aims at creating citizens who will make better choices about such issues in future. When polluting firms are exposed, the bad publicity they receive may force them to alter their practices.

The most appropriate pollution control policy depends upon the circumstances. While economists generally prefer market-based solutions such as Pigovian taxation and tradable permits there are situations when these policies might not be the best choice especially if pollution is localized and not dispersed.

With direct regulation and tradable permits, the government can set a cap on total emissions. With taxation, the resulting pollution level will be unknown in advance as it depends on how firms and even final consumers will adjust their behavior to the resulting increased prices. Thus, if the policy objective is to keep pollution levels below a predetermined level with certainty, regulations or a 'cap and trade' scheme may be the best options. On the other hand, if encouraging innovation in cleaner technologies is the objective, a Pigovian tax may be preferable. Still, enacting pollution taxes can be politically difficult as new taxes are typically unpopular. In theory, a pollution tax can be revenue-neutral if the revenues from the tax are offset by lowering other taxes—but this may or may not occur in practice. Tradable permit systems on the other hand tend to be more politically popular, especially if firms believe they can lobby policymakers to receive free permits.

Dealing with Negative Consumption Externalities (Demerit Goods)

– Indirect taxation

In the case of a negative consumption externality the goal is to reduce the consumption of the good generating the external costs. Indirect taxes are one option. In most countries around the world there are taxes on tobacco products. Recently, taxes have also been placed on sugary drinks and perhaps a tax on red meat may soon follow. More specifically, a sugar tax is in place in the UK since 2018. Officially called the Soft Drinks Industry Levy (SDIL), the tax puts a charge of 24p on drinks containing 8g of sugar per 100ml and 18p a litre on those with 5–8g of sugar per 100ml.

An indirect tax equal to the external costs of consumption will decrease supply and so increase the price of the good. The higher price will induce a lower level of consumption. If the size of the tax is correct, the socially optimal level of consumption may be achieved. The figure below illustrates the case.

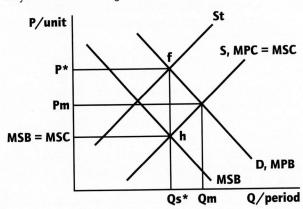

Market for sugary beverages: the impact of an indirect tax

The specific tax fh will decrease supply to St. As a result, the market price of sugary drinks will increase to P*. The higher price will lead to a decrease in the quantity consumed to Qs*, the socially optimal level of consumption.

Several issues arise with such a solution. Again, the optimal tax is difficult to determine. Let's take the examples of drinking and smoking. Alcohol and tobacco are addictive, so demand is quite price inelastic. This means that if the goal is to curtail smoking then a very high tax on cigarettes will be needed. The reason is that with a very high tax, the monthly expenditure on cigarettes will represent a large proportion of the monthly income for many households thus deterring consumption. Remember that price elasticity of demand also depends on the proportion of income spent on the good. The impact of even a high tax on higher income individuals will be minimal but studies point that the prevalence of smoking decreases with higher levels of income and the level of education.

On the other hand, in the case of alcohol, a tax aiming at decreasing heavy drinking is considered rather ineffective. The reason is that there are very many different types (whisky, vodka, wine, white cider etc.) and for each type there are very many different brands and qualities that differ dramatically in price. Thus, if, say, 20% tax is imposed on alcoholic drinks then a 'chain of substitutions' may start with many poorer addicted individuals just switching to lower priced and lower quality alcoholic substitutes so that overall consumption decreases very little.

Many consumers may also seek to buy the good in a black market where no tax is paid to the government. Consumption may therefore not decrease as expected and, even worse, health-related problems may result if the products are of a lower or dubious quality while the government earns less in tax revenue. Tax hikes on tobacco products that successive governments in Greece have implemented have contributed to a loss of tax revenues as many smokers switched to parallel markets.

Lastly, keep in mind that indirect taxes are *regressive*. Thus, low-income consumers will be burdened proportionately more.

– Legislation and regulation

Often governments regulate consumption of demerit goods and the behaviour of those who consume them. This may involve a ban just like has happened with smoking which has been banned from public spaces in many countries. Or, it may involve legal age limits whereby a minimum age at which a person can legally consume a good is set.

Another approach to reduce consumption of certain demerit goods is packaging warnings where manufacturers are forced by law to include health warnings on their products. This has been applied to both tobacco products and alcoholic beverages. Recently, packaging requirements for tobacco products have increased. Australia was the first country to introduce the plain packaging law, which refers to packaging that requires the removal of all branding, allowing manufacturers to print only the brand name in a standardized font in addition to the health warnings. All these laws and regulations aim to reduce demand and shift it closer to MSB.

– Minimum unit price

In the case of alcohol, a price floor may also be used to decrease consumption. Given that there are many types of alcohol and very many different brands, the minimum price imposed is analytically different from a minimum price on a farm product like corn and thus a simple demand and supply diagram cannot be used.

More specifically, the Scottish government was first to set a minimum price on a 'unit of alcohol' at 50p. The unit of alcohol was defined as 10ml of pure alcohol. For each alcoholic beverage, the number of units of alcohol contained is determined and thus the minimum price at which it can be sold is the number of units contained times 50p. This means that stronger alcoholic drinks that contain more units of alcohol become more expensive and since a 'chain of substitutions' cannot occur, their consumption will decrease. Heavy drinkers will be forced to quit or to switch to alcoholic drinks with less alcohol content that will be cheaper. Studies published in the BMJ have found that introduction of minimum unit pricing appears to have been successful in reducing consumption of alcohol in Scotland especially in lower income households and the purchase of cheap, high-strength alcohol.

– Increasing awareness and education

Governments use advertising to increase awareness about the risks of smoking and drinking. The goal is to inform the public of the health-related costs of smoking and drinking. However, given the nature of goods like cigarettes and alcohol or even sugary drinks, those already addicted may not be incentivized to reduce their consumption. Still, it may be that persuasion will actually prevent the young from taking up such habits. The effectiveness of advertising and persuasion can only be seen in the long term and must be complementary to other price-related policies and also regulations.

– Nudges

'Nudges' to reduce smoking and alcohol consumption are also used as a complementary strategy to pricing policies. Plain packaging mentioned earlier as well as visual display bans (placing tobacco products far from the checkout area of the store) are gaining in popularity. Removing information on cigarette packs regarding the amount of tar, nicotine and carbon monoxide in a brand may nudge smokers towards considering all tobacco products equally dangerous and threatening.

Framing a message sent to drinkers by telling them how their drinking ranks compared to others ('You are in the top 10% of heaviest drinkers') has been shown to lead to more individuals asking for help. Or, the default size for a draught beer in British pubs can change to a half pint instead of a pint thus requiring customers to ask for a pint.

Policymakers' perspective

Decreasing negative consumption externalities related to drinking or smoking is a complex issue that requires a multidimensional response. No single policy initiative is considered sufficient to reduce consumption of these goods. Any success that has been achieved cannot be attributed to any one policy.

Higher prices, either as a result of indirect taxes or as a result of some form of minimum price, are credited with significant success and policymakers agree that price signals are important to lower alcohol and tobacco use. Of course, higher prices are more effective in decreasing the consumption of lower income households which seems unfair but at the same time it is the poor who are often more at risk especially from heavy drinking, so if the policy is successful then, in the long term, they will reap the benefits of better health.

Regulations, being direct, have a more certain effect than higher prices which are favored in several settings. Banning tobacco use in public places to protect the health of non-smokers and prohibiting the sale of tobacco and alcohol to minors are more successful policy choices than taxation, since higher prices would not necessarily be sufficient to protect non-smokers or minors. It is thus generally agreed that a wide range of interventions is required. Higher prices, regulations and nudges are all important and should be used in a complementary fashion. Increasing public awareness, especially of the young, is also very crucial in this effort. Ignorance about the ill effects of smoking, drinking and even of excessive sugar consumption would make it much more difficult for policymakers to curtail consumption of demerit goods. Of course, increased information alone about the risks of consuming such goods without higher prices, regulations or nudges would prove insufficient.

Dealing with Positive Production Externalities
– Granting a subsidy

Granting a subsidy will decrease the costs of production associated with the activity generating the externality and will thus decrease price and induce a greater level of output. Using the James Meade apple farmer and beekeeper example presented earlier, the subsidy will lower production costs for the apple farmer and if the subsidy is equal to the external benefit of production then the MPC will become equal to MSC so that the level of apple production will reach the socially optimal level.

The problem once again is that it is difficult to estimate properly the size of the external benefits generated and so the correct size of the subsidy. Therefore, the subsidy may not be enough to correct market failure and ensure allocative efficiency or indeed the subsidy might lead to overproduction of the good. Also, a subsidy is associated with opportunity cost. The funds spent on the subsidy could have been used for spending in other areas such as public health or public education.

– Direct provision

The government may itself provide the good that generates positive externalities associated with its production. For example, the government typically funds infrastructure investments such as the construction of airports, power and communication grids, sewerage, sanitation and wastewater facilities etc.

It also engages directly (through public universities or research institutes) or indirectly (through providing research grants and other funding) with research and development (R&D) activities that advance scientific knowledge.

Note that both the granting of subsidies and direct provision require funding. Financing thus requires higher taxes now, or borrowing now and higher taxes later and has an opportunity cost.

Dealing with Positive Consumption Externalities (Merit Goods)

– Granting a subsidy

The government can grant a subsidy equal to the size of the external benefit created. The subsidy would lower production costs and increase supply leading to a lower price and a higher level of consumption which in principle would be equal to the socially optimal level, as illustrated in the figure below.

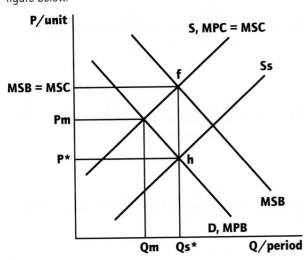

Market for flu vaccinations: the impact of a subsidy

The subsidy increases supply of the good (for example vaccinations) to Ss. The market price will consequently drop to P*. Consumers at the lower price P* will be willing to consume Qs* which is equal to the socially optimal level of consumption.

Again, estimating the proper size of the subsidy is not an easy task. Also, there is an opportunity cost associated with subsidies. The cost of the subsidy must be somehow financed. Either taxes must increase now, or the government must borrow now and tax later or some other government project must be scratched. All these options involve an opportunity cost so that the additional benefits accruing to society from any such subsidy must be weighed against these costs.

– Legislation

Governments may also try to increase consumption of goods with positive externalities through legislation. For example, many countries have legislation that makes education compulsory up to a certain level. Similarly, in many countries there are laws that require children to be vaccinated against certain types of disease.

– Direct provision

When a government considers that the external benefits are very significant to the economy and that any positive price may be prohibitively high for some, very poor, members of society it often directly provides the good or the service free at point of delivery. In many countries this is the case with state education, or with national health-care systems and public hospitals. Direct provision is of course costly and creates a significant burden on the government's budget. The state must run schools and hospitals equipped with trained professionals, or purchase and distribute vaccinations for free. All these government expenditures eventually are paid by taxpayers.

– Increasing awareness and education

Governments also resort to advertising the benefits from the consumption and use of such goods in an attempt to increase their demand to the level of the MSB curve. Many countries, for example, have campaigns and programmes that try to increase enrolment in schools and in colleges. Increased awareness about the benefits of education may convince parents in many countries to ensure that their children are not only enrolled but also attend school and may convince high school graduates to attend or not to drop out from college. Campaigns to increase awareness about the benefits of covid-19 vaccinations are also organized in many countries.

Dealing with...			
Negative production externalities	Negative consumption externalities	Positive production externalities	Positive consumption externalities
• Indirect taxes (Pigovian taxes) • Carbon taxes • Tradable pollution permits ("cap and trade" schemes) • Direct regulation • Increasing awareness and education	• Indirect taxes • Legislation and regulation • Increasing awareness and education • Nudges	• Subsidies • Direct provision	• Subsidies • Legislation • Direct provision • Increasing awareness and education

Common pool or common access resources

Common pool or common access resources are resources that are not owned by anyone but are available for anyone to use without payment. Examples include fisheries, forests, wildlife, irrigation systems (groundwater), hunting grounds, pastures and lakes. Note that since the atmosphere has been used as a 'sink' of many anthropogenic pollutants it is also considered a common resource. These are all renewable resources in the sense that they can replenish themselves unless they are overused by humans.

Technically speaking, a common resource is a **non-excludable good** because people cannot easily be excluded from using it. The other characteristic of a common resource is that it is a **rival good**, meaning that its use by one person diminishes the quantity or quality of the resource available to others. That is to say that one individual's use subtracts from the benefits available to others using the resource and for this reason the rivalrous characteristic of common pool resources is also referred to as subtractability.

Consider the open seas an example of a common pool resource. Fishing vessels can catch as many fish as they are able to as no one can be excluded from fishing in these waters. But if one vessel catches a ton of fish there will be one ton less available for all other vessels to catch. One person's use of a common resource subtracts from the amount available for all others. This implies that others will have to fish longer and harder to catch the same amount of fish.

The result is an overuse of common pool resources. Assume a pasture open to all ("the commons") with the adjacent land owned by a number of herdsmen. Each herdsman has the incentive to have more and more of his cattle graze on the commons because he enjoys the full benefits of this as his animals are fed. However, the costs are shared by all. As a result, there will be overgrazing and the commons will be destroyed. This is also why fish stocks in many parts of the world are severely depleted or why many forests are disappearing. According to the UN's Food and Agriculture Organization the percentage of the world's assessed fish stocks that are overexploited or fully exploited is 87% while 1.3 million square kilometers of forest have disappeared between 1990 and 2016. A resource that is non-excludable and subtractable is usually overused and this is referred to as the "Tragedy of the Commons", a term introduced by Garrett Hardin in his 1968 SCIENCE paper.

Analytically, the effect of such behaviour may be illustrated through a negative externalities diagram, as in the figure below, which illustrates the decisions of a fishing firm. What is important to notice in the diagram is that the MSC of fishing exceed the MPC the fishing firm takes into consideration. The activity imposes costs on all other fishing boats as they are forced to fish harder and for longer. It also imposes costs on future generations as unsustainable fishing practices risk depleting fisheries around the world. However, these are costs external to a fishing firm's decisions. The MSC curve is drawn steeper to illustrate that the external costs increase as the volume of fishing increases and the fishery is depleted.

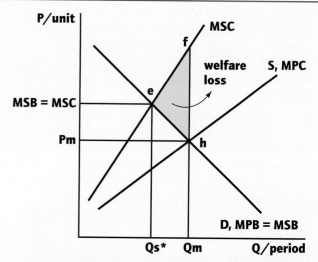

The fishing firm will choose to fish Qm units where the MPB of fishing an additional unit are equal to the MPC of the activity. The optimal level of fishing though is less at Qs*, where MSB is equal to MSC of the activity. More fishing than the socially optimal level takes place.

The depletion or degradation of common pool resources poses a threat to sustainability, as overexploitation implies that the resource will not be available for others to use in the future.

Responses to the threat to sustainability common pool resources face

(note that given that the atmosphere is a common pool resource all the responses to negative production externalities explained earlier also apply here)

– Regulation by the government ("top-down" approach)

In certain cases, regulation by governments may prove effective. Setting fishing quotas is an example. Fishing quotas are catch limits (usually expressed in tonnes) that are set for most commercial fish stocks. The EU has set fishing quotas for the managing of fisheries and for preventing depletion of fish stocks. But, even with fishing quotas, there may still be issues. For instance, a shipping company of a certain nationality is only subject to its national government's fishing quota. Yet, if its fleet is flagged under a different country it is no longer subject to the quota. Other regulations may involve restrictions regarding hunting seasons, issuing licenses or permits for particular activities (such as hunting or fishing), the establishment of protected areas for endangered ecosystems as well as emission standards. Nevertheless, such regulations may often involve significant costs of monitoring to detect possible violations.

– International agreements

Regulations are typically imposed by national governments. However, the overuse of common access resources often has international consequences, in which case international cooperation of governments is necessary. For instance, much of the open water of the oceans is a common-pool resource to governments as well as to individual fishermen. No single body can exercise control over it. As long as that continues to be the case, the corrective action will be difficult to implement. In recognition of this fact, there is now an evolving law of the sea defined by international treaties. The global scope of many common pool resources, therefore, requires new and reformed institutions that can manage common pool resources at an international level.

The Paris Agreement on Climate Change was adopted by 197 countries in Paris on 12 December 2015. Its goal is to reduce global greenhouse gas emissions and to ensure that the global temperature increase in this century is below 2 degrees Celsius above pre-industrial levels and hopefully even below 1.5 degrees. It is worth noting that the Paris Agreement does not guarantee these outcomes, but it requires signatories to commit to reduce emissions through plans for climate action referred to as nationally determined contributions (NDCs). It represents a step toward realization, on the part of the signatory countries, that there was a common interest in combatting climate change. Even though the US had withdrawn in June 2017 under President Trump, it rejoined under President Biden and the Paris Agreement will enter into force for the US on 19 February 2021. This is important as even though the US represents just over 4 percent of the world's population, it emits almost a third of the excess carbon dioxide in the atmosphere. By rejoining, countries producing two-thirds of all global carbon pollution will have committed to net-zero emissions, up from just half without the US.

Prior to the Paris Agreement there were a few noteworthy efforts concerning climate change. The 1992 Rio Earth Summit led to a first "Framework Convention" and in 1997 the Kyoto Protocol was signed but overall these were not successful.

– Education

Educating, especially the young, on the importance of adopting environmentally conscious behaviour may have considerable long-term significance.

– Collective self-governance ('bottom-up' approach)

A different approach is the self-governance of the commons as proposed by Elinor Ostrom (Nobel Prize in Economics 2009). The idea is that, under certain conditions, a group of users of a common pool resource can and has devised frameworks of use that effectively regulate access to the resource and balance resource use and resource renewal.

More specifically, if users can engage in face-to-face bargaining and have autonomy to change their rules, they may well attempt to organize themselves. For the self-organized management of the common resource to be feasible it must be that:

- The resource is not at a point of deterioration such that it is useless to organize or so overutilized that little advantage results from organizing.
- Reliable and valid information about the general condition of the resource is available at reasonable costs.
- Users are dependent on the resource for a major portion of their livelihood.
- Users have a shared image of the resource and how their actions affect each other and the resource.
- Users trust each other to keep promises and relate to one another with reciprocity.

Many scholars conclude that only very small groups can organize themselves effectively because they presume that size is related to the uniformity of a group, which is needed to initiate and sustain self-governance. For example, if groups from diverse cultural backgrounds share access to a forest, the key question affecting the likelihood of self-organized solutions is whether the views of the multiple groups concerning the structure of the forest, interpretation of rules, trust and reciprocity differ or are similar.

Overall, for users to contemplate changing the framework of use, they have to conclude that the expected benefits from an institutional change will exceed the immediate and long-term expected costs. Whether the self-governed management succeeds over the long term depends on whether the institutions the users develop have clearly defined boundaries, involve collective-choice arrangements and include monitoring and conflict-resolution mechanisms.

2.9 Market failure—public goods

Public goods

A good is considered a public good if it is characterized by the following two properties.

- It is non-excludable. This means that if the good becomes available to even one consumer it automatically becomes available to all. No one can be excluded from consuming it.

- Consumption of the good is non-rival. This means that each individual's consumption of the good does not decrease the amount available for all others.

Non-excludability leads to individuals hiding their true preferences and behaving as free-riders because they know that they can enjoy the good without having to pay for it once it becomes available for others. Non-rivalry in consumption implies that the marginal cost of an extra user is zero.

The externality aspect of public goods becomes apparent by realizing that if someone provides or maintains a public good, even at a cost, he or she cannot prevent others from enjoying the benefits. So, if the private benefits of providing a public good are small compared to the social benefits and the private costs are larger than the private benefits, then the good will not be supplied at all.

More generally, public goods are a case of market failure because private profit-oriented firms will not have the incentive to produce and offer such goods and services through the market. The market mechanism fails. Even though there may be sufficient demand for such a good, it will not be offered.

Few examples of pure public goods exist. National defence, traffic lights and lighthouses are examples. Once national defence is provided to one citizen it is impossible to stop others from enjoying the benefits of national security. Also, if one citizen enjoys the benefits, this does not diminish the amount available for others to enjoy. Similarly, if a traffic light is placed at an intersection it automatically becomes available to all drivers. No driver can be excluded from the benefits. In addition, the use of the traffic light by one driver does not diminish the benefits available for other drivers. Or, if a lighthouse is built and maintained, no ship can be excluded from its benefits. In addition, if the lighthouse benefits one ship, the same amount of benefit is available to all other ships. Peace and security of a community is a somewhat different example but satisfies both criteria of a public good. For example, if it is peaceful and secure for one citizen in a community then, probably, the same applies to others. Also, if that citizen benefits from peace and security there is no less benefit available for others.

A different example of a pure public good is radio and off-the-air television broadcasting. Both public good properties are satisfied. A radio broadcast is normally available to any household with a receiver (a private, separate good). Also, if one person listens to a programme there is no less

of it available for others to listen to. Interestingly, off-the-air television and radio broadcasting, despite their public good features, are produced and offered by private, for-profit companies. This is possible because broadcasters are not selling the programmes but the advertising time, which is both excludable and rival.

> **Recap**
>
> ### Public goods
>
> Public goods are:
>
> - **non-excludable:** if the good becomes available to even one consumer it automatically becomes available to all.
>
> - **non-rival:** each individual's consumption of the good does not decrease the amount available for all others.
>
> - Examples of public goods are traffic lights, peace and national security.
>
> - Public goods are a case of **market failure** because private profit-oriented firms will not have the incentive to produce and offer such goods and services through the market.

Government intervention in response to public goods

The government must provide public goods, using tax revenue. Note, though, that the government is not necessarily producing the public goods. For instance, traffic lights or military aircraft are not produced by the government but by private firms who are contracted by the state. However, the following points should be considered.

- There are opportunity costs associated with such expenditures on public goods, as these expenditures must be financed either by higher taxes now or by borrowing now and imposing higher taxes later—or by cutting other government expenditures such as on health care or education.

- Evaluating the benefits and costs is not easy and often open to debate. For example, should the local government of a town install traffic lights? If so, should there be traffic lights at all intersections? How many traffic lights should be installed? The local government should conduct a cost-benefit analysis but there is unfortunately room for corruption as some individuals may use the power of their office for their own private benefit. The result could be that we end up with more traffic lights or military aircraft than necessary. This could imply much less allocated on health care and education.

2.10 Market failure—asymmetric information (HL)

HL

Asymmetric information occurs in a market when one party in the transaction has access to more or better information than the other party. In such situations resources are not allocated efficiently and the market fails. There are two distinct problems that asymmetric information can lead to: adverse selection and moral hazard.

Adverse selection

HL

Adverse selection relates to limitations on information and occurs when one party knows more about the product being sold than the other party.

- Consider the used car market. Sellers have more information about the condition of their cars than potential buyers. Due to asymmetric information, buyers are willing to offer an "average" price based on the used cars offered. However, sellers of better than average cars withdraw from the market. This results in a decrease in the average quality of cars, as there are fewer good cars now being sold. The price buyers are willing to offer decreases, leading to a greater number of better than average cars withdrawn. The market thins out and may collapse.

- Something similar happens in the market for health insurance. A health insurance company cannot determine the health status of its potential customers. Individuals in good health know that they are less likely to incur medical expenses. As a result, they are discouraged from buying the company's insurance plan as they find it expensive. This leaves the health insurance company with exactly the customers it does not want: people with a higher risk of needing medical care. In response, the firm will raise premiums, trying to compensate for the payouts to its less healthy customers. This will also drive away more of the remaining healthier customers. Again, the market for health insurance becomes thin and possibly collapses.

Moral hazard

HL

Another problem of asymmetric information is moral hazard. Moral hazard occurs when individuals have the incentive to alter their behaviour after a contract has been signed, while someone else bears the cost. This can occur because they have better information regarding their behaviour compared to the other party, while the other party in the contract cannot easily monitor their behaviour. For example, buyers of car insurance may become less careful while driving, because

they will not bear the cost of any damage they might cause. Similarly, doctors with malpractice insurance may put less effort into avoiding malpractice because they know that the insurer will cover the costs. In both examples, this happens because individuals on one side of the contract have more information about their own actions than the insurers, while their behaviour cannot be easily monitored.

Responses to asymmetric information

HL

Government responses

- Governments can legislate minimum quality and safety standards and can regulate firms' behaviour in order to minimize information-related market failures. However, legislation and regulation are arduous, bureaucratic procedures. Also, regulatory and quality control activities have very large opportunity costs and may impose large costs on firms, especially if these activities are excessive.

- Governments may also choose to provide information to consumers that will protect buyers in their purchasing decisions. However, when the government directly supplies information, there are difficulties with respect to the collection and sharing of all the necessary information and possibly to its accuracy.

Private responses

- **Signalling** takes place when the party with superior information conveys information that will make them seem credible to the other party. For instance, reputable used-

car dealers often offer warranties—promises to repair any problems with the cars they sell that arise within a given amount of time. This is not just a way of insuring their customers against possible expenses; it is a way of reliably showing that they are selling good quality cars.

- **Screening** takes place when individuals try to infer additional information from other observable characteristics. If you apply to purchase health insurance, you will find that the insurance company will demand documentation of your health status in an attempt to "screen out" sicker applicants—customers they will refuse to insure or will insure only at very high premiums. Auto insurance also provides a very good example. Insurance company staff may not know whether you are a careful driver, but they have statistical data on the accident rates of people who resemble your profile—and they use those data in setting premiums. In some cases, this may be quite unfair. However, nobody can deny that the insurance companies are right on average.

2.11 Market failure–market power (HL)

Focusing on firms

Profits

Economic profits, typically denoted with the Greek letter π, are equal to the difference between the total revenues (TR) collected from selling Q units of a good minus the total economic costs (TC) incurred in producing these Q units, or:

$$\pi(Q) = TR(Q) - TC(Q)$$

Revenues

Total revenues or sales revenues (TR) collected from selling Q units are defined as the product of the price (P) per unit charged times the number of units sold, or:

$$TR(Q) = P \times Q$$

Average revenue

Average revenue (AR) is revenue per unit sold, so:

$$AR = \frac{TR}{Q}$$

Since TR = P × Q, it follows that average revenue is always equal to the price charged by the firm.

$$AR = \frac{TR}{Q} = \frac{P \times Q}{Q} = P$$

Note that since the demand curve a firm faces shows at each output level Q the price at which it will be absorbed and since average revenue is always equal to price, it follows that the demand curve that a firm faces is also its AR curve.

Economic costs

The concept of economic costs is tricky. Since resources are scarce, in economics we care about the value of all resources sacrificed in the production process, whether an explicit payment is made or not. Economic costs are thus distinguished into explicit and implicit costs. Explicit costs refer to "out-of-pocket" costs a firm has, for example when it has to pay a supplier. Implicit costs include, for example, the value of firm-owned resources. No payment is made for, say, premises owned by a firm, but they are "sacrificed" as no other firm can use them. Or, consider an entrepreneur also working in her firm. We must include the wages she would have earned had she been working for another firm.

Normal profit

Economic costs include something more. Remember that entrepreneurship is also a scarce factor. The entrepreneurial capital that an entrepreneur invests in a certain line of business cannot at the same time also be invested elsewhere. Economic costs thus also include the minimum return the entrepreneur requires to remain in a line of business. This minimum return is known as normal profit. It is equal to what could have been earned if this entrepreneurial capital was invested in the next best alternative with the same risk. If this return is not earned, then the firm is not viable—in the same way that if a firm is not prepared to pay workers the market rate then they will not be willing to work for that firm.

Paying the market wage rate is necessary to secure the scarce factor of production labour and is, of course, an element of economic costs. Normal profits are the necessary minimum return to secure the scarce factor of entrepreneurship. Since wages paid to labour are an element of economic costs, normal profit is also an element of economic cost. Economic profits thus differ from accounting profits in that they include the value of all resources sacrificed in the production process.

Average costs

Average costs (AC) are defined as costs per unit of output produced. This is total costs (TC) divided by the number of units (Q) so:

$$AC = \frac{TC}{Q}$$

Profit maximization

We typically assume in economics that firms aim to maximize profits even though, as we have seen, there may be other objectives. The question that a firm must answer is how much output to produce to achieve its profit-maximization goal. To answer this question, we must first introduce and explain the terms *marginal cost* and *marginal revenue*.

Marginal cost (and the law of diminishing marginal returns)

Marginal cost (MC) is defined as the additional cost of producing an additional unit of a good. More generally, it is the change in total cost (TC) following a change in output:

$$MC = \frac{TC}{Q}$$

This is the slope of the total cost function. Typically, marginal costs initially decrease and then, after some point, they start to increase. This behaviour is the result of the law of diminishing returns.

In the short run, when at least one factor of production is considered fixed (typically, capital; think of the firm's premises) it is initially easy to increase output because there is a lot of opportunity for labour specialization. The additional output produced from an additional worker rises. This implies that the additional cost of an additional unit of output produced (the MC) decreases.

After some point, though, there is less and less room for specialization and the additional output from an additional worker employed starts to decrease. This is when diminishing marginal returns set in. Total output continues to rise as workers are added to the production process but at a diminishing rate. It follows that the additional cost (the MC) of an additional unit of output produced will at that point start to rise. The behaviour just described for the MC gives rise to the "Nike-swoosh" shape of the MC curve shown in Figure 2.11.1. At output level q1, the law of diminishing marginal returns begins to take effect and MC starts to rise.

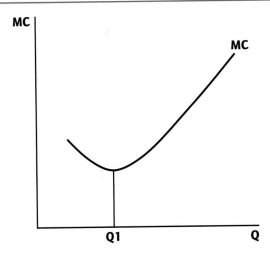

Figure 2.11.1 The MC curve

Marginal revenue

Marginal revenue (MR) is the additional revenue collected from selling an additional unit of a good. More generally, it is the change in total revenues (TR) following a change in output:

$$MR = \frac{TR}{Q}$$

There are two cases.

Case 1

In this case, the firm is very small compared to the size of the market in which it operates and produces a good identical to what the other firms in this market offer (the good is known as homogeneous). This firm must accept the market price. It is a price taker. In this case marginal revenue is constant, as shown in Figure 2.11.2. The additional revenue collected from selling one more unit will always be equal to the price prevailing in the market.

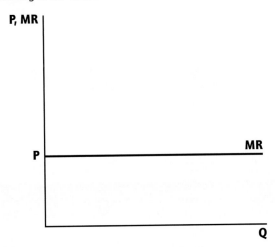

Figure 2.11.2 The MR curve if the firm is a price taker

Case 2

In this case (shown in Figure 2.11.3), the firm faces a negatively sloped demand curve and so it can choose the price at which it wishes to sell its product. It is a price maker. If it wishes to sell more units per period, it must lower the price. However, this lower price will apply to all units sold per period, not just the additional (last) unit. Marginal revenue collected will thus be less than the new lower price charged for the firm's output. A firm that faces a negatively

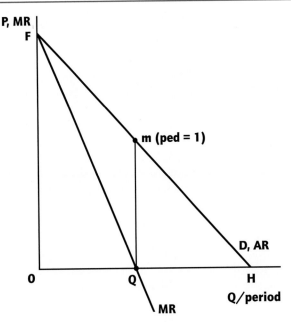

Figure 2.11.3 The MR curve if the firm is a price maker

sloped demand curve will have a marginal revenue curve with double the slope of the demand curve.

Note that since marginal revenue has double the slope of the demand curve it cuts the midpoint Q of line segment (OH). Right above output Q, where MR is equal to zero, the PED of the demand curve is 1 because point m is the midpoint of line segment (FH). Remember that as price decreases, if demand is price inelastic, then total revenues decrease, so that marginal revenue must be negative.

Rule for profit maximization

To maximize profits, a firm must choose a level of output Q for which:

$$MR = MC$$

Very often, students incorrectly infer from the above condition that the level of profits enjoyed by a firm at that level of output is zero. It will become clear that if MR = MC then we know that profits are maximum but these maximum profits can be: positive, in which case we say that the firm enjoys abnormal (or supernormal) profits; zero (in which case we say that the firm enjoys just normal profits, the minimum return required by the entrepreneur to remain in that line of business); or even negative (in which case the firm is making economic losses and is not even earning normal profits).

To understand the above, consider a firm producing pencils. Assume that currently it is producing 5 pencils per period (say, per hour) and is making profits equal to $18.00. If the additional revenue it can collect by producing and offering a 6th pencil is $3.00 (so MR = $3.00) and the additional cost of producing it is equal to $1.00 (so MC = $1.00), should it produce it? What will its profits be if instead of 5 pencils per period, it is producing 6 pencils per period? Profits would increase and equal $20.00. What if for an additional pencil (the 7th), MR is equal to $3.00 and MC is equal to $2.00? Should the firm be increasing output to 7 pencils per period? Yes, as by increasing output to 7 pencils, it would further increase profits to $21.00. Pushing this logic further, it should be clear that *as long as* MR exceeds MC then it pays a firm to increase output per period because by doing so, its profits will be increasing.

if MR > MC, keep on increasing output ...

... until, for the last unit produced, MR = MC

At that level of output at which MR = MC, profits will be maximum

So: What if the firm was producing 5 pencils per period and was making losses equal to, say, $30.00? Assume that again, the additional revenue it can collect by producing and offering a 6th pencil is $3.00 (so MR = $3.00) and the additional cost of producing it is equal to $1.00 (so MC = $1.00). Should the firm produce the 6th pencil? What will its profits be if instead of 5 pencils per period, the firm was producing 6 pencils per period? Losses would decrease to $28.00. What if for one more (an additional) pencil (the 7th), MR is equal to $3.00 and MC is equal to $2.00. Should the firm be producing and selling 7 pencils per period? Yes, as by increasing output to 7 pencils, the firm would be further decreasing losses. Pushing this logic further, it should be clear that *as long as* MR exceeds MC then it pays this loss-making firm to increase output per period because by doing so, its losses will be decreasing. So, for this firm:

if MR > MC, keep on increasing output ...

... until, for the last unit produced, MR = MC

At that level of output at which MR = MC, losses will be minimum

Summing up, if a firm is producing a level of output for which MR = MC for the last unit produced, then it is either making maximum profits or minimum losses. To determine whether these are positive, zero or negative profits, we need to compare average revenue (AR) and average cost (AC).

- If AR > AC then profits are positive (abnormal or supernormal).

- If AR = AC then profits are zero (the firm is just making normal profits).

- If AR < AC then the firm is making losses (negative profits).

Market structures

In economics, there are four types of market structure. The distinction is based on the following three characteristics.

- The number of firms in the market. There can be very many firms, few firms or just one firm in the market.

- The type of the product offered in the market. The product offered can be differentiated or homogeneous. A product is differentiated if it differs across firms in terms of characteristics, quality or even just packaging. Examples include nearly everything: laptops, cars, hair salon services, banking services, mobile phone service providers or plain vanilla ice cream sold in supermarkets. A product offered in a market is homogeneous if it is considered identical across firms in the eyes of consumers. If it is branded, like the vanilla ice cream or the bottled water offered by different firms in supermarkets, it is not considered homogeneous. Very few products can be considered being homogeneous, as all firms have the incentive to somehow differentiate what they offer from what other firms in the same market offer. By differentiation firms can increase price without risk of losing all customers or sales. So, what are examples of homogeneous products? One is copper offered by different mining companies in the world to manufacturers. Another is the wheat that food companies, such as Kellogg's or Nestlé, buy from farmers around the world. Examples are found in the primary sector as commodities are considered "gifts of nature".

- Whether or not barriers exist preventing entry of other firms into the market. A barrier is anything that deters entry into a market. There are different types of barriers, which will be discussed later.

Recap

Characteristics used to distinguish market structures

The three characteristics are:

- the number of firms in the market—it can be very many, few or one

- the type of product offered—it can be homogenous or differentiated

- the entry conditions—barriers may or may not exist.

On the basis of the above, four market structures are distinguished in economics.

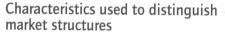

	Perfect competition	Monopoly	Monopolistic competition	Oligopoly
Number of firms	Very many	One	Very many	Few
Type of product	Homogeneous	(Unique)	Differentiated	Either homogeneous or differentiated
Entry conditions	No barriers exist	Barriers do exist	No barriers exist	Barriers do exist
	(and perfect information)			
	(and perfect factor mobility)			

"Structure–Conduct–Performance" and market power

The characteristics or structure of each of the different types of market determine to a large extent their market behaviour. Their market behaviour, in turn, affects their performance. Performance refers to the degree to which firms in each market structure achieve relevant societal goals. In a market economy, these goals refer to producing the level of output that is optimal from society's point of view and charging the lowest possible prices.

Another most important performance outcome is the extent to which firms innovate. Innovations refer to new products and new production processes and are considered a most desirable market outcome in a vibrant and dynamic economy.

These goals are closely related to the degree of market power firms have. Market power refers to the ability of a firm to influence price and is prevalent in most real-world markets. We will see that even though lack of any market power is desirable, it is, on the other hand, usually necessary for firms to innovate.

Policymakers' perspective

In most countries, specialized offices exist that monitor market and firm behaviour. Examples include the Directorate-General for Competition in the European Union, the Antitrust Division of the Department of Justice in the USA, the Competition and Markets Authority in the UK and the Competition Commission of India.

The degree of market power that a firm possesses is extremely important for policymakers who focus on the way different markets operate. We will later see that if in a market the degree of market power is very high, policymakers, and specifically the competition authorities, may have sufficient reason to intervene. They definitely have reason to intervene if policymakers suspect abuse of market power. The goal of competition authorities is to ensure that consumers have access to goods and services at the most competitive prices and that firms have the incentive to innovate.

Perfect competition

A market is considered perfectly competitive if the following applies.

- The market includes very many firms.
- The product is homogeneous.
- There are no entry barriers.
- In addition, perfect information and perfect factor mobility are assumed.

Perfectly competitive firms are price-takers

The above assumptions imply that such firms are price-takers. This means that each firm must accept the market determined price. Why? A firm cannot charge a higher price because there are very many other firms in the market, all producing the identical product. Buyers in the market are aware of this as a result of also assuming perfect information. Why not sell at a lower price? A firm has no incentive to do so. Why not? The firm is so small compared to the whole market that it can sell all it wants at the going market price. If a firm is so small that it can sell more output

without pushing down the price, what incentive is there for it to lower the price? There is no incentive.

The perfectly competitive firm is thus a price-taker. It faces a horizontal, perfectly elastic demand curve at the market determined price which is also its average revenue (AR) curve and also its marginal revenue (MR) curve. In perfect competition, the additional revenue (MR) the typical firm collects from selling an additional unit is equal to the market-determined price.

Short-run equilibrium for the perfectly competitive firm

Think of the quinoa market, a good example of a perfectly competitive market. Let's give a name to the typical quinoa firm we are focusing on. Let's call it Felipe. Figure 2.11.4b shows the quinoa market and Figure 2.11.4a shows Felipe's firm.

Market demand and market supply for quinoa determine the equilibrium market price P. Note that the scale of the horizontal axis differs. It is thousands of kilos for the

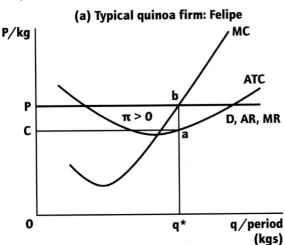

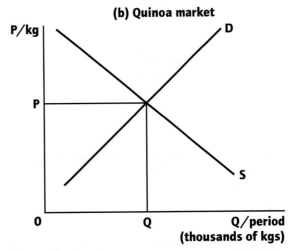

Figure 2.11.4 Perfect competition: short-run equilibrium—case with abnormal (or supernormal) profits

market (Figure 2.11.4b) but only kilos for the typical firm (Figure 2.11.4a). Felipe, as explained above, will have to accept the market determined price P. He thus faces a perfectly elastic (horizontal demand) at P as he knows that consumers will buy any amount he offers (remember it is very small compared to the market) at that price P. Demand always reflects his average revenue and here it also reflects his marginal revenue.

Profit maximization for the typical perfectly competitive firm

Focusing on Figure 2.11.4, to maximize profits, Felipe will choose to offer q* units of quinoa, as at q*, MR = MC. To determine whether these maximum profits are positive, zero or negative, we have to compare the firm's AR with its ATC.

Note that the ATC curve in Figure 2.11.4a is U-shaped and that the MC on its way up cuts the ATC curve at its minimum. This is the result of a strict relationship between marginal costs and average costs, which is explained in the box below.

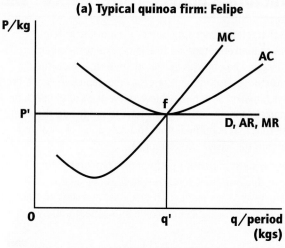

(a) Typical quinoa firm: Felipe

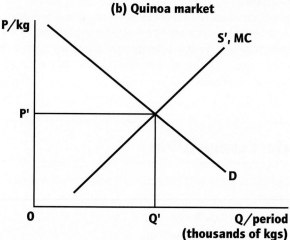

(b) Quinoa market

Figure 2.11.5 Perfect competition: long-run equilibrium

Unit costs (ATC) when Felipe is producing q* units are equal to segment (q*a) or (OC). Since price (= AR) is greater than average total cost, this firm is making positive economic profits equal to segment (CP) per unit. Multiplying by the number of units (Oq*) Felipe sells which are equal to segment (Ca), we arrive at the size of the positive economic (abnormal or supernormal) profits Felipe is earning, which are equal to the rectangular area (CabP).

From short-run to long-run

If the typical firm in a market is making positive economic profits, it is earning more than normal profits (more than what entrepreneurs could earn in the next best alternative with the same risk). There is an incentive for more firms or entrepreneurs to enter. There are no barriers in perfect competition, so new firms will start entering the quinoa market. As the number of firms in the market increases,

market supply will increase and the supply curve will start shifting to the right. Excess supply will start pushing the quinoa market price down. Entry will stop when abnormal (or supernormal) profits are competed away and driven down to zero (that is, to normal). If profits earned are normal, the quinoa firms are making the minimum return they require to remain in the quinoa market. There will be no incentive for more firms to enter and also no reason for existing firms to exit. Each firm is achieving its profit-maximizing goal (MR = MC) and no entry or exit takes place (as AR = AC). This is referred to as long-run equilibrium. So, the condition for long-run equilibrium is that at the chosen output Q': P (= AR) = MR = MC = AC. This position is shown in Figure 2.11.5.

Figure 2.11.5 depicts long-run equilibrium in a perfectly competitive market. In Figure 2.11.5a, the typical firm, Felipe, is achieving its goal to maximize profits as at Q': MR = MC. In addition, there is no reason for new firms to enter or for any of the existing firms to exit as the typical firm is earning at Q' zero economic profits; that is, it is earning normal profits, as much as these entrepreneurs could earn in the next best alternative with the same risk. At Q', AR = AC = (OP').

If the typical firm was making losses in the short run, it means that it would not be earning normal profits, the minimum it required. This case is illustrated in Figure 2.11.6.

Firms in this case have the incentive to exit this market and switch to their next best alternative with the same

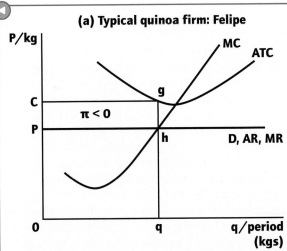

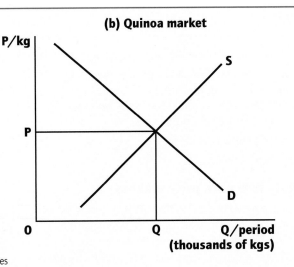

Figure 2.11.6 Perfect competition: short-run equilibrium—case with losses

risk. Remember, we also assume perfect factor mobility. As the least efficient firms exit, the market supply will shift left and the market price would start rising. Exit will stop when the typical firm is earning just normal profits (that is, zero economic profits).

Efficiency issues in perfect competition: Allocative efficiency

If markets are perfectly competitive then market forces alone, without the need of the state, will lead to just the right amount of the good being produced from society's point of view. Scarce resources will be optimally allocated (appointed to their best possible use) and social welfare, the sum of the consumer surplus and the producer surplus will be maximized.

Why is this the case? It is because for the last unit produced, both in the market and by the firm, P = MC. This means that all units of the good that are worth to consumers more than the additional cost of producing each (that is, the value of

whatever is sacrificed) are indeed produced, up until and including that unit for which P = MC. Focusing on the typical firm, we realize that at Q': P = MC and focusing on the market, at Q': P = MC. Remember that for each level of output how much it is worth to consumers is measured by their willingness to pay, P.

Since in perfectly competitive markets all units for which P > MC are produced up until and including that unit for which P = MC, allocative efficiency is achieved and the price charged to consumers is the lowest it can be.

Policymakers' perspective

Perfect competition does not exist in real-world markets. Few markets can be perhaps considered good approximations of perfect competition. In many markets, few large firms dominate. Market power is often present that usually leads to higher prices for consumers and less than the socially optimal level of output enjoyed. Real-world markets often fail as they are allocatively inefficient.

So, why is perfect competition considered important? The reason is that it manages to answer in the best possible way the first fundamental question of economics, the "what" question. It guarantees that just the right amount of a good is produced from society's point of view: that is, it guarantees

that allocative efficiency is achieved. In addition, since in the long run the typical firm is forced to produce with minimum average cost, it is also technically efficient. This means that the "how" question is also answered in the best possible way, as no scarce resources are wasted.

Perfectly competitive markets thus lead to the optimal output at the lowest possible price. Policymakers use this market structure as a measuring rod against which actual market performance is judged. Thus, when in real-world markets prices charged by firms are significantly higher than the marginal cost of production it means that consumers enjoy less and pay more. Policymakers may decide to intervene.

Recap

Two benefits of perfect competition

Perfectly competitive firms have no market power.

- Firms cannot charge more than the competitive equilibrium price (P).
- Consumers enjoy the good at the lowest price possible.

Allocative efficiency is achieved.

- At the competitive equilibrium output (Q): MB = MC
- Just the right amount of the good is produced; resources are allocated in the best way and social surplus is maximized.

Monopoly

A monopoly is a market where the following conditions apply.

- There is only one firm producing a good or one firm dominating the market. For example, Google's parent company, Alphabet, controls 92.5% of the world search engine market, with Bing controlling 2.5%.
- The product is considered unique.
- There are high entry barriers.

Monopoly firms are price-makers

Assuming there is only one firm in the market, it becomes clear that the monopoly firm faces the negatively sloped market demand curve. The monopoly firm can choose the price it wishes to charge and in this sense such firms are price-makers or price-setters. Monopoly firms thus have market power. **Market power is also often referred to as monopoly power.**

Keep in mind that a monopoly is still constrained by the demand curve it faces so it cannot choose both the output it wishes to sell per period and the price it wishes to charge. If it decides to choose the output rate it wishes to sell per period then it is the market that will determine the price at which it will be absorbed; if it decides the price it wishes to charge then the market will determine the quantity that will be absorbed at that price. Figure 2.11.7 shows the equilibrium position of a profit-maximizing monopoly firm.

To maximize profits the monopoly firm will choose that level of output Q for which MR is equal to MC. This is the case at output level Qm. To determine the price at which the market will absorb this output per period we need to draw a vertical line up from Qm to meet the demand curve. This price is Pm. To determine now the level of profits (or, losses) we need to compare price (Pm), which is also the average revenue earned by the firm, with the unit costs

incurred when producing Qm units which is equal to segment (QmA) or (OC). Since in this case average revenue exceeds average cost, this monopoly firm is earning profits per unit equal to segment (PmC). Multiplying this by the number of units (OQm) or segment (CA), we arrive at the size of the positive economic profits this monopoly firm is earning, which is equal to the rectangular area (CABPm). These economic profits are positive, so the monopoly firm is earning abnormal (or supernormal) profits. Consequently, other firms or entrepreneurs would like to enter this market. However, in monopoly we assume that barriers to entry exist and so entry cannot take place. It follows that these abnormal (or supernormal) profits will persist in the long run and that Figure 2.11.7 shows both the short-run and the long-run equilibrium position of the monopoly firm.

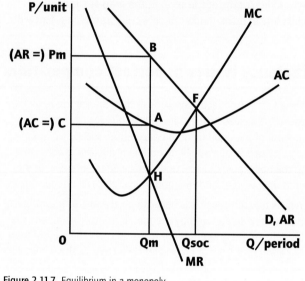

Figure 2.11.7 Equilibrium in a monopoly

Efficiency issues and the monopoly firm

A monopoly firm is allocatively inefficient. Referring to Figure 2.11.7, at the chosen profit-maximizing level of output Qm, price (P) exceeds marginal cost (MC). Specifically, price is equal to segment (QmB) while marginal cost is equal to segment (QmH). Society would have wanted more units of this good produced. Society would have wanted all units up until unit Qsoc, as Qsoc price, which measures the willingness to pay, is equal to MC (since at that level of output the AR curve intersects the MC curve). Since the monopoly firm does not produce units (QmQsoc), a welfare loss results equal to area (HBF). The welfare loss reflects net value lost by society from units (QmQsoc) not being produced by the monopoly firm even though they should have been produced from society's point of view. A monopoly firm is also not forced to produce with minimum average cost, as perfectly competitive firms are, so it is also technically inefficient.

It is instructive to make a direct comparison of a perfectly competitive market and a monopoly market. In Figure 2.11.8, a perfectly competitive market is shown. The interaction of market demand and market supply (which also reflects marginal cost) leads to an equilibrium price Pc and an equilibrium quantity Qc. Assume now that this market is somehow monopolized. In addition, assume that the technology used, and the cost conditions faced by the

monopoly firm are the same as those that perfectly competitive firms faced. The MC curve thus remains the same. This is a rather restrictive assumption and will be relaxed later when we will examine the possible benefits of larger size.

Comparing perfect competition with monopoly: Same cost conditions

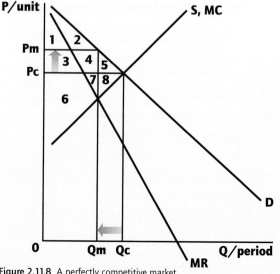

Figure 2.11.8 A perfectly competitive market

The profit-maximizing monopoly firm will choose to produce Qm units where MR = MC. The price that will be charged will be Pm. It is clear that the monopoly firm restricts output to raise price. Monopoly produces and offers less than the competitive market (Qm < Qc) and charges a higher price (Pm > Pc). In addition, whereas the competitive outcome is allocatively efficient (as at Qc, P = MC), the monopolist is allocatively inefficient (since at Qm, P > MC).

A welfare analysis is revealing.

- The consumer surplus is the area below the demand curve, above the price paid for the units actually consumed.
- The producer surplus is the area below the price earned, above the supply curve (or the MC curve for the monopoly as MC reflects the minimum the firm requires to offer each additional unit) for the units actually sold (which in the case of monopoly are up to Qm).
- The social surplus is the sum of the consumer and producer surplus.

Perfect competition	
Consumer surplus	Area (1 + 2 + 3 + 4 + 5)
Producer surplus	Area (6 + 7 + 8)
Social surplus	Area (1 + 2 + 3 + 4 + 5 + 6 + 7 + 8)
Monopoly	
Consumer surplus	Area (1 + 2)
Producer surplus	Area (3 + 4 + 6 + 7)
Social surplus	Area (1 + 2 + 3 + 4 + 6 + 7)

The above analysis reveals the following.

- Consumers are worse off as they lose area (3 + 4 + 5).
- The firm is better off as it loses area (8) but it gains area (3 + 4).

- A welfare loss results equal to area (5 + 8) since monopoly restricts output and units that should have been produced from society's point of view are not produced.
- Area (3 + 4) represents a transfer of income from consumers to the monopoly as it used to be part of the consumer surplus but is now appropriated by the monopoly firm. If in an economy market power is increasing in more and more industries, income distribution will become more unequal because firms with market power can charge consumers a higher price. This is one of the reasons that income inequality in many economies has been increasing in the past 20 years or so.

Note that price is set by the monopolist above marginal cost. The ability of a firm to set price above marginal cost is the formal definition of monopoly power. The degree of monopoly power is measured by the Lerner Index of Monopoly Power defined as the difference between price and marginal cost expressed as a proportion of price:

$$\left(\frac{P - MC}{P} \right)$$

Monopoly power and market power can be used interchangeably. If a firm is a perfectly competitive firm, then the Lerner Index of Monopoly Power measurement is zero, as price is equal to marginal cost. The firm has no monopoly power (no market power) as it cannot influence price. However, a monopoly can set price. It does have market power, and the degree of monopoly power it has depends on how much higher than marginal cost it can set its price. This of course depends on the number and closeness of available substitutes to consumers. The fewer the available substitutes, the greater the ability to raise price above marginal cost and the greater the degree of monopoly or market power the firm possesses.

Monopoly firms: A report card

Monopoly firms or, more generally, firms that dominate in their market have significant market power, so they are typically not considered desirable from society's point of view.

There are quite a few reasons for this. Their market power permits them to restrict output below the competitive level. Consumers then enjoy less of the good. Restricting output allows these firms to charge a higher price. This hurts consumers, especially lower income households, since it decreases their purchasing power. Consumer surplus shrinks and part of this surplus is transferred to the monopoly firm. This transfer of income that is accomplished through the higher prices charged by firms with significant monopoly power increases income inequality.

Sometimes the existence of monopoly firms or, more generally, large firms that dominate a market may benefit society. It will be explained later why under certain conditions having only one firm in a market may even be preferable. This is the case of a natural monopoly where having two firms splitting the market would result in an unnecessary waste of resources; the price natural monopolies can charge consumers is typically regulated by the state. It will also be explained that large firms may often be able to produce at a lower average cost (this is known as benefiting from economies of scale) allowing them to decrease the price they charge. Also, because of entry barriers such firms may maintain in the long run any supernormal profits earned. They thus have the necessary resources to invest in research and development, which leads to innovations that benefit society.

Policymakers' perspective

Keep in mind that it is the existence of barriers to entry that permit a firm to maintain abnormal (or supernormal) profits in the long run and keep price significantly higher than the competitive level. The extent to which barriers prove successful in protecting a monopoly position in the real world depends on the type of barriers that exist in any particular market. Some barriers may lead to what are

referred to as "entrenched" monopoly positions, while others may eventually be overcome by entrepreneurs who develop a new product or a new competing technology. Entrenched monopoly positions are typically a result of state-created barriers but in the recent past, even in the absence of state-created barriers, there are some questionable tactics by firms that have been very successful in fending off potential competition in their markets.

Entry barriers

What is an entry barrier?

An entry barrier can be anything that deters entry of new firms into a market. Barriers can be distinguished into three types. They are:

- state-created barriers
- firm-created barriers
- natural barriers.

State-created barriers

State-created barriers include patents, licenses and trade barriers.

Patents are granted by governments to firms that introduce a new product or a new technology. A patent permits the owner to produce the good or to use the technology exclusively for 20 years. This creates a monopoly in order to protect the incentive to invest in research and development (R&D) and to generate innovations. Pharmaceutical corporations apply for and are granted patents for new drugs they develop. Patents are obviously necessary, but the particulars of the law may prove counterproductive.

Licenses are exclusive permits that governments issue to one or few firms for a variety of reasons. Licenses are granted to radio and television stations in order to allocate bandwidth. Medical doctors and lawyers are also licensed to protect the public from unqualified individuals. Of course, to the extent that medical associations also restrict entry into the field of medicine they also are responsible for maintaining higher fees, in other words to exert some degree of monopoly power.

Trade barriers will be examined in detail in section 4.2. They include taxes on imports (tariffs), quantitative restrictions on imports (quotas) and other policies that limit competition from abroad. They aim at protecting domestic firms and their workers but they do lead to higher prices for buyers.

Firm-created barriers

Firms also try to prevent entry of new firms into their market. Restricting competition will lead to higher prices and will permit these firms to maintain abnormal (or supernormal) profits. These firms may maintain excess productive capacity so that a potential entrant is aware that the incumbent firm can easily increase output and drive the price down to unprofitable levels. They may engage in excessive advertising and create a distinct brand name, or they may extensively differentiate their product and offer very many different varieties to make it more difficult for others to find a niche and enter the market. They may even set price only slightly above average cost so that the potential entrant knows that if it decides to enter, price will be depressed to unprofitable levels as a result of the additional supply entering in the market.

In the recent past another old questionable tactic has resurfaced. Large firms with very significant market power have been buying out competitors or any start-ups that may threaten their dominance. For example, Oracle acquired PeopleSoft, Siebel, BEA, Sun Microsystems and more than 60 other firms. Google "vacuumed-up" more than 100 companies including YouTube and DoubleClick. Facebook even managed to block multi-homing of all social media applications under one host. It has since also acquired Instagram and WhatsApp, cementing its dominance in social media. Amazon has acquired more than 100 companies and has established itself as the centre of e-commerce by providing the infrastructure that other rival businesses crucially rely on to exist. An example of this is when Amazon delisted a French publisher's books from its website for a while. Such behaviour is considered by several legal experts to constitute abuse of market power and we will examine it again later.

Natural barriers

Economies of scale and the case of the natural monopoly

The production technology for some goods or services requires huge set-up costs. Examples include laying out a railway network, a water distribution network or a power grid to deliver electricity. Such infrastructure costs imply that the average cost of one large firm supplying the whole market is much lower than the average cost that each of two firms supplying the same market would have. Significant *economies of scale* are present.

Economies of scale are defined as decreases in average costs that are a result of a firm's larger size. They refer to the long run when firms can change all factors and so can change their scale (size) of operations. Firms of larger size may enjoy a cost advantage for many other reasons. They may be able to buy their inputs in bulk, extracting lower prices from their suppliers. They may be able to borrow from banks at better terms (lower interest rates) by being considered more creditworthy and less risky. Indivisibilities of certain types of capital equipment or of certain technologies imply that they can be adopted only by very large firms. An example is the assembly line in car manufacturing. Indivisibilities also explain why production processes such as those involved in electricity, water and natural gas distribution, or a railway or subway network, require firms that are very large in size and can spread these huge set-up costs across a huge scale of output, resulting in lower average costs.

A natural monopoly may emerge if, given market size, only one firm can profitably exist. Two firms splitting the market would both be unprofitable. Figure 2.11.9 shows this.

Assume that the profit-maximizing level of output is at Q*.

(Note: the profit-maximizing level of output is where MR and MC intersect. This is not shown, to avoid cluttering Figure 2.11.9).

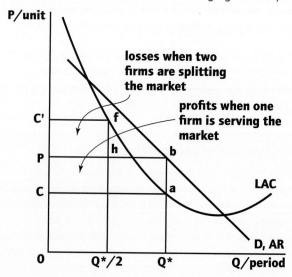

Figure 2.11.9 The case of a natural monopoly

The price at which this market will absorb Q* units is P. Average costs for this firm are equal to (OC). It thus makes abnormal (or supernormal) profits equal to area (CabP). If now two firms were to split this market, each producing $\left(\dfrac{Q^*}{2}\right)$ units, then together they would still be producing Q* units and the market price would still be P (remember the good is homogeneous). Now, though, these smaller in size firms will not be able to enjoy the cost savings that the single large firm enjoyed. Average cost for each would be (OC') and thus each would make losses equal to area (PhfC'). The size of

this market, together with the huge economies of scale present, permit only one firm to profitably operate. This is a natural monopoly. Natural monopolies are usually regulated by the government. Prices charged are set below the profit maximizing level to ensure affordability.

Note that a natural barrier leading to monopoly is also exclusive ownership of a vital natural resource that prevents others from offering the good or the service. For example, if one person owns all the land surrounding a pristine beach in Mykonos, then only he or she decides who can buy land in order to build a resort hotel there.

Oligopoly

An oligopoly has the following characteristics.

- It is a market in which only a few firms operate.
- The firms produce either a homogeneous product (such as steel, cement, oil or copper) or a differentiated product (such as cars, laptops or mobile phones, or products offered by the banking or insurance industries, or providers of mobile phone services).
- High barriers to entry exist, which explains why there are only a few firms. Barriers are the same as those that give rise to monopolies (for example, economies of scale that permit only a few firms to operate profitably, licenses, creation of brand names, limit pricing and product proliferation).

As a result of only a few firms operating in the market these firms are interdependent. Interdependence exists in a market if the outcome of any action of one firm depends on the reaction of its rival or rivals. We can say that a market is oligopolistic if the firms in the market are interdependent.

Concentration ratios

To determine the extent of concentration in a market a concentration ratio (CR) is used that measures the proportion of total sales accounted for by the "n" largest firms in a market. For example, the four-firm concentration ratio (CR_4) is given by:

$$\frac{\text{Sales of largest 4 firms in the market}}{\text{Total market sales}} \times 100$$

Researchers often calculate a series of concentration ratios for a market, for example the CR_4, the CR_8 and the CR_{20}, in order to provide a more comprehensive picture of the degree of concentration. The higher the concentration ratio of a market, the more oligopolistic it is, as it indicates that few firms dominate. In the USA, the CR_4 in the dry cat food industry is 97%, the CR_3 in the car rental industry is 50% and the CR_2 in smartphone operating systems is 99%. Not only is a series of concentration ratios useful to derive safer conclusions about the degree of concentration in a market, but historical data are also necessary to determine whether there is a trend towards more or less concentration.

To collude or to compete?

Interdependence in oligopolistic markets is responsible for this dilemma that oligopolistic firms face. Through competition these firms may increase their own market

share and their profits at the expense of rivals, but at the risk of starting a price war which could prove catastrophic for all firms involved. By colluding they decrease uncertainty and maximize joint profits as if they were a monopoly, but at the risk of getting caught and facing the consequences of the law, namely fines and even imprisonment. This dilemma and much more can be clearly visualized through the "Prisoner's dilemma".

The "Prisoner's dilemma"

A branch of mathematics known as game theory is widely used to analyse oligopolistic set-ups. We will examine the simplest form of a game, known as the "Prisoner's dilemma". Through this game we will clearly understand interdependence in such markets, why a price war may be initiated, why such firms have an incentive to collude and also why there is sometimes cheating involved.

We assume two firms, A and B, each with two possible strategies. Each can either maintain price high or it can cut price. Figure 2.11.10 shows their "pay-off matrix". Each number is the profit each firm will earn from each strategy adopted, given the strategy its rival will adopt. Firms are aware of the pay-offs, but initially we assume that there is no communication between the two firms.

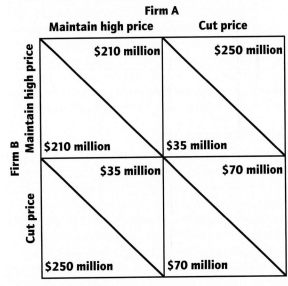

Figure 2.11.10 Pay-off matrix

Interdependence

Interdependence is clear. Assume that firm A chooses to maintain a high price. It does not know the outcome—whether it will earn $210 million or $35million—because it depends on the reaction of its rival firm B; namely, whether firm B will also maintain a high price or whether firm B will cut its price.

Risk of a price war

We can see why without some kind of coordination there is risk of a price war occurring. Consider firm A. It realizes that if firm B maintains a high price it will earn more by cutting price ($250 million) than by maintaining price ($210 million). Firm A also realizes that if firm B cuts price, firm A will again earn more by cutting price ($70 million instead of $35 million). So, no matter what firm B chooses to do, firm A will cut price. The same logic applies to firm B thinking about its best strategy given firm A's action. It follows that both firms under this set-up will choose to cut price, each earning $70 million.

Incentive to collude

The set-up above assumes no communication and can be called a "one-shot" game. In the real world, there is repeated or, more precisely, continuous interaction between firms in a market. It would become evident to both firms that if they were to make an agreement and coordinate price changes, they would both be better off: each would earn $210 million. Less uncertainty and the possibility of greater profits makes collusion very tempting for firms in oligopolistic markets.

Risk of cheating

The structure of the pay-off matrix in Figure 2.11.10 may also explain why firms sometimes do not abide by the terms of the collusive agreement made. Firm A realizes that if, following the agreement with firm B to maintain a high price, it alone decided to cut price it would earn even higher profits ($250 million) while its rival would have earned only $35 million. In such a case, both firms would return to cutting price so only under very particular circumstances would this incentive to cheat materialize. If the pay-off of $35 million was instead a loss of $20 million, then cheating may have been a much more tempting strategy to pursue.

Collusive oligopoly

Collusion exists when two or more firms agree to fix or to raise price in order to restrict competition. The agreement can be written, verbal or inferred from conduct. When firms collude, they collectively behave as if they were a monopoly. Collusion can be formal—in which case a cartel is formed—or tacit, where the agreement is informal. When a tacit collusive agreement is uncovered by the competition authorities, it is referred to as a cartel by the press. Collusive agreements are in general illegal. The best known formal collusive agreement is OPEC, the Organization of Petroleum Exporting Countries. This is an international exporting cartel of 14 countries.

In collusive oligopoly, member firms behave as if they were a monopoly. Their aim is to maximize joint profits. This is shown in Figure 2.11.11, which can be used to represent an oil cartel.

Collusive oligopoly acting as a monopoly

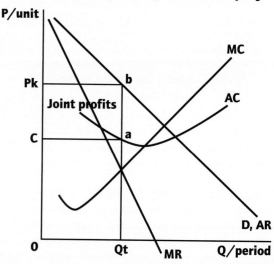

Figure 2.11.11 Collusive oligopoly: an oil cartel

In order to maximize joint profits, the total output all cartel members together must sell is at Qt where MR = MC. If the members adhere to the agreement, then the cartel price will be Pk. Joint profits will then be equal to area (CabPk). Members will have to agree on their quotas—the quantity each member will produce and sell.

In the case of OPEC, member countries negotiate and agree on how much oil each will sell in the market to achieve a certain price for oil. Despite the formal structure of OPEC, for the following reasons the organization's goal is difficult to achieve.

- Price still also depends on demand conditions.
- There are quite a few large oil producers who are not members (such as the USA, Canada and Russia).
- For various reasons, members do not abide by the rules.

In other collusive cases, executives of companies secretly agree to fix price and then each firm sells as much as it can at that price. Secret agreements often take place in cafés, restaurants or hotels. It has been reported that executives of a yogurt cartel met at a Parisian café "Au chien qui fume" while executives of a car parts cartel met in Tokyo at "Café Renoir".

Note that oligopolistic firms face a negatively sloped demand curve and, independently of whether or not collusion is present, allocative efficiency cannot be achieved. Output is less than the socially optimal level because:

- profit maximization requires MR = MC
- P > MR because demand is negatively sloped; so P > MC, while allocative efficiency requires that P = MC.

Non-collusive oligopoly

If oligopolistic firms decide to compete by cutting price there is a very significant chance that they will become involved in a price war. A price war refers to a situation where a firm attempts to gain market share at the expense of its rivals by cutting price, triggering retaliation and further price cuts. Usually, all firms end-up worse off, as shown in the "Prisoner's dilemma" earlier. Rarely, price

wars may deliberately start when circumstances are such that a firm confidently expects to gain market share at the expense of rivals by cutting price. An example is T-Mobile, which initiated a price cut to attract more subscribers and was considered the winner in a relatively recent mobile telecoms price war in the USA. Often such firms have a "deep pocket", meaning that they can sustain losses for a while.

Since starting a price war is typically not in the interest of most oligopolistic firms, it follows that such firms usually adopt non-price competition as a strategy to increase sales, even if a price agreement has been made. Fear of triggering a price war as well as collusive agreements result in prices being "sticky" in oligopolistic markets. Even if production costs decrease, firms do not decrease price.

Non-price competition can take many forms. Perhaps the single most important method of non-price competition is heavy advertising and creation of brand names (an example is the soft drinks industry). Firms also compete by:

- developing and marketing new products (smartphones and cars)
- continuously differentiating their products (breakfast cereals)
- offering volume discounts (for shampoos, conditioners and detergents)
- providing customers with after-sale service (customer plans in the car industry)
- offering lengthy guarantees (for electronics products)
- offering gifts and coupons (in newspapers and supermarkets)
- organizing competitions (as radio stations often do).

Policymakers' perspective

Oligopolistic firms face a negatively sloped demand curve and thus charge a price higher than marginal cost so they are allocatively inefficient. If in an oligopolistic market firms collude then price may even be as high as if the market was a monopoly. But we must bear in mind that if there is a price war then price may approach marginal cost and thus the extent of allocative inefficiency will be diminished. Also, as we shall see later, if these oligopolistic firms are large they may enjoy other benefits, such as those resulting from economies of scale. The issue of efficiency in such markets is thus rather complicated.

Monopolistic competition

A market is considered monopolistically competitive if the following applies.

- It has very many firms.
- The firms produce differentiated products.
- There are no entry barriers.

Typical examples of monopolistic competition include hair salons, restaurants, bars, opticians or fuel stations. Since each firm is producing a differentiated product, it faces a negatively sloped demand curve. If it raises price it will lose some, but not all, of its customers. It follows that monopolistically competitive firms have some market (or

monopoly) power. However, that market power is small. This is because there are very many firms in each market and consumers thus face many close substitutes. A restaurant can raise the price of the pasta dish it offers, but not too much as there are many other restaurants around that offer the same or similar pasta dishes. The same issue affects fuel stations and hair salons.

Monopolistic competition: Short-run equilibrium

Figure 2.11.12 shows the short-run equilibrium position of a monopolistically competitive firm.

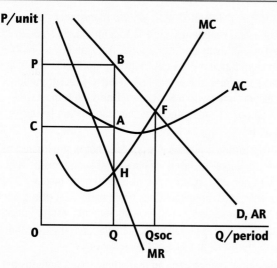

Figure 2.11.12 Monopolistic competition: short-run equilibrium

Assuming that it aims at maximizing profits it will choose to produce and offer Q units per period, where MR = MC, and sell at price P. It will be thus earning abnormal (or supernormal) profits equal to area (CABP).

Since firms in this market are earning abnormal (or supernormal) profits other entrepreneurs will have the incentive to enter this market. Why? It is because firms in this market are earning more than normal profits, which means more than what they could have been earning in the next best alternative with the same risk. More firms will enter the market as there are no barriers in monopolistic competition. As they enter, the demand that each firm faces "shrinks and tilts". It decreases and the demand curve shifts left. This is because at each price they will be selling less because of their diminishing market share. Demand also becomes flatter, meaning more price elastic. Why? It is because consumers will be facing even more and even closer substitutes. This process of entry will stop when firms in this market are earning zero economic profits (that is, normal profits). If entrepreneurs earn in this market as much as they could earn in the next best alternative with the same risk, then there will be no reason for more firms to enter or for any of the incumbent firms to exit. Long-run equilibrium will have been reached. Figure 2.11.13 shows long-run equilibrium in a monopolistically competitive market.

Monopolistic competition: Long-run equilibrium

Entry of new firms and the existence of even more and even closer substitutes for consumers have shifted the demand curve to the left for each firm and made it quite price elastic and flat. It can never be horizontal because products are differentiated. Profit-maximizing monopolistically competitive firms will choose Q units, where MR = MC, and sell at price P. Economic profits are zero as at Q, AR = AC. The demand curve has shifted left until it became tangent to the U-shaped AC curve. Since firms are earning normal profits, this represents long-run equilibrium in the market.

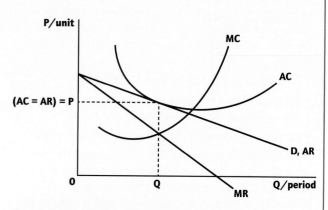

Figure 2.11.13 Monopolistic competition: long-run equilibrium

Efficiency issues in monopolistic competition

Monopolistically competitive firms are allocatively inefficient. They produce less output than the socially optimal level because at the chosen level of output, P > MC. Remember, they face a negatively sloped demand curve and so have some degree of market (or monopoly) power. However, the degree of monopoly power they possess is quite limited. They cannot charge a price that is significantly higher than marginal cost. Consumers have very many close substitutes to choose from. For example, if the price of a popular meal rises too much in a restaurant in town, people can easily switch to another restaurant. The degree of allocative inefficiency in monopolistically competitive markets is usually rather small. In addition, demand faced may not be horizontal, but since the existence of very many close substitutes makes it quite flat, such firms will produce with an average cost only slightly above the minimum. This may also be the result of their constant attempt to differentiate their product even more. So, even the extent of technical inefficiency will be small.

Most importantly, monopolistically competitive markets present consumers with great variety and this is a highly valued characteristic of this market structure. There are restaurants and hair salons, for example, that cater to every taste and if there is a niche, an entrepreneur will soon enter the market to satisfy it.

Policymakers' perspective

Monopolistic competition is allocatively and technically inefficient but the extent of these inefficiencies is very small compared to monopoly or oligopoly. The market power and resulting pricing power of monopolistically competitive firms are minimal. These firms offer tremendous variety to consumers. The fact that there are many monopolistically competitive firms implies that for any such market there will probably be a firm located near consumers, which is also an advantage.

Advantages of large firms

Firms that are large in size and have significant market or monopoly power have certain advantages when compared with the small firms in perfect and monopolistic competition.

Being large in size allows firms to benefit from economies of scale. These firms can often produce at a lower average cost compared to smaller firms. This allows larger firms to set a price lower than the price found in a perfectly competitive market and to offer an even greater quantity. Of course, there is no guarantee that the cost savings resulting from economies of scale will be passed on to consumers in the form of lower prices. The extent to which this will be the case depends on the actual and potential competition these firms face. Entrenched monopoly positions or successful collusive agreements that are maintained for long and are not exposed may not lead to the lowest prices that competition guarantees.

Large firms in monopoly or oligopolistic markets are in position to maintain abnormal (supernormal) profits in the long run. This enables them to invest in research and development (R&D) activities which is of tremendous importance because R&D leads to innovations. Innovations refer to new products and new production processes. There is no question that consumers have benefited from striking innovations. The question that remains is what market characteristics make innovations more likely to result.

Lastly, there is the Schumpeterian argument in favour of large firms with monopoly power that can maintain abnormal (supernormal) profits in the long run. Schumpeter, an Austrian economist at Harvard University, held that in the absence of entrenched monopoly power, large firms are not only able to innovate but are forced continuously to innovate to avoid being swept away by the "perennial gale of creative destruction".

Abuse of monopoly power

Monopoly power may be necessary to permit a firm to grow and to invest in R&D and innovate but there are many instances where a firm's dominant position has led to abuse of such a position. A dominant position does not in itself constitute a reason for governments or competition authorities to intervene. However, abuse may be present if it is suspected that a firm is acting with the intention to eliminate competitors or to prevent entry of new firms. Tech giants such as Google, Facebook, Apple, Intel and Amazon, among others, have been suspected of abusing their market power. They have been accused of acting in precisely the manner described above. They have restricted competition in their markets by aggressively buying out their competitors. The USA Justice Department has complained that some hi-tech companies have reached agreements that deprived engineers and scientists working for them of seeking better job opportunities elsewhere. Some have used their extensive legal resources to suppress competition by restricting access to their platforms to rival firms. This may not directly lead

to higher prices for final consumers but it has caused competing producers to suffer and may have decreased the rate of innovation.

When firms collude and behave as if they were a monopoly, pricing abuses result that harm consumers (who are forced to pay higher prices). The European Commission has fined members of many cartels in a vast area of markets including canned vegetables, electronics products, car safety equipment, apple sauce, beer, vehicle sales and many others. In all cases of collusion, the resulting market power led to much higher prices paid and less choice for consumers. In the market for pharmaceuticals there is a lot of discussion on how some firms have managed effectively to extend patents on drugs to more than 40 years instead of the 20-year current limit. Some drugs companies have also been accused of "paying for delaying" tactics, where they pay firms to delay entry into a market after a patent has expired. Such abuse of monopoly power has led to exorbitant prices for drugs, harming consumers and taxpayers.

Policymakers' perspective

The typical set of available responses in the policymakers' toolkit includes, among other tools:

- imposing heavy fines
- prohibiting mergers
- prohibiting acquisitions
- forcing firms to sell off parts
- imposing a maximum price.

It is important to stress that in the case of enforcing competition the USA and the European perspective diverge. The USA has shifted its focus exclusively towards consumer welfare so that a major guiding principle is whether the final consumer is harmed from higher prices or not. The 2020 Economic Report to the President claimed that rising concentration is driven by economies of scale that decrease prices for consumers and that successful firms tend to grow, so it is important that competition authorities do not punish firms for their success.

Others, including the Europeans, have in addition focused on: the rights of excluded competitors; the impact of firm practices on workers; whether certain large firms have too much buying power, forcing down prices and suffocating suppliers; and the possible negative impact of rising concentration on the rate of innovation.

The job of the policymaker is not easy. It is a balancing act often with many conflicting considerations. For example, the EU competition commission recently blocked the merger between the German firm Siemens and French firm Alstom, Europe's largest suppliers in the rail market. The reason was that the merger would have "harmed competition in markets for railway signaling systems and very high-speed trains". The proposed merger "would have led to higher prices, less choice and less innovation", according to EU Competition Commissioner M Vestager. There was another side to the argument, though. It relates to the discussion of what constitutes the relevant market. According to this perspective, the real markets for these European manufacturers are outside Europe where they would have to compete for international contracts with CRCC, a huge Chinese competitor, as well as with other Japanese and South Korean companies. There was need, according to this side, for a "European champion" that could better compete in international markets. It was not an easy question to decide.

Or, if policymakers set price ceilings or other restrictions on, for example, pharmaceutical corporations, there is a risk that it would decrease their incentive to innovate and spend billions to find new life-saving drugs. These are questions that are not easily settled.

In general, it is not easy to decide whether there is abuse of market power and what kind of response is optimal for society. The particulars of each case matter a lot.

3.1 Measuring economic activity and illustrating its variations

Measuring economic activity involves measuring an economy's national income or total output and is referred to as national income accounting.

We cannot evaluate the performance of an economy: that is, determine whether an economy is doing better or worse this year compared with last year or five years ago, if there is no measurement of economic activity. We cannot compare the performance of one economy against other economies at a point in time or over some period if we do not know how total output and income have behaved. If performance has been judged unsatisfactory, policymakers will need to devise and implement policies to improve its performance and also to judge the effectiveness of their policy choices later.

National income accounting therefore helps in assessing economic performance through time, across countries, as well as in devising and evaluating policies.

How is economic activity measured?

Gross domestic product (GDP)

GDP is the most often used measure of economic activity and it is defined as the *value* of all *final* goods and services produced *within* an economy over a period of time, usually a year or a quarter.

Let's add some points to explain this definition.

- The "value" of a good or a service is simply its quantity produced multiplied by its price.

- Goods can either be "final" or intermediate. Only final goods and services are included in GDP. Intermediate goods, which are inputs to the production of final goods and services, are excluded to avoid double counting. For example, steel is an input to the production of cars and so it is an intermediate good while cars are the final good. Steel is thus already included in GDP as part of cars. Considering it separately would only lead to counting it twice.

- In some cases a good can be both final and intermediate. For instance, flour produced by McDougall's flour mill is final when bought by individual consumers at the supermarket but also intermediate when bought by Warburtons bakery to produce bread. This shows that, instead of trying to work out which goods are final, the "value added" contributed by each firm in the country can be counted. The value added is defined as the difference between the total revenues collected by each firm and the cost of raw materials, services and components the firm purchased to produce the good or service.

- "Within an economy" means that the goods and services are produced within the physical borders of the country.

- Also, measurement of the GDP of an economy does not include transactions involving used goods, financial transactions or transfer payments, as these do not represent contributions to current production of goods and services.

There are three conceptually equivalent methods to calculate GDP. Government statisticians use all three methods.

- The **output approach** adds up the value of all the final goods and services produced by each economic sector, such as agriculture, manufacturing, transport, banking and so on.

$$\text{GDP} = \text{sector 1} + \text{sector 2} + \text{sector 3} + \ldots + \text{sector n}$$

- The **expenditure approach** measures the total amount spent on domestically produced final goods and services. Total spending includes:

  – consumption spending (C) : spending by households

  – investment spending (I) : spending by firms

  – government spending (G)

  – net exports (X – M): spending by foreigners on domestic goods and services (that is, exports) minus domestic spending on foreign goods and services (that is, imports).

$$\text{GDP} = C + I + G + (X - M)$$

- The **income approach** adds up all the income generated in the production process and by the factors of production in the economy.

$$\text{GDP} = \text{rents} + \text{wages} + \text{interest} + \text{profits}$$

The three methods described above are equivalent and with some minor adjustments all three approaches yield the same result. The idea rests on the circular flow of income, which was presented in section 1.1 (see page 5).

The circular flow model shows that the value of output produced is equal to the expenditures made to purchase that output, which is equal to the total income generated in producing that output. That is to say, in an economy the value of goods and services produced is equal to the expenditures made to purchase these goods and services. These expenditures did not disappear but they ended up in the pockets of all those who were responsible for the production of these goods and services as income. For example, if in an economy only 100 haircuts were produced in 2020 valued at $1000.00 (value of output), then $1000.00 was spent by all those who got their hair cut (expenditures on this output) and this $1000.00 was collected by all those responsible for the production of these haircuts (income generated by the production of this output).

Gross national income (GNI)

As explained above, the income approach of calculating GDP is to add up all the income earned by factors of production from firms operating within the economy—but consider two questions. What happens when profits are paid to foreigners who own stocks in domestic firms? Where do the profits earned by domestic companies operating overseas fit in? The answer is that they go into GNI but not GDP, where GNI is given by:

GNI = GDP + factor income from abroad − factor income sent abroad

GNI thus includes factor income earned abroad by a country's residents, such as the profits of Microsoft's European operations that accrue to Microsoft's US shareholders and the wages of US consultants who work temporarily in East Asia. However, it excludes factor income earned by foreigners, such as profits paid to Chinese investors who own US stocks and payments to Venezuelan workers temporarily in the USA.

In practice, it does not make much difference which measure is used for large economies like that of the USA, as the flows of net factor income to other countries are small. For smaller countries, however, GDP and GNI can diverge significantly. For example, much of Ireland's industry is owned by US corporations and their profits must be deducted from Ireland's GDP.

Nominal versus real values

Nominal GDP is the value of output of a certain period valued using the prices that prevailed at that period. Nominal GDP or nominal GNI for, say, 2020 are expressed in terms of current prices, the prices prevailing in 2020.

Now consider the following. If GDP was $10 million in 2017 and 10% more in 2018 (that is, $11 million) we cannot know whether the higher figure was due to an increase in output produced. If prices had increased by 10% then output produced was the same. To measure actual changes in output, we need real GDP or real GNI.

More specifically, real GDP is a measure of output of a certain year (say, year "t") valued at the prices prevailing at some reference period (known as the base period or base year). So, the output of each good in year "t" is multiplied by its price that prevailed in the base year chosen. Real GDP is therefore a measure of output after having isolated (or, adjusted for) the effect of inflation. Real GDP figures reflect the volume of production, not the value. The same applies to real GNI.

Define the GDP deflator as the ratio of nominal GDP to real GDP of a year times 100:

$$\text{GDP deflator} = \frac{\text{nominal GDP}}{\text{real GDP}} \times 100$$

By manipulating the above we arrive at:

$$\text{Real GDP} = \frac{\text{nominal GDP}}{\text{GDP deflator}} \times 100$$

The GDP deflator is a comprehensive price index that measures the average level of prices of all goods and services included in the GDP of a country.

Real GDP or real GNI must be used when making comparisons over time, as it is important to isolate the effect of changing price levels.

Per capita figures

By dividing GDP or GNI by the population of a country we arrive at per capita GDP and per capita GNI respectively. Per capita figures provide an indication of average or per person output or income in the economy. Per capita income figures can be used as a measure of the standard of living in a country as they provide a very rough indication of the access to goods and services that the population of a country has.

Real GDP/GNI per capita at purchasing power parity (PPP)

To have a basis of comparison across countries we need to convert each country's per capita income figure to a common currency, which is typically the US dollar. Yet, prices of goods and services can vary significantly across countries. A haircut in Lagos is much cheaper than a haircut in New York. Cost of living differences must be considered in the conversion of per capita income to US dollars. Therefore, instead of the market exchange rate we use "purchasing power parity" (PPP) dollars. These are dollars of equal purchasing power: that is, they buy the same basket of goods and services that the national currency buys. As such, PPP dollars incorporate cost of living differences and make cross-country comparisons more meaningful.

What do all these national income statistics tell us?

National income statistics can:

- provide a measure of the size of the economy
- be used to assess the performance of an economy over time
- help policymakers devise and evaluate appropriate policies
- be used to make cross-country comparisons
- be used as a measure of the standard of living in a country.

Using GDP or GNI statistics to measure economic well-being

Bear in mind that if any such attempt is made it is better to use GNI rather than GDP figures, as GNI focuses on incomes earned by the nationals of a country while GDP focuses on output produced inside the country. Such a figure must be divided by the population to adjust for the size of the country. Also, if comparisons are made through time, then real and not nominal figures must be used to adjust for changing prices.

The major argument in favour of using per capita income as a measure of living standards is that if it is higher it implies that people command more output on average, and access to more output is considered better than access to less output.

However, this per capita statistic suffers from major deficiencies and should be employed with extra care. The following is a list of the associated problems.

- As an average, a per capita statistic provides no information about the distribution of income in a country. Per capita income of a country may be high because people in the top 1% earn extraordinarily high incomes but the bottom 99% earn very little. For example, the USA and Denmark have both high per capita income levels but income inequality in the USA is much higher and so we cannot claim that living standards in these two countries are the same.

- Per capita income rises when production levels rise but it may be rising at a huge cost to the environment. Any damaging effect of increased production on the environment is ignored. If per capita incomes double over a decade but at a cost of epic pollution and environmental degradation, is it safe to conclude that living standards have also doubled? For instance, in India per capita incomes have grown dramatically but at the same time in 2020 India was home to "21 of the world's 30 most polluted cities" (CNN 2020). Green GDP is an attempt to correct this problem as it factors in the detrimental effect of production on the environment. Green GDP is estimated by subtracting from GDP the cost of natural resource and environmental depletion.

- Per capita income statistics fail to include the value of leisure. Leisure is a most important dimension of the well-being of people, but its importance is not accounted for. Per capita income levels may be the same in two countries, but it makes a difference whether people work 60 or 35 hours per week.

- Living standards are not only affected by current income but also by the stock of wealth of the population. The house or the car a family owns provides services that significantly contribute to their well-being.

- The level of public health care and public education available to citizens may differ between two countries with the same per capita income greatly affecting living standards. High quality health care and education services available free at point of delivery permit families to spend more on other goods and services.

- Some expenditures may be recorded as positive contributions to economic activity and so to income although they have been made to counteract activities that have caused harm. For example, the expenditures for cleaning up the oil spill in the Gulf of Mexico were an addition to the US GDP with no adjustment made for the environmental catastrophe.

- Per capita statistics fail to reveal the composition of output. Two economies with equal per capita income levels may differ with respect to economic well-being because of different output mix. A country that devotes a large proportion of its GDP to, say, defence, sacrifices resources that could otherwise have been used in the production of pro-development goods.

For all these reasons, alternative measures to assess well-being have been developed.

Better Life Index (BLI)

The Better Life Index (BLI) has been developed by the Organization for Economic Cooperation and Development (OECD) and is designed to produce an overall well-being index. The BLI includes 11 topics that reflect what the OECD has identified as essential to well-being in terms of material living conditions and quality of life. The topics include:

- housing
- income
- jobs
- community
- education
- environment
- civic engagement
- health
- life satisfaction
- safety
- work and life balance.

Each of the 11 topics of the index is based on one to four indicators that are averaged with equal weights. For example, the Jobs topic is based on four separate measures: the employment rate, personal earnings, the long-term unemployment rate and job security. The BLI can then be used to assess well-being within countries and across countries. For instance, the USA, despite having a high per capita GDP (much higher compared to the OECD average), ranks below average in terms of work and life balance because it is faced with significant income inequality. In contrast, Colombia has a relatively low per capita GDP (significantly lower than the OECD average), but ranks above average in health status as well as environmental quality, which are important dimensions of well-being.

Happiness Index

The Happiness Index has been developed by the United Nations Sustainable Development Solutions Network and is published annually in the World Happiness Report, a survey of the state of global happiness that ranks 156 countries by how happy their citizens perceive themselves to be. To estimate the Happiness Index the "Cantril Ladder" is used, where the sample population is asked to rank their satisfaction with respect to their present living conditions from 0–10 (where 10 represents the best possible life and living conditions and 0 presents the worst possible life and living conditions). The Happiness Index is then calculated by averaging the answers to this Cantril Ladder to a single number. According to the Happiness Index of 2018, the happiest countries in the world are: Finland (7.63), Norway (7.59) and Denmark (7.56) whereas the unhappiest countries in the world are: Burundi (2.91), Central African Republic (3.08) and South Sudan (3.25).

Happy Planet Index (HPI)

The Happy Planet Index (HPI) has been developed by the New Economics Foundation of London and is designed to assess whether a country is able to promote the well-being of its residents. It is made up of the three variables of:

- average life expectancy
- average subjective well-being
- ecological footprint (the impact of a person or community on the environment, expressed as the amount of land required to sustain their use of natural resources).

Surprisingly, the top five countries in the Happy Planet Index ranking have GDP per capita levels below $10,000. Costa Rica is on the top of the ranking, with Costa Ricans having a significantly higher well-being than the residents of many rich nations.

The business cycle

The real GDP of a country does not increase continuously over time. Typically, periods during which the economy expands are followed by periods during which the economy contracts. The business cycle, shown in Figure 3.1.1, refers to these short-term fluctuations of an economy's real GDP over time.

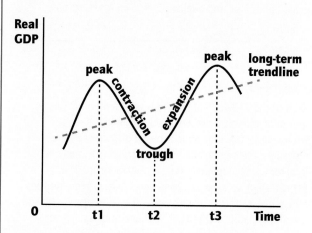

Figure 3.1.1 The business cycle

Between time t1 and t2 the economy is contracting (contraction phase) since real GDP is decreasing. We say that it is in recession (technically, an economy is in recession if real GDP decreases for at least two consecutive quarters). At t1 it was at a peak and just about to enter recession. The major characteristic of a recession is rising unemployment. At t2 it is at a trough and just about to enter recovery–expansion. Between time t2 and t3 the economy is growing (expansion phase) since real GDP is increasing. However, if the expansion is too rapid it may give rise to inflationary pressures.

This economy is also growing over the long term as the trendline is upward sloping. The trend line is the average annual long-term growth of the economy.

An economy is growing when real GDP is increasing, and it is contracting when real GDP is decreasing. The growth rate of an economy is the percentage change of real GDP between two years. If the percentage change in real GDP is positive, then real GDP is increasing, suggesting that the economy is growing. However, if the growth rate is negative, then real GDP is decreasing, and the economy is in recession. Note that if the growth rate is positive but decreasing (from, say, 2.1% to 0.8%) real GDP continues to increase but at a slower rate. It is not in recession.

Calculations

The following data refer to Lalaland in 2015.

Variable	Amount ($ billion)
Consumption expenditures (C)	35.86
Investment expenditures (I)	6.52
Government expenditures (G)	22.82
Export revenues (X)	8.6
Import expenditures (M)	9.8
Factor income earned abroad	1.1
Factor income paid abroad	1.3

1. Calculate nominal GDP from the expenditure approach.

Nominal GDP can be calculated from expenditure data using the relationship:

$$\text{nominal GDP} = C + I + G + (X - M)$$

So: nominal GDP = 35.86 + 6.52 + 22.82 + (8.6 – 9.8) = $64.0 billion

2. Calculate nominal GNI for Lalaland.

To calculate Lalaland's GNI we need to add net factor (or property) income from abroad to its GDP figure. This is equal to income earned abroad ($1.1 billion) minus income paid abroad ($1.3 billion):

$$1.1 - 1.3 = -\$0.2 \text{ billion.}$$

It follows that in 2015 Lalaland's GNI was 64.1 – 0.2 = $63.8 billion.

The following table shows additional data for Lalaland.

Year	Nominal GDP ($ billion)	GDP deflator	Population (million)
2016	308.12	98.9	13.27
2017	321.99	100	13.34
2018	332.65	102.2	13.47

3. Calculate the level of real GDP for Lalaland for 2016 to 2018.

To calculate real GDP from nominal GDP data we need to divide the nominal GDP data by the GDP deflator that year and multiply your result by 100.

2016: $\text{real GDP} = \dfrac{308.12}{98.9} \times 100 = \$311.55 \text{ billion}$

2017: $\text{real GDP} = \dfrac{321.99}{100} \times 100 = \$321.99 \text{ billion}$

2018: $\text{real GDP} = \dfrac{332.65}{102.2} \times 100 = \$325.49 \text{ billion}$

4. Calculate the real GDP per capita for Lalaland for 2016 to 2018.

To calculate real GDP per capita we must divide real GDP by the population of the country.

2016: $\text{real GDP per capita} = \left(\dfrac{311.55 \times 10^9}{13.27 \times 10^6}\right) = \$23,478$

2017: $\text{real GDP per capita} = \left(\dfrac{321.99 \times 10^9}{13.34 \times 10^6}\right) = \$24,137$

2018: $\text{real GDP per capita} = \left(\dfrac{325.49 \times 10^9}{13.47 \times 10^6}\right) = \$24,164$

3.2 Variations in economic activity—aggregate demand and aggregate supply

Aggregate demand

Aggregate demand refers to the *total planned spending* on *domestic* goods and services at different *average price levels* per period of time.

Spending on domestic goods and services can originate from households, firms, the government and foreigners. This means that aggregate demand (AD) includes consumption expenditures (C), investment expenditures (I), government expenditures (G) and exports (X). However, since some of the expenditures that households, firms and the government make are on foreign goods, we must subtract imports (M).

$$AD = C + I + G + (X - M)$$

If this looks familiar, it is because GDP measured by the expenditure approach is the same sum—but GDP and aggregate demand are not at all the same concepts. GDP is *actual* output produced, say $5.15 trillion in Japan in 2019, whereas aggregate demand shows the *planned* level of spending at different price levels in a country. So GDP is a number whereas aggregate demand is a function.

In Figure 3.2.1, aggregate demand is illustrated by the AD curve. On the horizontal axis is real output and on the vertical axis is the average price level (APL), an index of the average of the prices of all final goods and services in the economy.

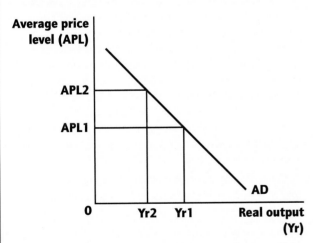

Figure 3.2.1 The AD curve

So, if the average price level is at APL1 then planned level of spending on domestic output is at Yr1. If the average price level is at APL2 then planned level of spending on domestic output is at Yr2.

The AD curve is downward sloping but not for the same reasons that the demand for a single good is downward sloping, as on the vertical axis we have the average price of all goods and not the price of a single good. The AD curve is negatively sloped because of the wealth effect, the trade effect and the interest rate effect.

- The wealth effect: if the average price level increases then the real value of the money that people have in their pockets or in bank accounts, as well as the real value of other financial assets they own such as bonds, decreases.

If people feel poorer they tend to spend less; consumer expenditures fall (C). Thus, if the average price level rises then spending on domestic goods and services falls, leading to a downward sloping AD curve.

- The trade effect: if the average price level increases then exports become less competitive abroad while imports seem more attractive at home, so net exports (NX), a component of aggregate demand, decrease. Thus, if the average price level rises then net exports fall, leading to a downward-sloping AD curve.

- The interest rate effect: if the average price level increases, then people need to hold more money to buy the same goods and services. The demand for holding money (cash and cheque accounts) increases. If the supply of money by the central bank is constant then the "price" of money, which is the interest rate, rises. Higher interest rates decrease consumption (C) and investment (I) expenditures as people and firms will borrow less from banks to buy durables and capital equipment. So, if the average price level rises then consumption and investment decrease, leading to a downward-sloping AD curve.

As in all diagrams, the function will not shift when a variable on either of the axes changes. So, if there is a change in the average price level there will be no shift in the AD curve but only a movement along it.

Aggregate demand will shift only if a determinant induces a change in any of its components. An increase in aggregate demand means that there is a shift of the AD curve to the right from AD1 to AD2. A decrease in aggregate demand means that the AD curve shifts to the left from AD1 to AD3. These effects are shown in Figure 3.2.2.

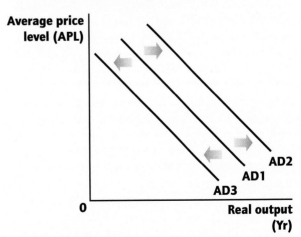

Figure 3.2.2 Shifts of the AD curve

Determinants of aggregate demand components

Consumption expenditures (C) are defined as spending by households on durables and non-durables and services and depend on the following.

- Interest rates: the interest rate is the cost of borrowing or the reward for saving money over a period of time expressed as a percentage. Households borrow to finance the purchase of durables, such as cars and appliances, and of houses. An increase in interest rates makes borrowing more expensive, resulting in less borrowing and so less consumer spending, decreasing aggregate demand and shifting the AD curve to the left. In addition, higher interest rates make saving more attractive. If people tend to save more then it automatically implies that they will tend to spend less. The reverse applies following a decrease in interest rates. Lower interest rates reduce the cost of borrowing while rendering saving less attractive and can lead to an increase in spending, boosting aggregate demand and shifting the AD curve to the right.

- Consumer confidence: this is a measure of how optimistic households are and how secure they feel about the future. Households feeling secure and confident about their future will tend to spend more. A stable and growing economy with low inflation and unemployment will boost consumer confidence and favourably affect household spending, shifting the AD curve to the right. On the other hand, uncertainty over future job prospects and insecurity about one's future income adversely affect present consumption. Spending on durable goods, such as cars and appliances, as well as on housing, is greatly affected by consumer moods.

- Household wealth: wealth refers to the value of what households own, such as stocks, bonds, deposits or real estate, minus what they owe. An increase in household wealth, for example due to a rise in property prices, leads to more spending, which increases aggregate demand, shifting the AD curve to the right. In contrast, if stock prices fall, wealth decreases and so will consumption. Aggregate demand will decrease and the AD curve will shift to the left.

- Personal income taxes: these determine the level of disposable income, which is the income left after taxes are paid. If the government raises personal income taxes, disposable income falls, spending drops with aggregate demand decreasing and the AD curve shifting to the left. On the contrary, a reduction in personal income taxes will lead to an increase in disposable income. Consumption will thus increase and so will aggregate demand.

- Household indebtedness: this refers to how much money households owe from taking out loans or from using credit cards. If they owe a lot, they will cut back on their spending, as they will first try to decrease their debt. Aggregate demand will decrease and the AD curve will shift left.

- Expectations of future price level: if households expect the average price level to decrease (deflationary expectations) they may delay purchases since they come to expect further price decreases. As a result, aggregate demand decreases and the AD curve shifts to the left. On the contrary, if consumers expect prices to increase (inflationary expectations) they may increase spending, leading to an increase in aggregate demand and a rightward shift of the AD curve.

Investment expenditures (I) are defined as spending by firms on capital goods (such as machines, tools, equipment and factories) per period of time. Investment increases the stock of capital of an economy. Investment is important both because of its influence on aggregate demand but also because of its influence on aggregate supply and so the rate of long-term economic growth. Investment spending depends on the following.

- Interest rates: if interest rates increase then borrowing to finance the purchase of capital goods such as machines, tools, equipment and factories will become more expensive so firms will find that fewer possible investment projects are now profitable. Even if a firm uses its own funds to finance an investment project, the opportunity cost of using these funds instead of keeping them in banks or as bonds increases. Investment expenditures by businesses are therefore expected to decrease, shifting the AD curve to the left. Decreases in interest rates have the opposite effect. Borrowing costs for firms fall leading to an increase in investment spending and aggregate demand shifting the AD curve to the right.

- Business confidence: this refers to how businesses feel about their future sales and about the economy. Economic and political stability are necessary for a positive business climate to evolve and so for more investments to take place. If firms are optimistic, they are more likely to invest and expand, aggregate demand will increase and the AD curve will shift to the right. Business pessimism, though, results in a decrease in investment spending and a decrease in aggregate demand, so the AD curve shifts to the left. Keynes considered the behaviour of entrepreneurs with respect to investment decisions similar to that of a herd (imitation) and, in his opinion, the observed instability of investment was due to these "animal spirits". Expectations can be greatly changed by many unpredictable factors, leading to swings in the prevailing business climate and so to changes in the level of investment spending.

- Technology: industries where technology improves fast will witness more investments, thus causing increases in aggregate demand and a rightward shift in the AD curve.

- Business taxes: these affect firms' profits. A decrease in business taxes increases the profitability of investment projects. More investment projects will be approved so investment spending will tend to increase. Aggregate demand will increase and the AD curve will shift to the right. An increase in business taxes may result in decreased investment and a leftward shift of the AD curve.

- Corporate indebtedness: if firms have high levels of debt due to past borrowing, they will be hesitant to take out more loans and make more investments as they will first try to decrease debt. Hence, aggregate demand decreases and the AD curve shifts to the left.

Government expenditures (G) are in many economies a large proportion of total expenditures on goods and services. Government spending is categorized as:

- current spending on goods and services
- capital (public investments) spending, which refers to spending on roads, ports, telecommunications, schools and other infrastructure
- transfer payments, which refer to pensions and unemployment benefits; note that transfer payments are not included in national income since they do not represent rewards to current productive effort.

Governments spend to ensure that adequate amounts of public and merit goods and services are available, such as national defence, education and health care. They spend to regulate markets in their attempt to guarantee product safety, environmental standards, competitive conditions and so on. They may also spend to redistribute income so that a socially acceptable minimum is guaranteed for all. Such spending, for example, includes funding state pensions, unemployment benefits, subsidies and disability benefits. Lastly, governments spend to affect aggregate demand. An increase or decrease in government expenditures will cause aggregate demand to increase or decrease, with the AD curve shifting to the right or to the left. This is part of what is known as fiscal policy (explained in section 3.6). We may therefore conclude that economic and political priorities affect the level of government spending. For instance, it may be a political priority to equip all public schools with smartboards and each student with a tablet, while it may be an economic priority that taxes on higher incomes must increase to decrease widening income inequality.

Net exports (X – M) are defined as the difference between spending by foreigners on domestic output minus domestic spending on foreign output or, more simply, as the difference between export revenues and import expenditures per period of time. They depend on the following.

- Income of trading partners: if income of our trading partners increases, their level of spending will increase. Part of their increased spending will be on imports, which are our exports. Thus, the exports of an economy will tend to increase if the income of its trading partners increases, increasing aggregate demand and shifting the AD curve to the right. For example, if the USA grows and income of Americans rises they will buy more Mexican goods so Mexico's exports will increase and so will Mexico's aggregate demand: the AD curve will shift to the right. If, however, the income of our trading partners decreases, say, as a result of a recession, then our exports will tend to decrease, leading to a decrease in aggregate demand and a leftward shift in the AD curve.
- Exchange rates: an exchange rate is the price of a country's currency expressed in terms of another country's currency. For example if €1.00 = USD1.13 it means that the price of one euro expressed in terms of US dollars is 1.13. If the exchange rate depreciates (so, in this example, if €1.00 now is equal to USD1.05) then EU exports become cheaper and more competitive abroad (in the USA) while imports (from the USA) become pricier and less attractive domestically (in the EU). As a result, net exports

increase, increasing aggregate demand and shifting the AD curve to the right. An increase in the exchange rate (appreciation) will have the opposite effect; net exports decrease, shifting the AD curve to the left.

- Trade policies: these refer to restrictions to international trade such as tariffs or quotas often imposed by governments (see section 4.2). If the government of one country imposes restrictions on the imports of another country, then imports will fall and so net exports will rise, increasing aggregate demand and shifting the AD curve to the right. For example, the US administration's decision to impose tariffs on Chinese steel and aluminum is expected to reduce imports and in turn increase net exports and aggregate demand. Relaxing trade restrictions can have the reverse effect. Reducing tariffs or quotas can lead to an increase in imports and so to a fall in net exports, which will decrease aggregate demand, shifting the AD curve to the left.

Recap

Aggregate demand

Movements along the AD curve are caused by changes in the average price level that lead to:

- the wealth effect
- the trade effect
- the interest rate effect.

Shifts in aggregate demand are caused by:

changes in consumption expenditures (C) resulting from changes in

- interest rates
- consumer confidence
- household wealth
- personal income taxes
- household indebtedness
- expectations on future price level

changes in investment expenditures (I) resulting from changes in

- interest rates
- business confidence
- technology
- business taxes
- corporate indebtedness

changes in government expenditures (G) resulting from changes in

- economic priorities
- political priorities

changes in net exports (X – M) resulting from changes in

- income of trading partners
- exchange rates
- trade policies.

Aggregate supply

Aggregate supply is defined as the planned level of output domestic firms are willing to offer at different average price levels per period time. Note that aggregate supply is not the same as real GDP. Aggregate supply shows how much output domestic firms are planning to offer at different average price levels. The shape of the AS curve is rather controversial in macroeconomics as it reflects the different assumptions used by different schools of thought. We will initially discuss aggregate supply under the Monetarist/New Classical model and, then, we will present aggregate supply under the Keynesian model.

Aggregate supply under the Monetarist/New Classical school

Monetarists (and New Classical economists) make a distinction between the short run and the long run. As a result, there is a short-run aggregate supply (SRAS) and a long-run aggregate supply (LRAS).

Short-run aggregate supply

Within the aggregate supply framework, the short run is the period during which money wages are fixed and unable to adjust to changes in the average price level. The money wage is basically what is written on a pay slip (that is, the "dollars" earned per time period).

On the other hand, the real wage is what you can buy with your money wage, or the purchasing power of your money wage. The real wage is thus:

$$Wr = \frac{Wm}{APL}$$

For example, if the Edgar's money wage is $60 per day and the price of a small carton of fruit juice is $2.00 then his real wage can be thought of as being 30 small cartons of juice per day. If Edgar continues to earn $60 but the price of a fruit juice rises to $4.00 per small carton, his real wage decreases to 15 of these cartons of juice per day. Of course, instead of using the price of one good, we use the average price level to determine whether the real wage increased or decreased.

Money wages are usually determined by labour contracts. This means that if the price level in the economy changes, as long as contracts are in effect, money wages will not adjust to match the change in the price level. There is also a second explanation based on the idea that workers are slow to adjust their expectations of inflation (of a rising average price level) and only after some time do they realize that rising prices have affected their purchasing power.

The reason money wages are closely related to aggregate supply is that they account for the largest part of firms' production costs. As long as money wages remain fixed, if the average price level changes only the real wage will be affected and so workers, in real terms, will either become "cheaper" or "pricier" to firms, inducing an output response. More specifically, if the average price level increases, then the real wage decreases and in turn firms will be willing to offer more output. On the contrary, if the average price level decreases, then the real wage increases and in turn firms will be willing to offer less output. The SRAS curve is therefore upward sloping, where real output is on the horizontal axis

and the average price level is on the vertical axis. This is shown in Figure 3.2.3.

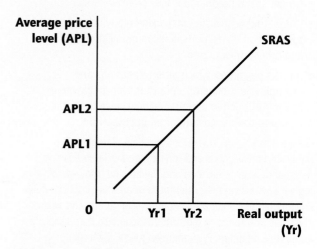

Figure 3.2.3 The SRAS curve

If the average price level rises from AP1L to APL2 while money wages remain fixed, then the real wage decreases and firms enjoy greater profitability, which induces them to offer more output: Yr2 instead of Yr1.

Changes and thus shifts in short-run aggregate supply are mainly caused by changes in production costs. Note that these would have to be changes in costs of production that will simultaneously affect most firms in the economy, not only firms of a particular market. Thus short-run aggregate supply will increase or decrease and thus the SRAS curve will shift in the following cases.

- Money wages change: money wages can change if, for example, there is a change in the minimum wage. So, if money wages increase, firms' costs of production rise, resulting in a decrease in short-run aggregate supply and a leftward shift in the SRAS curve. In contrast, if money wages decrease, for example because a government weakens the power of labour unions, short-run aggregate supply increases and the SRAS curve shifts to the right.

- Energy prices change: changes in the price of oil affect short-run aggregate supply in the same way as changes in wages. An increase in the price of oil decreases short-run aggregate supply and shifts the SRAS curve to the left; a decrease increases short-run aggregate supply and shifts the SRAS curve to the right.

- Indirect taxes or subsidies change: indirect taxes, such as sales taxes, affect costs of production. Therefore, higher taxes increase production costs and so decrease short-run aggregate supply and shift the SRAS curve to the left. Lower taxes on the other hand, lower production costs. For example, if the VAT in Greece decreases from 24% to 10%, firms will face lower costs of production leading to an increase in short-run aggregate supply and to a shift of the SRAS curve to the right. Subsidies also affect firms' production costs. An increase in government subsidies will reduce costs of production and so increase short-run aggregate supply, which will shift the SRAS curve to the right. A decrease in government subsidies, on the other hand, will raise production costs for firms, causing a decrease in short-run aggregate supply and a leftward shift of the SRAS curve.

An increase in short-run aggregate supply means that there is a shift of the SRAS curve to the right, shown in Figure 3.2.4 as a shift from SRAS1 to SRAS2. A decrease in short-run aggregate supply means that the SRAS curve shifts to the left from SRAS1 to SRAS3.

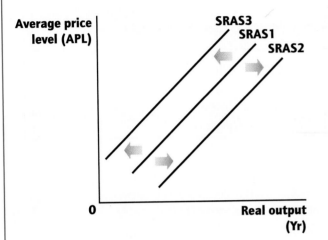

Figure 3.2.4 Shifts in the SRAS curve

Long-run aggregate supply

In the long run, money wages are assumed by the Monetarist/New Classical school to be flexible and fully adjusting to changes in the average price level. So, if the price level rises by 2.4% then money wages will also increase by 2.4%. It follows that the real wage is constant. As such, firms no longer respond to changes in the price level by changing their level of output.

Long-run aggregate supply is therefore drawn as a vertical (the LRAS curve) to show that changes in the average price level do not affect real output. The reason is that in the long run money wages fully adjust and thus the real wage and firms' profitability do not change to induce an output response. This is shown in Figure 3.2.5.

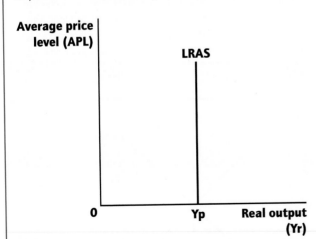

Figure 3.2.5 The LRAS curve

More specifically, according to the Monetarist/New Classical school, the LRAS curve is vertical at the economy's potential level of real output, Yp, since in the long run an economy produces whatever its resources and technology allow it to produce. Output is at its potential or natural level, which is considered the economy's full employment level of output.

Note that even though at this level of potential output we say that there is full employment, it should not be taken to mean that there is no unemployment in the economy. At the potential level of real output there is some unemployment, which is referred to by the Monetarists as natural (or normal) unemployment, and is the unemployment that exists when the labour market is in equilibrium (see section 3.3).

If long-run aggregate supply increases and the LRAS curve shifts to the right then this implies that the potential level of output has increased, meaning that the economy's productive capacity has increased. This is shown in Figure 3.2.6.

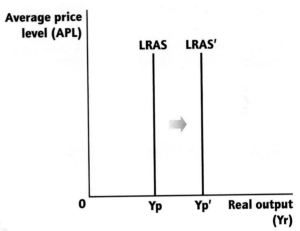

Figure 3.2.6 The LRAS curve shifting to the right

An increase in long-run aggregate supply can be a result of the following.

- The quantity of factors of production increases. An increase in the quantity of labour due to immigration means that the economy is capable of producing more real output and so the LRAS curve shifts to the right.

- The quality of factors of production improves. Greater levels of education and skills improve the quality of labour. Workers become more productive and the LRAS curve shifts to the right.

- There are improvements in technology. Technological innovation can lead to improved machines and equipment, which will be able to produce more output, and so the LRAS curve will shift to the right.

- Efficiency increases. When an economy makes better use of its resources, it can as a result produce a greater quantity of output. Therefore, the LRAS curve shifts to the right.

- There are institutional changes. Improvements in the institutional framework increase the economy's productive capacity. Reducing the amount of bureaucracy facilitates economic activity and can increase the output produced; the LRAS curve will shift to the right.

Recap

Monetarist/New Classical aggregate supply	
Short-run aggregate supply (SRAS)	**Long-run aggregate supply (LRAS)**
Money wages are assumed fixed.	Money wages are assumed flexible.
The SRAS curve is upward sloping:	The LRAS curve is vertical at the potential level of output:
• if average price level (APL) increases, the real wage drops, so firms offer more output	• changes in average price level (APL) do not affect real output because the real wage is not affected.
• if APL decreases, the real wage increases, so firms offer less output.	Shifts of the LRAS curve can occur due to:
Shifts of the SRAS curve can occur due to:	• an increase in the quantity of factors of production
• changes in money wages	• an improvement in the quality of factors of production
• changes in energy prices	• improvements in technology
• changes in indirect taxes or subsidies.	• increases in efficiency
	• institutional changes.

Aggregate supply under the Keynesian school

In the Keynesian school there is no distinction between the short run and the long run and so there is only one AS curve, which has three sections, as shown Figure 3.2.7.

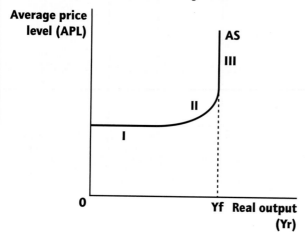

Figure 3.2.7 The Keynesian AS curve

Section I is horizontal, implying that higher levels of output can and will be produced without the average price level rising. The explanation lies with the realization that the real output levels corresponding to this region are significantly below the full employment level of real output denoted with Yf. Such an economy operates presumably in deep recession or depression-like conditions. Unemployment is very high and there is a lot of spare or unused capacity.

Section III is vertical at the full employment level of output Yf. This full employment level of output is typically considered within the extreme Keynesian framework of analysis as a "wall", implying that there is no unemployment in the economy. Real output cannot increase beyond Yf.

Section II illustrates an upward sloping AS curve. It depends on the realization that an economy consists of many different sectors and industries that employ differing types of resources, which do not reach full employment conditions together. Some industries may reach full employment earlier than others. This situation is referred to as bottlenecks in production: spare capacity in some industries may coexist with full employment in others. Real output may continue to rise but as a result of the capacity constraints in some industries, wages and, more generally, production costs may also be rising and so will prices.

Note that, strictly speaking, it is a mistake to refer to long-run Keynesian aggregate supply as Keynes was not interested in the long run in his analysis of the workings of an economy. We will thus make the distinction between short-run and long-run aggregate supply only for the Monetarist/New Classical model.

Macroeconomic equilibrium

Equilibrium in the Monetarist/New Classical model

Short-run equilibrium

Macroeconomic equilibrium in the short run exists at that level of real output at which aggregate demand is equal to short-run aggregate supply, as shown in Figure 3.2.8.

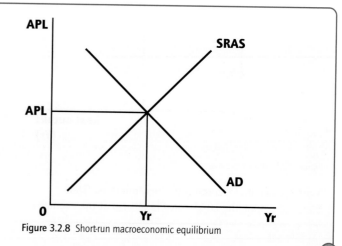

Figure 3.2.8 Short-run macroeconomic equilibrium

The equilibrium level of real output Yr is determined at the intersection of AD with SRAS. The average price level of the economy is also determined at level APL.

Any shift in aggregate demand will induce a change in the equilibrium average price and output levels in the same direction as the change in aggregate demand. For example, if aggregate demand increases, say, as a result of lower interest rates, then the AD curve will shift to the right from AD1 to AD2. This will lead in the short run to higher real output Yr2 as well as to a higher average price level at APL2, as shown in Figure 3.2.9.

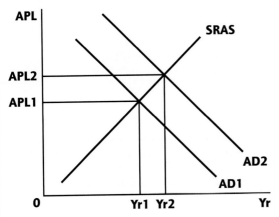

Figure 3.2.9 A shift in the AD curve

Shifts in short-run aggregate supply will induce changes in the average price level and of equilibrium output that are in the opposite direction. For example, if oil prices increase then, since production costs will rise, short-run aggregate supply will decrease, with the SRAS curve shifting to the left from SRAS1 to SRAS2 in Figure 3.2.10. There will be a higher average price level, APL2, accompanied by lower equilibrium real output Yr2.

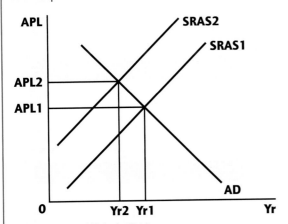

Figure 3.2.10 A shift in the SRAS curve

Long-run equilibrium

In the long-run, equilibrium will necessarily be at the economy's potential or full employment level of output, as any deviation from the potential level of output can only exist in the short run because money wages are assumed fixed. Deviations of short-run equilibrium from the potential level of output will be temporary and the economy will always return in the long-run to its potential or full employment level of

output as a result of money wages being flexible and fully adjusting to any change in the APL. Figure 3.2.11 shows this.

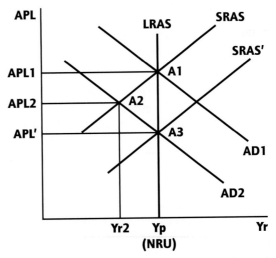

Figure 3.2.11 Returning to full employment following a decrease in aggregate demand

Assume an economy in equilibrium at point A1 where real output is at its potential level Yp, unemployment is at its natural or, normal rate (NRU) and the average price level is at APL1.

Now assume that business and consumer confidence in the economy decrease, leading to a decrease in consumption and investment expenditures. Aggregate demand decreases, with the AD curve shifting to the left from AD1 to AD2. The average price level drops from APL1 to APL2 and, since in the short run money wages are assumed fixed, the real wage increases and thus profitability for firms decreases so that real output falls to Yr2. There is a movement in the short run along the SRAS curve from point A1 to point A2.

Short-run equilibrium is at point A2 at the intersection of AD2 with the SRAS curve. Real output is below its potential (full employment) level and so unemployment rises above its natural rate (NRU). The economy is characterized by a deflationary (recessionary) gap equal to the difference between the potential level of output and the lower equilibrium level of output Yr2Yp.

> A deflationary gap (also referred to as a recessionary gap) exists when equilibrium real output is below the potential (full employment) level of output.

In the long run, however, according to Monetarists, money wages are flexible, which means that money wages will decrease to match the decrease in the price level. Remember that money wages is a shift factor for short-run aggregate supply. For this reason, short-run aggregate supply increases and the SRAS curve shifts to the right to SRAS'. Since the adjustment of money wages is assumed full, the real wage returns to its original level. Also, since the real wage is unchanged, unemployment must return to its natural rate (NRU) and consequently real output back to its potential level Yp. The economy has therefore moved automatically at point A3.

According to Monetarists, an economy will bounce back (that is, the deflationary/recessionary gap will close), only through the adjustment of money wages. There is no need for the government to intervene. The question is, of course, how fast the economy will return to full employment. It is not specified and thus the "long run" may prove too long a period, especially for the unemployed.

Something similar happens if there is an increase in aggregate demand. This is shown in Figure 3.2.12.

Assume an economy in equilibrium at point A1 where real output is at its potential level Yp, unemployment is at its natural or normal rate (NRU) and the APL is at APL1.

Now assume that a reduction in interest rates leads to an increase in aggregate demand, which shifts the AD curve to the right from AD1 to AD2. The price level rises from APL1 to APL2 and since in the short run money wages are assumed fixed, the real wage decreases and thus profitability for firms increases so that real output rises to Yr2. There is a movement in the short run along the SRAS curve from A1 to A2.

Short-run equilibrium is at A2 at the intersection of AD2 with SRAS. Real output is above its potential (full employment) level and so unemployment falls below its natural rate (NRU). The economy is characterized by an inflationary gap equal to the difference between the potential level of output and the greater equilibrium level of output YpYr2.

> An inflationary gap exists when equilibrium real output is greater than potential (full employment) output.

However, in the long-run, money wages are assumed flexible and they will fully adjust, matching the increase in the average price level. Short-run aggregate supply decreases, shifting the SRAS curve to the left to SRAS'. Since the adjustment of money wages is assumed full, the real wage returns to its original level. Also, since the real wage is unchanged, unemployment must return to its natural rate (NRU) and consequently real output back to its potential level Yp. The economy has therefore moved automatically at point A3.

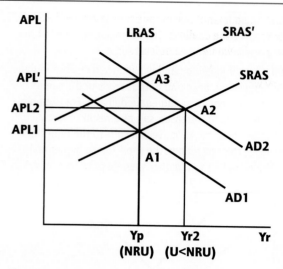

Figure 3.2.12 Returning to full employment following an increase in aggregate demand

According to Monetarists, an inflationary gap will close only through market adjustments, namely the increase in money wages. There is no need for government intervention.

Equilibrium in the Keynesian model

The major difference between the Monetarist/New Classical model described above and the Keynesian model is that the latter is not equipped with an automatic adjustment mechanism. Within the Keynesian framework an economy may find itself stuck at an equilibrium level of real output with less than full employment. No endogenous forces exist that will restore full employment.

More specifically, money wages are assumed "sticky downwards" (money wages may increase but they do not easily adjust downwards). It follows that within the Keynesian model, aggregate demand is the driving force behind the equilibrium level of economic activity. Instead of believing in "supply creating its own demand" (Say's law from the Classical school of thought, which included the intellectual fathers of monetarism and the New Classical school), Keynes turned things inside out, postulating that

Recap

Adjustments in the Monetarist/New Classical model	
The case of a deflationary gap	**The case of an inflationary gap**
• A decrease in aggregate demand in the short run will lead to a decrease in the average price level. Since money wages are assumed fixed, the real wage will increase, inducing firms to reduce output.	• An increase in aggregate demand in the short run will lead to an increase in the average price level. Since money wages are assumed fixed, the real wage will decrease, inducing firms to increase output.
• A deflationary gap will arise since the equilibrium level of real output will fall below the potential output level.	• An inflationary gap will arise since the equilibrium level of real output will exceed the potential output level.
• In the long run, money wages are flexible and will adjust and decrease to match the decrease in the average price level. The real wage will be restored and so will the potential level of output.	• In the long run, money wages are flexible and will adjust and increase to match the increase in the average price level. The real wage will be restored and so will the potential level of output.
• There is no need for government intervention.	• There is no need for government intervention.

it is "effective demand" (which we call aggregate demand) that determines the equilibrium level of real output in an economy. If, for whatever reason, aggregate demand proves insufficient to establish full employment then a market economy will suffer a system-wide failure, as it will be unable on its own (that is, without the help of the government) to restore full employment conditions.

Consider the economy shown in Figure 3.2.13, initially operating at full employment. A collapse in business and consumer confidence causes a decrease in aggregate demand, and the AD curve shifts to the left from AD1 to AD2. Equilibrium real output Yr2 is below the full employment level of output Yf. Thus, there is a deflationary (recessionary) gap equal to Yr2Yf.

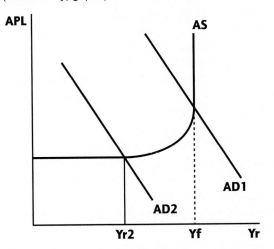

Figure 3.2.13 The deflationary (recessionary) gap within the Keynesian diagram

As mentioned above, according to the Keynesian school, money wages are "sticky downwards". There is no automatic adjustment mechanism to push the economy back to the full employment level of output. Therefore, an economy may remain stuck in a deflationary/recessionary gap; that is, at a level of real output that is below the full employment level. The government must therefore intervene in order to increase aggregate demand and restore full employment. This can be achieved either through expansionary fiscal policy or loose monetary policy (see sections 3.6 and 3.8).

An inflationary gap is more cumbersome to illustrate within a Keynesian diagram, as Keynesian analysis was originally not interested in investigating inflationary conditions. In any case, if aggregate demand increases within the vertical section of a Keynesian AS curve (section III) then an inflationary gap is said to be created.

Figure 3.2.14 shows an economy at the full employment of output Yf. A rise in business and consumer confidence now causes aggregate demand to increase and thus shift the AD curve to the right from AD1 to AD2. Equilibrium real output will remain at Yf (remember the "wall"). The APL will though rise from APL1 to APL2.

Vertical distance ab can be referred to as the inflationary gap. Unlike the Monetarist/New Classical model, the gap is now on the vertical axis as in the strict interpretation of the Keynesian model, full employment refers to zero unemployment.

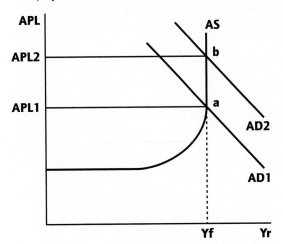

Figure 3.2.14 The inflationary gap within the Keynesian diagram

Note that the idea of the natural rate of unemployment can still be incorporated in the Keynesian model. The way to do it is to define as the full employment level of output some level of real output to the left of where the vertical section of the AS curve would intersect the horizontal axis. This is shown in Figure 3.2.15.

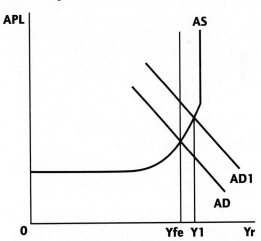

Figure 3.2.15 An alternative on the Keynesian inflationary gap

The increase of aggregate demand to AD1 creates an inflationary gap equal to distance YfeY1 on the horizontal axis.

Economic growth

Meaning of the term

Economic growth refers to an increase in the size of an economy over time: it is defined as an increase of real GDP through time.

Measuring economic growth

The growth rate is the percentage change in real GDP between two periods. The periods are usually two years but they could be two quarters. So, for example, the growth rate for an economy in, say, 2020 (compared to 2019) would be:

$$\text{Growth}_{2019\rightarrow2020} = \frac{\text{rGDP}_{20} - \text{rGDP}_{19}}{\text{rGDP}_{19}} \times 100$$

Using actual data to calculate the US growth rate in 2019:

real GDP in 2019 = $19,220 billion

real GDP in 2018 = $ 18,783 billion.

$$\text{Growth in 2019} = \frac{19220 - 18783}{18783} \times 100 = 2.33\%$$

This means that the US economy grew in 2019 by 2.33%. If the growth rate figure for a country in 2019 was −2.5% it would mean that this economy's real GDP *decreased* between 2018 and 2019, so this economy was in recession. If the growth rate for another economy in 2018 was 3.45% and then one year later it was at 2.85% this lower growth rate does *not* mean that real GDP decreased or that the economy is in recession. Since the growth rate is still positive, the economy continued to grow in 2019, but at a slower rate.

Growth rates can also be calculated using per capita real GDP figures.

Growth over the short term

This refers to growth that is a result of greater use of existing resources. Potential (or full employment) output is not affected.

Growth over the short term is a result of aggregate demand increasing as an increase in aggregate demand will lead to an increase in real GDP (assuming the economy is not at its potential, or full employment, output).

Aggregate demand can increase, shift to the right and lead to growth for a variety of reasons. Technically, any factor that increases any component of aggregate demand will shift it to the right and increase real output. Remember that aggregate demand includes consumption (C), investment (I) and government (G) expenditures as well as net exports (NX).

The most important factors that may lead to short-term economic growth include the following.

- Improved consumer and business confidence leading to increased spending by households (C) and firms (I) may increase economic growth in the short term.

- Short-term growth may result from a decrease in interest rates as lower interest rates decrease the cost of borrowing for households and firms, who may borrow more to buy or build houses, to buy consumer durables or to buy machines or build factories. Lower interest rates may also lead to a depreciation of the exchange rate which makes exports cheaper and more competitive, and imports pricier and less attractive, so that net exports, another component of aggregate demand, increase.

- An increase in government expenditures (G) which, being a component, would directly increase aggregate demand.

- A decrease in (direct) taxation would increase disposable income, which could lead to an increase in consumption expenditures (C). Note that an increase in government expenditures and a decrease in direct taxes are referred to as expansionary fiscal policy.

- A depreciation of the exchange rate, faster growth of our trading partners and a decrease in the degree of protection domestic firms face can all lead to an increase in net exports and thus growth.

Illustrating short-term growth

To show short-term growth you can use a Keynesian or a Monetarist/New Classical diagram where the AD curve shifts to the right, leading to an increase in real output and thus economic growth. The effect of such an increase in aggregate demand on real GDP depends on the size of the increase in aggregate demand but also on the original equilibrium level of real output.

In the Keynesian model, the increase in aggregate demand could prove ineffective in generating growth if the economy was operating close to its potential (full employment) as the rise in aggregate demand would mostly lead to a rise in prices with only a small, if any, increase in real GDP.

In the Monetarist/New Classical model (Figure 3.3.1b), an increase in aggregate demand would prove ineffective if the economy was operating past potential real output. The original equilibrium level of real output must lie to the left of potential output to illustrate any growth in real GDP that is not temporary.

The Keynesian diagram (Figure 3.3.1a) should be used to show that an increase in aggregate demand may not lead to any increase in the average price level.

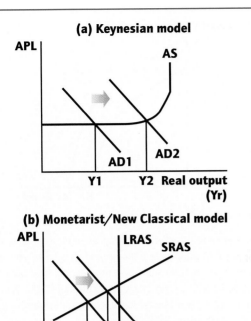

Figure 3.3.1 Growth in the short term through a shift right of aggregate demand (AD)

In Figure 3.3.1a and 3.3.1b, aggregate demand shifts to the right from AD1 to AD2 leading to an increase in real output from Y1 to Y2 and thus to short-term growth.

You can also illustrate short-term growth using a production possibilities curve (PPC) diagram. Think of an economy initially located at a point inside the PPC and then moving towards the northeast, closer to the boundary. Such a movement would indicate more being produced of both goods. Total output would be greater and since the production possibilities boundary will not have shifted outwards, this growth would be the result of greater use of existing resources and not of more resources or better technology becoming available. In Figure 3.3.2, the economy was initially producing X1 units of good X and Z1 units of good Z (combination F). Greater use of existing resources permits it now to produce combination H with X2 units of good X and Z2 units of good Z. Since more of both goods are produced while the production possibilities remain the same (AB), actual growth has been achieved.

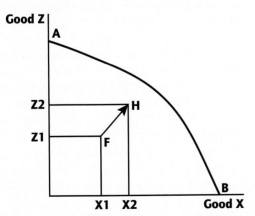

Figure 3.3.2 Growth in the short term through an outward shift of the PPC

Growth over the long term

Growth over the long term is a result of more or better resources becoming available and/or of improved technology. Any factor that will increase potential (full employment) output implies growth over the long term.

The following are some of the most important factors.

- An increase in the size of the labour force. The number of workers available for work may increase for a variety of reasons. For example, an increase in population, an influx of migrant workers, or an increase in the participation rate of some population group (for example, of women) will increase the size of the labour force.

- An increase in the stock of human capital. Past investments in education and health care will increase labour productivity.

- An increase in the stock of physical capital. If there are more machines and more factories, then the productive capacity of the economy increases, leading to long-term growth. Note that more and better infrastructure becoming available is a most significant contributing factor for a country to achieve and sustain economic growth over the long term.

- Historically, the main drivers of long-term economic growth are technological advances. Advances in technology in agriculture, industry and health services have been responsible for dramatic increases in potential output for all economies in the past two centuries.

- Advances in information and communication technologies are considered to further increase potential output.

- An improved institutional framework (the rules and regulations within which economic activity takes place) may also help achieve growth in the long term. Less bureaucracy, a more flexible labour market and more competition in the product markets can also shift long-run aggregate supply (LRAS) to the right and lead to an increase in potential output.

Illustrating long-term growth

Long-term growth can be illustrated through a shift to the right of the Keynesian AS curve or the Monetarist/New Classical LRAS curve so that full employment real output (potential output) increases (see Figure 3.3.3).

Growth in the long term can also be illustrated using a production possibilities curve (PPC) diagram. Since growth in the long term requires more or better resources, or better technology, a diagram where the PPC shifts outwards can be used to illustrate economic growth over the long term.

The PPC for the economy shown in Figure 3.3.4 was initially AB. As a result of more or better resources and/or better technology, the production possibilities of this economy expanded, and it is now able to produce combinations of goods that initially were not feasible. Its PPC has shifted out to FH. This illustrates growth in the long term.

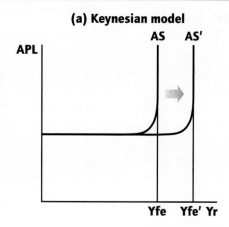

(a) Keynesian model

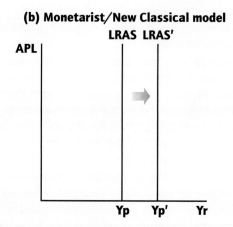

(b) Monetarist/New Classical model

Figure 3.3.3 Growth in the long term using the AD/AS models

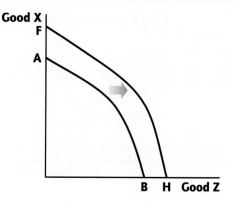

Figure 3.3.4 Growth in the long term using the PPC model

Note that certain factors that lead to an increase and shift to the right of aggregate demand and thus to an increase in equilibrium real output (short-term economic growth) may also to an increase and shift to the right of long-run aggregate supply and lead to an increase in potential output (long-term growth).

For example, an increase in government spending on infrastructure or on education and health care will increase aggregate demand, increasing equilibrium real output—but it will also increase long-run aggregate supply and thus potential output. Or, higher level of private investment spending now will increase aggregate demand and thus equilibrium real output but the increase in the stock of capital (more machines and factories available) in the economy will also increase its potential level of output as long-run aggregate supply will also shift to the right. In other words, increased private or public investment spending increases aggregate demand and thus real output but also increases the productive capacity of the economy and thus long-run aggregate supply and potential output.

Consequences of economic growth

Impact of economic growth on living standards

Economic growth is defined as an increase through time of an economy's total output (real GDP). Given that the value of an economy's total output is the flip-side of the income generated in the production process (in other words, the country's national income) it follows that if an economy is growing faster than its population, then income per person (referred to as per capita income) is rising. Higher per capita income levels permit individuals greater access to goods and services, so in this sense living standards improve. This explains why the release of growth statistics make headlines in most countries.

Unfortunately, economic growth may not imply improved living standards for the population. The reason is that there is no guarantee that the fruits of growth are shared by all. They may accrue only to the wealthiest. For growth to lead to improved living standards it must be inclusive. Per capita income figures are just an average and this average provides no information about the underlying distribution of income. As a famous Nobel Prize economist explained, if Jeff Bezos walks into a bar then

automatically the average income of its customers increases to several billion dollars. But have any of non-Bezos customers become any richer? Economic growth accompanied by increased income inequality is fragile and not desirable because the living standards of ordinary people do not improve. This is one reason why we need to re-evaluate laudatory headlines about the rate of economic growth of any country.

Also, to the extent that economic growth negatively impacts the environment in which people live, it is highly controversial to accept that economic growth necessarily improves living standards. If the means with which economic growth is being achieved are responsible for the extreme weather conditions experienced in many parts of the world that have resulted in floods, droughts, fires, rising sea levels and crop failures, then it cannot be argued that this type of growth has improved living standards for the affected people.

Economic growth may not improve living standards if it is jobless. It will be jobless if it is a result of adopting labour-saving technologies. Widespread adoption of technologies relying on robotics, automation and artificial intelligence further increase the risk of jobless growth in the near future.

It must be noted that living standards also depend on very many other factors that are not captured by economic growth and rising per capita incomes. The idea of improved living standards is closely related to the idea of human development, which is discussed later in this book. Even Simon Kuznets (the creator of national income and product accounts for which he earned the Nobel Prize in 1971) noted that increase in per capita income (that is, growth) is an imperfect measure of living standards.

Impact of economic growth on the environment

The relationship between economic growth and the environment is not simple. Economic growth may have both a positive and a negative impact on the environment. It may have a positive impact because richer countries have more resources at their disposal to deal with environmental issues, they rely more on the production of services and on information intensive industries and they have tougher environmental regulations.

It was believed that the relationship between environmental degradation and growth exhibited an inverted U-shape. As countries grew and per capita incomes increased, pollution would initially rise and then, after some critical level of per capita income, it would decrease. This relationship is referred to as the environmental Kuznets curve (EKC). If such a relationship was generally true, then economic growth would lead to eventual environmental improvement. Several considered the EKC as a justification for adopting a "business as usual" approach to the issue of sustainability. More recent research has shown that even if such a relationship is true, it applies only to certain types of pollutants typically associated with "local externalities" (such as indoor household pollution from cooking using polluting open fires). Also, if the EKC was more generally true for some advanced economies, it may have been the result of the effect of international trade on the distribution of polluting industries across countries so that the adverse global environmental impact is not reduced.

The EKC does not seem to apply to what are known as "dispersed externalities", such as carbon emissions. Economic growth is a result of increased levels of production, but increased production has predominantly relied on the use of fossil fuels or on the use and depletion of common access resources. Growth that neglects the impact on the environment is not sustainable. Economic growth that comes at the expense of pollution and environmental degradation has an adverse impact on the living standards of the present and future generations. Such economic growth has been labelled by the UNDP as "futureless". It is not sustainable and, if unchecked, it is thus undesirable.

Is it possible for economic growth to be sustainable? The optimistic answer is yes. Perhaps the first step in this direction is for governments to stop subsidizing use of fossil fuels and other unsustainable economic activities. For example, many governments around the world continue to subsidize their fishing industry heavily, which of course accelerates the depletion of fish stocks.

Government could adopt and enforce stricter environmental regulations. Policies that force polluting industries to internalize the external costs they generate are necessary. These include imposing carbon taxes which incentivize firms to adopt cleaner technologies, and the broader adoption of cap and trade schemes so that pollution decreases more by those firms that can do it effectively (with the least cost). Investments in green technologies and subsidies to firms that adopt clean technologies are also necessary.

Lastly, parties to the Paris Agreement must ensure that their Nationally Determined Contributions (NDCs) are met. NDCs include the goals and the means each of the signatory countries commits itself to adopt in order to meet the goals of the Paris Agreement. It has become clear that these NDCs should successively become more ambitious when they are reviewed every five years.

Impact of economic growth on the distribution of income

Economic growth may both decrease and increase income inequality. It may decrease income inequality because of the "fiscal dividend" that the government collects through growth. Growth implies higher incomes, which lead to more income and expenditure taxes collected. Higher tax revenues allow governments to adopt policies that alleviate poverty. For example, more can be spent to create or improve a social safety net. The government can set up or improve a pension system to increase the disposable incomes of older people. Higher tax revenues enable the government to establish or to increase unemployment benefits and to pay cash transfers to the disabled and the destitute. Such short-term programmes decrease income inequality.

Growth also allows a government to embark on longer-term programmes that lift people out of poverty and decrease income inequality. Growth over the long term enables governments to invest in policies to increase agricultural productivity and to improve sanitation and basic infrastructure, especially in rural areas of the country. It allows higher investment in education and health care programmes that favour the poor by improving their access to these services, thus increasing their human capital. Their resulting increased productivity increases their income-earning capacity and so decreases income inequality.

However, income inequality has increased in many growing economies. Leading experts on the issue have documented that in the past three decades, income inequality within countries has risen dramatically as they have grown. The fiscal dividend that has resulted from growth may allow, but does not force, governments to adopt policies that decrease income inequality. There is no guarantee that market forces alone will ensure that the benefits of growth are fairly distributed.

Growth may be driven by only a handful of industries or it may be concentrated in certain regions of a country (often the coastal regions). It may rely only on certain skills, often of the more educated. This is referred to as the "skill-biased technological progress" where the wages of the highly skilled workers have been rising much faster than the wages of the less skilled, widening income inequality.

Another contributing factor is that in some countries there has been a very significant increase in corporate concentration and monopoly power. This is responsible for a transfer of income away from consumers to a few firms. Firms with high monopoly power can charge consumers more for products and services and pay their workers less. Research shows that this rise in corporate power is more pronounced in the USA than in Europe, even though it has been rising in most countries.

Rising income inequality may also be the result of increased trade liberalization and globalization. Many workers in industries where import penetration has been high have lost their jobs. Even though, as it will become clear, the gains of the winners from free trade are greater than the losses of the losers, there have been few, if any, government programmes in most countries to compensate displaced workers for their losses. Workers in import-competing industries lose their income and face dislocation, whereas workers in booming export-oriented industries maintain or increase their income.

Tax and transfer systems may also be responsible. In many countries, taxation has become much less progressive since the 1980s, while at the same time transfer payments decreased both in size and in scope. Tax and transfer systems affect the level of disposable income in a country. Disposable income is defined as factor income plus transfers (such as benefits and pensions) minus income taxes. According to the Luxemburg Income Study Center (LIS) the USA has the highest inequality among advanced economies when considering disposable income. This may be the result of the belief that high income taxes decrease incentives to work and to invest, while generous welfare payments disincentivize recipients to increase their income earning potential, thus slowing down growth of the economy. However, research has shown that northern European countries with more progressive income taxes and more generous payments have not, over the long term, grown more slowly.

More generally, even the International Monetary Fund (IMF) is now re-evaluating growth resulting from market-based supply-side policies that many countries of the world have implemented since the 1980s. These policies, which will be explained later, decrease the role of the government and increase the role of unregulated markets. They aim at accelerating growth, but they do not pay attention to the distribution of the growth that results. As this growth is not inclusive, income inequality is increased.

Recap

How growth may affect income inequality

The resulting higher tax revenues permit the government to create or improve a social safety net by spending more on:

- pension schemes to support older people
- unemployment benefits
- other cash transfers, to support other groups of people who are deprived and in need.

The resulting higher tax revenues permit the government to invest more in:

- improving policies that increase agricultural productivity that raise rural incomes
- infrastructure projects that improve sanitation, electrification, transport and telecommunications and so improve the lives and prospects of the poor

- education and health care for the poor to increase their human capital, productivity and income-earning capacity.

Growth may increase income inequality:

- if it relies only on certain skills, the highly educated or is concentrated in certain areas, often coastal regions
- if market concentration is rising, as it permits firms to charge higher prices and pay lower wages
- as a result of trade liberalization that displaced many workers without any compensation or retraining provided
- as a result of income taxes becoming less progressive and transfer payments decreasing in size and scope
- as a result of market-based supply-side policies implemented since the 1980s that decreased the role of the state and of labour unions.

Policymakers' perspective

Growth is an important economic objective for any economy. It permits the government to make or increase investments in infrastructure, in human capital and in R&D. Such investments lay the foundation for further growth. In addition, higher growth rates imply that incomes are rising faster. However, faster growth rates that make the headlines must be carefully evaluated. If these higher levels of income are enjoyed only by the top 1% or the top 10% of the population, then there may be less to applaud. If the rising levels of output and incomes come at a high environmental cost, then there may be less to cheer about. Growth must be inclusive and sustainable. Otherwise it may prove fragile.

Low unemployment

Meaning and measurement

An individual is considered unemployed if he or she is actively looking for a job but cannot find one.

The unemployment rate is the ratio of the number of unemployed over the size of the labour force (also referred to as the workforce) times 100. The labour force includes the employed and the unemployed.

$$\text{Unemployment rate} = \frac{\text{Number of unemployed}}{\text{Labour force}} \times 100$$

Note that the labour force or the workforce is not the same as the population of working age, which includes everyone typically aged between 15 and 64, even if they are not looking for a job.

Difficulties of measuring unemployment

The above formula seems straightforward but there are many difficulties in arriving at an accurate estimate of the unemployment rate of a country. The official statistic may underestimate or overestimate true unemployment.

The official unemployment statistic may underestimate true unemployment for the following reasons.

- The population includes discouraged workers. These are individuals who would like to work and would happily accept a job offer but who have stopped actively searching for one because they have remained unemployed for too long and their past search effort was unsuccessful. Since they are demonstrating no effort in seeking employment, they are not considered unemployed and they are not included in the official unemployment statistic.

- Some individuals are underemployed. They are involuntary part-time workers who do have a job so they are considered employed but they are working fewer hours per week than desired. Underemployed individuals also include workers who do not fully utilize their skills or experience so they may be overqualified for the job they hold.

The term *hidden* or *disguised unemployment* is often used to refer to underemployed individuals and to discouraged workers.

The official unemployment rate may overstate true unemployment because of the following.

- Some individuals may intentionally conceal their true employment status, either fearing loss of transfer payments such as unemployment benefits that are granted only to the unemployed, or to avoid paying income taxes.

- Some individuals are employed in illegal activities and report that they are unemployed.

The official unemployment statistic is also nothing more than an average for the whole country so it does not reveal disparities between:

- different regions of the country
- female and male unemployment rates
- different ethnic or religious groups
- different age groups.

Youth unemployment refers to unemployment among workers aged between 15 and 24 and it is typically the unemployment category with the highest rate. Unemployment is also usually higher for women and for minorities. Studies show that there are often significant

differences among regions within countries. Therefore, it is important to examine disaggregated unemployment data to get a clearer picture of the labour market of a country.

Lastly, of significant importance is the long-term unemployment rate of a country, which is defined as the ratio of those unemployed for 12 months or more as a proportion of the labour force.

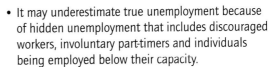

Recap

Limitations of the official unemployment statistic

- It may underestimate true unemployment because of hidden unemployment that includes discouraged workers, involuntary part-timers and individuals being employed below their capacity.

- It may underestimate true unemployment because of individuals concealing their employment status to avoid paying income taxes or because their work is illegal.

- It is just an average for the economy, so it may conceal differences between regions, gender, ethnicities and age groups.

Causes of unemployment

Not all unemployment is the same. Individuals who are unemployed are unemployed for different reasons. This is very important because the policies used to decrease unemployment differ depending on the cause. Policies that may be effective to decrease one type of unemployment may be ineffective to deal with another type.

Unemployment is categorized into four types: seasonal, frictional, cyclical and structural. The first two are relatively insignificant and they are typically low. Cyclical and structural unemployment are much more serious. These are examined separately below.

Seasonal unemployment

Seasonal unemployment is a result of unavoidable and predictable variations in the demand and supply of labour. Weather patterns mean that construction workers are often laid off for several weeks in the winter months in places where freezing temperatures and ice may prevent their work and will increase the risk of work-related accidents. In many areas farm workers are unemployed for some periods of time relating to work schedules for different crops. Another seasonal variation is the surge in labour supply every year in June in the USA, and other countries, as many college and secondary school graduates start looking for a job but only gradually find employment.

This type of unemployment is expected and there is not much governments can do about it. Monthly unemployment statistics are corrected by statisticians (seasonally adjusted) though, so that policymakers can determine true changes in unemployment, not those due to seasonal factors.

Frictional unemployment

Frictional unemployment refers to people who are between jobs as it takes time to match a job-seeker with an available job vacancy. This unemployment is of a short-term nature and is also largely unavoidable in an economy since people will always voluntarily switch jobs, searching for better ones, or choosing to relocate. Faster and better information related to the labour market will decrease but not eliminate frictional unemployment. Governments can minimize frictional unemployment by ensuring that job vacancies as well as the profiles of those available for work become known wider and faster. The internet has considerably helped as vacancies and availabilities can be posted and matched in real time.

Cyclical (demand deficient) unemployment

This type of unemployment is directly related to the business cycle. Higher unemployment will necessarily accompany a recession because of the lower level of economic activity.

Assume that aggregate demand decreases for some reason. This could be the result of a decrease in consumer or business confidence levels. Or it could be the result of lower exports because of lower incomes abroad. The resulting decrease in economic activity forces some businesses to shrink and others to shut down.

As production levels fall, demand for labour will decrease. However, money wages do not easily decrease for many reasons, for example because of contracts. They are "sticky downwards". Firms will need to fire workers. The resulting unemployment is cyclical unemployment. It is a result of the downturn of the business cycle.

Cyclical unemployment can be illustrated using a Keynesian diagram (see Figure 3.3.5). Initially the economy is assumed to be at its full employment level of real output Yf. Aggregate demand decreases from AD to AD'. As a result, real output decreases below full employment to Y' and a deflationary gap forms equal to Y'Yf. This lower level of economic activity leads to cyclical unemployment as workers are laid off by firms that are shrinking or forced to exit the market. Again, the greater the size of the deflationary gap, the greater the size of the resulting cyclical unemployment.

It should be clear that in order for policymakers to decrease cyclical unemployment they should try to decrease the size of the deflationary gap by increasing aggregate demand and thus economic activity. The expansionary demand-side policies that may be used to increase aggregate demand will be explained and evaluated later.

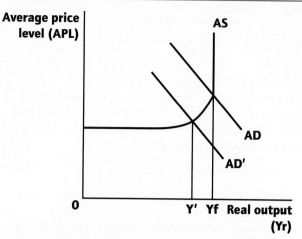

Figure 3.3.5 Illustrating cyclical unemployment (Keynesian model)

Structural unemployment

Structural unemployment is the unemployment that remains way past economic recovery. The causes of structural unemployment may be summarized by two words: mismatch and rigidities. Mismatch describes the situation where job vacancies exist but the skills of the unemployed are not the skills that employers demand.

New technologies render certain jobs obsolete while at the same time creating new job opportunities. Artificial intelligence will be responsible for many losing their jobs. Driverless trucks are already used in some countries, slowly making truck drivers unemployed.

Loss of export markets to more competitive, lower cost, foreign firms may also lead to job losses in a country. Very many industrial jobs were lost in the USA and in other countries due to lower cost imports. Job vacancies may be plenty in exporting and other industries but those unemployed due to import competition often lack the necessary skills to be offered a job.

Figures 3.3.6a and 3.3.6b illustrate this case. They show structural unemployment as a result of a fall in demand in a particular industry: ship repair.

Assume the market for shipyard repairs in Greece. As a result of more efficient and cheaper ship repair services offered in Korea, China and other countries, demand for ship repair services in Greek shipyards dramatically decreased and thus demand for the highly specialized labour working in this industry also decreased.

In Figure 3.3.6a demand for ship repair services in Greece decreased, from D to D'. As a result, far fewer ship repair services

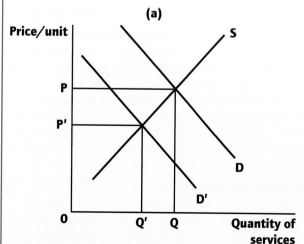

Figure 3.3.6a Market for ship repair services

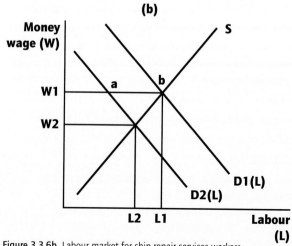

Figure 3.3.6b Labour market for ship repair services workers

were produced: Q' instead of Q per year, and at a much lower price. Shipyards in Greece were thus forced to fire very many highly specialized and highly paid workers. Unemployment in towns where shipyards were the biggest employer reached 90%.

In Figure 3.3.6b, the labour market for these highly specialized workers is shown where demand for their services decreased from D1(L) to D2(L). If money wages are "sticky downwards" and remain at W1, then structural unemployment equal to (ab) will result. Even if money wages do decrease to W2, you will note that only L2 workers would be employed in these shipyards. This implies that L1L2 highly specialized shipyard workers were laid off. Some may have accepted lower paying jobs elsewhere, perhaps as gas attendants, but the vast majority remains structurally unemployed. It should be realized from Figure 3.3.6b that the number of employed workers is lower and the resulting unemployment higher if money wages in such industries are indeed "sticky downwards" and remain at, or below but close to, W1.

The mismatch can also be geographic, with the unemployed clustered in one region of the country while job vacancies exist elsewhere. Newer research reveals that geographical mobility of labour is much lower than previously thought as the unemployed, especially older individuals, are reluctant to move because of family ties, home ownership and the often high cost of moving.

Structural unemployment may also be a result of labour market rigidities. These refer to labour market related laws and regulations that do not permit the labour market to adjust to changing labour demand and labour supply conditions.

Minimum wage laws are examples of labour market rigidities. If money wages are set above the market equilibrium level, then firms will be willing to hire fewer workers while more individuals will be offering their labour services.

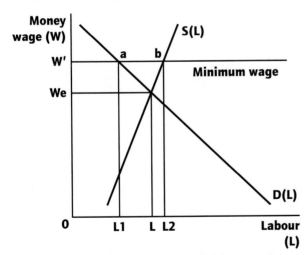

Figure 3.3.7 Structural unemployment as a result of minimum wage laws

In Figure 3.3.7, at the minimum wage rate W', excess supply of labour results equal to L2 – L1 or line segment (ab). It should be noted though that many empirical studies have shown that reasonable minimum wage laws have not led to higher unemployment. One explanation could be that wages paid by many employers were originally below the competitive level or that employers do not object to a reasonable increase in the wage rate paid because it may elicit greater effort from workers and decrease turnover, which is costly.

Other labour market rigidities leading to structural unemployment include the following.

- High non-wage labour costs that burden businesses: these refer to national insurance contributions (for pensions and health care benefits) that employers pay for their workers. Higher labour costs imply fewer workers hired.

- High money wages achieved by powerful labour unions for their members: again, this implies higher production costs for businesses and fewer workers hired. Union members ("insiders") benefit at the expense of "outsiders" who do not get hired.

- Laws that guarantee job security aiming at protecting workers: if it becomes difficult and more costly for firms to fire workers then they may become more reluctant to hire workers.

- High unemployment benefits: these may decrease the incentive of the unemployed to accept a job offer.

To decrease structural unemployment, governments offer training and retraining programmes or they may subsidize or grant tax breaks to firms that hire and retrain long-term unemployed individuals. Governments may also provide low-cost loans to individuals enrolling in skill-creating courses or who are willing to relocate to areas with better job prospects. To force the unemployed to faster accept a job offer, governments may also decrease the size of, and limit the duration of, unemployment benefits. These policies are referred to as labour market related supply-side policies and will be discussed in section 3.7.

Recap

Types and causes of unemployment

The four types of unemployment and their causes are:

- seasonal—a result of seasonal variations in the demand or the supply of labour

- frictional—a result of people between jobs

- cyclical—a result of recession as firms will be forced to shed labour

- structural—a result of a mismatch between skills the unemployed have and skills that firms demand, or a result of labour market rigidities.

The natural rate of unemployment (NRU)

The idea of the natural rate of unemployment (NRU) was introduced earlier (see section 3.2, page 81). Some unemployment is unavoidable in any economy. There will always be people who are out of work because of seasonal factors or because they are between jobs. Given that any economy is always in a constant state of change, some people will be also unemployed because of advances in technology or changes in global competitive advantage. Some will be unemployed because the labour market cannot always adjust fast enough to changing labour market conditions. What has just been described amounts to seasonal, frictional and structural unemployment. So, we can state that natural unemployment comprises seasonal, frictional and structural unemployment.

Figure 3.3.8 can be used to illustrate the NRU. It shows a labour market in equilibrium. The vertical axis is the real wage rate (Wr) and the horizontal is the number of workers (L). The labour demand (LD) curve shows how many workers firms are willing to hire at different levels of the real wage. At a higher real wage, firms will try to employ fewer workers. The LF (labour force) curve shows the number of individuals willing to join the labour force at each level of real wage. As the real wage increases, the opportunity cost of leisure increases so more people will substitute work for leisure and thus join the labour market. The AJ (accept jobs) curve shows at each real wage rate, the number of individuals in the labour force who, given the level of unemployment benefits, will accept a job offer. As the real wage rises compared to the level of unemployment benefits, the probability of one accepting a job offer increases. Therefore, the horizontal difference between the AJ and the LF curves becomes smaller. Equilibrium in the labour market is at Wre where the number of individuals that firms are willing to hire is equal to the number of individuals who are willing to accept a job offer (Le). The unemployment that continues to exist when the labour market is in equilibrium is the equilibrium or NRU. It is equal to distance (ab).

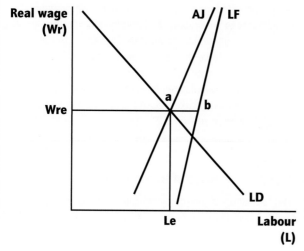

Figure 3.3.8 The NRU

Figure 3.3.8 implies that those included in the natural rate are voluntarily unemployed. This may be true for some workers. For example, certain high paid workers who lost their jobs because of foreign competition may simply reject offers to work as gas attendants or farm workers. On the other hand, it is also unfair to label all unemployed at the natural rate as voluntarily unemployed, as many can simply not find a job that will permit them and their families to afford a relatively decent standard of living. This figure is still very useful as it does show that the NRU is equilibrium unemployment and it also permits discussion on the extent to which some of the unemployed here may be considered voluntarily unemployed. It also shows that if, for example, policymakers decrease unemployment benefits, the AJ curve will shift right and so the NRU will decrease.

Costs of unemployment

One of the most significant goals of macroeconomic policy is achieving and maintaining high levels of employment in the economy. This implies that unemployment should be kept low. The reason is that unemployment imposes many costs on the economy, on the individual and on society, especially if it is high and prolonged.

Economic costs of unemployment

- Perhaps the most important economic cost of unemployment in a country is the "lost output forever". Goods and services that could have been produced are not produced. Remember that resources are limited. It becomes clear what a complete waste unemployment represents. Higher unemployment is associated with a loss in real GDP as the economy is operating inside its production possibilities curve.

- Rising unemployment decreases the tax revenues the government collects. The unemployed lose their incomes so they do not pay income taxes. They may collect unemployment benefits, but these are lower than their income, so they spend less. The government thus collects less in both direct and indirect taxes. At the same time, government expenditures rise, as a result of:
  - unemployment benefits that most governments pay the unemployed for some period of time
  - funding more training programmes that are implemented to help retrain unemployed workers
  - additional expenditures to remedy social costs that often arise as a result of unemployment.

- Perhaps the most significant economic costs arise when unemployment is high and prolonged. High and prolonged unemployment increases income inequality in the country as the unemployed lose their income while others maintain theirs. Many people may slip into poverty, especially the less educated, because even if they manage to find a job later it is often a low pay, part-time, insecure job. Rising income inequality is responsible for many economic, social and political problems.

- High and prolonged unemployment may force many, especially the younger and the better educated, to try to find a job abroad. In this way, emigration shrinks the economy's human capital. A country is often deprived of its best and brightest members of its labour force. The lower human capital decreases labour productivity, compromising future growth prospects. Growth may as a result be lower for many years to come.

Personal costs of unemployment

- The single biggest cost for people losing their job is lost income. Even if they receive unemployment benefits, these will be less than what they earned while working—and the benefits will be temporary. Suddenly the set of goods and services these people can access becomes smaller. The unemployed may even lose their house if they are unable keep up with their monthly mortgage payments to the bank. Some end up homeless.

- In some countries matters become much worse because individuals losing their job may also lose their health insurance. If there is no national health-care service that covers all individuals independently of their employment status this may prove disastrous for the unemployed.

- Long-term unemployed people also lose their skills. This decreases their job prospects when competing against others with up-to-date skills.

- In addition, an employer offering a job may prefer to hire a person currently working elsewhere rather than someone who is unemployed. This is because the employer cannot be sure why the unemployed person lost his or her job or is no longer working.

- Long-term unemployed individuals often suffer family breakdown, accumulation of debt, alcohol or drug abuse, loss of self-esteem or depression. Some may even commit suicide.

Studies have shown that a 1% increase in the unemployment rate is associated with a rise in suicides between 0.8% and 1.3% among people under the age of 65.

Social costs

Unemployment also burdens society with very significant costs in both the short term and the long term.

- Society may experience a higher incidence of crime and violence and other negative externalities resulting from increased drug and alcohol abuse. Unemployment, if high and prolonged, imposes costs on businesses, law enforcement and the judicial system, and health care.

- Matters become much worse if unemployment is regionally concentrated. If the major employer in an area is forced out of business, populations of whole towns may suffer. Recent research finds that even if economic conditions are terrible, contrary to what was believed, people find it very difficult to move elsewhere with better jobs and financial prospects. The opioid crisis in many towns in the USA points to this conclusion. Society suffers in the long term from the breakdown that follows.

- Problems also become more pronounced and difficult if unemployment is concentrated in certain age groups such as the young. High youth unemployment may be responsible for a lost generation of productive workers who without some assistance from the state to improve their condition may also become a burden over the long term as they will never be able to land jobs with a secure and promising future. With insecure, part-time, low paying jobs they may never be able to save enough for retirement and this will create further social problems in the future.

- Over the long term, society may suffer from political costs. Long-term unemployment concentrated in areas and age groups may create heightened levels of discontent that may erode the social fabric and even risk democratic institutions.

Recap

Costs of unemployment

The **economic** costs are:

- lost output
- lower tax revenues and higher government expenditures
- rising income inequality
- erosion of human capital.

The **personal** costs include:

- loss of income and, in some countries, of health insurance
- erosion of skills
- family breakdown
- debt accumulation
- alcohol and drug abuse
- deterioration of mental health.

The **social** costs are:

- higher rates of violence and crime
- the social costs of drug and alcohol abuse
- longer-term social and political problems.

Policymakers' perspective

Achieving and maintaining high levels of employment is one of the most significant macroeconomic goals. Unemployment is a terrible waste and it imposes many costs on the economy, on individuals and on society.

Economic costs are more pronounced if unemployment is high and prolonged. It is the resulting increase in income inequality and the erosion of the stock of human capital that are the most significant economic costs of unemployment. The loss of tax revenues is of secondary importance because governments can typically borrow any shortfall in funds while any increase in government expenditures is also relatively small.

The personal costs are of obvious importance to the unemployed individuals, especially if unemployment benefits are low and paid for a short period of time and their health insurance is lost.

It has also become clear that policymakers should be very mindful of areas suffering a persistently very high rate of unemployment. Social costs rapidly escalate in such communities and in the long term may even transform into serious political costs.

Policymakers must ensure that the appropriate polices are chosen to tackle unemployment. No policies are adopted for seasonal unemployment. Reducing frictional unemployment requires better and faster transmission of labour market information. Dealing with cyclical unemployment is straightforward as the policy goal is to increase aggregate demand. Later it will become clear that different levels of cyclical unemployment may require different policy approaches in achieving this. Decreasing structural unemployment that is a result of a mismatch of skills requires that retraining of workers is somehow achieved. Policies necessary for dealing with structural unemployment that is a result of rigidities may seem straightforward, but their implementation and their possible long-term side effects often render them difficult to pursue in practice. This will also be explained later.

Policymakers should be aware that measuring the size of unemployment is not as easy as it seems. First, it is just an estimate. In addition, individuals may misrepresent their true employment status. Also, many previously discouraged workers may be re-entering the labour force and finding a job if aggregate demand is rising and the economy is growing fast. The unemployment rate may therefore be decreasing below what was considered the NRU without any pressure on wages or on prices to increase, complicating the job of the policymakers. Lastly, differences between regions or groups may necessitate a policy response even if overall unemployment is low.

Inflation

Inflation is defined as a sustained increase in the average price level. The inflation rate is the percentage change in the average price level between two periods. So, if the inflation rate in India in 2016 was 4.94% it means that prices in India, on the average, increased in 2016 by 4.94% compared to 2015.

One year later, in 2017, the inflation rate in India was recorded at 2.49%. What does this mean? It means that prices in India, on the average, continued to rise but at a slower rate, compared to 2016. This is referred to as **disinflation**. It follows that disinflation exists when the inflation rate decreases so that the average price level is still increasing but at a slower rate.

In Switzerland the inflation rate for 2016 was recorded at –0.43%. What does this mean? The negative inflation rate in 2016 means that the average price level in Switzerland decreased compared to 2015. This describes deflation.
Deflation exists if prices in an economy, on average, are decreasing or, more formally, deflation refers to a sustained decrease in the average price level.

Measuring inflation

The average price level that is used to measure the inflation rate is the Consumer Price Index (CPI). The CPI is the weighted average of the prices of all the goods and services the typical consumer in a country buys per period. Statisticians determine the basket of goods and services that the typical household buys through household surveys conducted every few years. This basket is fixed for a few years. By keeping the goods and services included the same, the changes in the cost of buying the basket can be recorded.

This average is "weighted", which means that not all prices included in the basket are of the same significance when deriving the average. Is the significance for consumers the same when rents increase by 10% and when the price of chocolate-chip ice cream increases by 10%? The impact on households of a 10% increase in rents is of much greater significance than a 10% increase in the price of ice cream. To account for differences in the significance of goods and services in the budget of consumers, the price of each product is multiplied by the proportion of total expenditures the typical consumer makes on each product. Goods for which the typical consumer devotes a bigger proportion of his or her total spending will thus "weigh" more (that is, "count" more) in the derivation of the average.

So, the CPI would be:

$w_1P_1 + w_2P_2 + w_3P_3 + \cdots + w_nP_n$, where the w's are the weights and $w_i = \dfrac{\text{expenditure on good i}}{\text{total expenditures}}$

The cost of purchasing this basket is recorded and then expressed as an index number. What does this mean? It means that, using statistical criteria, some year is chosen to be the "base" (or reference) year and all other years are then expressed as a percentage of the cost of the basket that year. It follows that the price index for the base year will be equal to 100. By expressing a variable as an index number, we get rid of its units of measurement, which makes comparisons through time a lot easier.

Once the CPI is available, calculating the inflation rate is easy. It will be the percentage change in the CPI between two years. So, the inflation rate for 2019 will be:

$$\text{Inflation rate 2019} = \frac{CPI_{19} - CPI_{18}}{CPI_{18}} \times 100$$

Note that in this IB course we simplify matters by using the quantities purchased of each good as weights. We multiply the price of each product by the number of units bought by the typical consumer. The worked example on page 99 illustrates the process.

Limitations of the CPI in measuring inflation

Measuring the rate of inflation using a consumer price index (CPI) may not be accurate. There are a few problems that we need to be aware of.

- As already explained, the CPI is the average of the prices of the goods and services that the "typical" consumer purchases. This "typical" consumer is no actual individual. Instead, this fictitious individual is both a bit old and a bit young, rich and poor, lives in a city but also in the countryside and is a man and a woman. Since different groups of people buy different baskets of goods and services, the actual buying patterns and so the cost of living of any specific group, say of young urban professionals with an average income, is not measured. This makes it problematical to use the published inflation rate to determine, for example, by how much a government should increase pensions, because older people consume more health-care services and perhaps less entertainment than others and it could very well be that the cost of purchasing their basket of goods and services has increased by a lot more than other groups' baskets.

- Some products may become more expensive, but their quality may have improved so much that they are effectively cheaper for the buyer. Think of car tyres. A new set may be 10% more expensive but it may last 50% more miles. Quality improvements are often not sufficiently accounted for, so published inflation may overestimate true inflation. This is referred to as the "quality bias".

- New products enter our lives almost daily but are included in the CPI only after a long delay. For example, many consumers in Greece subscribe to Netflix and to Spotify but neither service is yet included in Greece's CPI. This is referred to as the "new product bias".

- More and more people now buy more and more goods online where prices are usually lower than prices in "brick and mortar" stores. Many consumers buy electronics, books, clothing and groceries online. If the statistical agency of a country sends its employees every month to collect prices mostly from physical stores and not so much from online retailers then the published inflation rate will again tend to overestimate true inflation. This is referred to as the "new retail outlet bias".

- The "substitution bias" results from the fact that the weights are fixed for some time. If a good becomes more expensive then consumers will tend to switch to cheaper substitutes. The significance of this good for the typical consumers will thus diminish. However, if its weight in the calculation of the CPI remains fixed, this now lower significance will not be reflected. This means that inflation will be overestimated.

Recap

Limitations of the CPI in measuring inflation

- The average refers to the buying patterns of the typical consumer, a fictitious person.
- Improved quality of more expensive products may not be sufficiently accounted for.
- New products that consumers buy are included in the CPI only after a significant time lag.
- Lower prices from new retail outlets such as e-shops are not adequately sampled.
- Weights are fixed so if a good becomes pricier even though its significance for consumers decreases, its weight does not.

Costs of a high inflation rate

Maintaining price stability is a most significant goal for policymakers because, as will be explained, a high rate of inflation creates many problems for an economy.

- Inflation increases the uncertainty that businesses face. This makes it even more difficult for firms to judge whether an investment project will be profitable and worth undertaking or not. How fast will wages and other production costs increase? At what price will it be possible to sell the good produced two or three years into the future? How fast will prices of substitutes and complements rise? How much will interest rates increase? Increased uncertainty discourages investment spending. Long-term economic growth and so employment generation will be slower.
- The purchasing power (real income) of those earning fixed money incomes decreases. Individuals with fixed money incomes include wage earners as well as pensioners. This is not the case though for those individuals who can adjust their earnings as prices increase. These groups include professionals such as lawyers, architects, consultants and others. Entrepreneurs who can raise their prices faster than inflation also gain. Income inequality thus widens.
- Low income families cannot easily borrow from banks. In addition, if their income permits them to make any savings,

they can only save in simple bank accounts. The interest rate paid on such savings accounts is usually not only low but also less than the rate of inflation. The real interest rate, defined as the interest rate minus the rate of inflation, is thus negative. For example, if the interest rate paid on a savings account is 3% per year but prices are rising at 5% per year then the saver loses money as the real rate of interest is –2%. In a year's time $100.00 will buy roughly only as much as $98.00 can buy now. On the other hand, higher income households can protect themselves against inflation by borrowing from banks and purchasing assets such as houses or land, or art or gold, the price of which is expected to increase faster than inflation. In this way, inflation may redistribute national income away from the poor to the rich, widening income inequality.

- If actual inflation proves higher than anticipated inflation then borrowers will gain income at the expense of lenders. The money they will be paying back to lenders will be worth less than what had been expected when the loan was agreed. Banks, in an attempt to protect against the possibility of inflation proving higher than expected, may charge even higher interest rates. This though decreases borrowing and spending, and aggregate demand, which also slows down economic growth.
- Inflation hurts the exports of a country. They become more expensive and therefore less competitive in foreign markets. Inflation also makes imports more attractive to domestic buyers so import expenditures rise. Decreasing export revenues and increasing import expenditures decrease aggregate demand and widen a trade deficit. This may exert pressure on the currency to depreciate and lead to more inflation, as will be explained in sections 3.5 and 4.5.
- Inflation is "noise". It distorts the signalling power of relative price changes that is responsible for resource allocation in a market economy. If the price of quinoa rises, this sends a signal to producers that people want more quinoa. If all prices are rising as a result of inflation, though, the price signal is not clear anymore and producers cannot be sure that consumers actually demand more quinoa. Misallocation of resources is the result.
- Inflation may induce people to save less. They may choose to buy durables now before these become even more expensive, spending more and saving less. Saving may also decrease because during inflationary periods the real interest rate is often negative. Savings in a bank account will be worth less and less.

However, inflation does have some benefits.

- Mild inflation slowly reduces the real wage and so the real cost of labour to firms. This is especially important for firms since money wages do not easily adjust downward. Lower production costs induce firms to produce more.
- Inflation also reduces the real value of debt. Households, firms and the government own less in real terms if there is some inflation in the economy.

Causes of inflation

Analytically, it is easy to understand why inflation may occur by examining a simple AD/AS diagram. Any factor that persistently increases aggregate demand or that leads to an adverse shift to the left of AS curve may lead to an increasing price level (that is, to inflationary pressures). The former is referred to as demand-pull inflation and the latter is referred to as cost-push inflation, even though once an inflationary process begins it is difficult or even meaningless to distinguish between the two.

Demand-pull inflation

Any factor increasing any component of aggregate demand may potentially initiate inflationary pressures. Of course, the risk of inflation increases the closer to full employment an economy is operating. The smaller the size of the deflationary gap in the economy, the greater the chance that an increase in aggregate demand will lead to an increase in the average price level. Unfortunately, it cannot be easily ascertained whether the economy is about to reach its potential level of real output.

The most common causes of demand-pull inflation include the following.

- Profligate government spending. *Profligate* is the word used to describe excessive spending by a government. Politicians historically have often increased spending to maximize their re-election chances, as even a temporary boost of economic activity and a resulting decrease in unemployment will serve this purpose. Government expenditures (G) are a component of aggregate demand, so if G rises, then aggregate demand will increase and the AD curve will shift to the right, potentially, but not necessarily, proving inflationary.

- According to the Monetarist School, and quoting Milton Friedman, inflation results when "too much money is chasing after too few goods". Monetarists consider that "inflation is always and everywhere a monetary phenomenon". If the central bank increases the money supply too fast and thus too much money is pumped into an economy, then this excess liquidity will be spent. Inflation could follow. Many consider that this is a serious risk of quantitative easing, which will explained later.

- Households and firms can be overly optimistic, resulting in excessive spending in the expectation that good times will persist. Since consumption and investment are components of aggregate demand, aggregate demand will be increasing and the AD curve will be shifting to the right, potentially proving inflationary.

- A sudden surge in exports may also prove inflationary, if the economy is operating near full employment.

- Inflationary expectations are considered a most important driving force of inflation. If businesses expect prices to rise, then they will their set prices higher, creating or increasing inflation as a result. Also, households expecting prices to rise may prefer to spend more now, before prices rise even further, which will lead to higher aggregate demand and higher inflation. This explains why it is important that policymakers are credible that price stability will be maintained.

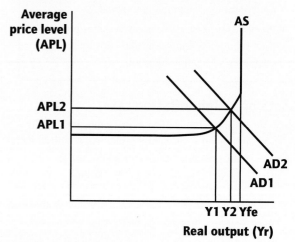

Figure 3.3.9 Demand-pull inflation

In Figure 3.3.9, a simple AD/AD is used to illustrate demand-pull inflation. Aggregate demand increases, perhaps as a result of excessively optimistic households and firms. The AD curve shifts to the right from AD1 to AD2. As a result, the average price level rises from APL1 to APL2. It should be clear from Figure 3.3.9 that the same increase in aggregate demand will prove more inflationary the closer to potential output the economy is operating. Unfortunately, policymakers are never sure in advance how close to full employment an economy is and this creates significant policy response problems. Policymakers closely examine economic data that may signal inflationary pressures and lead them to take action but there is a lot of uncertainty that makes their job difficult.

It is perhaps worth noting that the Monetarist/New Classical diagram is strictly speaking ill equipped to illustrate demand-pull inflation. Since the short-run aggregate supply (SRAS) curve is upward sloping, it shows that demand-pull inflation results whenever aggregate demand is increasing even if the economy is operating way below its potential and is suffering from a large deflationary gap, which is misleading.

Demand-pull inflation is caused by:

- profligate government spending
- "too much money chasing after too few goods"
- overly optimistic households and firms
- a sudden surge in exports
- inflationary expectations.

Cost-push inflation

This is the result of a decrease in aggregate supply. This shifts the AS curve to the left and leads to an increase in the average price level as well as to a lower level of real output. Aggregate supply may decrease, and the AS curve shift to the left, for a variety of reasons.

- Historically, the most common reason for cost-push inflation has been a sustained and significant increase in the price of oil. Oil is still the predominant form of energy and it is also used as an input in many production processes e.g. in the plastics industry. If the price of oil increases, production costs for many firms will increase. Aggregate supply will decrease (the AS curve will shift left), leading to rising prices but also to slower growth (or even a decrease in real GDP) and rising unemployment.

- More generally, production costs may increase because other commodity prices rise. Commodities are primary products that are used as inputs in manufacturing. Crop failures increase the price of agricultural products and this may increase the cost of food production. Disruptions in extraction industries may also lead to higher prices of metals and minerals.

- Powerful labour unions in many countries have been successful in increasing money wages for their members and thus production costs for firms, especially in the past. More generally, keep in mind that the standard way policymakers assess the risks of rising inflationary pressures has been to monitor closely the state of the labour market and whether money wages are rising. Even if inflationary pressures originate from rising aggregate demand, these pressures will show up as rising money wages in the labour market and will be an early signal of inflation.

- Another significant reason that may increase production costs and lead to cost-push inflationary pressures is a depreciation of the exchange rate. The reason is that a depreciation increases the domestic price of imports. If the country imports a lot of raw materials and intermediate products, then production costs for many firms will increase. There is more on depreciation of the exchange rate in section 4.5.

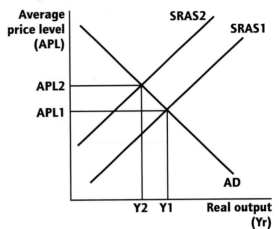

Figure 3.3.10 Cost-push inflation

Figure 3.3.10 shows cost-push inflation. A sustained increase in the price of oil has increased production costs for most firms. As a result, aggregate supply decreases and the AS curve shifts left from SRAS1 TO SRAS2. The average price level increases from APL1 to APL2. Real output also decreases from Y1 to Y2 even though it is more likely that growth will just slow down, but that would be more difficult to show on this diagram.

Deflation

Deflation is a sustained decrease in the average price level. If the inflation rate is negative it means that the average price level has decreased and thus there is deflation.

So, if the CPI in 2019 was 145.65 and in 2020 it was 142.95 then the rate of inflation in 2020 was −1.85%. There was deflation in 2020 as prices decreased compared to 2019.

Causes of deflation

Typically, deflation results from a prolonged decrease in aggregate demand. If aggregate demand in an economy is decreasing so that inflation is very low (say, at 0.6%) and growth is also very low (say, at 0.4%) then a further decrease in aggregate demand could easily result in negative growth and deflation. Figure 3.3.11 shows deflation resulting from a decrease in aggregate demand.

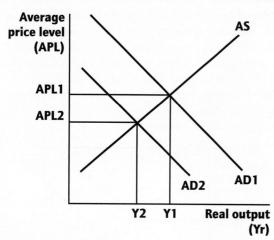

Figure 3.3.11 Deflation: aggregate demand decreasing and the AD curve shifting left

The decrease in aggregate demand from AD1 to AD2 was responsible for a decrease in real GDP from Y1 to Y1 and for the average price level decreasing from APL1 to APL2.

It is feared by many that Covid-19 will result not only in severe economic contraction but perhaps even deflation as a result of the dramatic decrease in aggregate demand.

Technically, deflation may also result from aggregate supply increasing. Since a falling average price level is in this case accompanied by an increase in real output, this is sometimes referred to as "good deflation", which is considered rather misleading. Deflation, as will be explained below, if it becomes expected, is very difficult to reverse.

> ## Recap
> ### Causes of deflation
> Deflation is caused by:
> - sustained decrease in aggregate demand
> - an increase in aggregate supply.

Costs of deflation

- Deflation induces consumers to delay purchases of durables since they come to expect further price decreases. Why buy a smartphone now, if you can buy it later at a lower price? As a result, aggregate demand decreases even more, pushing the average price level even lower.

- Deflation decreases firms' revenues, reducing profit margins and forcing them to cut costs. Wages fall and workers are made redundant. Some firms may go bankrupt.

- Since deflation is a result of a persistent fall in aggregate demand, it is not only the average price level that falls but also real output. Deflation is accompanied by higher levels of unemployment.

- What households and businesses owe to banks increases in real terms. Households become hesitant to borrow and spend; indebted firms are also hesitant to make investments. Aggregate demand decreases even more.

- Since the real value of outstanding debt increases, some households and some firms may not be able to service their loans. Banks may thus start to accumulate non-performing ("bad" loans). The risk of a banking crisis increases.

- Low confidence levels and increased uncertainty may also induce households to defer consumption and deter firms to make investments.

- The biggest risk of deflation is that the economy may enter a deflationary spiral. A vicious cycle may start, where deflation creates more deflation.

- Resources are misallocated as prices lose their signalling power and incentives are distorted. It becomes difficult for producers to determine whether demand for their product is falling when there is a general tendency for prices to fall.

- If an economy becomes caught in a deflationary spiral, policymakers may not have many policy options available. Monetary policy may be ineffective as interest rates are probably already very close to zero. A "zero lower bound" (ZLB) on interest rates was considered a limit for using monetary policy to help an economy grow and exit deflation. More recently though, negative interest rates policies (discussed later) are being considered and have even been employed by some central banks. Using expansionary fiscal policy by increasing government expenditures is also not always an option as many economies face debt constraints and are fearful of raising the debt to GDP ratio by too much.

> ## Recap
> ### Consequences of deflation
> - Consumers postpone purchases of durables, further decreasing aggregate demand.
> - Firms' revenues and profits are reduced, leading to redundancies and bankruptcies.
> - Since aggregate demand is falling, real GDP is decreasing and unemployment is rising.
> - Real debt levels rise so there is less borrowing and spending, which further decreases aggregate demand.
> - There is increased risk of a banking crisis because banks accumulate bad loans.
> - The low level of confidence decreases spending and so decreases aggregate demand.
> - There is a risk of a deflationary spiral as deflation brings about more deflation.
> - There is resource misallocation and inefficiency.
> - The policy options available are very limited.

Relative costs of unemployment versus inflation

Which is worse—inflation or unemployment? The simple answer is that it depends.

It depends on who you are. Much of the income earned by wealthy households is in the form of interest payments from fixed income assets they own, such as bonds. Inflation erodes the real value of the income earned from bonds. If a wealthy household earns $1 million per year from interest payments, inflation slowly decreases the real value of this $1 million.

On the other hand, the primary concern for workers is keeping their job. Inflation for workers is of lesser importance. Losing their job and the wage they earn (often even their health insurance) is much more costly, even if inflation shrinks their real wage. The threat of unemployment represents to them a much greater cost than inflation does.

Whether inflation or unemployment is more costly also depends on one's ideological leanings. Monetarists such as Milton Friedman considered inflation as the true enemy of an economy for many reasons. Inflation distorts the workings of markets and of the price mechanism and leads to inefficient allocation of resources. It increases uncertainty for businesses, decreasing investment spending. On the other hand, if price stability is achieved and maintained, the economy can theoretically grow faster and, in the long term, even more jobs will be created.

Whether inflation or unemployment is more costly to the economy also depends on the particulars. High and prolonged unemployment can destroy the social fabric of the economy as poverty increases and income inequality widens. In addition, if the youngest and the brightest members of the country's labour emigrate, then the future growth of the country is compromised. In this sense, high unemployment may be considered costlier than inflation. The opposing view is that accelerating inflation is also very costly and dangerous, especially for countries that rely on export-led growth. Runaway inflation severely damages savings and has led in many instances to social unrest.

Policymakers' perspective

One of the biggest problems that policymakers face is to determine early when a growing economy enjoying lower and lower unemployment is about to experience rising inflation. As long as an economy is growing, incomes are rising, and more jobs are created. To the extent that this growth is inclusive and sustainable it is, of course, much desired. However, if the potential level of real output is being approached then there is a risk of inflation accelerating. It is thus important for policymakers to try to slow down growth to avoid the inflation rate increasing above their target, which is usually set at 2%.

Policymakers therefore closely monitor the labour market. If they see that the unemployment rate is decreasing and approaching historically low levels, they realize that money wages and subsequently inflation will soon start to increase. At that point they will want to try to slow down the expansion.

The problem lately faced by policymakers was that despite unemployment decreasing fast in several countries,

notably the USA, money wages were not rising and neither was inflation accelerating. So, if policymakers had decided to adopt too soon the policies that would slow down growth then many workers who did find jobs would have remained unemployed.

There are many explanations for the persistently low growth in wages and in prices but one that should be easily understood is that many discouraged workers (known as "workers on the sidelines") were joining the labour force again, encouraged by the sustained expansion. If more workers join the labour force and accept jobs there is no reason for wages to start rising and subsequently for prices to increase.

The opposite side of the above is the problem faced when policymakers try to decrease inflation. Some of the measurement problems discussed earlier may lead to an overestimation of inflation. A positive inflation rate may be officially recorded, but in reality the average price level may have already started to decrease. This explains why the target rate of inflation is never 0%.

Worked example

Calculating a weighted price index and the rate of inflation from a set of data

You may be asked to calculate from a set of data a weighted price index (HL) and then use the price index to calculate inflation rates (SL and HL). This exercise takes you through the process.

Assume that in Laylaland, the basket of goods the typical consumer purchases includes only five products, A, B, C, D and E. The table below includes the quantities bought of each by the typical consumer per period and their prices in dollars for the years 2017 to 2020.

Product	Quantities bought per period	Price per unit in 2017 ($)	Price per unit in 2018 ($)	Price per unit in 2019 ($)	Price per unit in 2020 ($)
A	5	2.15	2.25	2.30	2.30
B	8	1.20	1.25	1.30	1.28
C	2	3.40	3.50	3.55	3.45
D	10	1.10	1.25	1.30	1.20
E	8	0.80	0.90	0.95	1.00

In order to calculate a weighted price index (HL) for each of the four years we first will have to calculate the cost of this basket of goods in each of these years. For each year we multiply the quantity bought of each good (the "weight") by its price. We then add the expenditures together to arrive at the cost of the basket in each year, as follows.

For 2017: (5 × 2.15) + (8 × 1.20) + (2 × 3.40) + (10 × 1.10) + (8 × 0.80) = $44.55

For 2018: (5 × 2.25) + (8 × 1.25) + (2 × 3.50) + (10 × 1.25) + (8 × 0.90) = $47.95

For 2019: (5 × 2.30) + (8 × 1.30) + (2 × 3.55) + (10 × 1.30) + (8 × 0.95) = $49.60

For 2020: (5 × 2.30) + (8 × 1.28) + (2 × 3.45) + (10 × 1.20) + (8 × 1.00) = $48.64

One of the years will be the base year. Assume that the base year is 2017. To derive the price index for each year we have to divide the cost of the basket in each year by the cost of the basket in the base year (in this case 2017) and multiply the result by 100. (Remember the two decimal places in economics calculations.)

$$\text{CPI for 2017} = \left(\frac{44.55}{44.55}\right) \times 100 = 100$$

$$\text{CPI for 2018} = \left(\frac{47.95}{44.55}\right) \times 100 = 107.6318743 \text{ or } 107.63$$

$$\text{CPI for 2019} = \left(\frac{49.60}{44.55}\right) \times 100 = 111.335578 \text{ or } 111.34$$

$$\text{CPI for 2020} = \left(\frac{48.64}{44.55}\right) \times 100 = 109.1806958 \text{ or } 109.18$$

Now the inflation rates can be calculated (SL and HL). The inflation rate for each year will be the percentage change in the CPI between two years.

$$\text{Inflation rate for 2018} = \left(\frac{107.63 - 100}{100}\right) \times 100 = 7.63\%$$

$$\text{Inflation rate for 2019} = \left(\frac{111.34 - 107.63}{107.63}\right) \times 100 = 3.45\%$$

(note that if you had not rounded off the CPI figures this would be 3.44%; the IBO has accepted both in all past exams)

$$\text{Inflation rate for 2020} = \left(\frac{109.18 - 111.34}{111.34}\right) \times 100 = -1.94\%$$

We realize that since the rate of inflation in 2019 was lower than 2018 there was disinflation. This means that prices in 2019 continued to rise but at a slower rate compared to 2018. It should also be realized that in 2020 there was deflation because the rate of inflation was negative. Prices in 2020 decreased by 1.94% compared to 2019.

All of the results of our calculations are included in the following table.

	2017	2018	2019	2020
Cost of basket	44.55	47.95	49.60	48.64
Weighted price index (CPI) base year: 2017	100	107.63	111.34	109.18
Annual inflation rate		7.63%	3.44%	−1.94%

The government (national) debt

Meaning of the term

At the simplest level the term *government (national) debt* refers to what a government owes. Governments' expenditures must be financed. This is the reason governments impose taxes. They need to raise money to finance these expenditures. However, governments often spend more than they collect in taxes. A **budget deficit** then results. The way to finance this deficit spending is by borrowing. A government typically borrows by issuing and selling bonds. In contrast, if a government collects more than it spends then it is running a **budget surplus**. In this sense the government debt is the sum of all past budget deficits minus any repayments made through budget surpluses.

What is a bond? A bond as a promissory note: it promises to pay the holder of this note a specific payment at a specific future date. Bonds used to be "official" pieces of paper but now they are mostly electronic records. They are also referred to as IOUs for the obvious reason. Governments sell these promissory notes at a price that is lower than the amount each note promises to pay the holder in the future. This makes the bond attractive to buy because the owner earns interest. Effectively, when people buy government bonds they lend to the government. A bond that has not been paid off is an outstanding bond. It follows that the government (national) debt is equal to the total value of all outstanding government bonds.

Why is the national debt expressed as a percentage of GDP?

The reason is very simple: the size of a country's debt must be scaled for the size of its economy. The same dollar amount of debt has different implications for a small economy compared to a large economy. The size of an economy is measured by its GDP. Dividing debt by GDP provides us with a more accurate picture of the size of the debt. Greece's debt in 2018 was around $375 billion. This number by itself conveys very little information—but if expressed as a percentage of the size of the Greek economy in 2018, it amounted to about 172% of the country's GDP. The same level of debt for the UK, a much bigger economy, would amount only to around 13% of that country's GDP. The implications are significant. The same debt implies a much higher debt burden for Greece than for a larger economy.

It should also be clear that the ratio of $\frac{\text{debt}}{\text{GDP}}$ could increase not only because the size of the country's debt is increasing but also because its GDP is decreasing as a result of recession. If GDP decreases faster than the size of the country's debt decreases, then the debt to GDP ratio will be increasing. More generally, the $\frac{\text{debt}}{\text{GDP}}$ ratio will increase if the size of the debt rises *relatively* faster than GDP.

Why is the debt to GDP ratio of importance? The reason is that it is a measure of how easily an economy is able to pay off its debt. A high debt to GDP ratio could imply that the economy's output and income may not be sufficiently high to pay off its debts, forcing investors to demand higher interest rates.

Costs of a high national debt

Cost of debt servicing

Debt servicing (that is, paying back the principal and the interest) carries a high opportunity cost. Governments facing a very high debt-to-GDP ratio must devote a share of their expenditures on debt servicing.

Rising debt-servicing costs will squeeze a government's ability to undertake discretionary spending. Resources that could have been invested on infrastructure, education and health care will have to be diverted to servicing the debt and poorer households will suffer the most.

The cost may also deny the country the ability to adopt expansionary fiscal policy (explained in section 3.5) if there is a sudden and severe recession. The government will not be able to borrow in order to finance the necessary increase in government expenditures. Lenders (that is, buyers of government bonds) will not be willing to lend unless interest rates paid rise sufficiently to compensate for the increased risk they face.

Governments may choose to service debt held by domestic residents by issuing new money. This is referred to as "monetizing" the debt. This will though increase the risk of inflation and of a subsequent depreciation of the currency. A depreciating currency, as will be explained in sections 3.5 and 4.5, will increase the cost of repaying any debt held by foreigners and thus denominated in dollars and may further increase inflation.

Credit ratings

The term *credit ratings* refers to a grade assigned by certain agencies, such as Moody's or Standard and Poor's, on the borrowing risks a prospective issuer of debt (for example, of a bond) presents to lenders. The highest rating assigned by Moody's is "Aaa" and is for bonds judged to be of the highest quality issued by governments presenting the lowest risk to creditors. A rating of "B" is for bonds considered speculative and subject to high credit risk. A "C" is the lowest grade, and is assigned to bonds typically in default, where the prospect of recovering the principal or interest is low.

As the debt to GDP ratio of a country increases, there is greater risk that a credit agency will downgrade the country's bonds. Investors will lose confidence in the government's ability to pay back borrowed funds and will demand higher interest rates on the debt. The higher interest rate governments are forced to pay is referred to as a "risk premium" and it may lead to a feedback loop: higher risk premiums lead to higher debt, which may lead to even higher risk premiums and increase the risk of default. The economy becomes trapped in a debt crisis.

Impact on future taxation and government spending

If the debt to GDP ratio is high, governments will be forced to cut spending and raise tax revenues. They will need to achieve a "primary budget" surplus, which refers to tax revenues exceeding government expenditures excluding debt servicing costs, so that debt is slowly reduced. Efforts to reduce budget deficits by decreasing government expenditures and increasing taxes are referred to as austerity policies.

Spending cuts can be painful as they often include reductions in pensions and unemployment benefits that hurt vulnerable population groups. The wages of public sector employees are also decreased. Infrastructure investments may also be scrapped and repairs of existing infrastructure may be postponed, negatively impacting the economy's potential output.

Increasing taxation is painful especially if the government decides to increase indirect taxes because indirect taxes are regressive in nature and affect lower income households disproportionately more than those on higher incomes.

Such policies, which are considered necessary when debt is growing at unsustainable rates, clearly impose a lot of hardship on the population of a country, especially the poor. It is worth noting that austerity policies typically lead to a decrease in economic activity and in national income which will, at least in the short term, further increase the debt to GDP ratio, even if the absolute level of debt decreases.

When is debt sustainable?

This is not an easy question to answer. An increase in government debt may increase welfare if it increases the growth rate of the economy. However, higher debt levels lead to higher risks. In addition, there may be a certain threshold level of debt beyond which further accumulation of debt decreases growth and may even lead to financial collapse or default. Examples show great variation: Japan can sustain debt levels above 200% of GDP without any pressure on interest rates whereas Ukraine defaulted on debt roughly equal to 30% of its GDP. The literature shows how difficult it is to determine when a country's debt to GDP ratio signals heightened economic risks and there are a few indicators that help.

The relationship between interest rates and growth rate of the country is important. It reveals how fast the country's income and debt repayment ability is rising compared to how fast its debt obligations are rising.

The condition of the "primary budget" balance is also important. If debt is rising and a government fails to improve its primary balance, then future debt problems become more likely. Similarly, it makes a difference whether debt is used by the government to finance productive capital expenditures that will permit faster future growth or mostly current expenditures that do not add to the stock of the nation's capital. Debt that accumulates as a result of budget deficits from tax cuts is also risky since the literature shows that corporate tax cuts lead to small, if any, additional private investment.

Lastly, explosive debt problems are less likely if most of a country's national debt is held by domestic investors, as in the case of Japan, and denominated in its domestic currency. Countries heavily depending on external borrowing in foreign currency face greater debt-related risks.

Policymakers' perspective

Historically, it has become painfully clear to a number of countries that the debt-to-GDP ratio is an economic variable requiring very close monitoring. Debt financing of increased government expenditures may help a country recover from a recession (as will be explained later) and grow and it will be necessary if a country suddenly faces a natural disaster.

However, if unchecked, then a high and rising debt-to-GDP ratio may become unsustainable. It may lead to a debt crisis that will require very painful adjustments for the population of the country and it may also jeopardize the country's growth prospects for a long time.

The Phillips curve
Trade-off between unemployment and inflation

The original Phillips curve

Since the early 1960s and until the mid-1970s economists relied on an empirical result that Alban W Phillips, a New Zealand economist at the London School of Economics, published in 1958. His work, the Phillips curve, became one of the most famous relationships in macroeconomics.

His original statistical work examined UK data on the annual percentage change in money wages and the annual unemployment rate over a period of 96 years (from 1861 to 1957). He found that the percentage changes in money wages and the unemployment rate were inversely related.

- If unemployment was low (which implied a "tight" labour market) then money wages increased a lot because employers were forced to offer higher wages to find workers.

- If unemployment was high (a "slack" labour market), then money wages would increase but only by a little, or could even decrease because firms could find and hire additional workers without having to offer more than last year's prevailing money wage.

Moving from wage inflation to price inflation was the next step. Since wages typically form a big proportion of production costs and since firms in the real world often set prices by adding a percentage mark-up on their average cost, it seemed sensible to expect that decreasing unemployment would lead to an increase in the average price level. The empirical results showed that there was indeed a trade-off between the inflation rate and the unemployment rate of an economy. When the unemployment rate decreases, inflation increases as businesses compete for fewer workers and this drives up wages, which leads to an increase in prices.

This inverse relationship is referred to as the Phillips curve and it is compatible with our simple AD/AS model.

Why the Phillips curve is compatible with shifts in aggregate demand

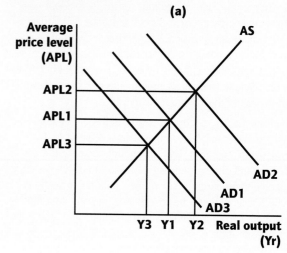

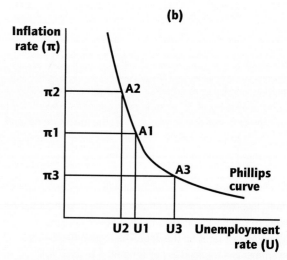

Figure 3.3.12 The effect on the Phillips curve of shifts in aggregate demand

Focusing on Figure 3.3.12a, assume the economy at equilibrium with real output Y1 and the average price level at APL1. Now look at Figure 3.3.12b. There is some inflation in this economy equal to π1 and some unemployment equal to U1, shown at point A1. Let aggregate demand increase to AD2. Equilibrium real output will increase to Y2. The higher level of economic activity will decrease unemployment to U2. The average price level rises though, so inflation is now higher at π2. We have moved from point A1 to point A2. Following the increase in aggregate demand, unemployment has decreased from U1 to U2, while inflation has increased to π2. If aggregate demand had instead decreased from AD1 to AD3, real output would have decreased from Y1 to Y3. The lower level of economic activity will increase unemployment from U1 to U3. The decrease in the average price level implies that inflation decreases from π1 to π3. We have moved from point A1 to point A3 on Figure 3.3.12b. Following the decrease in AD, unemployment increased and inflation decreased. This inverse relationship between unemployment and inflation is exactly what the Phillips curve described so Figure 3.3.12b is the original curve resulting from the work of AW Phillips.

If this inverse relationship between inflation and unemployment was stable, then governments could perhaps exploit it. The Phillips curve was considered for many years as presenting policymakers with a "menu of choices" inviting them to intervene. It seemed policymakers could achieve a lower unemployment rate but at the cost of higher inflation, or they could achieve lower inflation but at the cost of higher unemployment. The issue was for the government to determine the politically desired combination of the two variables and then by manipulating aggregate demand (by using demand-side policies), policymakers could achieve it.

For many years, policymakers in many countries were trying to achieve whichever combination of inflation and unemployment the government considered most desirable.

In the 1970s, not only did this stable relationship between inflation and unemployment break down but also Milton Friedman, the most prominent Monetarist economist, showed that in the long run there is no such trade-off between inflation and unemployment.

In the long run, policymakers cannot decrease unemployment below what Friedman called the natural rate by pursuing policies that aimed to increase aggregate demand. He showed that any such attempt could only temporarily lower unemployment at the cost of higher inflation. In the short run, an inverse relationship between inflation and unemployment did exist, but in the long run unemployment would return to its natural rate. According to Friedman, the long-run Phillips curve is vertical at the natural rate of unemployment, which is also the equilibrium rate of unemployment.

The logic of the vertical long-run Phillips curve

The distinction between a short-run Phillips curve (SRPC) and a long-run Phillips curve (LRPC) was introduced by Milton Friedman and, independently, by another economist, Ed Phelps. Their theory became known as the Phelps-Friedman critique or the expectations-augmented Phillips curve.

According to this theory, any short run trade-off between inflation and unemployment was only the result of workers suffering from money illusion. Specifically, workers expect next year's inflation rate to be the same as previous inflation rates (referred to as backward-looking or adaptive expectations). Workers are slow to realize that inflation is increasing when the government uses (expansionary) policies to increase aggregate demand.

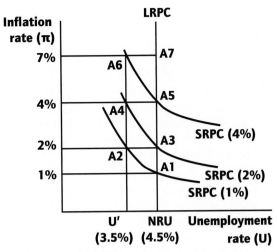

Figure 3.3.13 The long-run Phillips curve

Figure 3.3.13 shows an economy initially at point A1 with unemployment at the natural rate of unemployment, the example used being 4.5%, and inflation for some time now equal to 1%. Workers expect 1% inflation next year.

Assume now that the government attempts to decrease unemployment below the 4.5% natural rate to 3.5% by increasing aggregate demand (using expansionary policies). It is essentially trying to expand real GDP beyond its potential level Yp. As a result of the higher aggregate demand, inflation will now accelerate to 2%. Since in the short run money wages are assumed fixed, the real wage rate will decrease, and firms will want to produce more output so they will hire more workers. Unemployment decreases to 3.5% and the economy has moved on Figure 3.3.13 to point A2 along the short-run Phillips curve SRPC (1%) that reflects workers expecting 1% inflation. This movement along a negatively sloped short-run Phillips curve is only the result of workers being temporarily fooled. They expected inflation at 1% but it increased to 2%. Workers are slow to realize that inflation is higher than they had expected and that consequently their real wage is lower. If we refer back to the Monetarist AD/SRAS diagram we have moved along the economy's SRAS curve: at a higher average price level, real output is greater and so unemployment is lower.

In the long run, though, workers' expectations about inflation will adjust. They realize that inflation is now higher (at 2%) and will demand higher money wages. Since in the long run money wages are assumed flexible, they will start to increase. As money wages increase, the SRAS curve in the Monetarist AD/SRAS diagram will start to decrease and shift to the left. Firms will be firing workers. Since money wages are assumed to adjust fully to changes in the average price level, the real wage will return back to its original equilibrium level. We say that in the long run the real wage is "restored". Unemployment will return to its equilibrium natural rate at 4.5% (see Figure 3.3.13). Real output will thus also return to its potential level Yp. The economy is at point A3 in Figure 3.3.13. Workers' expectations have adjusted and they expect inflation at 2%. The short-run Phillips curve has shifted to the right to SRPC (2%) because workers now expect higher 2% inflation.

If the government insists on trying to decrease unemployment below its natural 4.5% rate by increasing aggregate demand, it would need to engineer even higher inflation so that workers would again be temporarily fooled and accept job offers without realizing immediately that their real wage has decreased. In Figure 3.3.13, inflation would have to rise to 4% for unemployment to drop again to 3.5% (point A4). The movement from point A3 to point A4 along the SRPC (2%) was because workers were fooled again. They expected inflation 2% but inflation increased to 4%.

In the long run, since money wages are assumed flexible, they will adjust and increase so that the real wage is restored. The economy would move to point A5 on SRPC (4%) with unemployment back at its 4.5% natural rate and output at its potential level Yp. The short-run Phillips curve will have shifted to SRPC (4%) as workers' expectations have adjusted and they now expect 4% inflation next period.

It follows that in the long run, when expectations have adjusted so that the money wage has increased and the real wage has been restored, the Phillips curve will be vertical at the NRU. There is no trade-off in the long run between unemployment and inflation.

This analysis is symmetric to the earlier analysis of why any inflationary gap will automatically close according to the Monetarist model. Remember, the long-run aggregate supply (LRAS) is vertical at the potential level of real output (Yp) where unemployment is at its equilibrium natural rate.

Recap

The short-run and the long-run Phillips curve

- In the short run there is a trade-off between unemployment and inflation.

- In the long run, there is no trade-off.

- In the long run there is only one rate of unemployment, the natural rate of unemployment (NRU).

- Any attempt to lower unemployment below the NRU by increasing aggregate demand will be futile and only lead to inflation.

- The problem is that policymakers do not know for sure what the NRU of the country is equal to.

- The NRU is not the same across time or for all countries.

- It follows that policymakers run the risk of slowing down growth fearing that the NRU has been reached when unemployment could decrease even more and thousands more workers could have found a job. In contrast, they may not apply the brakes soon enough to slow down growth and, as a result, allow inflation to rise.

Policymakers' perspective

The policy implication of this analysis is clear. Governments should not adopt policies to increase aggregate demand in order to increase real output above its potential level and to decrease unemployment below its natural rate. Any attempt to do this will increase inflation and in the long run prove futile.

Practically, this means that policymakers must keep monitoring how much unemployment is decreasing and whether it is approaching what is considered the country's natural rate. If unemployment is decreasing fast to very low levels, policymakers may suggest that it is probably time to slow down growth. They will fear that higher inflation is just around the corner. The idea of a negatively sloped short-run Phillips curve relationship is responsible for this fear.

In the USA, though, during the last decade something strange was going on. The country had been experiencing falling unemployment since the end of the 2008–09 global financial crisis without an increase in money wages

or in inflation. The unemployment rate had decreased below 4% to a historic 3.5% low, which was significantly below what was believed to be the NRU for the USA. Still, inflation did not rise. Many questioned whether the inverse Phillips curve relationship still holds. Articles were written wondering whether the Phillips curve was dead or flattening or, perhaps, just "hibernating". One explanation of the observed phenomenon is that it is impossible to know precisely how much unemployment is structural and how much is cyclical. Since structural unemployment—the dominant type of unemployment in the NRU—can change through time, the NRU is not constant either. The NRU is not a fixed percentage through time or across countries. In addition, as we have mentioned earlier, discouraged workers rejoining the labour market and finding a job may also obscure the issue as this causes the unemployment rate to decrease without wages or prices rising. Lastly, it could be the result of expectations of future inflation remaining very low so that workers do not demand higher wages and firms do not start asking for higher prices.

3.4 Economics of inequality and poverty

Equality versus equity

The ideas of equality and equity often arise in relation to the distribution of income. Equity means fairness, which is not the same as equality. Different societies have different perceptions of what is equitable. Although there is a consensus that extreme inequality is unfair, there is little general agreement on the desirability of greater income equality for its own sake or on what constitutes a fair distribution of income. Nonetheless, equity is typically interpreted as less inequality in the share of income received by members of society.

Economic inequality

The meaning of economic inequality

Economic inequality relates to the unequal distribution of income and of wealth.

Income and wealth are often used interchangeably but they are not the same. A pensioner living in a house valued at $500,000 might be considered wealthy, but if her pension pays her just $100 a week, most would consider her as having a low income. This is why it is important to understand the difference between income and wealth.

Household income is generated from the payments received per period of time from the use of factors of production that include rent, wages, interest and profit. Wealth consists of what households own—the value of their assets at some point in time—minus what they owe (that is, their debt). Assets include bank deposits, shares, bonds, houses, cars and boats. Households can use wealth to consume more than their income, or may consume less than their income and add to their wealth. Given that wealth is accumulated over time it is typically higher on average than income. For instance, in 2016, the average household income in OECD countries was $25,908 a year but average household net wealth was $67,139.

Wealth is distributed more unequally than income, that is to say inequalities in wealth tend to be more prominent than income inequalities. In fact, across the OECD countries, wealth

The Organisation for Economic Co-operation and Development (OECD) is an intergovernmental economic organization with 37 member countries. The OECD works to shape policies that foster prosperity, equality, opportunity and well-being for all.

inequality is twice the level of income inequality on average. This is important because wealth can itself generate income and so as wealth inequality widens, it fuels income inequality.

Wealth inequality is highest in the USA where households in the top 10% in terms of their wealth own 80% of total wealth and those in the bottom 40% own just over 2% of total wealth. The next two countries on the scale of high wealth inequality are the Netherlands and Denmark. Wealth inequality is lowest in Japan, Poland, Greece and Belgium where households in the top 10% own a little over 40% of total wealth.

Interestingly though, countries with high wealth inequality, such as the Netherlands and Denmark, where households in the bottom 60% owe more than they own, are countries with a very equitable income distribution. Also, households with low net wealth are not necessarily "poor" in terms of their income and some may own substantial wealth but combined with high levels of debt.

Measuring economic inequality

The income distribution in an economy can be represented graphically using a Lorenz curve.

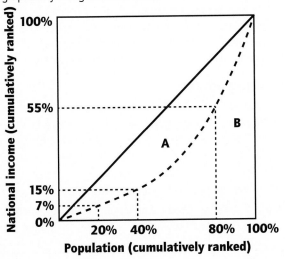

Figure 3.4.1 The Lorenz curve

Population is represented on the horizontal axis of the graph, in cumulative percentages, from the lowest to the highest income households. On the vertical axis, the percentage of national income received by each percentage of the population is represented. So, the poorest 20% of people receives only 7% of national income, the poorest 40% of the population receives 15% of national income while the richest 20% receives 45% of national income.

The diagonal line is the line of perfect income equality, where the "poorest" 20% earns 20% of income and the "poorest" 40% earns 40% of national income. As we move further to the right of the diagonal, the distribution of income becomes more and more unequal. So, more income inequality is shown by a shift of the Lorenz curve further to the right of the diagonal and less income inequality by a move towards the diagonal.

The degree of income inequality can be measured through the Gini coefficient. The Gini coefficient is defined as the ratio of the area between the Lorenz curve and the diagonal over the area of the half-square.

$$\text{Gini coefficient} = \frac{\text{Area (A)}}{\text{Area (A + B)}}$$

It can vary from 0 to 1, where 0 represents a society where everyone has the same income and, therefore, there is no inequality. At the other end of the scale, 1 represents a society where only one person has all the income and so there is maximum inequality.

Real world Gini coefficient values are between 0.25 and 0.60. The lowest values are recorded in Northern European countries such as Sweden, Norway, Denmark and Austria, while the highest values are to be found in Lesotho, South Africa and Latin America. The USA has the higher income inequality of advanced nations as according to recent data (2018) the Gini coefficient has increased from 0.40 to 0.48, while China is reaching a Gini coefficient of 0.50.

Constructing a Lorenz curve from income quintile data

The income distribution for an economy by quintile appears in Table 3.4.1.

Year	Lowest 20%	Second 20%	Third 20%	Fourth 20%	Highest 20%
2018	3.2	8.4	14.3	23.0	51.1

Table 3.4.1

Each column shows what share of the total income is earned by each quintile in the year 2018. The first quintile is the lowest 20% ,the second quintile is the next lowest and so on.

Given that a Lorenz curve shows cumulative shares of income received, to plot the curve we begin with the lowest quintile and mark a point to show the percentage of total income those households received. We then add the next quintile and its cumulative share and mark a point to show the share of the lowest 40% of households. Then, we add the third quintile, and then the fourth. Since the share of income received by all the quintiles will be 100%, the last point on the curve always shows that 100% of households receive 100% of the income.

Using the data above, the lowest 20% receives 3.2% of total income, which will be the first point on the Lorenz

curve (see Figure 3.4.2). Then the lowest 40% receives 11.6% (= 3.2% + 8.4%), which is the second point on the Lorenz curve. Adding the third quintile leads to 60% of households receiving 25.9% (= 11.6% + 14.3%) of total income and to the third point on the Lorenz curve. Adding the fourth quintile leads to a total income share of 48.9% (= 25.9% + 23.0%) and to the fourth point. The last point on the curve derives from adding the fifth quintile (that is, 48.9% + 51.1% = 100%).

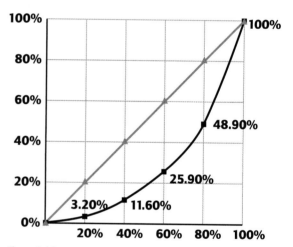

Figure 3.4.2

Meaning of poverty

Poverty refers to the inability to cover minimal consumption needs. There is a distinction between absolute and relative poverty, as follows.

- Absolute poverty refers to the case where a household does not have sufficient income to meet basic needs. Absolute poverty is often discussed in terms of an income below which people cannot afford a basic basket of goods and services.

- Relative poverty compares the income of households in a society with the median national income. The more unequal the distribution of income within the total population, the more significant is the degree of relative poverty. The idea behind relative poverty is that people may still be poor, even if they can afford basic necessities, when they cannot afford the typical lifestyle in their society—relative poverty gauges where people stand compared to everyone else in their society.

Both absolute and relative poverty relate to people's income and material conditions. Poverty has more dimensions, though: it can be thought of in terms of possessing the basics of life, such as shelter or nutritious food; having access to services that improve people's lives, such as education and health care; being free of the threat of violence; and being able to contribute to decisions that will shape the future of someone's community. The impact of these dimensions of poverty is increasingly recognized.

Measuring poverty

Poverty should be measured in order to provide estimates of the magnitude of the problem, and raise its visibility (that is, to keep poor people on the policy agenda). Also, poverty measures are needed to target appropriate policy interventions.

Poverty is usually measured in terms of income.

To measure absolute poverty, a minimum income level called the "poverty line" is identified. That is the basic minimum that families need in order to get by. Once the poverty line is defined, the amount of poverty can be measured by taking the percentage of the population, who earn an income below the poverty line. These poverty lines can be set both at a national and an international level. The World Bank sets the international poverty line at periodic intervals. It was first set in 1990 at $1.00 a day. Some years ago, it was revised to $1.25 and, in 2015, it was revised again—to $1.90 per day. At that time, households living on less than $1.90 a day were in absolute poverty. Note that these thresholds are not actually in "real" US dollars but rather in purchasing power parity (PPP) dollars in order to take account of differing cost of living between countries.

Relative poverty can be measured by specifying a percentage of the median income, usually set at 50%. Households earning less than 50% of the median income will be considered relatively poor. More specifically, statisticians examine the full range of incomes in a country—from lowest to highest—and identify the point that separates the top half of earners from the bottom half. This is the median income. The poverty line is then calculated at 50% of the median income. For instance, say the median annual household income in an economy is $20,000. Taking 50% of this, we have $10,000. Any household with an annual income that falls below $10,000 is considered poor in relative terms.

The measures of absolute and relative poverty described above provide poverty estimates on the basis of income. Yet, as already explained, poverty is a phenomenon that can neither be described in a single word nor accurately be captured by a single indicator. For this reason the Multidimensional Poverty Index (MPI)—a composite indicator—has been constructed.

Oxford Poverty & Human Development Initiative (OPHI) as well as the United Nations Development Programme (UNDP) developed this index in 2010 in order to determine poverty beyond measures that are based solely on income. It covers over 100 developing countries and helps to determine the most vulnerable people among the poor in different societies around the globe.

The MPI captures the acute deprivations that each person faces with respect to education, health and living standards. These three dimensions are assessed by ten indicators, which are:

- child mortality
- nutrition
- years of schooling
- school attendance
- cooking fuel
- sanitation
- drinking water
- electricity
- housing
- assets.

If individuals are deprived in three or more of these ten indicators, the index identifies them as "MPI poor", and the intensity of their poverty is measured by the percentage of deprivations they are experiencing.

According to the MPI, at least 1.57 billion people are living in multidimensional poverty, representing deprivations in health, education and their standard of living. This is much higher than the roughly 800 million people worldwide estimated to be living in absolute poverty.

Difficulties in measuring poverty

Measuring poverty accurately is important in assessing the scale of poverty, formulating policies and evaluating their effectiveness. However, measurement is not a simple task.

- Issues arise from the very first step, which is defining what is meant by the term *poverty*. There are differences in the perceptions of those who define and measure poverty. As such, poverty can be difficult to measure because of the difficulty in agreeing a definition.

- Household surveys are currently the source of most poverty-related data. However, in many countries the surveys are conducted on an irregular basis. Even if countries have a regular household survey in place, the data provided by the survey may be insufficient.

- In addition, household poverty surveys frequently omit from the sampling people who may be likely to be poor but who do not live in households. This includes a range of people such as the homeless, drug users, sex workers and street children, who all face acute deprivations but who are still not represented in the surveys and in turn in poverty statistics.

- There are also limits to the disaggregation of data in relation to gender, disability and age. More disaggregated poverty data would enable a better understanding of poverty and its impact on different groups of people, including women for example.

- There is evidence to suggest that the poverty lines underestimate the actual severity and intensity of poverty, as poverty lines tend to provide no more than arbitrary cut-off points that have no specific relevance to the lives of the poor. Poverty lines often produce an overly simplistic portrait of poor people's lives.

Minimum income standards can be misleading and can create a sense that people living in poverty have a reliable, albeit very small, income. However, in reality, incomes can be unpredictable and sporadic. Farmers, for instance, may earn all their money just once or twice a year after harvest time.

Recap
Difficulties in measuring poverty

There are difficulties in:

- defining poverty
- having insufficient and irregular household surveys to collect poverty data
- sampling; people in acute poverty may be omitted
- having limited disaggregation of data
- relying on poverty lines, which may underestimate the severity of poverty
- relying on minimum income standards, which can be misleading.

Causes of economic inequality and poverty

There is a whole range of factors—economic, social and the role of the state—driving economic inequality and poverty. Examples are explored below.

Inequality of opportunity

This occurs when people living in the same society do not have access to the same opportunities. Parental background is the key circumstance influencing inequality of opportunity, followed by gender and place of birth. Inequality of opportunity is strongly correlated with income inequality.

Countries with high levels of inequality of opportunity tend to have high levels of income inequality. The reason is that people's circumstances at birth such as their parental background, the place where they were born, their ethnicity or their gender determine to a large degree the educational qualifications they obtain, the type of job they get and, ultimately, their level of income.

For example, due to the Covid-19 lockdown in 2020 and schools switching to remote learning strategies, children have not had the same opportunities within and across countries. In some cases, distance-learning programmes were launched within a few days of schools closing but in other cases it took much longer. At the same time, wealthier households were able to seek distance-learning opportunities at higher rates than poorer households. Overall, because of these disruptions current students stand to lose $10 trillion in earnings over their working life. Yet, as a result of the disparities in opportunities the learning loss will not be uniformly distributed; the income level of the parents and the place where these children were born will determine how much this may set them back over their lifetime.

Remarkably, there are no cases where a country with high levels of inequality of opportunity enjoys moderate or low levels of income inequality. In contrast, there are a few rare instances where inequality of opportunity is relatively low, but income inequality is still high. This suggests that inequality of opportunity is an important determinant of income inequality but not the only one.

Different levels of resource ownership

Income depends on the payments households receive by offering the factors of production they own. Remember that factor payments take the form of rents (for land), wages (for labour), interest (for capital) and profits (for entrepreneurship). A highly unequal ownership of the factors of production would lead to a highly unequal income distribution.

Over the past few decades there is increasing evidence that the share of national income going to capital and entrepreneurship is rising and that the share going to labour is falling. This decline in labour's share of income is fuelling inequality. For instance, a report by the International Labour Organisation on G20 countries suggests that a 1% decrease in labour's share of income increases inequality in income by 0.1% to 0.2%.

Different levels of human capital

Human capital refers to the skills, education and experience embodied in the labour force. Some workers are able to receive higher wages because of special skills and education or experience, while others who are less skilled, educated or experienced may receive extremely low wages. At the same time, lower wage jobs are often associated with poorer working conditions and less stability.

Over the years, the proportion of workers who have mid-level skills has declined. Between 1995 and 2010, the share fell from 53% to 41% of the workforce in OECD countries. However, the share of people working at the two ends of the skills spectrum, high skilled workers such as designers and lower skilled workers such as drivers, has increased. This trend is likely to increase income inequality.

Discrimination

Discrimination against gender, race, religion or any other factor plays an important role in perpetuating inequality. Groups of the population facing discrimination may have greater difficulty in finding a job and may receive lower earnings than workers who are not discriminated against.

In the case of gender discrimination, for example, evidence suggests that women are generally at higher risk of poverty than men as they are less likely to be in paid employment, they tend to have lower pensions, they are more involved in unpaid caring responsibilities and when they are in work they are frequently paid less for the same job. Similarly, in cases of racial discrimination, members of minority ethnic groups and immigrants may have less chance to access employment and may end up earning less than other workers, often without social security or insurance.

Unequal status and power

Inequality can also arise when there are disparities in market power and social power. Significant market power concentrated in the hands of a few firms may lead to economic inequality. More specifically, in some countries there has been a very significant increase in corporate concentration and monopoly power. This leads to a transfer of income away from consumers to a few firms, as they can charge consumers more for what they sell and pay their workers less. At the same time, certain powerful social groups may be granted exclusive privileges and preferences, which could boost their income and wealth, widening inequality.

Government tax and benefits policies

Governments can mitigate inequality through public policy—primarily taxes and payments such as public retirement benefits or unemployment benefits. Typically higher-income individuals tend to pay proportionately more in taxes than their lower income counterparts; while lower income individuals tend to receive more support from the state. Combined, these systems of taxes and benefits can narrow income disparities.

However, many countries have now seen an increase in income inequality, indicating gaps in existing tax-and-transfer systems to counteract rising inequality. Particularly, in some advanced economies the tax rate on high incomes has declined. Across OECD countries, the average top tax rate fell from 66% in 1981 to 41% in 2008. High earners have benefited from other changes in tax regimes, too. Tax on property and on inheritances has tended to fall, allowing high earners to build up wealth. At the same time, transfer payments have decreased both in size and in scope; the welfare state is shrinking. As a result, economic inequality has been rising.

See page 110 for a more detailed explanation of the role of taxation.

Globalization and technological change

The world economy has become increasingly integrated and interconnected. All of the flows that constitute globalization can have some impact on inequality, but perhaps the most important one is technology. Technological change affects the job market, devaluing and revaluing skills and, of course, creating whole new skills and jobs—think of app developers and social media strategists. People with the devalued skills suffer from a decline in wages while those with the revalued or new skills see their earnings rise, potentially widening inequality—so the relationship between skills and technology can be regarded as an important factor behind rising income inequality.

Increased international trade as a result of globalization has also impacted income inequality. Many workers in industries where import penetration has been high become redundant. As such, workers in import-competing industries lose their income and face dislocation whereas workers in booming export-oriented industries maintain or increase their income, widening the income gap.

Market-based supply side policies

The basic principle of market-based supply-side policies is to have less government and more free and unfettered markets in order to achieve long-term growth. Based on this principle many countries have reformed the rules covering products, services and employment, and so market forces are generally allowed freer rein. However, this has also tended to widen inequality.

Deregulation and privatization have increased monopoly power and concentration in many countries, which has led to higher prices and to a transfer of income from consumers to businesses. The increased labour market flexibility resulting from lower minimum wages, lower labour union power, lower employment protection laws and lower unemployment benefits is responsible for the shrinking share of wages in national income. Lastly, the benefits of tax cuts have accrued mostly to the wealthiest.

Recap

Causes of inequality and poverty

Inequality and poverty can arise from:

- inequality of opportunity
- different levels of resource ownership
- different levels of human capital
- discrimination (gender, race, others)
- unequal status and power
- government tax and benefits policies
- globalization and technological change
- market-based supply-side policies.

Impact of income and wealth inequality

Impact on economic growth

There is rising evidence—from the OECD, IMF and others—that inequality can have a negative impact on economic growth and that this impact can be substantial. Particularly, in OECD countries, the rising inequality over the past couple of decades is estimated to have cut GDP by around 8.5%.

Inequality lowers growth by depriving the ability of lower income households to access health care and education and to accumulate human capital. For instance, it can lead to underinvestment in education with poor children ending up in lower quality schools and less able to go to college. As a result, labour productivity will be lower than it would have been if it were not for inequality. Lower labour productivity then leads to slower economic growth.

With high inequality, the overall rate of savings in the economy tends to be lower, because the highest rate of savings is usually found among the middle classes, which are usually "squeezed" by inequality. High income individuals typically spend much of their incomes on imported luxury goods, jewellery, expensive houses and foreign travel, or they seek havens abroad for their savings in what is known as capital flight. Therefore, when savings are low, the level of investment is low. As a result, productive resources do not increase or improve, withholding economic growth.

High levels of inequality have also been linked to rent seeking, defined as "efforts that people take to get a larger share of the pie rather than to increase the size of the pie". Wealthy individuals may use their ability to, say, fund political parties to influence policies in a way that benefits them. When resources are allocated to such rent-seeking behaviours, they are diverted from productive purposes that could have led to faster growth.

The higher the inequality is, the smaller the fraction of the population that qualifies for a loan or other credit. When low income individuals cannot borrow money, they may not be able to educate their children sufficiently or start and expand a business. The result of these factors can be a slower growth.

In addition, according to several researchers, growth tends to be more fragile when inequality is high. That is to say that it is how the benefits from growth are distributed that will ultimately determine whether the growth will last. If growth is non-inclusive and its benefits remain with the wealthiest because of economic inequality, then growth will be less resilient. This implies that in an unequal society policies that would help deal with an adverse economic shock will not gain enough support since the long-term benefits will not be uniformly shared.

Lastly, a growing gap between rich and poor may also impede growth, because it may create political and social instability, which, in turn, may deter investment. Social divisions fuelled by inequality may also make it more difficult for governments to find the necessary consensus in society to meet economic and financial crises.

Impact on standards of living and social stability

High and sustained levels of inequality can have a harsh effect on societies, making them worse places in which to live. Such inequality will result in large social costs.

Inequality can reduce people's well-being by fuelling crime: disadvantaged people are more likely to commit and to be victims of crimes.

Inequality may also damage trust. In particular, citizens can lose confidence in institutions, eroding social cohesion.

Even worse, high inequality makes weak institutions very difficult to improve, because the powerful few are likely to view themselves as worse off from a socially efficient reform, and so they have the incentive and the means to resist it.

High inequality may also lead those on low incomes to support populist policies that can prove to be damaging. Moreover, high inequality also strengthens the political power of the rich and hence their bargaining power. Usually, this power will be used to encourage outcomes favourable to the rich.

In cases of extreme inequality, upheavals and civil conflict may result that can cost lives and set back any progress.

Recap
Impact of inequality

Impact on **economic growth** includes:	Impact on **standards of living and social stability** includes:
low levels of human capital → low labour productivity → slower growth	higher criminality
lower savings → lower investment → slower growth	damaged trust and social cohesion
inequality encourages rent-seeking behaviours → diverting resources from productive purposes	increasing support of populist policies
lack of access to credit → lower investment → slower growth	increasing power of the rich
inequality creates instability → discouraging investment → limiting growth	fuelling conflicts and upheavals.
high inequality → non-inclusive growth → fragile growth.	

The role of taxation

Taxes are distinguished into direct and indirect.

- Direct taxes are directly paid to tax authorities by taxpayers and include:

  - personal income taxes: paid based on all forms of income such as wages, rental income, interest income and dividends

  - corporate income taxes: taxes on the profits of a corporation

  - wealth taxes: taxes imposed on the ownership of assets; they include property taxes and inheritance taxes.

- Indirect taxes are taxes imposed on goods and services or on expenditures. They are called indirect because consumers are paying them indirectly through the sellers of the good or service being purchased.

Progressive, proportional and regressive taxes

Taxes can be progressive, proportional or regressive depending on the relationship between income and the percentage of income paid as tax.

- A tax is progressive if higher income individuals pay proportionately more so that as income increases the percentage of income paid as taxes also increases.

- A tax is proportional if higher income individuals pay proportionately the same so that as income increases the percentage of income paid as taxes remains constant.

- A tax is regressive if higher income individuals pay proportionately less so that as income increases the percentage of income paid as taxes decreases.

To understand the difference between progressive, proportional and regressive taxation consider two individuals, Alex and Bill, whose yearly earnings are different.

- If Alex earns $10,000 and pays $2,000 in income tax while Bill earns $20,000 and pays $5,000 then the tax system is progressive. Bill pays a larger proportion of his income in tax compared to Alex (25% > 20%).

- If Bill pays $4,000 in income tax then the tax system is proportional. Both Alex and Bill pay the same proportion of their income in tax (20%).

- If Bill pays $3,000 then the tax system is regressive. Bill pays a smaller proportion of his income in tax compared to Alex (15% < 20%).

Note that in all three cases Bill pays more. The key is whether Bill pays proportionately more or not.

Income taxes are never regressive; however, indirect taxes are. The following example shows why this is.

Assume that the VAT is 20% and both Alex and Bill have paid $400 in tax for a $2,000 laptop. As a proportion of his lower income, Alex is paying more; he is paying:

$$\frac{400}{10,000} \text{ or } 4\%$$

whereas Bill is paying:

$$\frac{400}{20,000} \text{ or } 2\%$$

Both individuals have paid the same "dollar" amount of VAT. Yet, since they do not have the same level of income, the amount of tax paid is a greater percentage of income for the poorer individual.

Calculating the total tax paid

Table 3.4.2 shows how much income tax Greek individuals were asked to pay, as of 2019.

Income (€)	Tax rate (%)
(0–20,000)	22
(20,001–30,000)	29
(30,001–40,000)	37
40,001 and above	45

Table 3.4.2

Nikos earns €35,000 per year. How much tax does he have to pay? Most will answer €12.950 (35,000 × 0.37) and they are wrong. The calculation is a bit more complicated.

Using the information in Table 3.4.2, the tax paid for the first €20,000 earned will be 22%; for the next €10,000 it will be 29%; and for the next €5,000 Nikos earns he will be taxed 37%. So:

$$(0.22 × €20,000) + (0.29 × €10,000) + (0.37 × €5,000) =$$

$$€4,400 + €2,900 + €1,850 = €9,150$$

The total tax paid by Nikos on the €35,000 he earns is €9,150.

Now consider Sofia, who earns €70,000 per year (so double the amount Nikos earns). To calculate how much tax she has to pay the same steps will be followed.

Using the information in Table 3.4.2, the tax paid for the first €20,000 earned will be 22%; for the next €10,000 it will be 29%; for the next €10,000 it will be 37%; and for the €30,000 that Sofia has above €40,000 she will be taxed 45%. So:

$$(0.22 × €20,000) + (0.29 × €10,000) + (0.37 × €10,000) + (0.45 × €30,000) =$$

$$€4,400 + €2,900 + €3,700 + €13,500 = €24,500$$

The total tax paid by Sofia on the €70,000 she earns is €24,500.

Average and marginal tax rates

To explain the difference between progressive, proportional and regressive taxes further we need to define the average tax rate (ATR) and the marginal tax rate (MTR).

The ATR is the proportion of income paid in taxes; that is, the ratio of the tax collected over income. More generally it is the tax paid as a proportion of the tax base, which

may be income, profits, wealth or spending. The MTR is additional tax paid as a result of additional income earned: that is, the tax paid on the last "dollar" earned. Table 3.4.3 shows the two rates.

Average tax rate (ATR)	Marginal tax rate (MTR)
$ATR = \dfrac{T}{Y}$	$MTR = \dfrac{\Delta T}{\Delta Y}$

Table 3.4.3

Let us turn again to the case of Nikos and Sofia.

As shown, Nikos earns €35,000 per year and pays €9,150 in tax:

$$ATR = \frac{€9,150}{€35,000} = 0.26 = 26\%$$

For the last euro earned Nikos paid 37% in tax, which is the MTR.

Sofia earns €70,000 per year and pays €24,500 in tax:

$$ATR = \frac{€24,500}{€70,000} = 0.35 = 35\%$$

For the last euro earned Sofia paid 45% in tax, which is the MTR.

	ATR	MTR
Nikos (income = €35,000)	26%	37%
Sofia (income = €70,000)	35%	45%

Table 3.4.4

What can be inferred from this case is that as income rises the ATR also rises, while the MTR is greater than the ATR for both individuals (see Table 3.4.4). The tax system in this case is progressive, with Sofia paying proportionately more than Niko.

In a proportional tax system the ATR remains constant as income rises so the MTR is equal to the ATR. In a regressive tax system the ATR decreases as income rises so the MTR is less than the ATR.

Recap
Effect of tax systems on ATR and MTR

- If the tax system is progressive then as income rises the ATR rises and MTR > ATR.
- If the tax system is proportional then ATR remains constant as income rises and MTR = ATR.
- If the tax system is regressive then ATR decreases as income rises and MTR < ATR.

In Figure 3.4.3 the horizontal axis measures the tax base (say, income) and the vertical the amount of tax paid. A proportional tax system is illustrated by any straight line through the origin. In a progressive tax system the slope of the line is increasing while in a regressive tax system the slope of the line is decreasing.

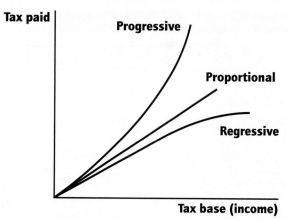

Figure 3.4.3 Progressive, proportional and regressive taxation

How can taxation reduce poverty, income and wealth inequalities?

Taxation can play a major role in making the after-tax income distribution less unequal. In addition, taxation is crucial for raising revenues to finance public expenditure on transfer payments, health care and education that tend to favour low-income households.

Progressive taxation of income is one of the main ways for governments to redistribute incomes. Progressive income taxes will require those on higher incomes to pay a larger proportion of their total income in taxes compared to those on lower incomes. Increasing the progressivity of the income tax system can lead to a less unequal after-tax distribution of income. This can be achieved by raising marginal tax rates on high earners.

However, higher marginal tax rates may encourage the development of selective tax reliefs, which can distort investment decisions. Also, they may lead to extensive tax avoidance through the exploitation of legal tax and accounting loopholes, with those on higher incomes ending up paying fewer taxes.

Perhaps an appropriate approach would be to reduce tax-induced distortions, including closing loopholes, and to achieve greater equity through other types of taxation and tax reforms.

Key economists, such as Emmanuel Saez and Thomas Piketty, have been documenting a massive rise in economic inequality in the USA that has been fuelled by tax cuts initiated after 1980 and which culminated after the recent 2018 tax cut. Their estimates show that the top tenth of 1% of Americans held 19.3% of all wealth in 2018. That was triple their share from four decades earlier. On these grounds, key economists are proposing a wealth tax as a way to reduce economic inequality by forcing the richest Americans to pay taxes on everything they own and diverting that money to public services such as improved health care and education for all. The wealth tax may thus serve as another way of using taxation towards narrowing economic inequality.

There may also be scope to raise taxation of residential property in particular, which is relatively lightly taxed in many countries. However, while the better off tend to own the most expensive residential property, there are many middle-class owners too. Nevertheless, many existing property taxes tend to be regressive (that is, they take proportionally more of the income of poorer households). Reform that would make property taxes more progressive will make the burden of the tax fall most heavily on the upper-income groups, rendering the taxes fairer and less distortive.

Lastly, reducing reliance on indirect taxes can also help towards reducing inequality and poverty. Indirect taxes are regressive with respect to income given that they fall on the consumption of goods and services that make up a larger share of the budgets of poorer households than of wealthier households. Hence, greater reliance on indirect taxes may make the tax system more regressive. On the other hand, indirect taxes such as VAT may be the only way to finance government spending. However, as some countries lack the capacity to make transfer payments to households, there may be a case for differentiating VAT rates to tax necessities at a lower rate, if at all.

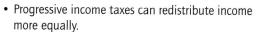

> **Recap**
>
> ## Taxation as a tool to reduce inequality and poverty
>
> - Progressive income taxes can redistribute income more equally.
> - A wealth tax can be used to redistribute wealth more equally.
> - Property taxes if increased and made more progressive can improve inequality.
> - Less reliance on indirect taxes can promote equity.

Further policies to reduce poverty, income and wealth inequality

Besides taxation, a government may also resort to the use of other policies. These include the following.

- **Policies to reduce inequalities of opportunities—investment in human capital.** Reducing inequalities of opportunities implies ensuring individuals' own background or circumstances—such as gender, ethnicity or parental status—are not allowed to limit the educational qualifications they can obtain, the type of job they can get and, in turn, their level of income. This can be achieved through improving the quality and access to education and health services for lower income groups. A healthier population with better education, training and skills will increase labour productivity and the income-earning capacity of the deprived, so they decrease income and wealth inequality.

- **Transfer payments.** These usually include pensions, unemployment and disability benefits as well as child and other allowances. These payments are made to the most vulnerable groups of the population using a part of the tax revenue collected from the working population, so they decrease income inequality.

It is important to note that there is a risk that the beneficiaries of such payments become overly dependent on them—but that may only necessitate that their design improves. For example, conditional cash transfers in Brazil have reduced the Gini coefficient from 0.62 to 0.49. These cash transfers are part of the Bolsa Familia programme that was initiated many years ago whereby a cash transfer is provided to poor mothers (as it has been shown that mothers are more likely than fathers to spend on the welfare of their children) under three conditions: their children have to attend school regularly, they have to be taken for regular medical check-ups and the mother has to attend neighbourhood nutrition and health classes. This programme managed to decrease the intergenerational transfer of poverty.

- **Targeted spending on goods and services.** The government can subsidize or directly provide services such as education and health care, and infrastructure in order to make them available to the most deprived groups. Examples include public health projects in rural villages and urban fringe areas, school lunches and pre-school nutritional supplementation programmes, and the provision of clean water and electrification to remote rural areas.

Often it is not sufficient that education is free of charge; poor rural families may need to keep their children at home to help in generating income so a cash subsidy may be necessary to induce them to send children to school; or it may not be sufficient to offer free vaccinations for children in remote villages. Esther Duflo (Nobel Prize, 2019) showed that the likelihood of mothers in Udaipur, India bringing their children to be vaccinated in a free immunization camp increased by six times if a 1 kilogram bag of lentils was also offered.

- **Universal basic income (UBI).** The UBI is a model for providing all citizens of a country or a geographic area with a given sum of money, regardless of their income, wealth or employment status. In its most common form, identical periodic payments are made to all individuals, which are funded through the taxes paid by those with higher incomes. The amount of money paid should be enough to take care of the individual's basic needs but not enough to provide a lot of add-ons. However, the UBI can be a huge draw on a government's funds, which could prevent its other priorities, such as infrastructure refurbishment or the building of hospitals or affordable housing. In June 2016 Switzerland's voters rejected such a plan.

- **Minimum wage policy.** The government can set or increase the minimum wage in order to support the incomes of low skilled workers. The result is that the minimum wage policy will benefit those workers, who will end up with a job at a higher wage. It may create unemployment. However, as mentioned in sections 2.7 and 3.3, research has shown that reasonable increases in the minimum wage have not led to higher unemployment and may even prompt greater effort on the part of workers.

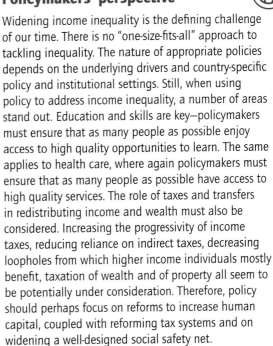

Policymakers' perspective

Widening income inequality is the defining challenge of our time. There is no "one-size-fits-all" approach to tackling inequality. The nature of appropriate policies depends on the underlying drivers and country-specific policy and institutional settings. Still, when using policy to address income inequality, a number of areas stand out. Education and skills are key—policymakers must ensure that as many people as possible enjoy access to high quality opportunities to learn. The same applies to health care, where again policymakers must ensure that as many people as possible have access to high quality services. The role of taxes and transfers in redistributing income and wealth must also be considered. Increasing the progressivity of income taxes, reducing reliance on indirect taxes, decreasing loopholes from which higher income individuals mostly benefit, taxation of wealth and of property all seem to be potentially under consideration. Therefore, policy should perhaps focus on reforms to increase human capital, coupled with reforming tax systems and on widening a well-designed social safety net.

3.5 Demand management (demand-side policies): monetary policy

Money, banking and monetary policy

In order to achieve policy objectives, policymakers use monetary, fiscal and supply-side policies. In this unit, each type of policy will be explained, their strengths and limitations will be examined and their effectiveness in achieving satisfactory growth, low unemployment, price stability and other objectives will be evaluated.

Figure 3.5.1 provides a "bird's eye view" of macroeconomic policies.

Demand-side policies aim at affecting aggregate demand. They are also referred to as short-run stabilization policies as they aim at stabilizing aggregate demand, and so the economy.

They include monetary policy and fiscal policy. Monetary policy is conducted by the central bank of the country and involves changes in the money supply or interest rates. Fiscal policy is conducted by the government and involves changes in the level of government expenditures and/or taxes.

Supply-side policies aim at increasing aggregate supply. They focus on the production side of the economy. They are often distinguished into market-based supply-side policies and interventionist policies. Fiscal and monetary policy may try to increase, but sometimes also to decrease, aggregate demand. Supply-side policies aim only to increase aggregate supply.

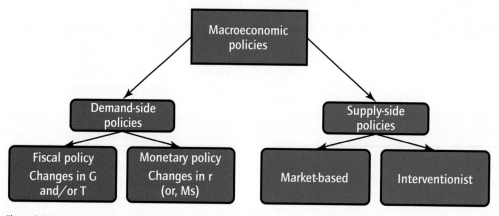

Figure 3.5.1 Macroeconomic policies

HL

Money

Money is defined as anything generally acceptable as a means of payment. If nothing serves this function, then it is a barter economy, where goods are exchanged for goods. Barter requires double coincidence of wants: if Joey wants to buy something that Jason is selling, Jason must want to buy something that Joey has and is willing to sell; otherwise the transaction will not take place. Individuals will therefore prefer to avoid specialization in order to minimize dependency on exchange. Introducing money permits specialization to take place and specialization expands dramatically the production possibilities of an economy.

In the past, various commodities had been generally accepted as a means of payment. For example, cattle, shells, salt and, of course, gold and silver coins were all used as money. Money had an intrinsic value. It had value independently of its value as a means of payment. At a later date, paper money was introduced that was backed by a commodity. This meant that one could always convert this paper money into something of value, such as gold or silver. Nowadays, money is "flat money". It has no intrinsic value, nor does it represent a claim on something else of value. It is backed by absolutely nothing. Flat money is considered money as a result of government decree. An Italian woman will accept a euro as a payment in the eurozone because

she knows that everyone else in the eurozone must also accept the euro when she wants to buy something.

So, what is generally acceptable as a means of payment? What is considered "money"? One can of course make a payment with notes and coins, so cash is definitely money. Payments can also be made by writing a cheque or by using your debit card linked to your bank account, so demand deposits (or cheque deposits or sight deposits) are also considered money. This means that the money supply of an economy must include currency in circulation and also demand deposits. This is a narrow definition of money.

However, it is now extremely easy to transfer funds from any savings account to a demand account. As a result, even though one cannot make a payment with a savings account, a broader definition of money includes what are often referred to as "near monies". Near monies are assets that can be quickly converted into cash or demand deposits. For our purposes we will consider as the money supply the currency in circulation and demand deposits.

The functions of money

What functions does money perform?

- Money is of course a "medium of exchange" as it is acceptable, by definition, as a means of payment in all market transactions.

- Money is a "unit of account". It is a yardstick used to express prices and so measure and compare values of goods and services.

- Money is a "store of value". It can be used to hold purchasing power and wealth over time. This is the first function of money that high inflation destroys.

- Money is also a "standard of deferred payment". Money links the past, the present and the future as it allows intertemporal contracts, which is just a way of saying that it permits people and firms to borrow and lend.

The banking system of a country

The banking system of a country comprises a central bank and commercial banks.

The functions of a central bank

- A central bank is the sole note-issuing authority of a country. Keep in mind though that the supply of notes is a small percentage of the money supply, which includes not just currency in circulation but mostly deposits that banks hold.

- It is the central bank that issues new government bonds, collects the proceeds and is also responsible for paying back bondholders when bonds mature.

- The central bank conducts monetary policy by influencing interest rates and bank lending practices. It is in charge of achieving and maintaining price stability, one of the most important macroeconomic goals.

- One of the central bank's responsibilities is exchange rate policy, which influences the competitiveness of a country's exports and the attractiveness of imports.

- The way in which commercial banks operate and behave is regulated and supervised by the central bank. Most importantly, the central bank makes sure that banks, in their quest for profits, do not engage in excessively risky lending as this could prove catastrophic for the whole banking system.

- The central bank is what is known as the "lender of last resort". Commercial banks must always have enough cash in their vaults to meet their cash obligations to depositors. The central bank is always ready to provide commercial banks with any required cash liquidity in case of a sudden emergency, to avoid a banking crisis.

Commercial banks and the fractional reserve system

Commercial banks are financial institutions that bring borrowers and lenders together. They collect deposits, for which they pay interest, and then use these to make loans, for which they charge interest. Their profitability thus largely depends on the difference between these two interest rates.

It is not necessary for a bank to keep in its vaults all of the funds deposited in it because it is highly unlikely that all depositors will want cash and withdraw all of their funds at the same time. On any day the amount of new deposits made will on average be roughly equal to the amount of money withdrawn. Most transactions (in terms of value) involve the transfer of funds, the electronic crediting of one account and the debiting of another bank account. A commercial bank will thus only be required to keep a *fraction* of the deposits it holds in the form of liquid assets, which can either be cash in its vault or deposits it holds at the central bank (as these can be converted into cash immediately).

The currency held by commercial banks in their vaults plus the deposits they keep at the central bank are referred to as bank reserves. The central bank determines the fraction of bank deposits that must be held as reserves by commercial banks and which cannot be lent out. This is referred to as the reserve requirement ratio (r_r). Excess reserves are the amount of reserves available for lending after required reserves are satisfied.

The process of money creation by commercial banks

Let's assume in the following example that the central bank has set r_r equal to 10%, or 0.10. What happens when Avinash decides to deposit $1,000 that he held in cash in the First National Bank? The money supply (currency in circulation plus demand deposits) has not changed because there will be $1,000 less of currency in circulation but $1,000 more in bank deposits.

Now though, First National Bank has $1,000 more in reserves. If the required reserve ratio is 10% it only needs to hold $100 in reserves (0.1 × 1000). The remaining $900 are "excess reserves". First National Bank can lend the $900 to Bob who uses the funds to pay for a new laptop. The seller of the laptop, Laptops R Us, will deposit the $900 to the Second National Bank.

The money supply has now increased. It is equal to the initial $1,000 that Avinash had as cash and was then converted into the demand deposit he has *plus* the $900 demand deposit of Laptops R Us in the Second National Bank, or $1,900.

The Second National Bank now has $900 additional reserves. It will keep $90 as required reserves (0.10 × 900) and will lend the remaining excess reserves of $810 to Carla, who will use the proceeds of the loan to buy a new cellphone from Best Cellphones. Then Best Cellphones will deposit the $810 to the Third National Bank. The money supply is now the initial $1,000 in Avinash's account plus the $1,810 in the accounts of Laptops R Us and Best Cellphones. The Third National Bank now has $810 of additional reserves of which 10% or $81 are required reserves and the remaining $729 are excess reserves. It can now lend out $729 to Daniel, who will use the loan to buy a Nakamura mountain bicycle from CrimsonBikes. CrimsonBikes will deposit the money in the Fourth National Bank, and the process will continue until no more lending can take place out of Avinash's original $1,000 deposit.

Commercial banks can thus lend and create money by the "stroke of a pen" or nowadays by the click of a mouse. Money is created when one bank's loan becomes another bank's deposit and that bank uses most of this deposit to make another loan. Table 3.5.1 shows the process.

Deposit	10% required Reserve ratio	Loans issued
$1,000	$100	$900
$900	$90	$810
$810	$81	$729
$729	$72.90	$656.10
$656.10	$65.61	$590.49
...	...	...
Total deposits	Total required reserves	Total loans issued
$10,000	$1,000	$9,000

Table 3.5.1 The money creation process

You may have noticed that, for simplicity, we are assuming the following.

• All currency is deposited in banks. The public holds no currency.

• Banks lend out all of their excess reserves.

If a bigger part of a loan is kept in cash and not deposited, or if banks decide to keep and not lend out all of their excess reserves, then the expansion of the money supply will be smaller.

The central bank can inject easily into the economy "fresh" reserves with tools we will examine later. If the required reserve ratio is r_r then simple mathematics reveals how much the money supply can increase from a $1,000 of "fresh" reserves (so $\Delta R = +1000$) entering the economy. Note that M_s below denotes the money supply and D denotes deposits while the Greek letter Δ denotes change, which in this case is an increase.

$$\Delta M_s = \Delta D = 1000 + 900 + 810 + 729 + ...$$

$$\Delta M_s = \Delta D = \Delta R + (1 - r_r)\Delta R + (1 - r_r)^2 \Delta R + (1 - r_r)^3 \Delta R + (1 - r_r)^4 \Delta R + ...$$

$$\Delta M_s = \Delta D = \Delta R \times [1 + (1 - r_r) + (1 - r_r)^2 + (1 - r_r)^3 + ...]$$

$$\Delta M_s = \Delta D = \Delta R \times \frac{1}{1 - (1 - r_r)} = \Delta R \times \left(\frac{1}{r_r}\right)$$

So, if the r_r is 10% then an increase by $1,000 in the banking reserves (the ΔR above) can increase demand deposits and the money supply by $10,000. The *money multiplier m* is equal to the inverse of the required reserve ratio r_r.

It follows that a fractional reserve banking system permits the money supply to grow many times more than the reserves in the banking system. This is the result of loans converted into deposits which allow more lending to take place and thus more deposits to be generated, and so on. It should also be clear that the central bank can affect the money supply by increasing or decreasing the amount of reserves commercial banks have available.

The demand for money

The term *demand for money* seems strange as most people would claim that the demand for money is infinite. Think of having $100 million of your own. Will you choose to hold this $100 million of your wealth as money stashed in your basement? In one year, you will still have $100 million. This would also be the case if you had your $100 million in a demand deposit (a cheque account or sight deposit) where in a year your balance will still be $100 million (as no, or extremely low, interest is paid on such deposits). If, though, instead you had bought a government bond then in a year's time you would have earned interest on your bond and your $100 million would have grown.

The term *demand for money* now has meaning. You demand money because you must be liquid enough to make transactions as you cannot go to the supermarket to buy groceries with a government bond. This is often referred to as the transactions motive for holding money. The higher the **nominal income** in a country, the more money will be demanded for transaction purposes. So, demand for money for transactions will increase if real GDP increases but also if the average price level increases.

However, there is an opportunity cost involved if you choose to hold money. You sacrifice the interest that you could have earned if instead you had chosen to hold a bond. There is a trade-off between the convenience of holding money that earns no interest, and sacrificing this convenience but earning interest. If Sammy is keeping funds in a demand deposit to take advantage of the convenience offered, he is foregoing the interest he would have earned by placing his funds in an interest-earning asset such as a bond. It follows that the demand for money decreases if interest rates increase.

Figure 3.5.2 shows what the above suggests—that the demand for money is negatively sloped if drawn against the interest rate (r) and that this money demand function will shift to the right if nominal income (money GDP) increases as at each interest rate people will want to hold more money.

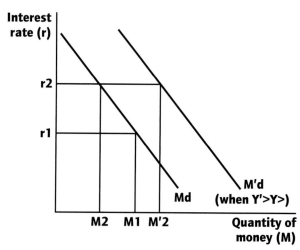

Figure 3.5.2 The demand for money

Given a level of nominal income (Y), demand for money is Md. If interest rates increase from r1 to r2 then demand for money will decrease from M1 to M2 as the opportunity cost of holding on to money balances is higher. There is a movement along the money demand function Md.

Now, if the average price level increases or real GDP increases then money income will increase from Y to Y'. At each level of interest rates, people will now need to hold more money for transactions. So, at r2, demand for money will be M'2, greater than M2. The money demand function has increased and shifted to the right from Md to M'd.

The supply of money

The supply of money is affected and determined by the central bank. We have established that if the central bank somehow changes bank reserves then the money supply will change. Even though commercial banks can also affect the money supply by altering how much they will choose to lend out after they satisfy the reserve requirement set by the central bank, we will choose for simplicity to consider the supply of money as determined only by the central bank and draw it vertical at some quantity of money (M) on the horizontal axis. This is shown in Figure 3.5.3.

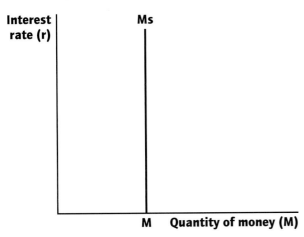

Figure 3.5.3 The supply of money

Determination of interest rates by the central bank

The equilibrium interest rate is determined in the money market by the interaction of the money demand curve and the money supply.

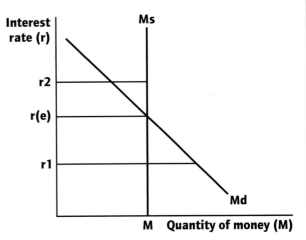

Figure 3.5.4 Equilibrium interest rate determination by the central bank

Assume that the central bank has set the money supply at Ms in order to achieve an equilibrium interest rate r(e). If the interest rate though is for some reason at r1, then the quantity of money demanded is greater than the quantity supplied. The public will try to switch from holding interest-bearing assets such as bonds into holding more money. As a result of the excess demand for money, the interest rate will increase to r(e) where the quantity of money demanded is equal to the quantity of money supplied by the central bank.

If the interest rate is at r2 then the quantity of money supplied by the central bank will exceed the quantity demanded at that interest rate. The public wants to hold more bonds and less money. The excess supply of money will decrease the interest rate to r(e) where money demanded is equal to money supplied.

Monetary policy

Monetary policy, as explained earlier, is a demand-side policy that is conducted by the central bank of a country. For example, in India it is conducted by the Central Bank of India, in China by the People's Bank of China, in Egypt by the Central Bank of Egypt, in New Zealand by the Reserve Bank of New Zealand, in the USA by the Federal Reserve Bank, in the UK by the Bank of England and in the eurozone by the European Central Bank. Most central banks are independent of the government, but their degree of independence varies. Monetary policy refers to changes in the money supply, and so interest rates, in order to affect aggregate demand.

Goals of monetary policy

• The single most important goal of monetary policy is to achieve and maintain price stability. A low and reasonably stable rate of inflation is necessary to avoid the adverse consequences explained earlier. Most central banks define price stability as inflation "below but close to 2%", even though a number of prominent economists consider that a slightly higher rate would for several reasons be preferable. Inflation close to 0% is not desired because, as explained earlier, the CPI tends to overestimate increases in the cost of living so there is a chance that if the measured inflation rate is close to zero, the economy may already be experiencing deflation. In addition, it is argued that a slightly higher than 2% inflation target gives central banks greater ability in a recession to decrease unemployment by cutting interest rates. Independently of the target rate of inflation set, a central bank must also ensure that it is stable through time.

• Many central banks have an explicit dual mandate not only to achieve and maintain price stability but also to pursue "maximum employment". More generally, signs of a recession and of a possible increase in unemployment instantly trigger a response by central banks. The possible trade-off between inflation and unemployment makes it difficult to achieve both goals. Central banks thus face a delicate balancing act. This is why it is argued that a slightly higher inflation rate target would help in achieving both goals.

- Monetary policy is used to minimize fluctuations in the business cycle. It has several advantages that permit central banks to act as "first responders" to any imminent risk of recession or to any inflationary pressures.

- Monetary policy, if successful, promotes a stable and less uncertain macroeconomic environment. If a low and stable rate of inflation is achieved and maintained, then the rate of investment spending in the economy will be higher. Higher long-term growth and so faster job creation will follow.

- Monetary policy influences the exchange rate of a currency. For example, a decrease in interest rates will (for reasons that will be explained) lead to depreciation of the currency, which will make exports cheaper abroad and

thus more competitive. This may be necessary if a country is to restore external balance as export revenues will tend to increase.

Recap

Goals of monetary policy

The goals of monetary policy are to:

- achieve and maintain price stability
- achieve high levels of employment
- stabilize economic activity
- promote a stable economic environment favourable to investment
- influence the exchange rate and achieve external balance.

HL

Tools of monetary policy

The central bank can change the money supply and affect the interest rate using the following tools.

The required reserve ratio (r₍ᵣ₎)

As explained earlier, in a fractional reserve banking system the commercial banks are required to hold reserves in the form of cash in their vaults or as deposits with the central bank. The minimum percentage of their demand (and other) deposits that they must keep as reserves is set by the central bank and is the required reserve ratio. Commercial banks can only lend out any excess reserves. If the central bank decreases the required reserve ratio then banks will have more excess reserves available and will be able to lend out more, so the money supply will increase. The money supply curve in Figure 3.5.3 will shift to the right. If the central bank increases the required reserve ratio then commercial banks will be able to lend out less so the money supply will decrease, and the money supply curve will shift to the left. Central banks rarely use the required reserve ratio as it would abruptly affect the profitability of commercial banks.

The discount rate

The discount rate is a special interest rate on loans that the central bank makes to commercial banks. It is also referred to as the refinancing rate or base rate. If a commercial bank is short of required reserves, it can always borrow from the central bank. If the discount rate is lowered commercial banks can, if necessary, obtain additional reserves by borrowing from the central bank. With additional reserves commercial banks can lend more, so the money supply increases. An increase in the discount rate discourages commercial banks from obtaining additional reserves through borrowing from the central bank. So, the central bank may raise the discount rate when it wants to restrict the money supply. The discount rate is not often used as a tool of monetary policy but in times of financial emergencies this special interest rate has been lowered to ease pressure on banks with bad loans.

Open market operations

Open market operations refer to the purchase or sales of outstanding short-term government bonds (bonds that mature in less than a year) from banks. The purchase of short-term government bonds increases the money supply, and the sale of government bonds decreases the money supply. Assume that the central bank decides to purchase $500 million of short-term government bonds from commercial banks. The central bank will pay commercial banks for these bonds by crediting the reserves that commercial banks maintain at the central bank. Commercial banks will thus be able to increase their lending. The money supply will increase. If the central bank wishes to decrease the money supply, it will sell short-term government bonds it owns to commercials banks. As a result, bank reserves with the central bank will fall, forcing banks to reduce their loans, and this leads to a decrease in the money supply. Note that open market operations are the principal tool of monetary policy that central banks use.

Quantitative easing

Lately, there is an additional tool that central banks in many countries have been using. Since the 2008–09 global financial crisis many central banks, including the US Federal Reserve, the Bank of England, the European Central Bank, the Bank of Japan and others, were forced to resort to a new unconventional type of open market operations that is known as quantitative easing.

Short-term interest rates were in many countries down to zero and central banks were faced with the zero lower bound (ZLB) problem. They could not decrease interest rates (much) below zero as people always have the option of holding cash. Further monetary easing thus became difficult.

Central banks responded by conducting large-scale purchases of a wide variety of longer-term assets that banks held that included long-term (5-year or 10-year) government bonds, mortgage loans owned by banks as well as a variety of other financial assets. The aim was to pump huge amounts of money into the banking system. Banks found themselves with a flood of non-interest earning reserves, forcing them to lend more aggressively.

Recap

Tools of monetary policy

Tools of monetary policy include:

- changes in the required reserve ratio (the proportion of deposits that cannot be lent out)
- changes in the discount rate (the interest rate central banks charge commercial banks in need of reserves)
- open market operations (purchases or sales of short-term government bonds that alter the reserves banks have)
- quantitative easing: purchases of long-term bonds and other assets by the central bank.

To **increase** money supply the central bank can:

- decrease the required reserve ratio
- decrease the discount rate
- buy short-term government bonds from commercial banks
- resort to QE which involves buying a wide array of many other longer-term financial assets from banks.

To **decrease** money supply, the central bank can:

- increase the required reserve ratio
- increase the discount rate
- sell short-term government bonds to commercial banks.

How does the central bank change interest rates?

If the goal of the central bank is to increase aggregate demand to fight off an imminent recession and a rise in unemployment, then expansionary (also referred to as easy or loose) monetary policy will be pursued. The central bank will decrease interest rates.

If the goal of the central bank is to decrease aggregate demand (or, better yet, to slow down its increase) in order to fight off inflationary pressures, then contractionary (also referred to as "tight") monetary policy will be pursued. The central bank will increase interest rates.

Figures 3.5.5 and 3.5.6 show how a central bank uses changes in the money supply to change the interest rate and thus achieve its goals.

Assume that the central bank wishes to lower interest rates from r1 to r2. In other words, assume that it has decided to pursue expansionary (that is, easier or looser) monetary policy. It will use its tools to increase the money supply from Ms1 to Ms2. It may decrease the required reserve ratio r_r or perhaps decrease the discount rate. Most probably though it will conduct open market purchases of outstanding (short-term) government bonds. Bank reserves will increase so that the money supply will increase to Ms2. At the original equilibrium interest rate r1, the supply of money exceeds the demand for money. There is excess supply of money in the money market, which will lower the interest rate to r2.

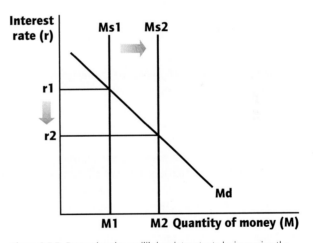

Figure 3.5.5 Decreasing the equilibrium interest rate by increasing the money supply

What if instead the central bank decided to pursue contractionary (tighter) monetary policy and thus wanted to increase the interest rate? It will use its tools to decrease the money supply. It may increase the required reserve ratio or increase the discount rate. Most probably though it will conduct open market sales of outstanding (short-term) government bonds. Bank reserves will decrease so that the money supply decreases from Ms1 to Ms2 in Figure 3.5.6. At the original equilibrium interest rate r1 the public will want to hold more money. The excess demand for money will increase the interest rate to r2.

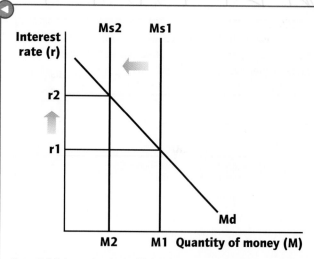

Figure 3.5.6 Increasing the equilibrium interest rate by decreasing the money supply

Effect of expansionary monetary policy on aggregate demand

What if an economy's growth is slowing down and policymakers fear a recession, or an economy is already experiencing recession? The central bank may use expansionary monetary policy, also referred to as "loose" or "easy" monetary policy, aiming at increasing aggregate demand and thus closing a recessionary (or, deflationary) gap. The central bank will decrease interest rates by increasing the money supply, typically through open market purchases of bonds. The resulting lower interest rate will increase consumption and investment expenditures as well as net exports. If C and I and NX increase, then AD will increase.

Lower interest rates will tend to increase consumption expenditures (C) for the following reasons.

- Lower interest rates decrease the cost of borrowing for households. Households borrow from banks to buy consumer durables such as cars and appliances but most importantly to buy a house. Borrowing will tend to increase and so household expenditures on durables and on houses are expected to increase. Aggregate demand will increase and shift to the right. The impact of lower interest rates on the housing market is considered the most significant route through which looser monetary policy increases aggregate demand.

- Lower interest rates decrease the incentive for households to save. If households save less, it means that they spend more. Consumption expenditures rise and aggregate demand increases and shifts to the right. This route is empirically rather insignificant.

Lower interest rates also increase investment expenditures (I) of firms for the following reasons.

- Typically, firms borrow to build new factories or to buy machines, tools and equipment. The cost of borrowing for firms will be lower so more investment projects will be considered profitable. Investment spending is expected to increase and since investment expenditures are a component of aggregate demand, aggregate demand increases and shifts to the right.

- Even if a firm uses its past profits to finance the purchase of capital goods and does not need to borrow from banks, if interest rates decrease then the opportunity cost of using these funds decreases, which will tend to increase investment spending.

Lower interest rates can also increase net exports (NX), as follows.

- A decrease in a country's interest rates implies a lower rate of return for financial investors who own bonds or have deposits in that country's currency. They will want to switch to financial assets of other countries where interest rates are higher. They will sell the currency to buy currencies of other countries. The increased supply of that country's currency in the foreign exchange market will decrease its value. However, depreciation of a currency makes exports cheaper abroad and thus more competitive. Exports will tend to increase and so aggregate demand will shift to the right. The impact of a change in interest rates and thus of the exchange rate on net exports is very important and will be fully explained later.

It follows that expansionary monetary policy will tend to increase consumption and investment expenditures as well as net exports, leading to an increase in aggregate demand.

In the Keynesian AD/AS diagram shown as Figure 3.5.7 an economy, as a result of a decrease in aggregate demand, is experiencing a recessionary (or deflationary) gap equal to Y'Yf. Aggregate demand has decreased, and equilibrium real GDP is at Y', way below the full employment level Yf. The economy is in recession and unemployment (cyclical) has increased.

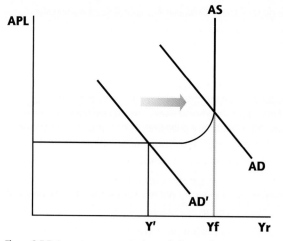

Figure 3.5.7 Impact on aggregate demand of expansionary monetary policy

The central bank, using its monetary policy tools, increases the money supply and decreases interest rates. Aggregate demand increases for the reasons explained above and shifts to the right from AD' to AD. The recessionary (or deflationary) gap is closed. The economy grew as real GDP increased from Y' to Yf and cyclical unemployment also decreased.

You should notice that as aggregate demand increases and the economy is approaching the full employment level of real output Yf, there may be pressure on the average price level to increase. The degree of any inflationary pressures depends on the shape of the aggregate supply curve.

A Monetarist/New Classical diagram can be used to show how expansionary monetary policy can increase aggregate demand and restore output back to its potential level and decrease unemployment back to the natural rate.

Effect of contractionary monetary policy on aggregate demand

What if an economy is experiencing inflationary pressures as a result of aggregate demand increasing too fast so that an inflationary gap arises? Policymakers will try to decrease inflation and restore price stability. They may use contractionary monetary policy, also referred to as tight monetary policy, aiming at decreasing aggregate demand or slowing down its increase. The central bank will increase interest rates by decreasing the money supply, typically through open market sales of bonds. The resulting higher interest rate will decrease consumption and investment expenditures as well as net exports. If C and I and NX decrease then AD will decrease.

Higher interest rates will tend to decrease consumption expenditures (C) for the following reasons.

- Higher interest rates increase the cost of borrowing for households so borrowing will tend to decrease and household expenditures on durables and on houses are expected to decrease. Aggregate demand will decrease and shift to the left. The impact of higher interest rates on the housing market is considered the most significant route through which tighter monetary policy decreases aggregate demand.

- Higher interest rates increase the incentive for households to save. If households save more, it means that they will spend less. Consumption expenditures fall and aggregate demand decreases and shifts to the left.

Higher interest rates also decrease investment expenditures (I) of firms for the following reasons.

- The cost of borrowing for firms increases so fewer investment projects will be considered profitable. Investment spending is expected to decrease and since investment expenditures are a component of aggregate demand, aggregate demand decreases and shifts to the left.

- Even if a firm uses its past profits to finance the purchase of capital goods and does not need to borrow from banks, if interest rates increase then the opportunity cost of using these funds increases, which will tend to decrease investment spending.

Higher interest rates can also decrease net exports (NX) as follows.

- An increase in a country's interest rates implies a higher rate of return for financial investors who own bonds or have deposits in that country's currency. They will want to buy that currency to buy bonds or make deposits in that country's currency. The increased demand for that country's currency in the foreign exchange market will increase its value. However, appreciation of a currency makes exports more expensive abroad and thus less competitive. Exports will tend to decrease and so aggregate demand will shift to the left.

It follows that contractionary (tighter) monetary policy will tend to decrease consumption and investment expenditures as well as net exports, leading to a decrease in aggregate demand.

In the Monetarist/New Classical AS/SRAS/LRAS diagram shown in Figure 3.5.8, an economy is experiencing an inflationary gap equal to YpY' as a result of an increase in aggregate demand from AD to AD'.

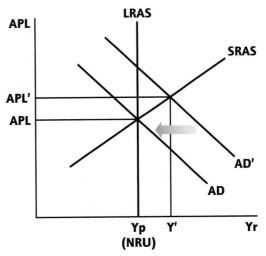

Figure 3.5.8 Impact on aggregate demand of contractionary monetary policy

Real GDP has increased above its potential level Yp and the average price level is rising from APL to APL'. The central bank, using its tools, decreases the money supply and increases interest rates. Aggregate demand decreases for the reasons explained earlier and shifts to the left from AD' to AD. The inflationary gap is closed.

A Keynesian AD/AS diagram can also be used to illustrate that tighter monetary policy will decrease aggregate demand and manage to eliminate inflationary pressures. However, both the Keynesian and the Monetarist diagrams must be interpreted loosely as the vertical axis denotes the average price level. The decrease in aggregate demand is not aimed at creating deflation but at lowering inflation.

Recap

Expansionary and contractionary monetary policy

- Expansionary monetary policy (easy; loose)

    $M_s\uparrow \rightarrow r\downarrow \rightarrow C\uparrow$ and $I\uparrow$ and $NX\uparrow \rightarrow AD\uparrow$

- Contractionary monetary policy (tight)

    $M_s\downarrow \rightarrow r\uparrow \rightarrow C\downarrow$ and $I\downarrow$ and $NX\downarrow \rightarrow AD\downarrow$

The real interest rate

The interest rates that banks quote for different types of deposits or for different types of loans are referred to as nominal interest rates. For example, if on a savings account the bank advertises a 4% annual interest rate, that is the nominal interest rate of the deposit. It means that if you deposit $200 you will get back in a year $208. If, though, inflation during that same year was at 4%, it means that the $208 that you will get back in a year will be able to buy the same amount of goods and services as the $200 could buy when you deposited the money. You received nothing extra. The real interest rate was 0%.

The real interest rate is more generally the nominal interest rate minus the (expected) rate of inflation:

$$r_r = r_n - \hat{p}$$

where r_r is the real interest rate, r_n is the nominal interest rate and $\hat{p}$ is the (expected) rate of inflation.

For our purposes we can simplify and remember that:

real interest rate = (nominal interest rate − inflation rate)

So, if nominal interest rate on a savings account is 2.25% annually, and inflation is 1.5% then the real rate of interest is 0.75%. If inflation was higher at 3.20% then the real interest rate would be −0.95%. In other words, you get less back in a year in real terms than what you had deposited. You will be able to buy fewer goods than what you were able to buy last year.

Now let the nominal interest rate on a car loan be at 0.50%. Further assume that there is deflation in the economy, so that the inflation rate is negative 1.50%. The real interest rate is:

$$0.50 - (-1.50) = +2.00\%.$$

So, very low nominal interest rates in a deflationary world that try to induce more borrowing and spending by households and firms lead to a *higher* real interest rate paid. This decreases the incentive to borrow and spend. Monetary policy is ineffective if there is deflation in an economy.

Remember: if there is inflation in an economy then the real interest rate is lower than the nominal interest rate and may even be negative. This benefits borrowers and penalizes savers. In contrast, if there is deflation in an economy then real interest rates are higher than nominal interest rates, which rewards saving and penalizes borrowing. Think whether this holds if nominal interest rates could be negative.

Effectiveness of monetary policy

Advantages

Monetary policy is the main choice for stabilizing an economy. It is considered the "first responder" when either a recessionary gap or an inflationary gap arises. Fiscal policy is also a demand-side policy and has been used to stabilize economic activity but certain advantages that characterize monetary policy render it the preferred tool for policymakers. Strengths of monetary policy include the following.

- It is flexible. Monetary policy can respond quickly to changing economic conditions. Monetary policy committees meet very often to decide on interest rate policy. Most central banks meet between six to eight times per year and they may even hold emergency meetings.

- It is incremental. A central bank can increase or decrease interest rates in a series of steps by 0.25% at a time. So, credit conditions can be tightened or loosened gradually.

- It is reversible. If it becomes clear to the central bank that interest rates increased or decreased more than necessary, it can easily reverse course.

- Central banks are typically independent from the government. This insulates them from political pressure in their monetary policy decision-making. In several cases though, politicians have tried to force central bankers to decrease interest rates at levels too low to be consistent with stable inflation in order to maximize their re-election chances. In 2018 President Trump openly criticized the US Central Bank for raising interest rates and later for not cutting rates more quickly. The degree of independence of central banks varies across countries.

- Monetary policy, just like fiscal policy, is characterized by time lags. Time lags weaken the effectiveness of demand-side policies. Time lags can be distinguished into these three types.

  - The detection or recognition lag. This is the time it takes for policymakers to realize that there is an economic problem they should deal with. It takes time to collect and process data. This lag is the same for both monetary policy and fiscal policy.

  - The administrative or implementation lag. This is the time it takes policymakers to decide on the appropriate policy response. This is much shorter for monetary policy. A central bank can decide much faster on a change in interest rates. It takes a lot longer for a government to change government expenditures and/or taxes as any change will also have to be approved by a long legislative political process, which can last months.

  - The impact or execution lag. This is somewhat shorter for monetary policy as some borrowing and spending decisions may change fast. Still, it may take months for an interest rate change to have full impact on the economy.

Overall, monetary policy faces shorter time lags and it is thus less likely to destabilize the economy. This is an additional extremely important argument in favour of using monetary policy as the preferred policy response for short run stabilization.

Disadvantages

Monetary policy faces certain significant constraints.

- Monetary policy may be very effective in reducing inflation but is less effective in fighting a recession. Lower interest rates affect spending by households and firms indirectly. The cost of borrowing decreases and this should induce households and firms to borrow more and so spend more. What if consumer and business confidence is very low though? What if the recession is deep and people and firms feel pessimistic, insecure and uncertain about their financial future? There is no guarantee they will decide that now is the right time to buy a house or a new car, if they fear losing their job. It is also unlikely that a firm will decide to expand during a severe downturn. In addition, banks may be reluctant to lend money, fearing that the loans they make will not be paid back. Monetary policy is like a string: you can pull it but you cannot push it.

- There is limited scope of reducing interest rates to help an economy avoid or exit a recession or deflation when they are already close to zero. This problem of monetary policy is referred to as the zero lower bound (ZLB) constraint.

Recap

Advantages and disadvantages of monetary policy

Advantages

- Monetary policy is flexible.
- It is incremental.
- It is reversible.
- It is independent (typically) of the government.
- It has shorter time lags than fiscal policy.

Disadvantages

- If confidence levels are low, monetary policy may prove ineffective.
- When nominal interest rates are close to zero there is not much room to lower them more (the ZLB problem).

Are negative interest rates possible?

Negative interest rates imply that depositors would pay to hold money in bank accounts, which is unlikely as they could just withdraw their funds and keep the cash. Even though the idea is strange, negative interest rates have lately been used. How did we get here?

To fight the 2008–09 global financial crisis, central banks decreased interest rates close to zero. Low borrowing and spending continued, though, and growth was still weak with inflation below the 2% target. This persistently low growth is referred to as *secular stagnation*, a term introduced by Harvard economist Lawrence Summers. Central banks have responded with quantitative easing, which was explained earlier. However, some also began to introduce negative interest rates on any excess reserves that commercial banks held with accounts at the central bank. The goal was to prevent banks for hoarding the cash inflows from the quantitative easing programmes and to encourage banks to lend more aggressively. Denmark's Central Bank and the ECB were first, followed by the Swiss, the Swedish and Hungary's central banks. Slightly negative interest rates were also introduced on certain accounts by some commercial banks and there were no widespread withdrawals, probably because the convenience and safety of a bank account outweighed the cost of paying instead or earning interest.

To move from mildly negative interest rates to "unconstrained negative interest rate policy" is not an easy task and it is also risky. It would require phasing out large denomination notes as well as changes in the legal, regulatory and tax framework. In a country suffering from deflation, though, it could provide the monetary stimulus required.

Policymakers' perspective

The advantages of monetary policy have made it the preferred policy choice to help stabilize an economy. Inflationary pressures are dealt with by the central bank, notching up interest rates to reduce consumer and business spending. Recessions have led to central banks decreasing interest rates to encourage borrowing and spending and stimulate the economy. However, the extremely low interest rates prevailing in many economies since the 2008–09 global financial crisis have left little room for central banks to conduct expansionary monetary policy and fight a severe recession or deflation. Negative interest rates and discussion of the necessary legal and regulatory changes now seem to be the issues for policymakers in an attempt to circumvent the zero lower bound (ZLB) problem they face.

3.6 Demand management (demand-side policies): fiscal policy

Fiscal policy

Fiscal policy is also a demand-side policy. It refers to changes in the level of government expenditures (G) and/or in (direct) taxes (T) in order to affect aggregate demand and so real output (growth), the level of employment and inflation.

Government expenditures

- Capital expenditures—which is really another name for public investments—include spending on infrastructure such as harbours, roads and highways, airports, telecommunication networks, electricity grids, water and sanitation networks, schools and hospitals.

- Current expenditures—these include salaries of public sector employees but also expenditures on public school and hospital supplies as well as subsidies. Interest payments made to owners of government debt are also included.

- Transfer payments—these include pensions, unemployment benefits and other cash transfers. Note that these expenditures are not included in GDP as they do not represent a contribution to current production.

Government revenues

Government revenues are mostly from taxes, direct and indirect. Revenues also include one-off receipts from the sale of state-owned assets (for example, firms, ports and airports) to the private sector (privatizations) as well as any profits collected from the goods and services that state-owned enterprises sell.

Terminology

If government expenditures (G) exceed tax revenues (T) in any given year, then the government is running a budget deficit.

If tax revenues (T) exceed government spending (G) in any given year, then the government is running a budget surplus.

If government expenditures (G) are equal to tax revenues (T) then the budget is balanced.

A budget deficit needs to be financed. The government finances a budget deficit by borrowing. It issues bonds that it sells to the general public. If you buy a government bond you are effectively lending money to the government. The government will pay you at a specified future date the principal plus interest. In this way, a budget deficit adds to the public debt whereas a budget surplus decreases the public debt.

Goals of fiscal policy

- Fiscal policy is considered a Keynesian-inspired demand management policy. It is the name of John Maynard Keynes that is associated with the idea of government intervention using fiscal tools; that is, government expenditures and taxes to help an economy restore full employment. It follows that perhaps the single most important goal of fiscal policy is to lift an economy from recession, especially a deep one. Fiscal policy is then the preferred policy choice to close a large recessionary or deflationary gap because of the ineffectiveness of monetary policy in such a situation.

- Fiscal policy is also adopted to decrease cyclical unemployment. If fiscal policy manages to lift an economy

from a recession it means that more jobs are created, so more people are employed.

- Fiscal policy can also be used to decrease inflation. Remember though that achieving and maintaining price stability is the responsibility of the central bank so tighter monetary policy is typically the preferred policy choice. However, policymakers will also use fiscal policy if inflation is the result of profligate government spending.

- Faster long-term growth may also result if fiscal policy is "prudent" which really means that large deficits are avoided, and the national debt does not increase to unsustainable levels. Why? Businesses feel less uncertain about the future so they are more willing to invest. They are less fearful of a need in the future to raise taxes or of interest rates rising (this is the "crowding out" idea, explained in the HL section on page 126).

- Fiscal policy may also reduce the short-term fluctuations of the business cycle. Automatic stabilizers (a type of fiscal policy explained in the HL section on page 126), are built-in fiscal characteristics that most economies have. These stabilizers help to protect an economy from short-term fluctuations in the business cycle.

- If the government expenditures are capital expenditures (that is, public investments) that increase or improve the available infrastructure, not only will aggregate demand and so real GDP increase in the short term but long-term growth will also accelerate. It is claimed that lower income and corporate taxes increase the incentive to work and to invest and so they may also accelerate growth, but there is scant evidence to support this claim.

- Fiscal policy can also be used to narrow income inequality in a country through cash transfers and more progressive taxation in the short term and through investments in education and health in the long term.

- Fiscal policy can also be used to decrease trade imbalances.

Recap

Goals of fiscal policy

Fiscal policy can:

- lift an economy from recession
- lower (cyclical) unemployment
- decrease inflation
- promote a stable macroeconomic environment that accelerates growth
- reduce business cycle fluctuations
- decrease income inequality
- decrease trade imbalances.

Fiscal policy in action

The government can increase government expenditures and/or decrease taxes to increase aggregate demand. It can also decrease government expenditures and/or increase taxes to decrease aggregate demand. These decisions describe what is referred to as "discretionary" fiscal policy. It is at the discretion of the government to decide how much to spend and/or to tax. The government "does" something. We will examine first how this kind of discretionary fiscal policy works and then (HL) we will also examine fiscal policy that could be described as "on automatic pilot" as it is conducted through the use of automatic stabilizers.

Expansionary fiscal policy

Expansionary fiscal policy increases aggregate demand and shifts the AD curve to the right, as in Figure 3.6.1. The goal is to lift an economy from recession. By increasing aggregate demand, expansionary fiscal policy closes a deflationary (recessionary) gap. The government will increase government expenditures (G) and/or decrease taxes (T).

If government expenditures (G) increase, then aggregate demand will *directly* increase as government expenditures (G) are a component of aggregate demand. Interestingly, the resulting increase in real GDP will be greater than the increase in government expenditures. Why? It is due to the work of the multiplier effect (HL), explained on page 126.

If taxes (T) decrease, then disposable incomes (Yd) of households increase. Remember that disposable income is defined as income minus direct taxes plus transfer payments. With higher disposable incomes, people will tend to spend more, increasing consumption expenditures (C) and thus aggregate demand. Also, if corporate taxes decrease then the resulting higher profitability that firms will enjoy may lead to an increase in investment spending (I) which also increases aggregate demand as I is also a component. Note that we are referring here to changes in direct taxation.

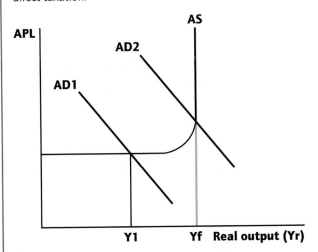

Figure 3.6.1 Expansionary fiscal policy closing a deflationary gap using a Keynesian diagram

In the Keynesian diagram shown in Figure 3.6.1 aggregate demand increases from AD1 to AD2 because government expenditures increased and/or because direct taxes decreased. As a result of aggregate demand increasing, equilibrium real output (Yr) increases from Y1 towards the potential (full employment) level of real output Yf (or Yp). The deflationary gap decreases and may even close. Unemployment (cyclical) in the economy also decreases.

We should note a few things here. As it should be clear from Figure 3.6.1, the increase in aggregate demand resulting from expansionary fiscal policy may also result to an increase in the average price level or, in other words, may lead to some inflation. This risk is lower if the economy is operating on the horizontal section of the Keynesian AS curve. Any increase in aggregate demand will prove less inflationary if there is still spare capacity in the economy.

Also, expansionary fiscal policy may actually aim at generating some inflation. This could be the case if the economy is on the verge of or already suffers from deflation. Given that monetary policy is ineffective if interest rates are very low and an even greater policy problem exists if there is deflation, expansionary fiscal has been used by policymakers to achieve higher inflation.

A Monetarist/New Classical AD/SRAS/LRAS diagram can also be used to show how a deflationary gap could be closed even though, if we rely on the extreme interpretation of the Monetarist/New Classical school, there is really no need for policymakers to intervene to close a deflationary gap. Market forces alone in the long run, namely the assumed decrease of money wages, guarantee that the economy will return to its potential output.

Contractionary fiscal policy

Contractionary fiscal policy decreases aggregate demand and shifts the AD curve to the left as in Figure 3.6.2. The goal is to decrease inflationary pressures and close an inflationary gap.

The government will decrease government expenditures (G) and/or increase taxes (T). If government expenditures (G) decrease, then aggregate demand will *directly* decrease as government expenditures (G) are a component of aggregate demand.

If taxes (T) increase, then the disposable income (Y_d) of households decreases. With lower disposable incomes, people will tend to spend less, decreasing consumption expenditures (C) and so aggregate demand. Also, if corporate taxes increase then the resulting lower profitability that firms will experience may lead to a decrease in investment spending (I) which also decreases aggregate demand.

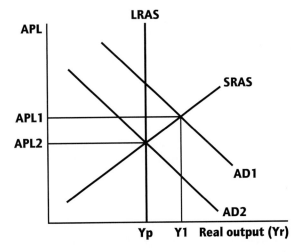

Figure 3.6.2 Contractionary fiscal policy closing an inflationary gap using a Monetarist diagram

In the Monetarist/New Classical diagram Figure 3.6.2, (note that a Keynesian diagram could also be used), an inflationary gap equal to (YpY1) exists. Contractionary fiscal policy will decrease aggregate demand from AD1 to AD2 because government expenditures decreased and/ or because direct taxes increased. As a result of aggregate demand decreasing, the average price level decreases from APL1 to APL2 and the inflationary gap (YpY1) closes or at least decreases. Within this Monetarist/New Classical framework, unemployment increases and returns to its natural rate. Within a broader analytical framework, contractionary fiscal that decreases aggregate demand to relieve an economy from inflationary pressures leads to an increase in cyclical unemployment.

However, both the Keynesian and the Monetarist diagrams must be interpreted slightly loosely as the vertical axis denotes the average price level but the resulting decrease in aggregate demand does not create deflation, it lowers inflation. Only a severe decrease in government spending (G) and an increase in taxes could lead to deflation. This was the case when Greece agreed with its creditors to implement austerity, which simply means to cut spending and to increase taxes, during its debt crisis. An interesting twist to contractionary fiscal policy was proposed by a few economists and is worth mentioning. They argued that decreasing government spending (but not increasing taxes) and trying to control widening budget deficits will increase business confidence, so it will foster investment

and accelerate growth. This idea became is referred to as "expansionary fiscal contraction" but most economist criticize it, claiming that the alleged "confidence fairy" doesn't exist.

It is perhaps necessary to make two more points. Contractionary fiscal policies, whenever applied, rarely include a tax increase. The reason is that politicians are worried that a tax rise will decrease their re-election chances. More generally, changing taxes is not considered prudent because firms and households require a degree of certainty regarding their future tax obligations.

Recap

Expansionary and contractionary fiscal policy

Expansionary fiscal policy:
$$G\uparrow \rightarrow AD\uparrow$$
$$T\downarrow \rightarrow Yd\uparrow \rightarrow C\uparrow \rightarrow AD\uparrow$$
Contractionary fiscal policy:
$$G\downarrow \rightarrow AD\downarrow$$
$$T\uparrow \rightarrow Yd\downarrow \rightarrow C\downarrow \rightarrow AD\downarrow$$

HL

The Keynesian multiplier

The term *multiplier* was introduced by JM Keynes and his student RF Kahn. It is often referred to as the Keynesian multiplier and it helps explain why expansionary fiscal policy in the form of increased government expenditures (G) is considered a very powerful tool to lift an economy out of a deep recession. The Keynesian multiplier states that an increase in government expenditures G will lead to a greater increase in national income Y:

$$\Delta Y > \Delta G$$

where ΔY is the resulting change in national income and ΔG is the change in government expenditures. This means that the change in national income Y will be "k" times the change in government expenditures, or:

$$\Delta Y = k\Delta G \text{ where k is the multiplier.}$$

So, if for example the government decides to increase government expenditures by $100 million and national income increases by $240 million then the multiplier, namely k, would be equal to 2.4:

$$240 = 2.4 \times 100$$

Why is that the case? The idea of the multiplier rests on the fact that one person's spending is automatically someone else's additional income, which in turn leads to additional spending that generates additional income and so on. Economic activity takes place in successive "rounds", as clearly illustrated by the circular flow model (see section 1.1, page 5).

An example will help to clarify the point. Assume that the government decides to increase expenditures by $100 million and hires unemployed workers to dig holes and bury

bottles, and other unemployed workers to dig the bottles up. National income has directly increased by $100 million, the income that these workers earned for the service they produced. Spending by the government is income for the workers. Economic activity will not stop there, though. There is a 2nd and a 3rd and an nth round that follow. Why? These workers will spend part of this additional income on domestic goods and services that others produce, and the process will continue. Note that the additional spending in each round creates additional demand, which leads to additional output (GDP) produced. If, for example, all workers hired by the government spend part of the additional income earned on domestically produced milk and all milk producers spend part of the additional income they earned on haircuts, then the economy's income will have increased and in addition more milk and more haircuts will have been produced. Remember that income and production are identically equal.

The size of the multiplier depends on the proportion of the additional income earned that is spent on domestic goods and services. The additional spending on domestic goods and services resulting from additional income earned has a name—it is called marginal propensity to consume (MPC).

$$MPC = \frac{\Delta C_d}{\Delta Y}$$

If for example, you spend $100 on a haircut and the hairdresser spends $80 of these dollars on domestically produced cheese, then the MPC is:

$$\frac{+80}{+100} = 0.8$$

If, though, 80 additional dollars were spent on domestic goods and services, where did the remaining $20 go? It is useful to remind ourselves again of the circular flow. We have defined withdrawals (leakages) as income not spent on domestic goods and services. It follows that part of these $20 (say $8) were saved, part was paid to the government as taxes (say $7) and part was spent but on foreign goods and services; that is, on imports (say $5). These are the withdrawals, namely savings (S), taxes (T) and import expenditures (M).

Some definitions of terms used below are:

• the marginal propensity to save (MPS)—the additional savings from additional income earned

• the marginal propensity to tax (MPT, also referred to as the marginal rate of tax)—the additional taxes paid from additional income earned

• the marginal propensity to import (MPM)—the additional spending on imports from additional income.

Using these definitions and the numbers in the example above:

$$MPS = \frac{\Delta S}{\Delta Y} = \frac{+8}{+100} = 0.08$$

$$MPT = \frac{\Delta T}{\Delta Y} = \frac{+7}{+100} = 0.07$$

$$MPM = \frac{\Delta M}{\Delta Y} = \frac{+5}{+100} = 0.05$$

It can be shown (see "Optional material", page 131) that the multiplier k is equal to:

$$k = \frac{1}{(MPS + MPT + MPM)} \text{ or } \frac{1}{MPW}$$

$$\text{which is equal to } \frac{1}{(1 - MPC_d)}$$

where MPW is the marginal propensity to withdraw, which is equal to the sum of the MPS, the MPT and the MPM. MPW is also found by subtracting from each additional dollar earned all that is spent on domestic goods and services; that is, MPW = $(1 - MPC_d)$.

It should be realized that the multiplier k is greater:

(a) the greater the MPC_d and (b) the smaller the marginal propensity to withdraw.

This makes sense if you check the circular flow: an increase in government expenditures will go around the circular flow of income many times (as your spending is someone else's income) but each time a fraction of the income generated leaks out of the flow because some will be saved, paid in taxes or spent but on imports. The size of the increase in national income that will result is greater, the bigger the part that is spent on domestic output or, equivalently, the smaller the part that is withdrawn.

There are a few points to keep in mind.

• The multiplier also works in reverse: if the government expenditures decrease, then national income (GDP) will decrease by more. This was the case in Greece a number of years ago when it agreed to cut government expenditures (G) drastically in order to receive the necessary bailout loans. Greece's GDP decreased by more

as a result of the multiplier. Interestingly, the IMF, one of Greece's creditors, had underestimated the size of the Greek expenditure multiplier, so the ensuing recession proved much deeper than expected. The IMF's chief economist at the time, Olivier Blanchard, acknowledged the error and published a revised estimate.

• Any change in any injection will initiate a multiplier process. In other words, GDP will change more not only if government expenditures (G) change, but also if investment expenditures (I) or exports (X) change. Again, this can be easily visualized using the circular flow of income illustration. Remember that injections, which are considered autonomous expenditures as they do not depend on domestic income, include G, but also I and X.

• The formulas to remember for simple exercises related to the multiplier are these two:

(a) $\Delta Y = k\Delta J$, where J symbolizes injections and can be G or I or X

(this relationship has three elements, ΔY, k and ΔJ, so if any two are given, you can solve for the third)

(b) $k = \frac{1}{MPW}$ or $\frac{1}{(1 - MPC_d)}$

(here, each relationship has two elements so if either is given, you can solve for the other).

• If in an exercise there is no government or, if it is referred to as a "closed" economy, it means that this economy has no taxes and/or no imports as withdrawals so its multiplier will be greater (the denominator, MPW, will be smaller).

To illustrate the multiplier, it is probably preferable to choose a Keynesian AS curve as the idea of the multiplier effect is indeed Keynesian. It is also preferable to assume an economy in equilibrium at a level of income (of GDP) way below the full employment level (at Y1 in Figure 3.6.3) so that there is a sizable deflationary gap (equal to Y1Yf). To illustrate the increase in government spending reflecting the expansionary fiscal policy chosen to close this gap, draw a new aggregate demand curve (AD2) somewhat to the right of the initial one and then, to illustrate the idea of the multiplier, draw a third AD3 even further to the right at AD3.

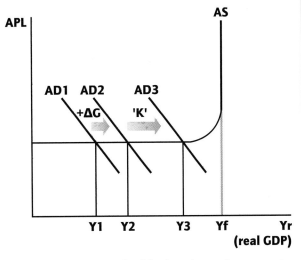

Figure 3.6.3 The multiplier effect following an increase in government expenditures (G)

Expansionary fiscal policy, namely the increase in government expenditures by ΔG, managed to decrease the recessionary (deflationary) gap from Y1Yf to Y3Yf, approaching full employment real GDP at Yf.

A 2020 paper by C Bayer and others estimated that following the massive March 2020 $2 trillion US stimulus response to the Covid-19 pandemic, the multiplier could be as high as 2. Following the 2009 Obama Stimulus Plan, which increased government expenditures in the USA by $787 billion to lift the US economy from recession, Christina Romer, then Chair the Council of Economic Advisers, estimated the US multiplier at 1.6, which meant that the US real GDP was expected to increase as a result by roughly $1.26 trillion. The size of the Keynesian multiplier depends on certain characteristics of an economy, for example on the degree of openness to international trade or on the debt–GDP ratio. In a more "open" economy imports, a withdrawal, will be greater. Characteristics vary across countries and through time, making it difficult to estimate the expenditure multiplier.

> ### Recap
> #### Keynesian multiplier
>
> - A change in any injection (G, I or X) will lead to a greater change in national income (GDP).
>
> - This is because one's spending is someone else's income, which leads to more spending and more income generation.
>
> - The size of the multiplier effect depends on the proportion of any additional income spent on domestic output. Or, equivalently, it depends on the proportion saved, paid in taxes or spent but on imports.
>
> - Since the multiplier is equal to $\frac{1}{MPW}$ it follows that the smaller the withdrawals in an economy, the greater the multiplier.

What are automatic stabilizers?

As explained earlier, discretionary fiscal policy involves the deliberate change by the government of government expenditures and/or of taxes. However, politicians may not move quickly enough to cut taxes or increase expenditures to mitigate the effects of a recession. Fortunately, most economies are equipped with automatic stabilizers. Automatic stabilizers are institutional features built into the budget of a country, such as the existence of unemployment benefits and of progressive income taxes, that reduce the ups and downs of the business cycle automatically.

> A tax is a progressive tax if higher incomes not only pay more but pay *proportionately* more, so that as income rises, progressive taxes rise faster. For example, if Brody earns $10,000 per year and pays $2,000 in income tax while Carrie earns $20,000 per year and pays $5,000 then Brody pays 20% of his income in taxes but Carrie pays 25% of her income in taxes. (For a full explanation see section 3.4, page 105.)

If an economy is entering recession, economic activity starts to decrease as some firms shrink in size while others shut down. People will be made redundant. Automatic stabilizers decrease the financial pain to households because they will owe less in taxes and they will be eligible to collect unemployment benefits. All this is accomplished automatically, without the need for the government to design and enact new laws. Their incomes (that is, wage earnings) may drop to zero as they lose their jobs but their *disposable incomes* (Yd) do not, because unemployment benefits automatically start and their tax burden will also be lower. Automatic stabilizers do not only help households in distress but also the economy as they stimulate aggregate demand when the economy is in great need for a boost. Consumption expenditures will decrease by less due to the effect on disposable income of automatic stabilizers and so will aggregate demand. The downturn will not be as severe. It will be milder.

In contrast, if the economy and incomes are growing too fast and there is increased risk of overheating and inflation, disposable incomes will rise but at a slower rate than incomes because of income taxes being progressive and thus rising faster than incomes. So, consumption expenditures will increase but at a slower rate and so will aggregate demand. The boom will be milder. Inflationary pressures will decrease. Automatic stabilizers smoothen the ups and downs of the business cycle without requiring legislative action. They are especially useful in a recession as they respond quickly.

Beyond responding quickly, automatic stabilizers also have a sizable impact on the economy. For example, the Obama Stimulus package was enacted in February 2019, five quarters *after* the start of the US recession—but by that time, spending by automatic stabilizers had already grown to almost 2% of the US potential GDP.

Recently, several economists are proposing to increase the size and scope of automatic stabilizers. For example, they propose offering lump-sum payments to households when unemployment increases by more than 0.5% compared to last year's low or introducing "shovel ready" local projects such as construction of additional schools that would automatically happen at the start of a recession without the need for action by the government.

> ### Recap
> #### Automatic stabilizers
>
> - Automatic stabilizers, which exist in most economies, are institutionally built-in characteristics that mitigate the short-term fluctuations of GDP.
>
> - Automatic stabilizers include unemployment benefits and progressive taxes.
>
> - As soon as an economy enters recession, tax burdens decrease and unemployment benefits are claimed.
>
> - Without any need for the government to act, disposable incomes and consumption decrease by less and the downturn is milder.
>
> - If an economy is growing too fast, progressive income taxes guarantee that disposable incomes and spending rise slower.

- Without any need for the government to act, aggregate demand rises slower; this slows down growth and reduces the risk of inflationary pressures.

What is the "crowding-out" effect?

If the government increases government expenditures (G) it will need to somehow finance these expenditures. It could increase taxes but if the goal is to increase aggregate demand that would defeat the purpose. Instead, it will prefer to resort to "deficit spending" and borrow the money from anyone willing to lend it. The government will turn to the loanable funds market, the market where those who want to borrow money (firms and households) and those who are willing to lend money (the savers) get together. Their interaction determines the interest rate for loanable funds.

In Figure 3.6.4a, demand for loanable funds D(LF)1 is downward sloping because at lower interest rates more investment projects will be profitable so firms will want to borrow more. Supply of loanable funds S(LF) is upward sloping because higher interest rates make saving and lending more attractive. The interest rate at which the demand for loanable funds D(LF)1 is equal to the supply of loanable funds S(LF) in Figure 3.6.4a is the interest rate in the loanable funds market. This is at r1.

Assume now that the government decides to employ expansionary fiscal policy in order to increase aggregate demand and that it increases government expenditures. As explained above, the government will need to finance these expenditures and will enter the loanable funds market to borrow the necessary funds. As shown in Figure 3.6.4a, the demand for loanable funds will increase and shift to the right from D(LF)1 to D(LF)2. The interest rate on loanable funds will increase from r1 to r2.

The resulting higher borrowing cost will dissuade many firms from borrowing to finance their own investment (I) plans. Private investment will decrease. It will have been crowded-out by the increased interest rates resulting from increased government spending. If the goal increasing government expenditures (G) was intended to increase aggregate demand then, since private investment (I) may decrease, aggregate demand will not increase as much as expected or even at all. This is shown in Figure 3.6.4b.

The increase in government spending would increase aggregate demand from AD1 to AD2 in the absence of crowding out. If, though, the increased borrowing needs of the government increase interest rates then investment spending, also a component of aggregate demand, will decrease. The result is that aggregate demand may not increase as much as expected, all the way to AD2, but only to AD3. Real GDP will perhaps rise, but only to Y2. Expansionary fiscal policy is not as effective as expected to close a recessionary (deflationary) gap, as private investment spending was crowded out.

As you might have guessed, this is a major criticism of Monetarists against the effectiveness of Keynesian-inspired expansionary fiscal policy and deficit spending. It makes sense, but only if the economy is booming and approaching full employment. In such a case the government will be competing with private firms for funds, which could drive up interest rates. What if the economy is in a deep recession? In this case crowding out is unlikely as business confidence will be low and firms will not be willing to invest.

Whether crowding out occurs or not crucially depends on the size of the deflationary gap. The risk is smaller, the deeper the recession. Also, in a deep recession it is expansionary fiscal policy in the form of increased government spending that can help an economy grow again.

Recap
Crowding out

$$\text{If } G\uparrow \rightarrow D_{LF}\uparrow \rightarrow r\uparrow \rightarrow I\downarrow \rightarrow AD\downarrow$$

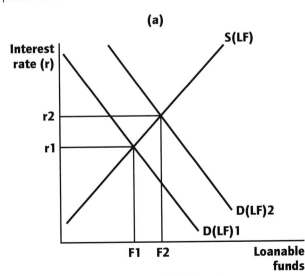

Figure 3.6.4a Crowding out: the loanable funds market

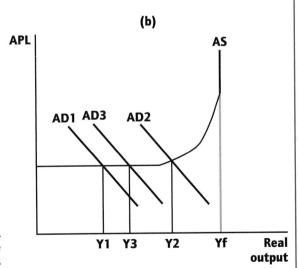

Figure 3.6.4b Crowding out: the impact on the economy

Effectiveness of fiscal policy

Advantages

- Perhaps the biggest advantage of expansionary fiscal policy in the form of increased government expenditures is that it is direct. Government spending is a component of aggregate demand. If it increases, aggregate demand will automatically increase. This is especially important in a deep recession when easy monetary policy may be ineffective as confidence levels are low but also because of the zero lower bound (ZLB) constraint explained in section 3.5, page 110.

- (HL) An increase in government expenditures will lead to an even greater increase in aggregate demand and in economic activity (that is, on GDP) because of the operation of the multiplier effect.

- Fiscal policy can be targeted. Increased government spending can target specific sectors of the economy, such as specific needs in infrastructure, R&D, the development of green technologies, education or health care. It can also target specific regions of a country that are growing much slower than average or are in decline.

- Tax cuts can also target the poor, who are not only in greater need for a boost in their disposable incomes during an economic crisis but who are also more likely to spend the resulting additional income than are higher income households, significantly increasing aggregate demand. In addition, tax cuts for the poor can help to decrease income inequality.

- An increase in government (capital) expenditures, such as on infrastructure, R&D, education and health care will also in the long term increase potential output, shifting aggregate supply to the right the long run.

- If an economy can issue its own currency and if most of its debt is domestically owned, then fiscal policy can be scaled up significantly. The response to the Covid-19 crisis in early 2020 clearly showed this. Advanced economies increased government spending by June 2020 by more than $7.6 trillion, representing roughly 11% of the 2019 world GDP. In the USA alone, a $2 trillion package had been enacted by March 2020 and an additional $2 trillion package was being discussed at the time of writing.

- (HL) A huge advantage to economies entering a downturn is the existence of automatic stabilizers. Automatic stabilizers do not require legislative action by the government so they are able to respond quickly to an economic downturn.

Disadvantages

- Discretionary fiscal policy is the responsibility of politicians. This presents some issues. Politicians aiming to maximize their re-election chances often push before elections for sizable increases in government spending as well as for tax cuts. Even if the fundamentals of the economy indicate the need for contractionary fiscal policy, it is not often adopted because cutting expenditures and raising taxes do not appeal much to the median voter. In contrast to monetary policy, fiscal policy is not independent of the political agenda of the ruling party. Fiscal policy therefore has an "expansionary bias".

- On the other hand, in many parliamentary democracies, opposition politicians often try to stall expansionary fiscal policy even if it is direly needed. Typically, opposition politicians claim that increasing government expenditures will increase the national debt to unsustainable levels (the country will "become like Greece" was the typical argument). Other opposition claims are that increasing government expenditures will lead to rampant inflation or that it will lead to increased interest rates. The result is that discretionary fiscal policy is often caught in endless debates and this explains why there are many economists who argue in favour of an increased role for automatic stabilizers.

- Fiscal policy is also characterized by very long time-lags. Time lags, as explained earlier (page 122), also characterize monetary policy but the administrative lag in fiscal policy is much longer. Not only will opposition politicians question the need for expansionary fiscal policy and stress its potential risks but even if there is agreement for a stimulus plan it can get stuck in further political debates about, for example, how much to increase expenditures, which expenditures to increase and which taxes to decrease and by how much. Long time lags may destabilize the economy instead of stabilizing it. For example, if the government decides to increase government spending in order to deal with a recession and close a deflationary gap, an inflationary gap may result if exports unexpectedly rise before the full impact of the fiscal stimulus.

- Expansionary fiscal policy may prove inflationary if the economy is already operating close to full employment or if time lags prove longer than expected.

- (HL) Expansionary fiscal policy may lead to private investment being crowded out if the economy is close to full employment.

- If it succeeds in raising incomes in the economy, expansionary fiscal policy may widen a trade deficit because higher incomes lead to more imports.

- Expansionary fiscal policy increases the national debt and under certain conditions this may prove unsustainable.

- Expansionary fiscal policy that relies on tax cuts may not prove effective if the tax cuts are mostly geared to higher incomes because those with higher incomes have a lower propensity to consume. More generally, tax cuts may not lead to increased spending if consumer and business confidence is very low.

Recap
Advantages and disadvantages of fiscal policy

Advantages

- Fiscal policy affects aggregate demand directly.
- Fiscal policy can be targeted.
- Certain expenditures may also increase potential output.
- Under certain conditions fiscal policy can be scaled up significantly.
- (HL) The multiplier renders fiscal policy powerful to fight a recession.
- (HL) Automatic stabilizers can be quick and sizable.

Disadvantages

- Politicians are responsible for fiscal policy.
- Fiscal policy is characterized by long time lags.
- It may lead to unsustainable debt.
- It may lead to inflation.
- It may widen a trade deficit.
- Tax cuts may not induce more spending.
- (HL) Fiscal policy may crowd out private investment.

Policymakers' perspective

It should be stressed that the role of fiscal policy in economic stabilization is becoming more important. Many policymakers are afraid that economies are ill-prepared to fight off a downturn. Monetary policy alone may not be able to mitigate recessions as a result of the zero lower bound (ZLB) constraint it faces with nominal interest rates. Research has shown that central banks typically decrease nominal interest rates by three to five percentage points in response to contractions. In recent years this is not possible in many countries because nominal interest rates are already below 5%. On the other hand, the long time lags that characterize expansionary discretionary fiscal policy may be a problem and may even worsen macroeconomic fluctuations. This is why policymakers are seriously considering relying more on automatic stabilizers.

Policymakers consider fiscal policy better equipped than monetary policy to prevent rising income inequality. Spending can be targeted towards regions and industries that are suffering more than others and tax cuts can be directed to improve the plight of the poor. Monetary policy, and specifically quantitative easing, is considered to have widened income inequality because much of the additional funding that central banks have pumped into economies has been fuelling stock market booms.

However, policymakers must be mindful of the risks associated with the expansionary bias of discretionary fiscal policies. The national debt may increase to unsustainable deficits and debt levels. Discretionary fiscal policy may also prove inflationary or it may crowd out private investment. Of course, with real interest rates so low, debt is not very costly.

Policymakers are aware though that the need for discretionary fiscal policy is the greatest when an economy experiences extraordinary shocks not as a result of cyclical economic conditions but as a result of exceptional circumstances. Its potency in such conditions was manifested at the outset of the Covid-19 crisis, as we saw with the example given earlier, when governments implemented extraordinary emergency fiscal measures to support economies.

Optional material

Algebraically the following holds:

(1) $\Delta Y = \Delta G + b\Delta G + b^2\Delta G + b^3\Delta G + b^4\Delta G + ... \rightarrow$

(2) $\Delta Y = (1 + b + b^2 + b^3 + b^4 + ...) \Delta G \rightarrow$

(3) $\Delta Y = \left(\dfrac{1}{1-b}\right) \Delta G \rightarrow$

(4) $\Delta Y = k \Delta G,$

where k is the multiplier

Since b is the marginal propensity to consume (MPC) domestic goods and services the multiplier k can be rewritten as:

$$k = \frac{1}{(1 - MPC)}$$

In (1) the change in income ΔY is equal to the initial change in government spending (ΔG) which workers earned and is the direct, first-round effect and the first term in the equation. The second term ($b\Delta G$) is the proportion b of this income that was spent on other domestic goods by these workers and which is income to others in the economy. For example, if I earned from the government £100 pounds for fixing a window in a government building and my MPC is 0.8 then I will spend £80 pounds, say on luxury cakes that the baker Roxanne across the street baked. Now, income has increased by 180 and represents the service (window fixing) and the good (cakes) produced up to this point. If Roxanne in turn spends 0.8 of her extra income on say, cheddar cheese that Bob produces, then his income will have increased by £64 pounds (this the third term, $b^2\Delta G$) representing the extra cheddar produced. Up to this point, national income has increased by 100 + 80 + 64 or, generalizing, by $\Delta G + b\Delta G + b^2\Delta G$. Bob will then spend a portion b of his extra income $b^2\Delta G$ or, $b^3\Delta G$ on some other goods, and so on.

In (2) the term ΔG is factored out and it should be realized that inside the parentheses we have the sum of infinite terms of a geometric progression that converges

(as $0 < b < 1$) to $\dfrac{1}{(1 - b)}$.

3.7 Supply-side policies

Supply-side policies focus on the production side of the economy. They attempt to enhance the institutional framework within which economic activity takes place, to increase the quantity and improve the quality of the available factors of production as well as to improve incentives. The goal is to increase potential output shifting the long-run aggregate supply (LRAS) curve to the right.

Supply-side policies may be distinguished into market-based policies and interventionist policies. In the former, the role of the government shrinks while the role of free markets expands. In the latter, the government takes on an active role in trying to influence the productive capacity of the economy.

Goals of supply-side policies

- The primary goal of supply-side policies is to expand the productive capacity of the economy and accelerate long-term growth.
- Supply-side policies aim to increase the degree of competition in product markets. More competition leads to lower prices, higher levels of output and improved efficiency.
- Supply-side policies aim to reduce wage and non-wage labour costs for firms. Lower labour costs render the labour market more flexible, permitting firms to hire more workers. Profitability also increases, which is also hoped to increase investment spending.
- Supply-side policies aim to improve firms' incentives to invest in new capacity and new innovative technologies.
- Supply-side policies aim to help reduce the risk of inflation, thus improving the international competitiveness of domestic firms.

Market-based policies

Market-based supply-side policies were championed for many years as the prime engine for economies to achieve long-term growth. The theory was that a shrunken government stimulates private investment and so stimulates growth. After the 2008–09 global financial crisis, these policies have come under greater scrutiny, forcing even the IMF, an ardent early advocate of such policies, to recognize that the growth that resulted from adopting some of these policies proved fragile and not sustainable.

Market-based supply-side policies can be distinguished into product market related policies, labour market related policies and incentive-related policies.

Product market related policies

Anti-monopoly regulation

Monopoly power leads to higher prices, lower output, slower rates of innovation and increased income inequality. Governments try to limit monopoly power by establishing competition commissions and passing antitrust laws. Competition commissions have been vigilant in detecting collusive agreements and other anti-competitive practices and have also blocked certain mergers and acquisitions. The interpretation, though, of what kind of behaviour should be regulated differs over time and between countries. For example, since the 1980s the USA has taken a much more permissive pro-business hands-off approach compared to the EU and other countries. The EU tries to prevent mergers and acquisitions that would allow a firm to grow excessively and strengthen its monopoly position. It has blocked several mega-mergers such as the one between German Siemens and French Alstom in the railway equipment and infrastructure market. It has also imposed significant fines on tech giants such as Google and Facebook for abusing their monopoly power. In the USA, intervention by antitrust authorities is only expected if firms' behaviour harms the consumer (for example, only if it leads to higher prices). So, for years the staggering growth of Amazon, Google and Facebook did not prompt any action in the USA despite the enormous market power these firms amassed. Only recently has there been some debate over the economic and even political risks of such market power; in September 2020 some US states started investigations of these large tech companies. It is also worth noting here that globalization has made it more difficult for policymakers to decide whether a large in size firm that results from a merger or an acquisition will abuse its monopoly power because the relevant market may now extend way beyond national borders.

Deregulation

Regulations are rules, restrictions and laws imposed by governments that aim to modify the behaviour of firms and the operation of markets. Of course, markets could not function effectively without numerous regulations. The challenge is to devise regulations that improve the functioning of markets. Often, regulations have been introduced as a result of political pressure by special interest groups that aim to shield specific industries from competition or ensure that they enjoy preferential treatment in the form of guaranteed prices, subsidies and so on. A different set of regulations, such as environmental or health and safety regulations, aim to promote social objectives when free markets fail to deliver.

Deregulation refers to the process of dismantling or relaxing inappropriate rules, restrictions and laws in the operation of firms or markets. Many industries in many countries including the airline industry, trucking, banking, electricity, communications and others have been, in the past 40 years, deregulated. For example, in Greece the trucking industry has recently been deregulated. Special licenses were required to start and operate a trucking firm to transport goods. For very many years the government succumbed to special interests and issued no new licences. The result was that a scarce licence could only be secured for more than €300,000, increasing the cost of transporting everything in the country. The OECD identified 555 regulatory restrictions in Greece that were considered to harm competition. Deregulation thus benefits competition and consumers if entry barriers are removed and prices are determined by market forces. Deregulation also decreases the costs that burden firms. More competition, greater levels of efficiency, and fewer costly rules and restrictions to comply with effectively shift both the SRAS and the LRAS curves to the right. Of course, not all deregulation has been successful. The deregulation of the US financial and banking industry has been considered by several economists as the root cause of the 2008–09 global financial crisis. The deregulation of electricity companies in California has also been severely criticized as suppliers were accused of deliberately limiting capacity, building investments to restrict supply artificially and steeply increase prices charged to consumers. The rolling back or elimination of many environmental regulations in the USA under President Trump is considered by many to have increased the risks of global warming and climate change.

Privatization

Privatization refers to the transfer of state-owned assets, usually enterprises, to the private sector. Many firms in many countries up until the 1980s were nationalized. Since then extensive privatization has taken place. Examples of privatized firms include utilities (water, electricity), telecoms, railways, steel, coal, airlines, airports, harbours, gas, oil and others. The logic is simple. Private owners of firms aim to make profits so they have the incentive to operate more efficiently by cutting costs and to try harder to meet the needs of consumers. Privately owned firms are also more likely to introduce new technologies. Critics claim that often a private monopoly simply replaced a state monopoly; that privatized firms led to higher prices and reduced employment as they often fired workers in their attempt to cut costs; or that the services provided were of inferior quality. The evidence from the privatization experience of many countries does not suggest that state-owned enterprises are necessarily inefficient or that privatized firms are necessarily more efficient. Performance of privatized firms has been mixed. Much depends on the specifics of each case.

Trade liberalization

A very fast way to unleash the power of markets and to increase competition and efficiency, forcing domestic firms to cut costs and improve quality, is through *trade liberalization*. The term refers to the elimination of policies that protect domestic firms from foreign competition. Such policies include:

- tariffs (which are nothing but taxes on imports)
- quotas (which are restrictions on the volume of imports allowed into the country)
- subsidies (that artificially lower production costs and render domestic firms more competitive)

- many regulatory health and safety barriers (that purportedly protect consumers but in reality often only protect domestic firms from foreign competition).

If trade is liberalized, then domestic firms with monopoly power immediately face competition from foreign producers. To survive, they have to cut costs, to lower prices and to invest in innovation, stimulating growth. Trade liberalization has lately been accused of displacing domestic labour as it has, in some cases, forced many smaller domestic firms to shut down and exit the market. As a result, some world markets are now dominated by a few large firms with very significant market power. Prices are higher than the expected competitive ideal and income inequality has increased.

Labour market related policies
Reducing the power of labour unions

Labour unions have historically been successful in achieving higher money wages for their members. This implies higher wage costs, so higher production costs for firms. By reducing labour unions' power, money wages and production costs decrease, permitting firms to reduce prices, expand output and hire more labour. Low labour union power in a country may also attract more inflows of foreign direct investment (FDI). On the other hand, it is argued that labour unions are necessary for several reasons. They ensure that safety and other regulations in the workplace are enforced; they protect workers from sexual and other types of harassment by some employers as well as against unlawful firing; and, if labour unions are abolished, the share of wages in national income decreases.

Decreasing or even abolishing the minimum wage

A high minimum wage increases the cost of hiring so demand for labour shrinks and unemployment rises. A lower or no minimum wage decreases production costs and induces lower prices, an increase in output and perhaps more investment. On the other hand, several studies have shown that reasonable increases in the minimum wage have not led to higher unemployment and have even contributed to higher labour productivity as a result of greater job satisfaction.

Reducing non-wage labour costs

Non-wage labour costs typically include employer contributions to national insurance and pension schemes for their employees. By decreasing these, production costs decrease, permitting firms to reduce prices and increase output. On the other hand, workers' disposable income decreases, which may prove devastating for unskilled labour, especially if minimum wage laws are also abolished.

Decreasing unemployment benefits

If a government offers high unemployment benefits compared to the average wage earned this reduces the incentive of an unemployed individual to accept a job offer. If the replacement ratio, the ratio of unemployment benefits to wage earned, is high, the probability of accepting the first job offer made available is low. Decreasing the size, but also the duration of unemployment benefits paid, increases the probability of unemployed individuals accepting a job offer, decreasing unemployment and increasing aggregate supply. However, workers may be forced to accept jobs that underutilize their skills, which will damage economic efficiency.

Incentive-related policies

Tax cuts are closely associated with a group of 1980s economists known as "supply-siders". They believed that high tax rates on personal income and on corporate profits discourage hard work and investments by individuals and firms respectively.

Cutting personal income taxes

Reducing personal income tax rates is expected to increase labour supply. As a result of lower personal income tax rates, more individuals may decide to join the labour force; the unemployed may be less willing to remain unemployed given a job offer; and workers may be incentivized to work longer hours. The increase in the factor of production labour will increase the economy's potential output, shifting the LRAS curve to the right. On the other hand, the higher disposable income that results from a tax cut may induce workers to choose more leisure and less work so that the labour supply does not increase.

Cutting business taxes and the capital gains tax

Tax cuts on corporate profits increase profitability of investments. More investments are expected and this will mean faster growth. The expected higher rate of investment in the country will increase potential output and shift the LRAS curve to the right. However, the empirical evidence on corporate tax cuts suggests that in most, if not all, cases investment spending did not in fact increase following a cut in corporate taxation.

Capital gains are the profits an individual earns from selling an asset at a higher price than it was purchased. It typically applies to the sale of stocks, bonds and real estate. By cutting capital gains tax, investments in stocks, bonds and real estate are encouraged. It is argued that a lower capital gains tax will have a large beneficial effect on output, growth and entrepreneurial activity. Many empirical studies conclude, however, that such cuts do not significantly boost economic growth, but they do increase income inequality, as it is the wealthy who mostly own such assets and so they benefit disproportionately.

> ### Recap
> Market-based supply-side policies
>
> **Product market related policies** include:
> - increasing competition in product markets that would lower prices, increase output and spur innovation
> - deregulation to open-up markets and decrease production costs for firms
> - privatization as the profit motive increases efficiency
> - trade liberalization to expose domestic firms to foreign competition.
>
> **Labour market related policies** include decreasing:
> - the power of labour unions, to decrease the ability of labour to raise wages
> - the minimum wage (or even abolishing it), to decrease wage costs for firms
> - non-wage labour costs to firms, to lower the cost of labour
> - unemployment benefits, to induce unemployed workers to accept sooner job offers.
>
> **Incentive-related policies** include decreasing:
> - personal income taxes, to increase the incentive to work
> - business and capital gains tax, to increase the incentive to invest.

Interventionist supply-side policies

These policies include increased government spending on education and health care, on infrastructure and on research and development (R&D), as well as a separate class of policies referred to as "industrial policies".

Increasing public investments in education, training and health care

The goal of such public investments is to increase the stock of human capital of the economy. Human capital refers to the education, training, skills and experience embodied in the labour force of a country. It is an intangible asset that increases labour productivity, employability and innovation.

Improving the quality of available education and training and ensuring greater access to these improved services, especially access for the poor, has been documented to significantly increase labour productivity and so potential output and growth. Education generates not only significant private benefits for the educated but also very sizable external benefits for the economy as a whole. Massive investments in education in East Asia increased the quantity of education. The quality also improved and the gap between male and female enrollments closed very quickly. These investments have paid off dramatically. The high returns of education are also evident in the Scandinavian countries where public spending on education are among the highest in the world. Note also the value of various retraining programmes offered directly or indirectly by governments and of lifelong learning programmes in decreasing structural unemployment.

Public investments in health care also increase and improve the stock of human capital of a nation. Better health-care services and greater access to them also generate significant private and external benefits. Workers who are skilled and healthy are more productive, and a more productive labour force accelerates growth.

Public investment in infrastructure

Infrastructure is defined as physical capital, typically financed by the state, that decreases the overall cost of economic activity as it generates massive external benefits. A better road and rail network in a country does not constrain firms to local inputs and local markets. It decreases the cost of accessing from more distant locations the inputs that exactly meet their specifications. It helps them to employ specialized labour based further from the firm. Most importantly, a better transportation network permits firms to sell in more markets. Harbours and airports allow a country's firms to engage in international trade. Water, sanitation and sewerage networks improve water quality and the level of health enjoyed by the population, increasing productivity. Power grids and telecommunication networks are crucial for an economy's growth. Electrification facilitates learning. It permits access to information. Electrification also permits refrigeration; the use of many time-saving appliances; it supplies lighting that, for example, increases the degree of safety enjoyed in towns and in driving; it permits the operation of clinics and very many businesses that need uninterrupted power. A telecommunications network is crucial for all, but especially for businesses, as it enables instantaneous access to necessary information related to their activities. Poor or crumbling infrastructure is considered a major obstacle to growth. Conversely, expanding and improved infrastructure raises potential output, shifting the LRAS curve to the right.

Public investment in research and development (R&D)

Technological developments matter. Improvements in technology are the most significant determinant of long-term growth. Governments, in their attempt to increase the productive capacity of the economy, fund research and development (R&D) projects. Public provision of basic R&D is also responsible for significant spillover benefits that a private firm would never be able to capture. This means that there is justification for an active role of the state. Markets alone would lead to fewer R&D projects being undertaken, which implies a slower rate of technological progress. Governments also provide incentives to private firms to invest R&D in the form of subsidies, tax allowances and patents granted for new products and new processes developed. Labour productivity does not only depend on the level of human capital of the labour force but also on the quality and the level of technology of the physical capital that workers use. It follows that a faster rate of technological advancement will increase labour productivity and so increase aggregate supply, shifting an economy's LRAS curve to the right.

Industrial policies

Industrial policies are a separate category of supply-side policies. Since they are highly interventionist, pro-market economists and politicians, who often overstate what markets alone can achieve and are critical of almost any public action, consider them counterproductive. However, industrial policies have been adopted by most, if not all, economies at various degrees. They are still employed around the world, although few governments admit this.

Industrial policies are championed by policymakers who consider government intervention and guidance necessary

for the productive capacity of an economy to increase. This group of policymakers considers market forces necessary but often inadequate to guide financial capital and investments to their most productive uses and so believe that government is necessary to do the job and "pick winners". These are industries and firms that are thought to be crucial for long-term growth. Direct or indirect subsidies, subsidized low interest loans, tax cuts and tax allowances, joint public-private research programmes and protection from foreign competition are some of the measures employed. Typical examples of industries that have received or are receiving preferential treatment include the cement and steel industries (as construction is considered an engine of growth for many economies), artificial intelligence and telecommunications, such as 5G technology (since in high-tech it is often "winner takes all"). A more specific example of successful industrial policy is the case of Hyundai in South Korea where the government in the 1960s financed its expansion into the shipbuilding industry only for South Korea to become one of the world's leading shipbuilders. Korea more generally successfully subsidized bank credit and rationed it to sectors and firms that invested in strategic industries. Also, China's manufacturing strength is not only the result of unconstrained market forces but also of active government guidance.

It must also be acknowledged that despite the widespread use of industrial policies many have been regarded as outright wasteful. Such waste is usually the result of *political capture*. The term refers to the case when industrial policies are captured by powerful business groups, closely linked to the ruling party, who manage to tailor these policies to serve their own narrow business interests instead of the country's long-term goals.

Recap

Interventionist supply-side policies

These policies increase:

- public investment in infrastructure as infrastructure decreases the overall cost of economic activity

- public investment in education and health care as the increased human capital increases labour productivity

- public investment in R&D as labour productivity also depends on the technology embodied in the economy's stock of capital

- economic growth—industrial policies are used in certain industries that are crucial for growth and may benefit from preferential treatment by the state.

Analysing the expected impact of supply-side policies using a diagram

The impact of successful supply-side policies, whether market-based or interventionist, can be illustrated using either a Monetarist/New Classical diagram (Figure 3.7.1) or a Keynesian diagram (Figure 3.7.2). In either case, you must shift the LRAS and the Keynesian AS curves to the right to show that potential (full employment) real output increases, from Yp to Y'p in the Monetarist/New Classical diagram and from Yf to Y'f in the Keynesian diagram. In the Monetarist/New Classical diagram you could also shift the SRAS to the right to show the impact of lower production costs resulting from deregulation, increased labour market flexibility and so on, but it is not necessary.

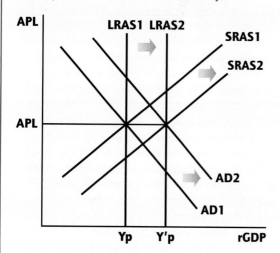

Figure 3.7.1 Impact of supply-side policies: Monetarist/New Classical diagram

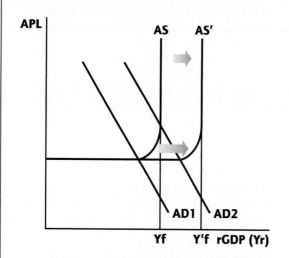

Figure 3.7.2 Impact of supply-side policies: Keynesian diagram

You could also include an increase in aggregate demand from AD1 to AD2. In such a case, you can illustrate that supply-side policies, by successfully increasing the productive capacity of the economy, decrease inflationary pressures that any increase in aggregate demand would exert. In both diagrams above, the increase in aggregate demand did not result in any upward pressure on the average price level because successful supply-side policies had managed to shift the AS curve to the right.

Demand-side effects of supply-side policies

Supply-side policies do not only have an impact on aggregate supply. Many also increase aggregate demand.

Any impact on aggregate demand will of course be in the short term whereas any impact on potential output and aggregate supply will be in the long term. All interventionist supply-side policies that call for public investments in infrastructure, health care, education and R&D activities also increase aggregate demand in the short term as these public investments require increased government expenditures. In addition, the tax cuts that aim at improving the incentive to work and to invest increase aggregate demand. If personal income taxes decrease, then households immediately enjoy higher disposable incomes, leading to an increase in consumption expenditures and thus an increase aggregate demand, so the AD curve shifts right. Corporate tax cuts may also increase aggregate demand if they manage to increase investment expenditures, a component of aggregate demand. In the long term, when the stock of capital of the economy increases, then the LRAS curve will also shift right.

Supply-side effects of fiscal and monetary policies

Fiscal policy is a demand-side policy, but an increase in certain government expenditures will also produce a supply-side effect in the long term. In a recession, a government may decide to increase spending in order to increase aggregate demand. If this spending is on infrastructure, health care, education and R&D, not only will aggregate demand increase, but in the long term, aggregate supply and potential output will also increase. In fact, during a deep recession when interest rates are low, increased spending on expanding or improving infrastructure is often undertaken, as borrowing to finance these expenditures will be cheap. More jobs are created, economic activity picks up and in the long term the productive capacity of the economy also expands.

If a corporate tax cut succeeds in increasing investment spending, aggregate demand will increase in the short term, but since it leads to an increase in the stock of capital of the economy, aggregate supply will also increase in the long term. A cut in personal income taxes will increase disposable income so, it is hoped, there will be an increase in consumption and aggregate demand in the short term. If, though, it increases the incentive to work, then the labour supply will increase and so, in the long term, aggregate supply will also increase.

Lastly, if fiscal policy is prudent (meaning that budget deficits are low and the level of national debt is considered sustainable), then businesses will feel less uncertain about the future. They will not fear a sudden acceleration of inflation or a sudden increase in interest rates. They will be more willing to invest, which positively affects aggregate demand in the short term, but also the productive capacity of the economy (that is, aggregate supply) in the long term. Also, if monetary policy is successful in maintaining low and stable inflation, then the associated lower economic uncertainty that firms enjoy may encourage more investment, positively affecting aggregate demand, and, in the long term, also aggregate supply.

Effectiveness of supply-side policies

Strengths of market-based supply-side policies

- A major advantage of market-based supply-side policies is that resource allocation will theoretically be improved. Less interference by the state will permit prices to emit the correct signals to producers and consumers; if deregulation opens up markets to greater competition and/or lowers production costs, then prices charged will decrease and closer reflect marginal costs of production. Privatized firms will typically waste fewer scarce resources. Labour will become cheaper relative to capital, permitting firms to choose the optimal combination of capital and labour for their production process.

- Market-based supply-side policies aim to decrease the involvement of the government and increase the role of markets. As these policies do not rely on increased government spending, they do not burden the expenditure side of the government's budget. In addition, tax cuts, according at least to their ardent supporters, "pay for themselves". By this they mean that as tax cuts theoretically stimulate more work and more investments, tax revenues will be higher despite the lower tax rates. Empirically though, this has not been the case.

Strengths of interventionist supply-side policies

- Interventionist supply-side policies directly target areas that are considered instrumental for accelerating long-term growth of nations. Public investments in education and health care, if properly designed and implemented, will increase the stock of human capital of the economy. Quality education and health-care services accessed by all, especially the poor, increase labour productivity and the income-earning capacity of all, permitting faster growth but also a more equitable income distribution. More and better infrastructure directly increases the productive capacity of an economy and indirectly permits business to grow faster. Over the very long term, growth has mostly been the result of better technology so the importance of public investment in R&D and government efforts to foster private investment in R&D cannot be overstated. As an example, the development of the internet was a product of publicly funded research by the US Defense department.

Drawbacks of market-based supply-side policies

- Perhaps the biggest drawback of market-based supply-side policies is that they have led to increased income inequality. Even the IMF, which for decades championed deregulation, reducing barriers to entry in product markets, privatization, trade liberalization and increased labour market flexibility, has questions about these policies. The IMF has acknowledged that despite empirical evidence that the policies have indeed been successful in accelerating economic growth, it now questions whether they alone can achieve "sustained" growth. There is now mounting evidence that the growth resulting from market-based supply-side policies proved fragile and not sustainable. The reason for this is that these policies are considered an important contributing factor for the observed increase in income inequality. Monopoly power and concentration has increased in many domestic and world markets as a result of deregulation, privatizations and the belief that markets should be unrestricted. Higher concentration in markets has led to higher prices and so to a transfer of income from consumers to businesses. The benefits of tax cuts have accrued mostly to the wealthiest. The increased labour market flexibility resulting from lower minimum wages, lower labour union power, lower job security and lower unemployment benefits is responsible for the shrinking share of wages in national income. It is now accepted by many policymakers that it is not just the size of the pie that matters but also its distribution.

- Market-based supply-side policies also suffer from very long time lags. The impact on the real economy of deregulating markets or any efficiency gains from privatizing a firm may take years to materialize. Any beneficial consequences resulting from rendering the labour market of a country more flexible also take time.

- Not only is the impact of any successful market-based supply-side policy felt long after it is implemented but vested interests in many countries have often managed to stall or even block efforts to privatize, to deregulate, to liberalize trade or to render the labour market more flexible. Politicians who are always apprehensive of the possible political cost of any game-changing decisions and who often rely on the support of large businesses or powerful professional associations (such as those of lawyers, accountants, tax consultants, engineers and architects) have in several countries proved to be unwilling to push hard for such structural reforms. Organized labour has also fought and often succeeded in stalling or blocking labour market reforms that would hurt their interests. Market-based supply-side policies are very long-term policies not only because once implemented it takes time for them to have an impact on the economy but also because vested interests in many countries stall their implementation.

- Regulations, as explained earlier, also include environment-related rules aimed at promoting social objectives when free markets fail to deliver. It has also been explained that such rules increase the cost of doing business for firms. It follows that rolling back or eliminating these rules will decrease production costs for firms, leading to higher levels of output and lower prices. This may sound good, but there may be significant drawbacks involved, which, if taken into consideration, render deregulation in such circumstances undesirable. For example, recent deregulation initiatives taken in the USA to relax or eliminate environmental rules may negatively impact the environment in the future. In March 2020, the US revised standards for average fuel economy in cars and for carbon dioxide emissions, making them less strict, so less costly, for US car manufacturers. The new less stringent rules will lead though to roughly an additional 2.0 billion barrels of fuel consumed and 900 more million metric tons of carbon dioxide emitted, compared to earlier standards. Many other examples of similar deregulation initiatives have been passed in other countries.

Drawbacks of interventionist supply-side policies

- A major issue with interventionist supply-side policies is that they need to be financed. The monetary cost of revamping or expanding the infrastructure of a country is a huge government expenditure. Even modest attempts to finance increased education, health-care services and R&D efforts need money. It follows that to fund improvement or expansion of infrastructure the government would have to increase taxes or resort to increased borrowing. Increased taxes are, in general, not politically popular, even if the increased taxes are taxes that aim to decrease the use of fossil fuels. Typically, governments resort to borrowing. In order to minimize the cost of borrowing, interest rates must be very low. This is why many economists are urging governments to improve or expand infrastructure, as well as to embark on human capital augmenting investments now, since interest rates in many countries are at historically low levels.

- Supply-side policies suffer from very long time lags. Interventionist supply-side policies may have a short-term impact on aggregate demand, reflecting the increase in government expenditures, but any impact on supply will take a very long time to manifest itself.
  - Infrastructure takes a very long time to build and complete.
  - Public investment in education that permits access to schools to all children takes even longer to show results.
  - Technological breakthroughs are uncertain and also take a long time to achieve.
  - The benefits of improved health for the population are also manifested in the long term.
  - Industrial policies are also, by definition, very long-term policies as their goal is to influence the structure of markets and of the economy.

Recap

Effectiveness of market-based supply-side policies	
Strengths of market-based supply-side policies are that they involve: • improved resource allocation • minimal burden on the government's budget.	**Drawbacks** of market-based supply-side policies are that they involve: • increased income inequality • very long time lags • vested interests that may stall or even block their implementation • deregulation of environmental rules that may worsen pollution and accelerate climate change.
Effectiveness of interventionist supply-side policies	
Strengths of interventionist supply-side policies are that they are targeted to: • factors critical for accelerating growth (infrastructure, human capital, R&D) • industries considered critical to drive growth.	**Drawbacks** of interventionist supply-side policies are that they involve: • costly financing, adding to the national debt • very long time lags.

3.8 Macroeconomic policies—strengths, limitations and conflicts

Macroeconomic objectives

The toolbox that policymakers can use in order to manage the economy and achieve their macroeconomic objectives includes fiscal policy, monetary policy and supply-side policies. Depending on the issue faced, each of these policies has certain advantages and certain disadvantages. Often though, to achieve one goal, another goal may be sacrificed. In this section we examine these issues.

Growth

Fiscal policy

- Since an increase in government expenditures (G) and/or a decrease in (direct) taxes (T) will increase aggregate demand, it follows that expansionary fiscal policy can promote growth. Remember that an economy is growing if real GDP is increasing.

- Since fiscal policy is characterized by long time lags, expansionary fiscal policy is typically not used if an economy is on the verge of entering recession (in other words, if growth is decreasing and close to 0%) or is already experiencing a mild recession. Any increase in government spending will take a long time to have an effect. It may destabilize the economy and risk creating an inflationary gap if, by the time of impact, it has already entered the recovery phase. Governments also avoid making frequent changes in their tax system as this creates uncertainty to households and businesses.

HL

Automatic stabilizers may have disadvantages but if they are significant in size, they may prove very helpful to rekindle growth in a weakening economy. Since the increase in government expenditures and the decrease in personal taxes are applied automatically, time lags are much shorter, increasing their effectiveness. This is why policymakers are considering increasing the size and scope of automatic stabilizers, especially since the effectiveness of easier monetary policy is now debatable because of the zero lower bound (ZLB) problem explained earlier (see section 3.5, page 114).

- If an economy is in a deep recession or, if there is significant risk of entering a deep recession (as was the case when Covid-19 forced lockdowns in many countries) then expansionary fiscal policy in the form of increased government expenditures is for many reasons the policy of choice.

  - First, increasing government expenditures is direct. If government expenditures increase, then automatically, aggregate demand increases: government expenditures (G) is a component of aggregate demand (AD). The increase in aggregate demand leads to an increase in economic activity and thus of real GDP.

HL

In addition, an increase in government expenditures will lead to a greater increase in aggregate demand and thus in real GDP because of the multiplier. In other words, expansionary fiscal policy in the form of increased government expenditures may prove to be a very potent tool.

  - Increased government expenditures can be targeted to specific geographical areas of the country suffering the most or towards sectors of the economy that are hit the hardest by the crisis.

  - By increasing and expanding unemployment benefits, fiscal policy can minimize the hardship felt by the vulnerable who lose their jobs. The poor typically spend a large proportion of any additional income leading to a significant increase in aggregate demand.

- In contrast, in a deep recession a tax cut, even if implemented, will probably not achieve much. The reason is that households will prefer to save instead of spending the resulting increase in their disposable income. Consumer confidence in a deep recession is low and workers fear that they may lose their job. Also, the theoretically presumed increase in labour supply and so in aggregate supply has had only very weak empirical support.

- Increased government spending on infrastructure, education, health care and R&D will, as explained, not only increase aggregate demand (so that real GDP increases) but will also increase potential output, over the long term shifting the AS curve to the right. The economy will not only achieve actual growth in the short term but also higher potential growth in the long term.

- Prudent fiscal policy implies that budget deficits are kept low and that the government (national) debt is considered sustainable. If fiscal policy is considered prudent then entrepreneurs will consider the risk of sudden inflation or of a sudden increase in interest rates low, leading to a higher rate of investment and faster long-term growth.

- Increased government expenditures to achieve or accelerate growth require financing. There are three choices. The government can increase taxes (direct and/or indirect) now, it can borrow now and tax later or it can lower spending elsewhere. Increasing taxes and cutting back on other government projects are both politically unpopular choices—so, usually such government expenditures are financed by borrowing. Borrowing, though, increases the budget deficit and adds to the national debt. It is therefore preferable to initiate such public investments when interest rates are low and inflation is below the target 2% rate. The resulting faster growth will lead to increased tax revenues which may be sufficient to pay off the increased level of debt.

Monetary policy

- Since a decrease in interest rates will increase aggregate demand and thus real GDP, it follows that easy monetary policy can promote growth.

- Monetary policy has several advantages over fiscal policy as a short-run stabilization tool. Monetary policy is flexible, incremental, reversible and it has shorter time lags compared to fiscal policy. It follows that if growth is weakening and there is risk of entering recession or if an economy has already entered a mild recession, policymakers will usually prefer to use easier monetary policy. It is said that monetary policy is the "first responder". Lower interest rates in such a case will induce more borrowing and more spending by households and perhaps by firms while the weakening (depreciation) of the currency will render exports cheaper and thus more competitive abroad and imports pricier and less attractive domestically. As consumer expenditures, investment expenditures and net exports will all tend to increase, aggregate demand will also increase, lifting the economy from recession.

- If interest rates are very close to zero, there is little room for central banks to decrease them. Thus, the ability of monetary policy to fight a recession and stimulate growth is limited. Central banks will lack the ammunition needed to stimulate economic activity.

- In a deep recession with cyclical unemployment rising and firms shutting down, even if the central bank has room to cut the interest rate significantly, it is unlikely that such a decrease will be able to induce more spending by households and firms. Low levels of confidence will discourage increased borrowing and spending. In a deep recession, policymakers are therefore more likely to resort to expansionary fiscal policy in the form of increased government spending to encourage growth than to looser monetary policy or even a tax cut.

- Very low interest rates (the zero-lower bound or ZLB problem) have forced several central banks to adopt massive quantitative easing programmes to support bank lending and to boost the economy. Some have even pushed short-term interest rates slightly below zero to provide a further boost to growth. The consensus on the effectiveness of such policies to stimulate growth is mixed. Significantly negative interest rates are also difficult for central banks to implement since earning zero interest by holding cash is preferable for savers to earning negative rates.

- If the central bank of a country is successful in achieving low and stable inflation over long periods of time, then the resulting decrease in business uncertainty may induce a higher rate of investment and faster long-term growth.

Supply-side policies

- Supply-side policies aim at expanding the productive capacity of an economy. As such they are the principal tool policymakers employ to achieve or accelerate long-term growth.

- The significance of public investments in infrastructure, education, health care and R&D is enormous, as the experience of all countries has demonstrated. Interventionist supply-side policies can and have helped nations achieve and also accelerate growth.

- Despite their role in achieving and accelerating growth, it must be noted that not all such expenditures are effective. Many infrastructure projects in developing and advanced nations proved wasteful. The returns to investments in education and health care that were not correctly targeted may also prove meagre. Building a bridge to nowhere or a school without teachers or students will not help a country grow.

- Industrial policies have also been successful in many cases in transforming economies and setting them on a successful growth path. China is the best example. The perceived economic threat from China perhaps also explains recent discussions for a new industrial policy in the USA and in Europe. Still, success of industrial polices is not guaranteed. In many countries, special interests have been able to secure preferential treatment by government officials that did not lead to economy-wide benefits but only to higher guaranteed profits for the protected industry and a waste of government funds.

- Market-based supply-side policies were considered for many decades as the winning recipe to boost economic growth over the long term. The idea was that decreasing the role of the government and unleashing market forces guaranteed growth. Recent empirical work has questioned the effectiveness of such policies as it has been pointed out that any resulting growth was not inclusive, so it was fragile. In economies with widening income inequality, there is less support by the poor for the, often painful, policies necessary to fight-off unfavourable economic setbacks because they fear that they will not enjoy any of the benefits.

Key issues

To accelerate long-term growth, interventionist and market-based supply-side policies are the primary policy choice. Each set has its advantages and disadvantages. On the other hand, to increase real GDP over the short term, expansionary demand-side policies are employed. Easy monetary policy is usually adopted to avoid a recession. Expansionary fiscal policy in the form of increased government spending is advised if the economy is stuck in a deep recession when confidence levels are very low.

Price stability

Fiscal policy

- To decrease inflation, contractionary demand-side policies are needed. Contractionary fiscal policy involves a decrease in government expenditures and/or an increase in (direct) taxes. Contractionary fiscal policy will therefore decrease aggregate demand and it could decrease inflation. In most real-world cases though, policymakers avoid using contractionary fiscal policy to fight inflation. One reason is that the responsibility for price stability lies with central banks, which are in charge of monetary policy. In addition, monetary policy has significant advantages compared to fiscal policy. It is flexible, incremental, reversible and has shorter time lags.

- However, if inflation is the result of past profligate government spending then policymakers will complement tighter monetary policy with contractionary fiscal policy. The result will be decreased government expenditures and, perhaps, increased taxes, dealing with the fundamental cause of the inflationary pressures.

- Remember that if an economy is approaching its potential (full employment) level of real output, then expansionary fiscal policy risks proving inflationary so it should be avoided. The problem is that it is not always easy for policymakers to know whether the economy is approaching its potential level of real output. They cannot be sure how low unemployment can decrease as the natural rate of unemployment (NRU) is not fixed through time. So, there is risk that expansionary fiscal policy will generate inflation.

- In an economy suffering from deflation policymakers have resorted to expansionary fiscal policy increasing, often dramatically, government expenditures to boost aggregate demand and help the economy exit the deflationary spiral. A good example is Japan. Remember that if an economy is suffering from deflation, then interest rates are very close to zero so there is not much room for the central bank to decrease interest rates further.

Monetary policy

- If inflationary pressures are building up in an economy, tighter monetary policy is the "first responder". When an economy is overheating and policymakers fear that inflation is an approaching threat, or if an economy is already suffering from inflation, then policymakers always resort to tighter monetary policy and increase interest rates. There are many reasons for this. First, it is the central bank that is responsible for price stability, and central banks are in charge of monetary policy. Central bank committees meet often to decide on the appropriate level of interest rates, usually every few weeks. They can increase interest rates by 0.25% at a time so that any change in monetary policy is gradual. If necessary, they can reverse their decision in the next meeting. They do not fear the political cost of slowing down the economy. Lastly, the associated time lags are shorter.

- What if inflation is not demand-pull but cost-push inflation? Many erroneously claim that in such a case supply-side policies are necessary as a policy response.

This is not true. First, the distinction between demand-pull and cost-push inflation is often vague. If money wages are rising, is it demand-pull or cost-push inflation? For analytical purposes it may be important to make the distinction but for policy purposes it is typically not that significant. No matter what the fundamental cause of any inflationary pressures arising in an economy, policymakers always respond with tighter monetary policy.

Interventionist supply-side policies are not appropriate because the necessary increase in government expenditures and resulting increase in aggregate demand would only add to inflationary pressures. Market-based supply-side policies are also never considered as it has been established that they are usually difficult to implement because of vested interests and they also have very long time lags. By the time they manage to increase the productive capacity of the economy, inflation will have risen massively and inflationary expectations will be entrenched in the decisions of both workers and firms, creating further inflationary pressures.

Supply-side policies can help keep inflation stable over the long term only in the sense that if they are successful and manage to shift the LRAS curve to the right then the economy can withstand increases in aggregate demand without any upward pressure on prices (see section 3.7, Figures 3.7.1 and 3.7.2).

- Monetary policy is considered ineffective to deal with deflation. The reason is that if there is risk of deflation in an economy, interest rates are already very low, close to zero. In this case, monetary policy faces the zero lower bound (ZLB) constraint. Nominal interest rates cannot be negative. Many central banks have adopted quantitative easing programmes with mixed success. A few have even experimented with mildly negative interest rates. The need to implement significantly negative interest rates may soon become clear in many economies.

Supply-side policies

- One of the goals of supply-side policies is to help reduce the risk of inflation, thus improving the international competitiveness of domestic firms. This should not be misinterpreted. It does not mean that supply-side polices are appropriate to fight inflationary pressures. Even if there is cost-push inflation, policymakers will still employ tighter monetary policy to get inflation under control because supply-side policies are characterized by very long time lags. Inflationary expectations cannot become entrenched because if workers and firms expect that inflation will continue in the next period they will demand higher wages and prices now, further increasing inflationary pressures.

- On the other hand, successful supply-side policies that render product markets more competitive, labour markets more flexible and increase the productive capacity of the economy help in reducing the risk of inflation. Of course, this helps domestic firms maintain or improve their international competitiveness.

Low unemployment

The decision on which policy is appropriate to decrease unemployment depends on the type of unemployment the policymaker faces.

Fiscal policy

- Expansionary fiscal policy is the best policy to use if unemployment is cyclical and the recession faced is deep. Cyclical unemployment is the result of aggregate demand decreasing. It follows that expansionary demand-side policies are needed that will manage to increase aggregate demand so that the resulting higher level of economic activity induces firms to expand and hire more labour.

  Demand-side policies include both easy monetary policy and expansionary fiscal policy. In a deep recession, though, expansionary monetary policy may be ineffective. Low business and consumer confidence may discourage firms and households from borrowing more and spending more. Also, the zero lower bound (ZLB) constraint applies: if interest rates are already very low and close to zero, there is little room, if any, for the central bank to decrease the cost of borrowing. On the other hand, expansionary fiscal policy in the form of increased government expenditures is effective as it is direct. If government expenditures increase, aggregate demand will increase. The operation of the multiplier effect (HL) can boost the increase in aggregate demand even more.

- Since structural unemployment is not the result of insufficient aggregate demand, fiscal policy is not relevant.

Monetary policy

- If unemployment is cyclical policymakers can use loose monetary policy, decreasing interest rates so that households and firms borrow more and spend more. If the recession is mild and cyclical unemployment is slowly rising then expansionary monetary policy is preferable. The reasons are clear. Fiscal policy has longer time lags, which may destabilize the economy whereas monetary policy is flexible, incremental and reversible.

- Since structural unemployment is not the result of insufficient aggregate demand, monetary policy is not relevant.

Supply-side policies

- Supply-side policies are required if unemployment is the result of a mismatch between the skills of the unemployed and the skills that firms demand, or if it is the result of labour market rigidities. Structural unemployment is the unemployment that persists way past recovery—so it is not a result of insufficient aggregate demand. Policies aiming to increase aggregate demand are not appropriate to deal with structural unemployment

- To decrease structural unemployment policymakers must try to equip the unemployed with the skills that firms demand. The government:
  - can and should provide lifelong training and retraining opportunities to labour
  - could provide incentives to firms to hire and train long-term unemployed individuals
  - could provide subsidized loans so that the unemployed, especially if young, can afford to enroll in training seminars that would equip them with the skills employers demand
  - could also provide subsidized loans so that the unemployed can afford to relocate to areas with jobs that require the skills they possess.

  Most of these initiatives are costly to the state but if properly designed their expected private and social benefits exceed the financing costs.

- If structural unemployment is the result of labour market rigidities, then market-based supply-side policies that aim to decrease or eliminate these rigidities are appropriate. A flexible labour market is one that adjusts easily to changing labour market conditions. Typical supply-side policies to decrease structural unemployment resulting from a rigid labour market include decreasing:
  - the minimum wage (or even eliminating it)
  - non-wage labour costs, such as national insurance contributions that employers pay for their workers
  - the degree of job security that workers enjoy
  - the power of labour unions.

  All these policies aim to decrease labour costs for firms so that they have an incentive to hire more workers and produce more. In addition, in some countries, governments have decreased unemployment benefits so that the unemployed are forced to accept a job offer. However, all of these policies have suppressed wages and decreased the disposable income of labour, so they have contributed to the observed rising income inequality in many countries.

- Note that if these policies are successful in decreasing structural unemployment, they also lower the natural rate of unemployment (NRU) as structural unemployment is the most significant type of unemployment included in the NRU.

- What about seasonal unemployment? It may come as a surprise, but governments do virtually nothing to decrease seasonal unemployment. The construction worker who is out of work because of freezing temperatures may only wait for a week or so for temperatures to rise while collecting unemployment benefits. The farm workers in rural areas who are out of work because the farm is between crops just wait for the next crop and in the meantime collect unemployment benefits. If every June unemployment statistics surge in many countries because of high school and college graduations, there is clearly not much for a government to do. The only thing that governments do for seasonal unemployment is to adjust monthly unemployment statistics seasonally. As for the snow ski instructor, for example, he or she is usually a water ski instructor during the summer and works at a gym as a trainer for the rest of the year, so this is hardly a case of seasonal unemployment.

- What about frictional unemployment? This type of unemployment is the result of people constantly trying to find a better job or to live in a better place. So, the only thing that can be done is to ensure that more and better labour market related information is quickly accessible to labour market participants. Government internet sites with listings of vacancies and of availabilities are extremely useful in reducing frictional unemployment and so is LinkedIn and other such specialized sites.

Potential conflict between macroeconomic objectives

Low unemployment and low inflation

It should be easy to realize that if policymakers increase aggregate demand though expansionary fiscal and/or easy monetary policies to try to achieve lower unemployment, then there is risk of higher inflation. If they try to lower inflation through tight monetary policy and/or contractionary fiscal policy, then there is risk of (cyclical) unemployment increasing. It seems difficult to achieve low unemployment and low inflation. There seems to be a conflict in achieving both policy objectives.

Assuming that an economy is facing an upward sloping Monetarist SRAS curve or that it is operating in the middle upward sloping section of a Keynesian AS curve. It becomes apparent that an increase in aggregate demand as a result of expansionary policies will increase economic activity (real GDP) and decrease unemployment but it will also increase prices (that is, it will generate inflation). This conflict is reflected in the (short-run) Phillips curve (HL).

Is this conflict unavoidable? The recent path of several economies following the 2008–09 global financial crisis suggests that it is not. At this time, unemployment in many countries had been decreasing, often at historically low levels, without inflation accelerating. In the USA unemployment had fallen below 4%, which is lower than what economists considered the natural rate of unemployment (NRU) for the country without any increase in wages or inflation. There are several explanations for this (see section 3.3, page 84). In any case though, the consensus is that typically there is an inverse relationship between inflation and unemployment. Whenever an economy is expanding and unemployment decreases below the NRU, inflation will accelerate. Some research examining historical data suggests though that for inflation to start to accelerate unemployment must fall more than one percentage point below the country's NRU. The issue becomes more complicated once it is realized that the NRU is not constant and may decrease. Policymakers therefore remain vigilant.

High economic growth and low inflation

Perhaps the easiest way to illustrate the possible conflict between achieving higher growth and maintaining low inflation is to use a Keynesian AS curve. The Keynesian AS curve begins to slope upwards as a result of "bottlenecks" arising in the economy. As explained in section 3.2, as aggregate demand rises not all sectors and industries reach full employment simultaneously. Capacity constraints (the "bottlenecks") are responsible for any inflationary pressures showing up in an economy as it grows.

The closer an economy is operating to potential (full employment) output, the more inflationary any further economic growth will prove. Again, the problem for policymakers is that they do not know in advance whether any further growth will lead to an acceleration of inflation. How much can they encourage growth and decrease unemployment before there is pressure on wages and on prices to rise?

Once again, the problem policymakers face is that the country's NRU can only be estimated with limited confidence. Since it may have decreased, they cannot know beforehand what its level is. Only after inflation has started to accelerate will they know that they had pushed growth too far and decreased unemployment below its natural rate.

On the other hand, if policymakers prematurely tighten monetary policy to avoid the possibility of inflation accelerating, they may succeed in keeping inflation very low (perhaps even lower than the common 2% target) but they will have inadvertently condemned very many individuals to remain unemployed for longer. It may have been the case that the economy could have continued to grow so that they also found a job without inflation rising.

The role of successful supply-side polices should be noted. Successful supply-side policies permit an economy to grow without experiencing inflationary pressures. If the productive capacity of an economy is increasing and its LRAS curve is shifting to the right, then increases in aggregate demand will not lead to a rising price level.

Lastly, it is worth noting that inflation has not been a serious issue for most economies for more than a decade. For example, since 2000, the inflation rate in the USA has never been higher than 4%. Very many countries are even struggling to increase inflation to meet the common 2% target. The world is more concerned with the risk of deflation and of very slow long-term growth.

High economic growth and environmental sustainability

Economic growth can have both positive and negative effects on the environment.

The possible benefits can be understood through the environmental Kuznets curve (see section 3.3, page 87). The basic idea is that as countries grow and per capita incomes increase, pollution initially rises and then, after some critical level of per capita income, it decreases. This implies that economic growth can eventually lead to environmental improvement and thereby become sustainable.

The issue is that economic growth not only requires the use of natural resources and the depletion of common access resources but also leads to more emissions and wastes that may exceed the Earth's carrying capacity. Growth may therefore be unsustainable. The environmental Kuznets curve provides an optimistic view but it may only hold for local externalities and not for many dispersed externalities such as carbon emissions. Nevertheless, a reduction in the production of pollution-intensive goods and a turn towards less pollution-intensive production technologies may allow for more sustainable growth.

In addition, to avoid "futureless" growth, governments should stop subsidizing use of fossil fuels or activities such as fishing that deplete common pool resources (see section 2.8). Governments should also adopt and enforce stricter environmental regulations. Carbon taxes as well as the broader adoption of cap and trade schemes may also help towards more sustainable economic growth. Lastly, investments in green technologies are also necessary, together with subsidies to firms that adopt clean technologies.

High economic growth and equity in income distribution

Economic growth can both improve and worsen income distribution.

Growth can alleviate income inequality as it permits a redistribution of income from the wealthy to the poor. Redistribution can be direct, through governments establishing or improving and expanding a social welfare net such as pensions and unemployment benefits, but it can also be indirect, through spending on programmes to alleviate poverty. These programmes may seek to increase agricultural productivity. They may also improve sanitation and basic infrastructure, as well as health and education facilities that increase human capital and labour productivity.

However, economic growth often leads to higher income inequality. In fact, income inequality has been increasing in many growing economies. This is because there is no guarantee that the benefits of growth will be fairly distributed. If growth is driven by only a handful of industries, if it is concentrated in certain regions, if it relies only on certain skills or if it is jobless, then many will be left out and inequality in the country may widen.

Lastly, if growth is non-inclusive and its benefits remain with the wealthiest then growth will be less resilient. This means that it is how the benefits from growth are distributed that will ultimately determine whether the growth will last. In an unequal society necessary policies to revive the economy may not gain enough support since the long-term benefits will not be uniformly shared.

4.1 Benefits of international trade

International trade refers to the buying and selling of goods and services across borders. The goods and services a country sells to other countries are referred to as exports (X). The the goods and services a country buys from other countries are referred to as imports (M). The importance of trade in the world has grown dramatically over the past decades. Examining the ratio of the sum of exports and imports over GDP, world trade has increased from about 27% in 1970 to about 60% in 2018. Perhaps the most important reason for this growth is that restrictions to the free flow of goods and services between countries (free trade) have decreased dramatically. What are the possible benefits for countries engaging in free trade?

Benefits of free trade

- Free trade permits specialization. The scarce resources of a country will specialize in the production of a range of goods and services, leading to higher levels of output and higher possible levels of consumption. A country engaging in international trade can consume combinations of goods and services outside its production possibilities curve (PPC).

- Free trade and specialization improve the allocation of scarce resources within an economy and in the world.

- Free trade automatically decreases any monopoly power that domestic firms may possess. All the benefits of increased competition will follow.
  - More competition leads to lower prices for buyers and improved product quality.
  - Increased competition as a result of free trade leads to greater efficiency in the use of resources as firms will be forced to cut costs. Firms cannot afford to waste resources.
  - Firms will also be forced to innovate to withstand competition from imports or to penetrate foreign markets and export more.

- Free trade allows firms to grow in size since the market in which they sell their products expands. This allows firms exporting from small countries with small markets to benefit from economies of scale.

- Free trade allows firms to import and use capital goods (machinery, equipment, tools and intermediate products) that meet much more closely their exact specifications. This further increases their productivity and profitability.

- Consumers enjoy a greater variety of goods and services to choose from due to free trade.

- Free trade enables faster transfer and diffusion of technology across borders as technology is embodied in traded capital goods.

- Natural resources are not distributed equally across countries. Free trade allows countries to import and use natural resources, such as oil, that they may not have.

- The benefits of specialization and of more competition, the faster diffusion of technology, the possibility of economies of scale and the increased exports a country enjoys all allow faster growth. This is why trade is referred to as an engine of economic growth.

Recap

Benefits of free trade

Free trade:

- permits specialization of resources increasing output and levels of consumption
- improves the allocation of resources
- increases competition, lowering domestic monopoly power
- leads to lower prices and improved quality
- forces firms to cut waste and become more efficient
- may induce domestic firms to grow and achieve economies of scale
- permits domestic firms to import capital goods that meet exactly their specifications
- presents consumers with greater variety
- permits technology and ideas to spread faster
- permits countries to acquire natural resources they are not endowed with.

Most importantly, free trade stimulates faster growth.

Exports, imports and the welfare increase resulting from free trade

Figures 4.1.1a to 4.4.1c illustrate the quantity of exports, the quantity of imports and the increased welfare that results from free trade. We assume the market for corn, a homogeneous product sold in perfectly competitive markets. We further assume that the country is "small". In the context of international trade, "small" means that the country can buy or sell as much of the product as it wants without the world price changing.

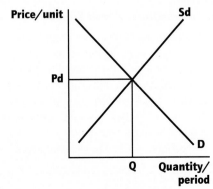

Figure 4.1.1a Closed economy—no trade; "autarky" case

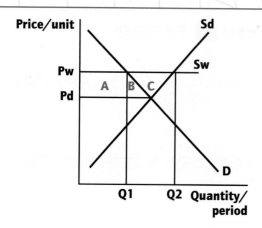

Figure 4.1.1b Open economy—Pw > Pd: country exports corn

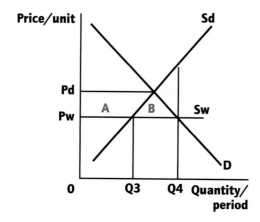

Figure 4.1.1c Open economy—Pw < Pd: country imports corn

Figure 4.1.1a illustrates the closed economy case when there are no imports or exports of corn. This is also referred to as the "autarky" case. Domestic demand and domestic supply of corn will lead to an equilibrium price of Pd per unit and an equilibrium quantity of Q units per period.

In Figure 4.1.1b we assume that the country is now an open economy and that the price of corn in the world market is higher at Pw. At the world price Pw domestic corn producers can sell as much as they want without affecting it (remember this is a "small" country). They face the world price Pw at which they will be willing to offer Q2 units. At that price, though, domestic consumers will only be willing to buy Q1 units of corn. Domestic corn producers will sell Q1 units in the domestic market and the remaining Q1Q2 units in the world market. Exports are equal to Q1Q2.

In this case, where the world price is higher than the domestic price resulting in exports, consumer surplus decreases by area (A + B) and producer surplus increases by area (A + B + C). A welfare gain thus results equal to area (C). Producers could in principle fully compensate consumers for their loss of income and still be better off. Free trade has increased social welfare but not everyone is a winner.

In Figure 4.1.1c we assume that the country is again an open economy but that the price of corn in the world market is lower at Pw. Domestic consumers can buy as much corn as they want at that price without affecting it (remember, this is a "small" country). At price Pw they will be willing to buy Q4 units while domestic corn producers will only be willing to offer Q3 units of corn. Units Q3Q4 will thus be purchased from abroad and reflect imports of corn.

In this case where the world price is lower than the domestic price resulting in imports, consumer surplus increases by area (A + B) and producer surplus decreases by area (A). A welfare gain thus results equal to area (B). Consumers could in principle fully compensate domestic producers for their loss of profits and still be better off. Free trade increases social welfare but not everyone is a winner.

Absolute and comparative advantage; specialization

HL

Absolute and comparative advantage

Free trade generates many benefits for an economy. It also increases social welfare even though not all parties involved are better off. The next step is to determine which goods should a country specialize in and export, and which goods should it import. We consider a world with two countries each producing two goods.

Absolute advantage: Adam Smith

The first explanation relies on Adam Smith's theory of absolute advantage. A country has an absolute advantage in the production of a good if compared to its trading partner, it can produce more units with the same resources or, equivalently, if it can produce a unit of the good using fewer resources. A country should specialize in and export that good in which it has an absolute advantage. Table 4.1.1 and Figure 4.1.2 show the production

possibilities of two countries, called Red and Green, each producing two goods, apples and bananas. We are assuming that both countries have the same amount of labour and of capital or, to simplify matters, each country has just one unit of labour. The numbers are the maximum amount of each good that each country can produce if it uses all of its resources in the production of that good.

	Country Red	Country Green
Apple production: maximum	30	10
Banana production: maximum	10	20

Table 4.1.1

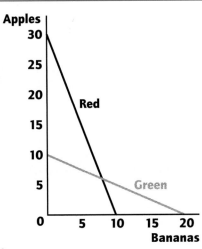

Figure 4.1.2

It should be clear from Table 4.1.1 that Red has the absolute advantage in apples, as with the same resources (say, one unit of labour) it can produce 30 apples whereas Green can produce only 10 apples. Green has the absolute advantage in bananas as it can produce 20 bananas while Red can only produce 10 bananas. So, Red can produce apples absolutely cheaper and should specialize in and export apples whereas Green should specialize in and export bananas.

What if one of the countries has the absolute advantage in the production of both goods? What if the production possibilities are as in Table 4.1.2 and Figure 4.1.3?

As shown in Figure 4.1.3, in this case Green (with the same

	Country Red	Country Green
Apple production: maximum	40	60
Banana production: maximum	20	90

Table 4.1.2

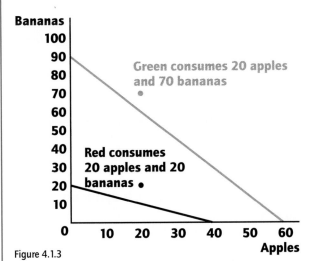

Figure 4.1.3

resources) can produce both more apples than Red (60 versus 40) and more bananas (90 versus 20). Green has the absolute advantage in the production of both goods. So according to Adam Smith, there is no room for mutually beneficial specialization and exchange.

Comparative advantage: David Ricardo

In 1817 David Ricardo showed that even in the case shown in Table 4.1.3 there is still room for mutually beneficial specialization and exchange. He showed that what matters is comparative and not absolute advantage. Relative, and not absolute, cost of production is important. This means that we should look at the opportunity cost of producing each good for each country. A country has a comparative advantage in the production of a good that it can produce at a lower opportunity cost than its trading partner. Table 4.1.3 focuses on which country sacrifices fewer bananas to produce an apple and which country sacrifices fewer apples to produce a banana.

Focusing on Red	Focusing on Green	It follows that:
Red can produce either 40 apples or 20 bananas. If it produces 20 bananas it will sacrifice 40 apples: opportunity cost of 20 bananas = 40 apples. Dividing by 20: **opportunity cost of 1 banana = 2 apples**	Green can produce either 60 apples or 90 bananas. If it produces 90 bananas it will sacrifice 60 apples: opportunity cost of 90 bananas = 60 apples. Dividing by 90: **opportunity cost of 1 banana = ⅔ of an apple**	Green can produce a banana at a lower opportunity cost: it needs to sacrifice ⅔ of an apple whereas Red must sacrifice 2 apples. Green has a comparative advantage in producing bananas: it should specialize in and export bananas.
Red can produce either 40 apples or 20 bananas. If it produces 40 apples it will sacrifice 20 bananas: opportunity cost of 40 apples = 20 bananas. Dividing by 40: **opportunity cost of 1 apple = ½ of a banana**	Green can produce either 60 apples or 90 bananas. If it produces 60 apples it will sacrifice 90 bananas: opportunity cost of 60 apples = 90 bananas. Dividing by 60: **opportunity cost of 1 apple = 1.5 bananas**	Red can produce an apple at a lower opportunity cost: it needs to sacrifice ½ of a banana whereas Green must sacrifice 1.5 bananas. Red has a comparative advantage in apple production: it should specialize in and export apples.

Table 4.1.3

We have established which country should produce apples and which should produce bananas. How can they now trade and increase their consumption bundles?

Green, which will specialize in bananas, sacrifices two-thirds of an apple to produce one banana so it will be willing to sell (export) one banana if it earns more than the opportunity cost to produce it (that is, more than two-thirds of an apple). Red will be willing to buy (import) one banana if it can pay less than two apples, which is the opportunity cost Red experiences of producing one banana.

A mutually beneficial exchange can occur if they trade one banana for one apple.

Green will sell (export) one banana to buy (import) one apple.

Note that looking at it the other way around leads to the same conclusion: Red will be willing to sell (export) one apple if it earns more than half of a banana, which is the opportunity cost of producing it. So, earning one banana for one apple is acceptable. Green will be willing to buy (import) an apple if pays less than the opportunity cost to produce one, which is one and a half bananas.

Red will sell (export) one apple to buy one banana.

If these two countries trade they will be able to consume combinations of the two goods that are outside their production possibilities. For example, Red can sell (export) 20 apples for 20 bananas. It could therefore consume 20 apples *and* 20 bananas.

Green can sell (export) 20 bananas for 20 apples. It could therefore consume 70 bananas *and* 20 apples. Both countries can consume outside their PPCs.

Note that there is room for mutually beneficial specialization and exchange only if the PPCs of the two countries are parallel because in this case the opportunity costs are the same.

Sources of comparative advantage

Ultimately, comparative advantage depends on differences in factor endowments and in technology.

- Differences in the quantity and quality of **factor endowments** result from differences in the stock of natural capital and its productivity, differences in the stock of human capital and its productivity and differences in the stock of physical capital and its productivity.

- Differences in **technology** are manifested indirectly as technology is embodied in the physical capital available and affects the productivity of human capital.

In addition:

- Actual trade flows can also be affected by movements in the exchange rate. For example, a stronger currency increases the foreign price of an exported good and may result in shrinking export markets.

- Changes in relative inflation rates also affect trade flows. Higher inflation in a country worsens the international competitiveness of the goods and services it exports as they become relatively more expensive over time.

- Many countries also pay export subsidies to lower the cost of producing a good or a service artificially and therefore increase its competitiveness abroad.

- Lastly, non-price factors can lead to the creation or the loss of comparative advantage and of international competitiveness. These factors include product design, reliability or quality of after-sales support. For example, exports of German capital goods are not significantly affected by an appreciating euro because of their good reputation in foreign markets.

Limitations of the model

Despite the model of comparative advantage being helpful in determining which goods a country should export and which goods it should import, it does not fully explain actual trade flows. The limitations arise from the underlying assumptions of the model.

- The theory of comparative advantage assumes that goods are homogeneous. This may be the case for agricultural goods, but it is definitely not the case for services or for manufactured goods. For example, both Italy and Germany produce, export and import cars because cars are highly differentiated products.

- It is assumed that opportunity costs are constant so that no matter how much of a good is produced the additional cost of producing one more unit remains the same and thus the PPCs are linear. In the real world, though, there are often economies of scale as increased levels of production are commonly associated with lower average costs.

- It is assumed that factors of production are perfectly mobile, easily switching from producing one good to producing another other. Is labour both geographically and occupationally mobile, though? A worker may not have the necessary skills to switch jobs or may not be able to move location.

- It is assumed that there are no transportation costs which, despite these often being very low because of container shipping, may sometimes impede trade.

- It is assumed that there are no trade barriers, but there are plenty of barriers that restrict trade flows in the world.

Complete specialization is risky

It should be noted that complete specialization in one good or service, or in a narrow range is very risky according to a strict interpretation of the theory of comparative advantage. If a country has a significant comparative advantage in tourism it should not specialize only in exporting tourism services because if something went wrong, its economy would be devastated. Export revenues would collapse, decreasing aggregate demand and real GDP. This was painfully realized after the outbreak of Covid-19 in countries relying almost exclusively on tourism. A country must try to diversify, specializing in and exporting a wide range of products. By doing so it minimizes risks. This is especially true for certain developing nations that often specialize in and export a narrow range of mostly primary products.

Comparative advantage is a dynamic concept

It should also be noted that comparative advantage is a dynamic concept as it can and does change over time. Governments invest in education, raising labour productivity. They may also import technology by attracting foreign direct investment (FDI) in high-tech sectors. In addition, they may pursue a variety of industrial policies in the hope of creating a comparative advantage over the very long term, as many countries have. For example, South Korea's exports of electronic and integrated circuits, as well as of cargo ships and cars, are to a large degree a result of successful industrial policies.

4.2 Types of trade protection

Despite the many benefits derived from free trade, many countries restrict trade flows and employ various degrees of trade protection. The most common forms are tariffs, quotas, subsidies and administrative barriers.

Tariffs

Analysis of a tariff

A tariff is defined as a tax imposed on imports aimed at restricting their flow into the country and protecting domestic producers. It has been the most common form of protection. It may be specific or ad valorem. For example, in May 2019 the USA imposed 25% on about $250 billion of Chinese products. A tariff will tend to raise the domestic price and domestic production of the good while lowering the amounts consumed and imported.

Figure 4.2.1 refers to the market for corn in some country. Let the world price of corn be at Pw. Assuming free trade, the world price will prevail in the domestic market in a small country. Remember that, in this context, "small" means that the country can buy or sell as much of the product as it wants without the world price changing.

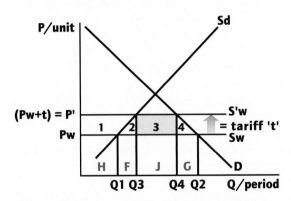

Figure 4.2.1 Effects of a tariff on the market for corn

With the price at Pw, domestic firms will offer Q1 units of corn per period while domestic consumption will be Q2 units of corn per period. The difference Q2 – Q1 = Q1Q2 is the quantity (volume) of corn imported. In addition:

- total revenues collected by domestic corn farmers = Pw × Q1 = area (H)
- total expenditures on corn by domestic consumers = Pw × Q2 = area (H + F + J + G)
- import expenditures = Pw × Q1Q2 = area (F + J + G).

Assume now that the government in order to protect domestic corn producers imposes a tariff equal to "t" dollars per unit of corn. The tariff will raise the domestic price to P' = (Pw + t). The tariff "t" is thus equal to P'Pw dollars per unit on Figure 4.2.1. The world price Pw is not affected if, as a result of the tariff, the country demands less corn because the country is small—its production and consumption decisions are insignificant and do not affect the world price.

Given the new price P' established in the domestic market, domestic production will rise to Q3 units of corn per period while domestic consumption drops to Q4 units of corn per period. The volume of imports shrinks to Q4 – Q3 = Q3Q4 of corn units per period. In addition:

- total revenues collected by domestic corn farmers = P' × Q3 = area (H + F + 2 + 1)
- total expenditures on corn by domestic consumers = P' × Q4 = area (H + F + J + 3 + 2 + 1); note that whether they increased or decreased depends on the price elasticity of demand (PED).
- import expenditures = Pw × Q3Q4 = area (J) as the tariff "t" per unit is collected by the domestic government so foreigners (exporters) still earn Pw dollars per unit of corn
- tariff revenues collected by the government = "t" × Q3Q4 or, P'Pw × Q3Q4 = area (3).

A welfare analysis reveals the following.

- Consumer surplus decreases by area (1 + 2 + 3 + 4) as a result of the higher price paid and the lower quantity enjoyed. Domestic buyers of corn are clearly worse off.

- Producer surplus increases by area (1) as domestic producers sell more corn and earn a higher price (remember that the tariff is collected from the imported units of corn).

- Area (3) is collected by the government and may be spent on schools, health care or infrastructure so it is money put back into the economy and it cannot be considered a welfare loss.

- It follows that a tariff leads to a welfare loss equal to area (2) and area (4).

Area (2) is referred to as production inefficiency because it costs more to produce units Q1Q3 domestically than it would have cost the country to import these units at the world price Pw. Analytically, the cost of producing Q1Q3 units domestically is area (F + 2), the area under the supply curve, as the supply curve is also the marginal cost of producing a good. The cost of importing these units is only area (F), the product of units Q1Q3 times the world price Pw at which they could have been bought under free trade. Area (2) therefore represents net value lost by society from units Q1Q3 being domestically produced even though they should have been imported instead.

Area (4) is referred to as consumption inefficiency because units Q4Q2 are now, as a result of the tariff, not being consumed by domestic consumers even though these units are valued by consumers more than what it would have cost to import them. Analytically, units Q4Q2 are worth to consumers area (G + 4), which is the area under the demand curve, and is the sum of how much consumers would have been willing to pay to consume these units. It would have cost to import and enjoy these units only area (G), the product of units Q4Q2 times the world price Pw at which they could have been bought under free trade. Area (4) therefore represents net value lost by society from units Q4Q2 not being consumed even though they should have been.

Quotas

Analysis of a quota

A quota is a quantitative restriction on the volume of imports. For example, in 2018 the USA imposed a quota on Korean steel imports equal to 2.68 million tons per year, which meant that the USA restricted annual steel imports of steel from Korea to that specific amount. This was a 21% decrease from the 2017 volume of imports. Figure 4.2.2 shows the effect of such a quota, using corn as an example.

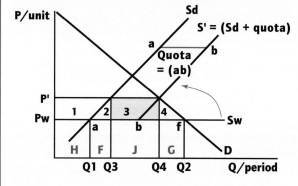

Figure 4.2.2 Effects of a quota on the market for corn

In Figure 4.2.2, the world price for corn is at Pw. At price Pw, domestic farmers are willing to offer Q1 units of corn per period while domestic consumption will be Q2 units. The volume of corn imports will be Q2 - Q1 = Q1Q2 = af units of corn per period.

The government now decides to limit the quantity of corn imports from af to only ab units per period. No more than ab units of imported corn may enter the domestic market. How much corn is supplied in this market?

Before the quota was imposed, at the world price Pw, the supply of corn faced by domestic buyers was infinitely elastic at Sw. At that price, foreign producers would offer as much corn as domestic consumers demanded. Therefore, at the world price Pw, given the demand for corn D, Q1 units of corn were offered by domestic farmers and Q1Q2 units were offered by foreign exporters.

The supply of corn in the domestic market is now restricted. At the world price Pw, domestic farmers are still willing to offer Q1 units of corn but only ab units are allowed to be imported as a result of the quota. So, at Pw, there is an excess demand for corn equal to bf. Total quantity supplied by both domestic and foreign producers is equal to line segment Pwb while quantity demanded is line segment Pwf. There is pressure for the domestic price of corn to rise.

What is the effective supply of corn in this market? At each price, it will be equal to whatever domestic producers are willing to offer plus the fixed quota amount of corn ab. We therefore draw from point b a line parallel and to the right of Sd at S' so that the horizontal rightward shift is equal at all prices to distance ab. Note that supply of corn in this market has decreased from Sw to S'. The world supply Sw pivoted to S'.

The new equilibrium price of corn in the domestic market will be at P' where demand D intersects the effective corn supply S'. At that price, domestic farmers are willing to offer Q3 units of corn and buyers are willing to purchase Q4 units of corn. The difference Q4–Q3 = Q3Q4 is the quantity of imports which is, of course, equal to the amount of the imposed quota ab.

Before the quota was imposed:

- total revenues collected by domestic corn farmers = Pw × Q1 = area (H)
- total expenditures on corn by domestic consumers = Pw × Q2 = area (H + F + J + G)
- import expenditures = Pw × Q1Q2 = area (F + J + G).

After the quota was imposed:

- total revenues collected by domestic corn farmers = P' × Q3 = area (H + F + 2 + 1)
- total expenditures on corn by domestic consumers = P' × Q4 = area (H + F + J + 3 + 2 + 1); note that whether they have increased or decreased depends on the price elasticity of demand (PED).

A welfare analysis reveals the following points.

- Consumer surplus decreases by area (1 + 2 + 3 + 4) as a result of the higher price paid and the lower quantity enjoyed. Domestic buyers of corn are clearly worse off.

- Producer surplus increases by area (1) as domestic producers sell more corn and earn a higher price.

- Area (3), the shaded area is known as "quota rents" and represents money typically earned by the foreign exporting firms that can now export the product at a higher price as a result of the restricted supply. The money represented by shaded area (3) may also go to foreign governments. The money that area (3) represents is rarely received by the domestic government. This would be the case only if the domestic government auctioned off the quota licences. Note that the term *rents* in economics refers to income earned as a result of some favourable policy decision.

- The effects of a quota are the same as those of an "equivalent" tariff (that is, a tariff that would also raise the domestic price to P') with one exception: the tariff revenues area (3) now represents quota rents that are usually collected by foreigners, so they represent an additional welfare loss.

- It follows that a quota typically leads to a greater welfare loss equal to area (2), which reflects the resulting production inefficiency explained earlier, plus area (4), which reflects the resulting consumption inefficiency also explained earlier, plus area (3), the quota rents.

The existence of quota rents helps explain why quotas are often imposed instead of tariffs even though the associated welfare loss is usually bigger. Foreigners are better off as they usually collect these rents. If the foreign exporting firms collect the quota rent, then their export revenues (and equivalently, the import expenditures of the importing country) are bigger than if an equivalent tariff had been imposed. Their export revenues may even be greater than they would have been under free trade. With free trade their export revenues (and, import expenditures) were equal to area (F + J + G)—whereas with a quota appropriated by the foreign exporter they are equal to area (J + 3), which could be greater. This possibility minimizes the probability of retaliation.

Recap

Effects of quotas

A quota:

- increases the domestic price of the protected good
- increases domestic production of the good
- decreases consumption of the good
- decreases the volume of imports
- decreases consumer surplus
- increases producer surplus
- creates "quota rents", which are usually collected by foreigners
- leads to production inefficiency and resource misallocation
- leads to consumption inefficiency
- is responsible for a welfare loss greater than that of an equivalent tariff (assuming that the quota rents are collected by foreigners).

Subsidies

Analysis of production subsidies and of export subsidies

A production subsidy is a per unit payment by the government on all units of the good produced by a firm. An export subsidy is a per unit payment by the government only on the units exported by a firm. In both analyses we keep the assumption that the country is small in the context of economics.

Production subsidy

A production subsidy is a per unit payment by the government to firms on all units of output produced, which leads to a decrease in their production costs. The lower production cost permits firms to produce more at each price so that imports of the good decrease. The effects of a production subsidy are illustrated in Figure 4.2.3.

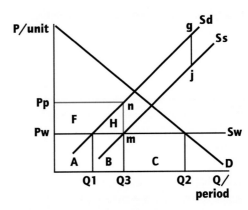

Figure 4.2.3 Effects of a production subsidy on the market for corn

In Figure 4.2.3 the world price of corn is at Pw. At that price domestic farmers are willing to offer Q1 units of corn per period while domestic consumption of corn will be at Q2 units per period. The quantity of corn imported, if trade is free, will thus be equal to Q2 – Q1 = Q1Q2 units of corn per period. In addition:

- total revenues collected by domestic producers = Pw × Q1 = area (A)

- total expenditures by domestic consumers = Pw × Q2 = area (A + B + C)

- import expenditures = Pw × Q1Q2 = area (B + C).

If the government now grants a production subsidy equal to jg dollars per unit of output, then the decrease in production costs will increase supply and shift the supply curve to the right or, better yet, vertically downwards by the amount of the subsidy jg to Ss. Remember the supply curve is the marginal cost (MC) curve so marginal cost decreases by jg dollars.

The world price will not be affected (given a small country case). At the world price Pw domestic firms will be willing to offer Q3 units per period because of their now lower production costs. Now, though, per unit sold they earn Pp, which is equal to what consumers pay (Pw) plus the subsidy mn paid by the government. Consumption remains unchanged at Q2. It follows that the quantity (volume) of imports decreased from Q1Q2 to Q3Q2. In addition:

- total revenues collected by domestic producers increase to Pw × Q3 = area (A + B + H + F).

- total expenditures by domestic consumers remain the same equal to area (A + B + C) since the price paid and the quantity consumed do not change

- import expenditures decrease to Pw × Q3Q2 = area (C); (remember that import expenditures are equal to the export revenues foreigners collect).

A welfare analysis reveals the following.

- Consumer surplus remains the same as consumers pay the same price and consume the same quantity.

- Producer surplus increases by area (F) because the price earned per unit by producers Pp is equal to the world price Pw plus the subsidy mn paid by the government, which is equal to jg, the vertical distance between the two supply curves.

- The cost of the subsidy to the government is equal to the subsidy per unit mn times the quantity produced Q3 or, area (F + H). This cost must somehow be financed. It can be financed by higher taxes now, by increased borrowing now and higher taxes later or by cutting back on some other government expenditure. An opportunity cost is therefore involved.

- It follows that a production subsidy leads to a welfare loss equal to area (H). This represents the production inefficiency because units Q1Q3 are now produced domestically even though it would have been cheaper to import them.

Export subsidy

An export subsidy is a per unit payment by the government to firms based only on the units of output exported. This payment means that a firm will find it more profitable to

Recap

Effects of production subsidies

A production subsidy:

- does not affect the domestic price of the protected good

- does not affect consumption of the good

- does not affect consumer surplus

- increases domestic production of the good

- increases producers' revenues

- increases producer surplus

- decreases the volume of imports

- decreases import expenditures (and thus export revenues foreigners collect)

- leads to increased government spending and financing, and imposes an opportunity cost

- leads to production inefficiency and resource misallocation

- is responsible for a welfare loss.

export the good than to sell it in the domestic market. The government's goal is to stimulate exports. Technically, export subsidies are illegal under World Trade Organization (WTO) rules but they are still granted by many countries in different forms. (See section 4.4, page 162 for information on the WTO.)

The effects of an export subsidy are illustrated in Figure 4.2.4. The world price is assumed at Pw so that quantity demanded is equal to Q1 units of corn per period while firms offer Q2 units per period. Units Q1Q2 are thus exported.

If a subsidy is paid to domestic firms equal to hj for each unit they export, then the domestic price of corn will increase to P'. This is because firms earn P' by selling abroad so they will not

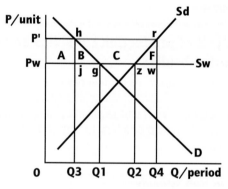

Figure 4.2.4 Effects of an export subsidy on the market for corn

be willing to sell any quantity domestically unless they also earn P' in the home market. The difference P'–Pw is equal to the export subsidy paid hj. At P', domestic consumption will decrease to Q3 while firms will offer Q4 units. The quantity of corn exports increases from Q1Q2 (= gz) to Q3Q4 (= jw) units per period. In addition:

- total revenues collected by domestic producers increase from area (0Q2zPw) to area (0Q4rP')

- total expenditures by domestic consumers change from area (0Q1gPw) to area (0Q3hP'); whether they have increased or decreased depends on PED
- export revenues increase from area (Q1Q2zg) to area (Q3Q4rh).

A welfare analysis reveals the following.

- Consumer surplus decreases by area (A + B) as a result of the higher price paid and the lower quantity enjoyed. Domestic buyers of corn are clearly worse off.
- Producer surplus increases by area (A + B + C) as producers sell a greater quantity and earn a higher price.
- The cost to the government of the export subsidy is equal to the subsidy per unit hj times the volume of exports jw (= Q3Q4), or area (B + C + F); the government must finance this cost by increasing taxes now, by borrowing now and increasing taxes later or by cutting back on some other government project.
- There is therefore a welfare loss equal to area (B + F). This becomes clear since the gains were equal to areas (A + B + C) while the losses were equal to areas (A + B) plus areas (B + C + F). Areas (A), (C) and one of the two (B) areas cancel out, leaving areas (B + F) as the welfare loss.

> ### Recap
> #### Effects of export subsidies
> An export subsidy:
> - increases the domestic price of the good
> - decreases consumption of the good
> - decreases consumer surplus
> - increases domestic production of the good
> - increases the revenues of domestic firms
> - increases the quantity of exports
> - increases producer surplus
> - leads to increased government spending and financing as it imposes an opportunity cost
> - leads to production inefficiency and resource misallocation
> - leads to consumption inefficiency
> - is responsible for a welfare loss.

Administrative trade barriers

Administrative trade barriers are also referred to as regulatory or legal barriers and are a common form of trade protection. Standards are set that imports must satisfy otherwise they are prohibited. These may be health-related standards, environmental standards or safety standards. For example, the EU and the UK do not permit imports of chlorine-washed chicken and hormone-treated beef from the USA. The USA maintains that these restrictions aim at blocking US exports of chicken and beef. Countries set environmental regulations such as specified emissions standards for car imports to protect the domestic population and combat climate change but some so-called "green regulations" may be used only to impede imports. Safety standards are set to protect consumers, for example regulations concerning automobile or electrical equipment, or chemicals or children's products. Some standards, though, may be set just to make it more costly for foreign exporting firms to comply and so they amount to disguised protectionism. The issue is to ensure that the standards are set to protect domestic consumers and are not just an excuse for protecting domestic producers.

In addition to such standards, the importing country may add more "red tape" to the necessary bureaucracy involved when importing a good. The country may increase the typical paperwork required for exporters to complete or it may lengthen the valuation, inspection and customs clearance processes. Perhaps the most absurd example of such administrative barriers is a very old one related to the city of Poitiers in France. The French government had ordered that all Japanese video imports were to be inspected and pass customs at Poitiers instead of at a major harbour or airport. Poitiers is located inland, is far from ports and was staffed

with only a few officers who were ordered to fully inspect each and every truck. You can imagine the delays that this seemingly innocent requirement created and that resulted in effectively reducing the volume of imports entering France.

Calculations

1. Tariff exercise

Assume that a tariff is imposed on some good X. Answer the following questions using the information in Figure 4.2.5.

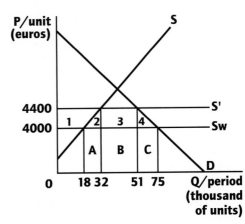

Figure 4.2.5 Tariff diagram: small country case

a. What is the size of the tariff imposed?

b. Calculate the pre-tariff volume of imports.

c. Calculate the import expenditures (or the export revenues of the foreign firms) under free trade.

d. Calculate the revenues earned by domestic producers under free trade.

e. Calculate consumer expenditures on the good under free trade.

f. Calculate the post-tariff volume of imports and their change.

g. Calculate import expenditures after the tariff was imposed and the change that occurred as a result of the tariff.

h. How much did consumers spend on the good after the tariff was imposed?

i. The money spent by consumers after the tariff was imposed was collected by foreign exporters, domestic producers and the government. Calculate how much each group collected.

j. What is the resulting production inefficiency equal to?

k. Calculate the resulting consumption inefficiency.

l. Calculate the resulting decrease in the consumer surplus.

2. Quota exercise

Assume that a quota is imposed on imports of some good X. Answer the following questions using the information in Figure 4.2.6.

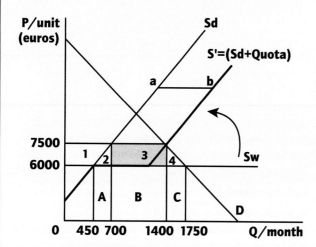

Figure 4.2.6 Quota diagram: small country case

a. What is the size of the quota imposed?

b. Calculate the import expenditures (or export revenues of the foreign firms) under free trade.

c. Calculate the revenues earned by domestic producers under free trade.

d. Calculate consumer expenditures on the good under free trade.

e. Calculate the change in the volume of imports as a result of the quota.

f. Calculate import expenditures after the quota was imposed and the change that occurred as a result of the quota.

g. How much did consumers spend on the good after the quota was imposed?

h. What can you infer about the price elasticity of demand (PED) for the good given the price change in the market?

i. Calculate the size of the quota rents. Who earns these rents?

j. Calculate the resulting decrease in the consumer surplus.

k. Calculate the resulting increase in the producer surplus.

l. What is the resulting production inefficiency equal to?

m. Calculate the resulting consumption inefficiency.

3. Production subsidy exercise

Assume that a subsidy is granted to the producers of some good X. Answer the following questions using the information in Figure 4.2.7.

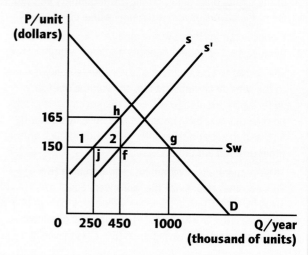

Figure 4.2.7 Production subsidy diagram: small country case

a. What is the size of the subsidy granted (on a per unit basis)?

b. Calculate the annual import expenditures (or export revenues of the foreign firms) under free trade.

c. Calculate the annual revenues earned by domestic producers under free trade.

d. Calculate annual consumer expenditures on the good under free trade.

e. Calculate the annual change in the volume of imports as a result of the subsidy.

f. Calculate annual import expenditures after the subsidy was granted and the change that occurred as a result of the subsidy.

g. How much did consumers annually spend on the good after the subsidy was granted?

h. Calculate the annual total revenues domestic firms collected after the subsidy was granted.

i. Calculate the annual cost of the subsidy to the government.

j. Calculate the change in the consumer surplus.

k. Calculate the resulting increase in the producer surplus.

l. What is the resulting production inefficiency equal to?

m. Calculate the resulting consumption inefficiency.

4. Export subsidy exercise

Assume that a subsidy is granted to the producers of some good X on each unit of X exported. Answer the following questions using the information in Figure 4.2.8.

a. What is the size of the subsidy granted (on a per unit basis)?

b. Calculate the annual export revenues that domestic producers earned before the export subsidy was granted.

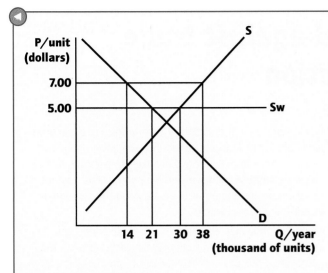

Figure 4.2.8 Export subsidy diagram

d. Calculate annual consumer expenditures on the good before the export subsidy was granted.

e. Calculate the annual change in the volume of exports as a result of the export subsidy.

f. Calculate annual export revenues after the export subsidy was granted as well as the change in export revenues earned as a result of the export subsidy.

g. How much did consumers annually spend on the good after the export subsidy was granted?

h. Calculate the annual total revenues domestic firms collected after the export subsidy was granted.

i. Calculate the annual cost of the export subsidy to the government.

j. Calculate the change in the consumer surplus.

k. Calculate the resulting increase in the producer surplus.

l. What is the resulting production inefficiency equal to?

m. Calculate the resulting consumption inefficiency.

c. Calculate the total annual revenues earned by domestic producers before the export subsidy was granted.

Arguments for and against trade control and protection

If the benefits from free trade are so many and—as shown in Figures 4.1.1a to 4.1.1c (section 4.1—net welfare of the country increases, why do so many countries restrict imports employing various degrees of protection? Why is "managed" trade so common?

The simple answer is that not all the parties involved gain from free trade. There are groups that are worse off. Free trade creates winners and losers. When the losses of the losers from free trade are significant then they may try to pressure the government for protection. This is often the case when free trade increases import penetration in a market.

Focusing on Figure 4.1.1c (page 146) it is realized that the increase in consumer surplus resulting from free trade and cheaper imports exceeds the decrease in the producer surplus that import-competing firms suffer. If there are only few affected producers then each one suffers a significant loss of revenues and profits and may also be forced to dismiss workers. In addition, these firms may be concentrated in a specific area of the country. Clearly, each of these firms has a big financial incentive to lobby the government and demand protection. Politicians are likely to succumb to these pressures because of the very visible political cost of firms shrinking or shutting down in an area and the consequent increase in unemployment.

Managed trade may also aim to increase exports. Even though consumers as a whole may be worse off when the government pursues policies that aim to promote exports artificially, the loss of income suffered from each consumer is small while the benefits enjoyed by each of the fewer exporting firms are large. This explains why governments are often active in promoting, directly or indirectly, their export-oriented firms.

Below we examine the most common arguments used in favour of protection. They are divided into non-economic arguments and economic arguments.

Arguments in favour of protection

Common non-economic arguments

- Governments often erect trade barriers to ensure that in case of a conflict a country is self-sufficient in the production of crucial goods for strategic reasons. The weapons and aerospace industries as well as the food industry are often classified as being of such strategic importance. The validity of this argument is doubtful, at least for countries belonging in wide strategic and/or political alliances.

- Trade barriers are employed to restrict imports of drugs and other harmful substances. Trade barriers are also used to pressurize and weaken politically unfriendly countries and in these cases are referred to as embargoes.

- Some countries resort to protection to preserve a way of life or their cultural identity as part of a broader social strategy. For example, the television stations in many countries restrict the number of broadcast hours of foreign language films and programmes.

- Trade barriers also exist to ensure that certain minimum safety and health standards are met. The goal is purportedly to protect the public but often such standards are a pretence through which domestic producers are protected.

Common economic arguments in favour of protection

- A most common argument in favour of restricting trade is to protect domestic jobs. Many claim that free trade decreases employment as cheaper and higher quality foreign products flood the domestic market, forcing domestic firms to shut down. Cheap foreign labour is typically blamed for the resulting higher rates of unemployment.

These claims must be carefully evaluated. First, higher domestic wages do not necessarily imply higher labour costs for firms because labour productivity is important. If domestic wages are higher because of higher labour productivity, then labour costs may be even lower than abroad and therefore there is no reason to fear imports.

If the higher domestic wages are not a reflection of higher labour productivity, then the domestic industry has a comparative disadvantage. Theory suggests that labour and other resources should be channelled to other, more efficient uses. Workers and owners of capital, and perhaps whole regions, will face real adjustment costs and, of course, will resist these changes. They will try to blame foreigners for their plight and will demand protection.

Instead of protection, which will reduce the incentive to restructure and adjust, other policies could be adopted to smoothen the adjustment, especially for displaced workers. Note that in many cases shifting resources from one use to another may be almost impossible without significant government assistance, which itself is costly to implement. In such cases, trade liberalization should proceed gradually. Also, if employment in a whole region relies on the distressed industry with few or no employment alternatives for the local population, then the trade liberalization process must be gradual to give sufficient time for owners of capital and workers to adjust. Recent research has found that people do not move easily to another location even if they have no job. Financial incentives do not matter as much as economists had thought, according to Esther Duflo (Nobel Prize, 2019). This significantly complicates the issue.

- Another common argument in favour of protection is to improve a trade deficit. A trade deficit exists if the value of imports of goods and services is greater than export revenues. The idea is that protection will render imports more expensive and less attractive. Spending on imports will then decrease, shrinking and correcting the trade imbalance.

  There are several potential problems with this argument. First, it invites retaliation from trading partners as any improvement in a country's trade balance comes at their expense. Second, restricting foreign products into the country will decrease foreign incomes and consequently their ability to buy the country's exports. Third, and most importantly, such a policy does not treat the fundamental cause of a widening trade deficit problem. The ballooning trade deficit may be the result of domestic products being expensive and therefore uncompetitive: domestic goods and services may be unable to penetrate foreign markets (so that exports decrease) and they are also not the preferred choice for domestic households who find it cheaper to buy imported products instead (so that imports rise). High inflation, rigid labour markets that result in high labour costs, uncompetitive domestic markets, as well as poor quality, lack of reliability, delivery issues, poor design or poor marketing may be the real reasons behind a growing trade deficit. In these cases, protection will not prove helpful and possibly may prove detrimental as it will delay the adoption of appropriate remedial policies.

- Governments may decide to erect import barriers to assist the growth of certain industries in their initial stages of development. The idea is that once these industries acquire the necessary know-how and lower their unit costs by achieving economies of scale, they will be able to meet international competition. At that point, theory dictates, protection should be removed. This is the well-known "infant industry" argument and is essentially a form of industrial policy.

  This argument also needs to be carefully evaluated. It is indeed theoretically sensible, and the policy has been adopted by all developed economies in the past including the USA, as well as by all Asian export achievers in varying degrees. However, it also suffers from the previously discussed drawbacks of industrial policies. How does a government pick a "winner"? It may be difficult to determine which industry qualifies for such treatment. If a mistake is made, will it be possible for the government to reverse its course and withdraw its support? Removing the protection could be fiercely resisted by the industry stakeholders. If protectionism is not lifted as theory dictates, then we have the case of the "perpetual infant". There is an inherent risk of making the industry over-reliant on state support, sluggish and inefficient.

- The World Trade Organization (WTO) permits a country to impose tariffs (taxes on imports) on a good if dumping is suspected. Dumping is said to exist if a firm is selling abroad at a price below the normal price it sells at in its own country, or below average cost. Often this could be because exporters are subsidized directly or indirectly by their government. The injured firm may file a complaint with the WTO (see section 4.4, page 162) and

its government may impose a tariff, referred to as "anti-dumping duty", to minimize the injury.

The WTO launches an investigation to determine the extent of any dumping taking place. It is not always easy to determine the "normal price" of the good as the price may vary depending on the region at which the good is sold, the buyers of the good or the time period during which dumping was allegedly taking place. As anti-dumping duties are automatically imposed when dumping is suspected and the investigation is lengthy, many industries make an accusation of dumping when imports flood their domestic market to gain time until a verdict is reached in order to restructure and (they hope) to become more efficient.

- Tariffs provide a government with revenues. Tax systems in certain developing countries are ineffective, making it difficult for their governments to collect sufficient revenue to finance pro-development activities. Since points of entry into a country are few, taxing imports may be a last resort to collect revenue, which cannot be given up. If this is the case then trade liberalization must be gradual to ensure that the provision of basic government services is not interrupted.

- Protection may be necessary when a developing country is trying to diversify its production and export base. Diversification refers to the process of increasing the variety of goods and services produced and exported in order to decrease risks (see section 4.10, page 198). Many developing countries still produce and export a limited range of products according to the principle of comparative advantage (an HL concept). If these countries are to decrease risks, they need to develop, through appropriate investments, a comparative advantage in new areas. Also, in the meantime they need to keep out imports from more efficient foreign producers. This is accomplished through protection of the new industries being established. It is again a form of necessary industrial policy.

Recap

Non-economic arguments in favour of protection

These include arguments that protection is needed to:

- ensure self-sufficiency in certain crucial industries such as weapons or food
- block imports of drugs and illegal substances
- protect a way of life (cultural issues)
- protect the health and safety of the population.

Economic arguments in favour of protection

These include arguments that protection is needed to:

- protect jobs from foreign competition
- correct a trade deficit
- protect against possible dumping
- enhance government revenues
- protect infant industries
- help a developing country diversify its produce and export base.

Arguments against protection

- Protection breeds inefficiency as domestic firms are exposed to less competition and are faced with captive domestic markets. Less competition implies greater domestic monopoly power.

- Greater monopoly power for domestic firms implies higher prices for buyers. Higher prices decrease consumer surplus and lower the purchasing power for households. Their ability to express demand for all other goods and services in the economy is therefore constrained. This could have negative effects on overall output and employment levels. Unfortunately, these effects are not conspicuous and may be ignored by politicians.

- Higher prices for domestic firms that import intermediate products (inputs in their own production process) imply higher production costs, so higher prices for these firms. Aggregate supply may decrease, and cost-push inflationary pressures may even arise.

- If these domestic firms happen to be export-oriented their competitiveness in international markets will be eroded, hurting their sales and adversely affecting overall employment levels in the economy. Protectionism usually destroys more jobs than it preserves or create.

- Protectionism may induce retaliation ("tit for tat") by foreign governments. If the trade frictions escalate then a trade war may result, in the long term hurting all parties involved.

- Consumers and firms are faced with limited options to choose from. The reduction in variety is a cost since buyers (consumers as well as firms) have to settle for their second-best or third-best choice. Utility decreases for households while competitiveness decreases for firms.

- Domestic firms will not be exposed to the technological advancements embodied in imported machinery (capital goods).

Recap

Arguments against protectionism

- It breeds inefficiency as a result of less competition and greater monopoly power, leading to waste and misallocation of resources.

- It leads to higher prices for consumers decreasing their purchasing power and their ability to express demand for other products.

- It limits choice for consumers and for firms as variety decreases.

- It increases the production costs of firms importing intermediate goods (inputs), forcing them to increase their prices.

- It may also reduce export competitiveness of domestic firms relying on more expensive imported inputs.

- It deprives domestic firms of taking advantage of the technological progress embodied in imported capital goods

- It increases the possibility of retaliation by trading partners.

Policymakers' perspective

Free trade versus trade protection

Just a few years ago there would have been no dilemma. Free trade has been responsible for much of the growth and rising incomes most countries have witnessed over the last few decades. Almost all economists agree that free trade is beneficial to economies. However, surveys suggest that only about one-third of the general public have a similar positive opinion on free, for reasons explained earlier. The benefits from trade, even though greater in size, are not as visible to the layperson as the costs. Most people can identify a firm or an industry that has shrunk or shut down because of free trade and may even know someone who has lost his or her job in such circumstances. Most of us, though, are not aware how much cheaper our clothes, appliances or cars are because of free trade.

The conclusion that free trade leads to a net welfare gain rests on one crucial assumption, namely that winners fully compensate losers. This compensation can be accomplished through targeted government policies. Governments can help displaced workers to retrain and move to industries and areas with plentiful jobs. Governments can help owners of capital to start new businesses that can compete more effectively in world markets. Too often though, losers, especially labour, have been neglected and this compensation has never materialized. This may help explain why, in the past few years, protection has increased and why there has been a backlash against globalization.

The best example of this new and dangerous trend is clear in the tariffs imposed by the USA on many goods ranging from solar panels and washing machines to steel and aluminum. These tariffs have led to retaliatory tariffs by the USA's trading partners. Studies have found the following.

- US companies, as a result of the recent tariffs, lost more than $1.7 trillion in the price of their stocks (www.nber.org).

- Overall, US employment decreased by almost 300 000 jobs (www.brookings.edu).

- These retaliatory tariffs by USA's trading partners were costing US exporters approximately $2.6 billion per month in lost exports (www.princeton.edu).

In addition, as our earlier tariff analysis suggests, American consumers and firms have borne almost entirely the cost of the tariffs imposed.

Slower growth in the USA, China and other major economies will decrease demand for commodities, affecting commodity exporters in Africa, South America and Australia. It will also slow down exports of all goods and services from the rest of the world with potentially devastating consequences for their economies.

The Covid-19 pandemic has only made these matters worse, especially for developing countries. The response of the advanced economies is crucial. Most policymakers, including world organizations such as the IMF and the World Bank, agree that perhaps the only solution is the return to free trade—accompanied this time with policies that compensate the vulnerable in each economy.

References

www.brookings.edu/podcast-episode/how-have-trumps-trade-wars-affected-rust-belt-jobs/

www.nber.org/system/files/working_papers/w27114/w27114.pdf; page 33

www.princeton.edu/~reddings/papers/CEPR-DP13564.pdf; page 15

4.4 Economic integration

Globalization implies greater interconnectedness of countries in the world. This greater interconnectedness is also expressed in the area of international trade. Economies have become more open, meaning that the size of exports and imports as a proportion of GDP has been increasing. The volume and value of annual trade flows has been rising in the past decades as a result of trade liberalization.

Trade liberalization, defined as a process of reducing or even eliminating trade barriers, may be achieved through preferential trade agreements or, multilaterally through the World Trade Organization (WTO) which currently has 164 member countries representing roughly 98% of world trade.

Preferential trade agreements

Preferential trade agreements are agreements between two or more countries to eliminate trade barriers between them on a narrow or wider range of goods and services.

If the agreement is between two countries it is referred to as a bilateral agreement. If it is between many, usually neighbouring countries, it is referred to as a regional agreement (a regional trading bloc). If it is between many countries that may not be in the same region it is referred to as a plurilateral agreement (but this distinction is not necessary here). Lastly, if it is between all countries who are members of the WTO it is referred to as a multilateral agreement.

Trading blocs

Regional trading blocs or agreements

According to the WTO, in 2020 there were 320 regional trade agreements in force up from 294 in 2019. There has been a proliferation of regional trading blocs because such agreements are faster to achieve and because of growing demand for deeper integration between countries.

Types of trading bloc

- Free trade area (FTA): this is formed when a group of countries agrees to phase out or eliminate trade barriers between them while each maintains its own tariff (trade barriers) toward non-members. Free trade areas require "rules of origin" to prevent non-members shipping goods into the area through the country with the lowest external tariff. For example, it may be required that at least 80% of the components of a laptop are manufactured within the group to qualify for 0% tariff.

- Customs union: an FTA may evolve into a customs union if, in addition, members agree to a common external tariff or, more generally, to a common trade policy toward non-members.

- Common market: a customs union may evolve into a common market if, in addition, to the free flow of goods and services within the bloc there is also free flow of:
  - capital (cross-border investments within the bloc)
  - labour (no work permits are required for a citizen of any member country to work in any other member country).

The highest form of integration is for the bloc to evolve into an economic and monetary union. Members of an economic union harmonize certain economic policies, particularly macroeconomic and regulatory policies. They coordinate tax and government spending policies. They share common regulatory policies (on, say, competition issues or bank supervision), as well as other policies such as on climate, the environment, health, security, justice and migration. Members of a monetary union adopt, in addition, a common currency and share a common central bank.

Examples of regional trading blocs

- **Free Trade Area (FTA)**. The prime example is the USMCA, the United States–Mexico–Canada Agreement, which came into force on 1 July 2020. It is referred to as the new NAFTA (the 1994 North American Free Trade Agreement) as it incorporates some minor changes. For example, the USMCA changed the "country of origin" rule for automobiles so that 75% of components, up from 62.5%, must be manufactured inside the area; it also stipulates somewhat greater protection of workers, so in factories making cars, workers must earn at least $16 an hour by 2023; US farmers have greater access to Canada's dairy market; it strengthens intellectual property rights, extending copyright protection of an author's work by 20 years, for example.

Other examples include:

  - the US–Israel FTA, which entered into force in 1985
  - the ASEAN Free Trade Area, established by the original ASEAN 6 (Brunei Darussalam, Indonesia, Malaysia, the Philippines, Singapore and Thailand) in 1992 and by 1999 had added Cambodia, Laos, Myanmar and Viet Nam.

- **Customs union**. The Southern African Customs Union (SACU) which includes Botswana, Lesotho, Namibia,

South Africa and Eswatini was established in 1910. It is the world's oldest Customs union.

The EU was initially a customs union when in July 1968 the six member countries of the European Economic Community (EEC)—Belgium, Germany, France, Italy, Luxembourg and the Netherlands—eliminated all customs duties between them and adopted a common external tariff.

- **Common market.** The Southern Common Market (MERCOSUR) was initially established by Argentina, Brazil, Paraguay and Uruguay, and subsequently joined as associate members by Bolivia, Chile, Colombia, Ecuador, Guyana, Peru and Surinam. Venezuela's membership was suspended in 2016.

The Common Market for Eastern and Southern Africa (COMESA) has included 21 African states since July 2018.

The European Customs Union was transformed into a common market in 1993 when adopting the four freedoms of movement of goods, services, people and money.

- **Economic and monetary union.** The European Union now has 27 member countries. Currently, 19 of these member states have joined in a monetary union with a common central, the European Central Bank, and the euro as their common currency.

Recap

How trading blocs are formed

- A **free trade area** is formed if members eliminate or agree to phase out trade barriers between them, but each member country maintains its trade policy towards non-members.

- A **customs union** is formed if free trade area members agree to adopt a common trade policy towards non-members.

- A **common market** is formed if members of a customs union additionally agree to permit the free flow of capital and labour.

- An **economic union** is formed if members of a common market additionally harmonize certain macroeconomic and regulatory policies.

- A **monetary union** is formed if members of an economic union agree to adopt a common currency and to establish a common central bank.

Advantages and disadvantages of trading blocs

The big question is whether preferential trade agreements are a "stumbling block" or a "building block" to multilateral trade liberalization through the WTO. Since almost all WTO members are also members of at least one preferential trade agreement but, at the same time, non-members of most agreements, the significance of evaluating the role of trading blocs becomes apparent.

Static effects

The static analysis of trading blocs rests on the work of Jacob Viner in 1950 who introduced the terms *trade creation* and *trade diversion*.

Trade creation refers to an increase in imports that displace less efficient domestic production. The elimination of the internal trade barriers in a trading bloc will lead members to import from one another goods and services that were previously produced domestically. Some domestic production will be replaced by imports from another member. This increases efficiency since production shifts away from a domestic producer with high costs to a foreign member producer with lower costs, leading to fewer scarce resources being wasted.

Trade diversion arises when imports shift from an efficient non-member to a less efficient member due to the preferences the latter enjoys. The external tariff for non-members may render some member artificially cheaper in the production of a good. Another member will then switch importing from the truly efficient and lowest cost non-member to the artificially cheaper member. This is inefficient since it implies production against what comparative advantage would dictate. However, it is still possible that the effect improves welfare as both consumers and producers within the importing country face prices closer to the true world price levels. For example, consider the USA, Mexico and South Korea. Assume that the USA has a 20% tariff on shoes imported from both Mexico and South Korea. Initially the USA is importing shoes from South Korea as this country is the cheapest, more efficient producer, despite the tariff. If, though, the USA and Mexico agree to sign a customs union then shoe tariffs will be scrapped for Mexican shoe exporters, but will still be in place for South Korean manufacturers. The USA may switch away from the more efficient South Korean shoe imports because Mexican shoes will now be artificially cheaper.

The relative size of trade creation and trade diversion will vary from case to case and it will determine whether the agreement enhances or diminishes static efficiency.

Dynamic advantages of trading blocs

- A trading bloc expands the size of the market for all firms so higher investment rates will follow. Higher rates of investment will accelerate growth. This has been a significant argument for developing countries. By forming a trading bloc, they could accelerate the process of industrialization.

- Phasing out and eliminating tariffs and other barriers exposes firms to more competition. More competition in turn leads to lower prices for consumers; greater efficiency in production, resulting in less waste; and a more efficient allocation of resources.

- Consumers will also have a greater variety of products to choose from.

- If within a regional trading bloc there is free movement of labour then employment opportunities increase, resulting in less overall unemployment.

- Seamless borders also permit faster technology transfer.

- The bargaining power of members increases: they can exercise greater economic leverage in negotiations than if they had acted individually. This is especially true for smaller countries but even a large country such as, say, France has more bargaining power in negotiations with the USA if it is negotiating through the EU.

- If the regional agreement leads to increased prosperity, then greater political stability may follow, and local conflicts are less likely.

- It is much easier for a country to reach an agreement when negotiating with only a few other countries than when negotiating with 163 other countries within the WTO. This is a major advantage that explains why the number of regional agreements has increased so much.

- Since the number of member countries is smaller than in the WTO these agreements permit member countries to integrate deeper than they would have within the WTO. Regional agreements have started to deal with areas such as investment and labour movement, competition issues, intellectual property rights, e-commerce and anti-corruption efforts that a country alone cannot deal with.

- (HL) Since firms will be selling in a bigger market they may grow and achieve economies of scale. This may lead to lower prices and increased competitiveness in world markets.

Possible disadvantages of trading blocs

- A major criticism of regional agreements and their proliferation is that they undermine multilateral trade liberalization through the WTO. Multilateral agreements that lower or eliminate trade barriers for all countries are superior to any regional trading agreement but have become more difficult to achieve. The latest WTO Doha round of trade negotiations has been deadlocked for many years to the extent that it is now considered effectively over. There is thus a risk that the world may end up split into a few major blocs, each a potential "fortress" to the others. This explains why many economists consider preferential trade agreements as "stumbling blocks" to trade liberalization.

- An additional risk arises when large economies (such as the USA, China, India or the EU) sign preferential agreements with smaller individual countries. Smaller countries are in a weaker position to defend their trade interests. Regional agreements may prove discriminatory against smaller, often developing, countries as they allow the powerful to use their huge bargaining power to achieve their preferred outcomes. This may explain the proliferation of such agreements.

- The proliferation of preferential trade agreements has also resulted in a "spaghetti bowl" of tariffs and rules of origin which increase business and administrative costs for trading firms.

- A country will sacrifice to various degrees its sovereignty, as some decisions will either be a compromise or will be made outside the country.

- (HL) It is likely that trading blocs are often formed as a result of lobbying efforts of self-interested member producers who hope to benefit from any resulting trade diversion effects.

Monetary union

A monetary union is formed when members of an economic union adopt a single currency and transfer the responsibility of monetary policy to a common central bank. In 1999 a subset of countries of the EU adopted a common currency, the euro, and established the European Central Bank (ECB). The eurozone has 19 member countries and since November 2019 Christine Lagarde is the President of the ECB.

Advantages of a monetary union

These are mostly of a microeconomic nature. They include the following.

- There are lower transaction costs as currency conversions are not necessary. Every time an individual or a business has to exchange one currency for another, a fee has to be paid to the bank. This cost is eliminated for any transactions within a monetary union.

- There is greater price transparency, which makes comparisons of prices of goods, services and resources much easier. Buyers (consumers and firms) are able to spot quickly the lowest price available in the market for whatever good or service they are looking for. This increases competition, forces inefficient producers to become more efficient and prices for tradable goods tend to gravitate towards the lowest offered in the union.

- Exchange rate risk and the resulting uncertainty costs are eliminated. Exchange rates tend to vary, and this implies increased uncertainty for businesses engaged in exports and imports of goods and services because the exchange rate may change between the time of purchase and that of payment. Investors who buy and sell stocks and bonds also face the same risk as they cannot be sure what the exchange rate will be at a future date when they may wish to sell their asset and convert the proceeds into their home currency. Note that exchange rate risk is greater for smaller businesses and investors who may therefore drop out of the market. This risk disappears with a single currency, encouraging more trade and a greater volume of investment within member countries. Many empirical studies have found evidence that membership in a monetary union has a positive impact on both trade and cross-border investments.

- A group of countries with a common market and a common currency will enjoy greater influence and bargaining power in world affairs.

Disadvantages of a monetary union

These are mostly of a macroeconomic nature. They may include the following.

- Member countries are deprived of an independent monetary policy. Since there is one currency and one central bank there is one monetary policy for all members. This "one-size-fits-all" approach may make things very difficult for some members if business cycles are "asynchronous". This term simply means that when one economy is booming and overheating another country may be losing steam and about to enter recession. Theory dictates that the former should tighten monetary policy, increasing interest rates, while the latter should loosen monetary policy, decreasing interest rates. If they are members of a monetary union, most probably the smaller country will suffer.

- Members are deprived of an independent exchange rate policy. A central bank is also responsible for conducting exchange rate policy. Being a member of a single currency area deprives a country the possibility to lower the value of its currency. Lowering its currency's value would decrease the foreign price of its exports, boosting export revenues and thus aggregate demand in a recession. It cannot increase the value of its currency in the face of mounting inflationary pressures either. Not only is there no exchange rate to manipulate between members, but also one member alone cannot influence the external value of the common currency as there is an independent central bank.

- There is limited room for pursuing independent fiscal policy. Even though each government can manipulate its own expenditures and taxes, the freedom to do so is limited because budget deficits and public debts must somehow be financed. Fiscal and monetary policies are not as independent as they may seem.

- Members lose economic sovereignty. If a country is deprived of an independent monetary policy, if it cannot exercise an independent exchange rate policy, if its ability to use fiscal policy is limited, then it has transferred at least part of its economic sovereignty outside the country. This has been a major argument for many EU countries against joining the euro.

Recap

Advantages and disadvantages of a monetary union

Possible **advantages** of being a member of a monetary union include:

- lower transaction costs as currency conversions are unnecessary

- greater price transparency, facilitating price comparisons

- no exchange rate risks and the associated uncertainty costs

- greater negotiating and bargaining power in world affairs.

Possible **disadvantages** of being a member of a monetary union include:

- no independent monetary policy

- no exchange rate policy

- limited room for independent fiscal policy

- loss of economic sovereignty.

The World Trade Organization (WTO)

The WTO was established in 1995. It is the successor of the GATT (General Agreement on Tariffs and Trade), a 1947 agreement between 23 countries to promote free trade by phasing out or eliminating tariffs and other trade barriers. GATT and the WTO agreements are known as multilateral agreements and are anchored on the most-favoured nation (MFN) principle that requires every member country to treat all other member countries as it treats its most-favoured trading partner, effectively not allowing discrimination.

Objectives and functions of the WTO

- The WTO has become closely associated with the process of globalization. It provides a forum for trade negotiations that cover goods, services and intellectual property. The WTO promotes free trade by persuading countries to abolish import tariffs and other trade barriers.

- It ensures that agreements are implemented and adhered to by requiring that national trade policies are transparent and by carrying out periodic reviews.

- It is the arbitrator of trade-related disputes. This means that all disagreements or grievances between member countries are settled within the WTO. The seven-member Appellate Body makes the final decision which all parties in any dispute must accept. The WTO empowers its members to enforce its decisions by imposing trade sanctions against countries that have broken the rules.

- It provides additional assistance to developing countries to build their technical expertise and their trade capacity.

Evaluating the WTO

- The GATT, and its successor the WTO, have been quite successful in decreasing trade barriers over the past 70 years and this has resulted in world trade growing dramatically. According to OECD and World Bank data, world trade (sum of exports and imports) as a percentage of world output (gross world product) increased from roughly 25% in 1960 to 59.4% in 2018.

- The greatest success resulting from the WTO is that, as an institution, it has established rules and order in the trading world and so it has managed, at least until now, to decrease uncertainty.

- The WTO proved instrumental in preventing national governments from resorting to escalating trade protection in response to the 2008–09 world recession. Members, bound by the rules of the WTO, did not resort to raising tariffs and quotas to appease domestic political pressure. As a result of Covid-19, the WTO estimates that the volume of world merchandise trade will contract by 13% in 2020 compared to a year before. For economies to rebound, the WTO must ensure that markets remain open and that members adhere to the rules of global business activity.

- Rules are enforced because members have agreed that the WTO has the authority to impose sanctions on the parties that lose in a dispute. The Appellate Body, the "supreme court" of the WTO, consists of 7 "judges" whose four-year appointment must be accepted by all 164 members, each with the right to veto a nomination. The USA, though, has been blocking the re-appointment of new judges since 2017. Since December 2019 the dispute settlement system of the WTO that prevented countries from resorting to trade protection has been paralyzed. The EU and 16 other members of the WTO agreed to develop a temporary arrangement that will allow members to maintain a dispute settlement system until the WTO Appellate Body becomes operational again. The hope is that countries will not resort to generalized successive rounds of protection.

- Of course, the WTO has been subjected to plenty of criticism. With 164 members it has been very difficult and time consuming to reach agreement, which has led to the proliferation of regional trade agreements.

- The WTO has been accused of mostly catering to the needs of advanced economies, neglecting those of the developing world. The WTO has pushed for the liberalization of services in developing countries so that multinationals from advanced economies gain access to their growing markets at the cost of local firms. At the same time, it has not done enough to force the USA and the EU to open up their own agricultural markets to imports. The inability to reach an agreement in agriculture is considered the main reason why the negotiations known as the Doha Round failed.

- It is claimed that the WTO has tried to force developing nations to change their policies, laws and regulations by declaring them in violation of its rules. It has also been accused of paying insufficient attention to the displacement of labour that trade liberalization unavoidably brings about, as well as to rising income inequality issues (even though one may argue that such policies are in the realm of national governments).

- According to critics the WTO also does not sufficiently consider the possible adverse effects of trade liberalization on the environment and it has not paid sufficient attention to child labour issues and to production processes in so-called "sweatshops".

However, few would disagree that as the net effect of the WTO on world welfare has been positive. There is of course room for improvement but the current scenario of no international body regulating the rules of world trade is alarming.

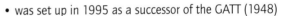

Recap

The World Trade Organization (WTO)

The WTO:

- was set up in 1995 as a successor of the GATT (1948)
- has 164 member countries responsible for 98% of world trade
- sets trade rules and ensures that they are followed
- is the arbitrator of trade-related disputes
- provides assistance to developing countries.

Evaluation—the WTO:

- has decreased tariff and other trade barriers and has helped world trade to increase dramatically, stimulating growth
- has prevented governments to resort to protection during crises
- has been able to enforce trade rules and to settle trade disputes
- is accused of being biased in favour of the USA, EU and other large economies while being inconsiderate to the needs of developing countries; for example, services and other markets in developing countries have been forced open whereas US and EU agriculture is still protected with subsidies and other barriers
- has been accused of paying insufficient attention to increasingly important issues such as the environment, child labour, health and workers' rights.

4.5 Exchange rates

The exchange rate of a currency is defined as the price of a currency expressed in terms of another currency. For example, on 2 July 2020:

- GBP 1.00 = USD 1.2471, so you needed 1.2471 US dollars to buy one British pound

- USD 1.00 = INR 74.682, so you needed 74.682 Indian rupees to buy one US dollar

- Euro 1.00 = NZD 1.7264, so you needed 1.7264 New Zealand dollars to buy one euro.

The exchange rate is one of the most important prices in an economy. It is determined in the foreign exchange market, which operates on a 24-hour basis, 365 days a year. Being a price, it is determined by the demand for the currency and the supply of it. When the exchange rate changes, it has consequences for almost everything and everyone.

Focusing on the exchange rate above of the British pound expressed in US dollars and dividing both sides by 1.2471

we get the price of one US dollar expressed in terms of pounds, or USD 1.00 = GBP 0.8019. You should realize that the one exchange rate is the inverse of the other, so if the price of the pound goes up with respect to the US dollar then this means that the price of the US dollar decreases in terms of the British pound.

If the exchange rate of the British pound with respect to the US dollar is equal to (e) then the exchange rate of the US dollar with respect to the British pound will be equal to $\left(\frac{1}{e}\right)$.

You should also realize that whoever is buying pounds in the foreign exchange market is at the same time selling dollars or, more generally, the buyer of one currency is at the same time a seller of another currency. This means that in a diagram of demand and supply for a currency, the demand for the currency that is being bought is also the supply of whichever currency is being sold.

Exchange rate systems

The exchange rate of a currency is affected by the demand for it and the supply of it but whether it is the result of only the interaction of demand and supply depends on the exchange rate system the country has chosen to operate by.

There are three different exchange rate systems within which exchange rates are determined: floating, fixed and managed exchange rate systems.

- **Floating** (or flexible) **exchange rate system:** this is when the exchange rate is determined only by the interaction of demand and supply without any government or central bank intervention.

- **Fixed exchange rate system:** this is when the exchange rate is set by the government at some level and is maintained at that level through appropriate intervention by the central bank.

- **Managed exchange rate system:** this is when the exchange rate is allowed to float but there is periodic intervention by the central bank whenever the direction or the speed of change is considered undesirable. The frequency of such interventions varies. Most currencies are traded in a "managed float" system.

Appreciation and depreciation versus revaluation and devaluation

When the price (the value) of a currency changes in a floating exchange rate system we describe the change using the terms *appreciation* and *depreciation*. On the other hand, when its price (its value) changes in a fixed exchange rate system we describe the change using the terms *revaluation* and *devaluation*.

More specifically, the term *appreciation* refers to an increase in the price of a currency in a floating exchange rate system. The term *depreciation* refers to a decrease in the price of a

currency in a floating exchange rate system. Consider the following.

- 5 August 2019: £1.00 = $1.2037.

- 9 December 2019: £1.00 = $1.3325.

- 16 March: £1.00 = $1.1650.

The value of the pound is obviously not fixed. The pound and the dollar operate in a floating exchange rate system. We say that between 5 August 2019 and 9 December 2019 the pound appreciated against the dollar. Between 9 December 2019 and 16 March 2020, the pound depreciated against the dollar. It should be clear that when the pound is appreciating against the dollar, the dollar is depreciating against the pound and when the pound is depreciating against the dollar, the dollar is appreciating against the pound. Remember, the one exchange rate is the inverse of the other.

In a fixed exchange rate system, when the central bank decides to set the exchange rate at a lower level, we say that there has been a devaluation of the currency. If the central bank decides to increase the official rate, we say that there has been a revaluation of the currency.

Denmark maintains a fixed exchange rate against the euro but keeps its currency, the krone (Kr), floating against all other currencies. Specifically, the Denmark's National Bank, Denmark's central bank, keeps the krone fixed against the euro at what is known as the central rate of €1.00 = Kr7.468 and permits it to fluctuate only within a +/- 2.25% band.

If for whatever reason Denmark's central bank decides to set the central rate of the krone at €1.00 = Kr7.60 then the Danish krone will have devalued (since the euro is more expensive, the krone is cheaper). Conversely, if the central rate was set at €1.00 = Kr7.30 then the krone will have revalued (since the euro is now cheaper).

Therefore, devaluation and revaluation are terms reserved for deliberate official changes in the value of a currency whereas depreciation and appreciation are reserved for exchange rate changes induced by market forces.

Who demands a currency and why; who supplies and why?

Let us for simplicity initially assume a world where only British pounds and US dollars are bought and sold by the participants in the foreign exchange market. We are also assuming that there is no central bank intervention, so we are analysing a floating exchange rate system.

For now, let's focus on the exchange rate of the British pound. Who would demand and buy pounds in this market and what for? Who will supply and sell pounds in this market and what for?

Pounds may be demanded by the following groups.

- Individuals who want to buy UK goods and services (that is, UK exports) demand pounds. If Americans are buying British goods and services, then dollars will have to be sold for pounds to be bought. Consider a New York department store planning to add to its selection a range of coats made by UK manufacturer Burberry. The store will need to buy pounds in order to pay Burberry. Now think of an American planning to attend the London School of Economics. She needs pounds to pay for her tuition so she will have to exchange her dollars for pounds. The demand for pounds therefore reflects UK exports of goods (Burberry's coats) and services (education).

- Investors will need pounds to make investments into the UK, meaning here to buy UK government bonds or shares sold in the London Stock Exchange, to make bank deposits in pounds, to acquire a British firm or to establish a new firm in the UK. If Americans wants to make deposits in British pounds, they will have to buy pounds with their US dollars. The same applies if they want to buy UK bonds or shares, a British company or to set up a factory in Manchester, UK. The demand for pounds therefore also reflects cross-border investments into the UK which are referred to as financial (or capital) inflows.

- Pounds may be bought by those who buy a currency because they expect it to rise in value. They may buy pounds now when its price is low and sell it later when its price increases. Buying and selling a currency hoping to make a profit from a change in its value is referred to as speculation.

Pounds are supplied by the following groups.

- UK importers of US goods and services supply pounds. A British firm buying (importing) Abercrombie and Fitch shirts will have to sell UK pounds to buy the necessary US dollars for the purchase of these shirts. An Englishman visiting New York for Christmas with his family will need to exchange his pounds for US dollars to pay for the holiday. The supply of pounds therefore reflects UK imports of goods (Abercrombie and Fitch shirts) and services (vacations in New York).

- British investors in the USA supply pounds. Such investments include buying US government bonds or shares sold in the New York Stock Exchange, buying a US

firm or establishing a new firm in the US. Think of British investors wishing to take advantage of higher US interest rates on dollar deposits. They will have to sell their UK pounds to buy the necessary dollars to make the deposit. The supply of pounds therefore also reflects cross-border investments into the UK, which are referred to as financial (or capital) outflows.

- Pounds may be supplied by those who want to sell a currency because they expect it to fall in value. They may sell pounds now when its price is high and buy pounds later when its price is lower.

So, trade flows and financial (capital) flows are two of the most important reasons why foreign exchange is demanded and supplied in foreign exchange markets. However, there are also other reasons for buying or selling a currency in the foreign exchange market.

- Pounds may be supplied in the foreign exchange market by migrant workers from, say, Bangladesh working in London and sending money back to their families in Dhaka. They will send them pounds which will have to be exchanged for Bangladeshi taka, the currency of Bangladesh. Amounts of money that migrants send to their country of origin are referred to as remittances.

- Lastly, central bank intervention will affect the demand and the supply of a currency and thus the exchange rate. For example, the Swiss National Bank, which is the central bank of Switzerland, may decide to buy euros by selling Swiss francs. The supply of Swiss francs will increase (as will the demand for euros).

Figure 4.5.1 illustrates the equilibrium exchange rate for the UK pound expressed in terms of US dollars.

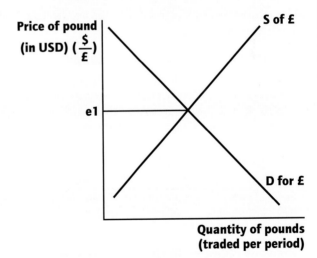

Figure 4.5.1 The market for UK pounds

Since Figure 4.5.1 focuses on the exchange rate of the UK pound with respect to the US dollar, the vertical axis is the price of the pound and the horizontal is the quantity of pounds traded per period. On the vertical axis, the price of the pound is expressed in US dollars, so it is US dollars per one UK pound or $\frac{\$}{£}$.

To avoid a common error, remember that whatever currency is on the denominator of this fraction is also on the horizontal axis of your diagram. In Figure 4.5.1, demand for pounds D1 is equal to the supply of pounds S1 at the exchange rate e1, say, $1.31 per pound. Any change in any factor affecting demand for pounds or supply of pounds will lead to appreciation or depreciation of the pound.

Why is the demand for pounds negatively sloped? The reason is that if the exchange rate decreases and the pound becomes cheaper then fewer dollars will be needed to buy a pound. British imported goods will become cheaper and more competitive for Americans to buy and it will also be cheaper for Americans to invest in the UK.

So, the quantity of pounds demanded at the lower pound exchange rate will increase. The supply of pounds is upward sloping for the symmetrical reason. If the pound becomes cheaper then UK residents will need more pounds to buy a US dollar. US imported goods will become more expensive in the UK. Investing in the USA will also become more expensive for British residents. They will therefore supply fewer pounds in the foreign exchange market at a lower pound exchange rate.

Changes in demand or supply for a currency

The exchange rate will appreciate or depreciate depending on whether excess demand or excess supply arises in the foreign exchange market. A currency will appreciate if there is excess demand. It will depreciate if there is excess supply. Excess demand will result either because demand for the currency increased or because supply of the currency decreased. Excess supply will result if demand for the currency decreased or because supply of the currency increased. More specific examples are given below.

Currency appreciation: Excess demand

If for whatever reason the demand for pounds increases and shifts to the right from D1 to D2 then excess demand for pounds equal to ab will put pressure on the exchange rate to increase to e2 in Figure 4.5.2. The pound will have appreciated from e1 to e2.

If for whatever reason the supply of pounds decreases and shifts to the left from S1 to S2 then excess demand of pounds equal to ab will put pressure on the exchange rate to increase to e2 in Figure 4.5.3. The pound will have appreciated from e1 to e2.

Currency depreciation: Excess supply

If for whatever reason the demand for pounds decreases and shifts to the left from D1 to D3 then excess supply of pounds equal to fh will put pressure on the exchange rate to decrease to e3 in Figure 4.5.4. The pound will have depreciated from e1 to e3.

If for whatever reason the supply of pounds increases and shifts to the right from S1 to S3 then excess supply of pounds equal to fh will put pressure on the exchange rate to decrease to e3 in Figure 4.5.5. The pound will have depreciated from e1 to e3.

Causes of changes in the exchange rate of a currency

Changes in trade flows

Remember that: when a country exports goods and services then foreigners need to buy its currency; when it imports goods and services it will need to sell its currency to buy foreign currencies.

Changes in the foreign demand of a country's exports

Assume that a country is experiencing growing demand for its exports. Growing exports implies that foreigners will need more of the domestic currency to pay for these exports. Demand for the currency by foreigners will therefore increase

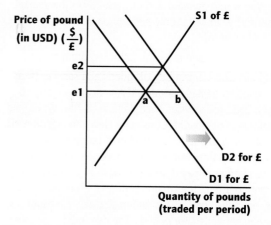

Figure 4.5.2 Impact of an increase in the demand for UK pounds

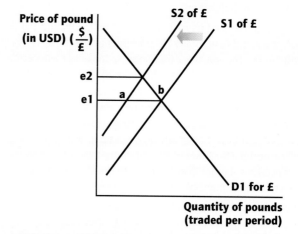

Figure 4.5.3 Impact of a decrease in the supply of UK pounds

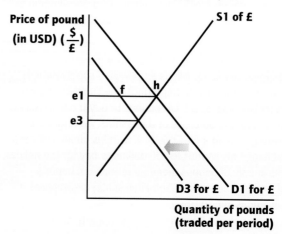

Figure 4.5.4 Impact of a decrease in the demand for UK pounds

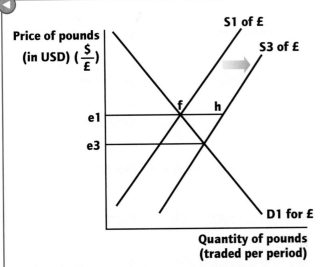

Figure 4.5.5 Impact of an increase in the supply for UK pounds

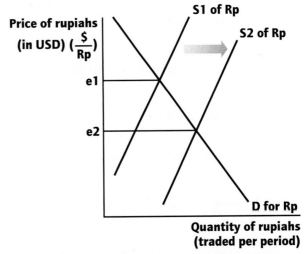

Figure 4.5.6 Effect of a growing economy on the exchange rate

and the demand curve will shift to the right. Excess demand for the currency will create pressure for the currency to appreciate. This is illustrated in Figure 4.5.2.

On the other hand, a decrease in the foreign demand for a country's exports will lead to a depreciation of the currency. This is illustrated in Figure 4.5.4.

Changes in the domestic demand for imports

Assume that domestic demand for imports increases. To buy more foreign products, importers must sell the domestic currency to buy the necessary foreign currency. The supply of the domestic currency will increase and therefore the supply curve will shift to the right. Excess supply for the currency will create pressure on the currency to depreciate. This is illustrated in Figure 4.5.5.

A decrease in the domestic demand for imports will lead to a decrease in the supply of the domestic currency and so the currency will appreciate. This is illustrated in Figure 4.5.3.

If the demand for a currency reflects the value of its exports and the supply of its currency reflects the value of its imports it follows that if exports rise faster than imports then, ceteris paribus, the currency will tend to appreciate. In contrast, if imports are rising faster than exports then, ceteris paribus, the currency will tend to depreciate.

Factors affecting trade flows

The above analysis shows that any changes in a country's trade flows will affect its exchange rate. Changes in growth rates and changes in inflation rates are two factors that will affect exports and imports of a country and thus the demand and the supply for its currency.

Changes in relative growth rates

A higher growth rate implies that incomes in the country are now rising faster than previously. Rising incomes imply rising consumption expenditures and household consumption expenditures include spending not only on domestic but also on foreign goods and services. It follows that in a growing economy, demand for imports will rise. Now let's focus on the Indonesian rupiah (Rp) and assume that the growth of the Indonesian economy is accelerating.

In Figure 4.5.6 the price of the Indonesian rupiah expressed in US dollars is initially at e1. If Indonesian growth accelerates then Indonesians' incomes are rising. Consumption expenditures will rise. This means that Indonesia will also buy more imports.

Indonesians will have to supply more rupiahs in the foreign exchange market to buy the necessary dollars to pay for the increase in imports. The supply curve for the rupiah will shift to the right to S2 as imports are now greater. The rupiah will therefore tend to depreciate to e2.

This is a very interesting result that is seemingly counterintuitive. A growing economy may witness a depreciating currency. It will be shown that this is not necessary if the growing economy attracts more investments.

Changes in relative inflation rates

If inflation in a country accelerates it means that prices of goods and services in that country are rising on the average faster than they used to. Its products will become less and less competitive abroad while imported goods and services will seem more attractive domestically.

Foreign demand for its exports will decrease and therefore so will the demand for its currency. In addition, domestic demand for imported goods and services will increase, increasing the supply of its currency.

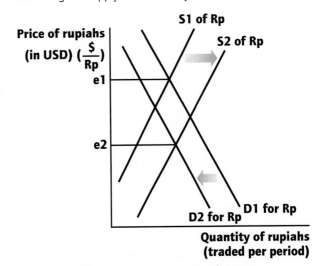

Figure 4.5.7 Effect of higher inflation on the exchange rate

Figure 4.5.7 shows the effect of higher inflation in Indonesia on the rupiah. Initially the rupiah exchange rate against the dollar was at e1. The higher inflation in Indonesia will decrease its exports as they will become less competitive abroad, decreasing the demand for the rupiah from D1 to D2 in Figure 4.5.7.

At the same time imported goods and services will seem more and more attractive to Indonesians. Imports will therefore tend to increase. More rupiahs will be supplied in the foreign exchange market, shifting the supply curve of rupiahs from S1 to S2. The decrease in the demand for rupiahs and the increase in the supply of rupiahs will lead to its depreciation to e2.

Inflation in an economy will tend to depreciate a currency.

Changes in cross-border capital flows

Inflows and outflows of financial capital for investment purposes will also affect the exchange rate of a currency. We distinguish two types of investment flows: portfolio investment and foreign direct investment (FDI).

Inward and outward portfolio investments

Portfolio investments refers to the buying and selling of financial assets, including stocks, bonds and deposits. If for some reason an economy attracts more portfolio investments, then the resulting inflows of financial capital will tend to appreciate the currency. For example, let's say that UK bonds or deposits in UK pounds or shares of UK firms listed in the London Stock Exchange become relatively more attractive to financial investors. Those investors will need to buy the UK pounds to be able to buy UK bonds, or make deposits in UK pounds or buy stocks in the London Stock Exchange. The demand for UK pounds will therefore increase. The pound will appreciate as a result of the inward portfolio investments. This case is shown in Figure 4.5.2.

If these financial investors later realize that it is now more profitable to switch to US bonds, or to deposits in US dollars or to stocks listed in the New York Stock Exchange, they will sell UK pounds to buy the necessary US dollars. The supply of UK pounds will increase. The pound will therefore depreciate as a result of outward portfolio investments.

Inward portfolio investments lead to an appreciation of the currency whereas outward portfolio investments lead to a depreciation of the currency. This is shown in Figure 4.5.5.

Inward and outward foreign direct investment (FDI)

Foreign direct investment (FDI) is of a long-term nature and refers to a firm establishing a new presence in a foreign country or acquiring controlling interest of a foreign company. If for some reason an economy attracts more FDI, then the resulting inflows of financial capital will lead to an appreciation of the currency. For example, if Côte d'Ivoire attracts more inward FDI then the demand for West African CFA francs (the currency of Côte d'Ivoire) will increase and so the currency will tend to appreciate. Conversely, outward FDI will tend to depreciate a currency.

Factors affecting cross-border capital flows

Whether deposits and bonds are attractive to financial investors depends, ceteris paribus, on their rate of return, in other words on the interest rate they pay the owner. Whether it becomes more attractive to own more shares in a foreign stock exchange or to establish a new presence in a foreign country critically depends on the growth prospects of that country. More specific examples are given below.

Changes in relative interest rates

If interest rates in an economy increase relative to interest rates in other economies then government bonds and deposits in that country's currency become more attractive as the owner of such assets will earn relatively more, ceteris paribus. Financial investors will have an incentive to buy the currency in order to make the deposits and/or to buy bonds. Demand for the currency will increase and the currency will tend to appreciate. For example, if the Bank of England increases interest rates then the higher rate of return will make UK bonds and deposits in UK pounds more attractive to financial investors. They will buy UK pounds in the foreign exchange market, increasing the demand for UK pounds and shifting the demand curve to the right, as shown in Figure 4.5.4. The UK pound will appreciate from e1 to e2.

If the Bank of England decreases interest rates, then the rate of return on UK bonds as well as on deposits in UK pounds is lower. These assets will be less attractive to financial investors so some will decide to sell these assets and switch to dollar deposits or US bonds. The supply of UK pounds will increase and shift the supply curve to the right, as in Figure 4.5.5, and the pound will tend to depreciate. In addition, demand for UK pounds will also decrease, further decreasing the value of the UK pound.

Note that this analysis raises an interesting question. If interest rates in say, Argentina, are the highest right now, why doesn't Argentina attract all financial investors? The answer is related to the fact that the decision also depends on the expectations financial investors have concerning the future value of the Argentine peso. If there is risk of a depreciation, then many will shy away from holding Argentinian assets.

To summarize, higher interest rates will, ceteris paribus lead to inward portfolio investment flows and an appreciation of the currency whereas lower interest rates will have the opposite effect.

Expectations concerning the growth prospects of an economy

When will investors be eager to buy more shares in a country's stock exchange? When will firms be eager to establish a new presence in an economy or to buy controlling interest in the shares of an existing foreign company?

There is a single answer, which is significantly related to the expected growth prospects of an economy. If the growth prospects of an economy are very promising, then investors will want to buy stocks and/or establish a new business presence themselves in the country so they can receive the expected profits. Demand for the country's currency will tend to increase, pushing upward the exchange rate.

A growing economy implies growing and profitable firms and plentiful business opportunities that foreigners will also want to take advantage of. The currency will therefore tend to appreciate.

Earlier it was explained that the currency of a growing economy may depreciate because of greater import absorption. It should be clear now that the currency may not depreciate if growth is expected to continue. Continued growth may also increase inward investments, exerting upward pressure on the currency.

Speculation

Buying or selling a currency for speculative purposes will also affect the exchange rate. If speculators buy the currency, demand for it will increase and the currency will tend to appreciate. If speculators sell the currency, supply of it will increase and the currency will tend to depreciate. Even small changes in the exchange rate of a currency can produce large profits for currency speculators when their bets involve large sums of money. Of course, errors may lead to large losses. What is the main driving force of currency speculation? It is the expected path of the exchange rate itself.

Anticipating an appreciation will lead to speculators buying the currency. Demand for it will increase and therefore the currency will tend to appreciate. Anticipating a depreciation will lead to speculators selling the currency. Supply of it will increase and therefore the currency will tend to depreciate. Note that these are examples of what are known as self-fulfilling expectations.

Remittances

When migrant workers send money back home, their families will have to exchange the money received for the home currency. This means that remittances increase the demand for the recipient country's currency and so lead to its appreciation. For example, if Mexican workers in the USA send money back home to their parents every month, they need to convert dollars to Mexican pesos. Demand for pesos will rise, and the peso will tend to appreciate. When these remittance inflows are large relative to the size of the recipient economies the appreciation may prove significant. Note that foreign aid may have a similar impact on the recipient country's exchange rate.

Central bank intervention (in managed and fixed exchange rate systems)

In a floating exchange rate system, there is no central bank intervention. However, central banks do intervene in a managed as well as in a fixed exchange rate system. If a central bank needs to make sure that the value of the currency does not decrease, it will enter the foreign exchange market and start buying it (using dollar or other foreign exchange reserves). In this way, demand for the currency increases or is maintained at the desired level.

If a central bank would like to make sure that the currency does not rise in value, then it will start selling the currency in the foreign exchange market, buying dollars or euros or some other major currency in exchange. For example, the Swiss National Bank (the central bank of Switzerland) was selling Swiss francs (SFr) during the coronavirus outbreak because in times of increased uncertainty financial investors consider the Swiss franc a safe haven and demand for it increases. If the Swiss National Bank sells it, its supply rises, and this prevents an undesired further appreciation of the SFr.

Recap

Factors affecting the exchange rate of a currency

Changes in trade flows

- Changes in the foreign demand for a country's exports

  If foreign demand increases then the exchange rate appreciates.

  If foreign demand decreases then the exchange rate depreciates.

- Changes in the domestic demand for imports

  If domestic demand increases then the exchange rate depreciates.

  If domestic demand decreases then the exchange rate appreciates.

  Trade flows are in turn affected by:

- changes in relative growth rates—faster growth increases import absorption so the currency will tend to depreciate (but see below)

- changes in relative inflation rates—faster inflation decreases exports and increases imports so the currency tends to depreciate.

Changes in investment flows

- Portfolio investment flows

  If these are inward then the currency appreciates.

  If these are outward then the currency depreciates.

  Portfolio investment flows are in turn affected by changes in relative interest rates.

- If domestic interest rates increase then the currency will tend to appreciate.

- If domestic interest rates decrease then the currency will tend to depreciate.

- Foreign direct investment (FDI) flows

  If these are inward then the currency appreciates.

  If these are outward then the currency depreciates.

  FDI flows are in turn affected by growth prospects of a country.

- If faster growth is expected in a country then, ceteris paribus, FDI inflows will increase and the currency will appreciate.

Speculation

- If speculators expect a currency to appreciate then they will buy the currency and it will tend to appreciate.

- If speculators expect a currency to depreciate then they will sell the currency and it will tend to depreciate.

Workers' remittances

Inflows will tend to appreciate the currency of the recipient country.

Intervention by the central bank

- If it buys the currency it will appreciate.

- If it sells the currency it will depreciate.

Consequences of changes in the exchange rate

Impact on the current account balance

The current account will be explained in some detail later but for our purposes it is sufficient here to understand it as the difference between the value of exports of goods and services and import expenditures on goods and services (that is, X – M).

If X > M then we say that there is a trade surplus whereas if M > X we say that there is a trade deficit. Remember that net exports, defined as X – M, are a component of aggregate demand.

Perhaps the most important thing to understand and remember is that if a currency depreciates then exports become cheaper abroad and therefore more competitive while imports become pricier domestically and less attractive.

To illustrate the impact of a depreciation on prices of exports and imports, assume for the sake of the example that initially £1.00 = €4.00 and that the pound depreciated so that £1.00 = €2.00. Further assume that the UK exports to the eurozone Celtic swords priced at £100 each and imports from France Bordeaux wine at €40 per bottle. Table 4.5.1 shows the impact of a depreciation of the pound on export and import prices.

Following a depreciation, we expect that a trade deficit will eventually decrease in size as exports become more competitive and imports less attractive. (HL will examine the necessary Marshall-Lerner condition—see section 4.6, page 177).

If, for example NX were equal to –$150 million then following the depreciation NX may have eventually decreased to –$110 million. It should be clear that this means that aggregate demand will increase, as exports became more competitive and imports less attractive.

The impact of an appreciation is the opposite. An appreciation will increase the foreign price of exports and render them less competitive abroad whereas it will decrease the domestic price of imports rendering them more attractive. A trade surplus will thus decrease and since net exports (NX) will be smaller, aggregate demand will also decrease.

Impact of a depreciating UK pound on the foreign price of exports and the domestic price of imports

Example: the UK exports Celtic swords and imports Bordeaux wine.

	Original exchange rate £1.00 = €4.00	New exchange rate £1.00 = €2.00
UK price of a Celtic sword £100.00	Price in the eurozone: €400.00	New price in the eurozone: €200.00 The UK export is now cheaper in the eurozone and more competitive.
Eurozone price of a bottle of Bordeaux wine €40.00	Price in the UK: £10.00	New price in the UK: £20.00 The EU import is now pricier in the UK and less attractive.

Table 4.5.1 Example of the impact of a depreciation on export and import prices

Recap

Currency depreciates			
• The foreign price of exports falls so exports become more competitive. • The domestic price of imports rises so imports become less attractive.	• Exports will tend to rise. • Imports will tend to decrease.	A trade deficit (when (X–M) is < 0) will eventually narrow (decrease).*	Aggregate demand will tend to increase (as the trade deficit is a smaller negative figure).
Currency appreciates			
• The foreign price of exports rises so exports become less competitive. • The domestic price of imports falls so imports become more attractive.	• Exports will tend to decrease. • Imports will tend to increase.	A trade surplus (when (X–M) is > 0) will eventually narrow (decrease).*	Aggregate demand will tend to decrease (as the trade surplus is a smaller positive figure).

*The role of the Marshall-Lerner condition (HL) is examined in section 4.6.

Impact on economic growth

Assume that a currency depreciates. Exports become cheaper abroad and more competitive while imports become pricier domestically and less attractive. Net exports will tend to increase and therefore aggregate demand will tend to increase. However, if aggregate demand increases and the AD curve shifts to the right then real GDP will tend to increase so the economy will grow. This explains why several countries have tried to maintain their exchange rate low—so that their exports remain cheap, and therefore competitive, in foreign markets. This is the idea behind what is known as "export-led growth".

We should note that this growth may prove inflationary if the economy is operating close to its potential output (see Figure 4.5.8).

In contrast, an appreciation will decrease aggregate demand and therefore slow down growth as net exports will tend to decrease.

Impact on unemployment

As depreciation leads to an increase in aggregate demand and so an increase in real output, it is expected that cyclical unemployment will decrease. A depreciation will not succeed in decreasing structural unemployment because the skills of the unemployed are not brought up to date, nor is the labour market becoming more flexible.

In contrast, an appreciation will, strictly speaking, decrease aggregate demand and so decrease economic activity and increase cyclical unemployment. However, if the appreciation succeeds in slowing down the increase in aggregate demand, mitigating rising inflationary pressures, then non-inflationary growth may persist and unemployment may decrease or at least not increase.

Maintaining the exchange rate high is, as explained later, sometimes used to diminish inflationary pressures in an economy and maintain price stability.

Impact on inflation

A depreciation may succeed in helping an economy to increase real GDP and increase employment levels, but it always runs the risk of creating both demand-pull and cost-push inflation. Demand-pull inflation may result if the economy is operating close to its full employment (potential) level of real output. Cost-push inflation may result if firms in the economy rely significantly on imported raw materials (such as energy) and intermediate products (such as parts) as a depreciation leads to higher domestic prices for imports so that production costs increase across a range of components.

In contrast, an appreciation by decreasing (or slowing down the increase) in aggregate demand and by lowering the cost of imported inputs may dampen inflationary pressures.

Note that a depreciation may help an economy avoid or escape deflation as more competitive exports may increase net exports and therefore aggregate demand, whereas an appreciation may push an economy into a deflationary spiral as net exports and so aggregate demand may decrease.

In Figure 4.5.8 the expected impact of a depreciation is shown. Since exports become cheaper and more competitive abroad and imports become pricier and less attractive domestically, the value of net exports (a component of aggregate demand) is expected to eventually increase. The AD curve will shift to the right from AD1 to AD2. Real GDP will increase from Y1 to Y2 and cyclical unemployment will decrease. There is no demand-pull inflation because the economy at Y1 was operating significantly below full employment output Yf. Had the economy been originally operating at Y2, the deflationary gap would have been much smaller so the depreciation could increase AD to AD3. In this case, real GDP increases to Y3 and cyclical unemployment decreases, but the possibility of demand-pull inflation is evident as the average price level (APL) will start rising.

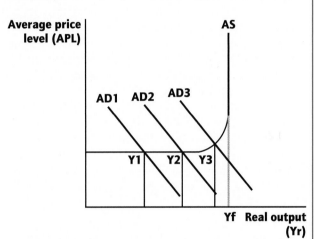

Figure 4.5.8 Impact of a depreciation on growth, unemployment and inflation

Impact on living standards

If, as a result of a depreciation or of maintaining a low exchange rate, growth accelerates, unemployment drops and incomes rise then living standards, on the average, will increase. Keep in mind that the biggest beneficiaries will be all those involved directly or indirectly with the export sector, which will be driving the country's growth. Whether a low exchange rate will benefit the population at large depends on whether the government adopts policies that will ensure the ensuing growth is inclusive.

An appreciation of the currency may slow down growth but may prove very helpful as inflationary pressures will decrease. Low income households will immediately benefit as the resulting lower import prices will decrease their cost of living. Remember that low income households spend a bigger proportion of their income on food and pharmaceuticals and if these goods are imported then their purchasing power will rise.

Beyond these general effects on living standards of a depreciation or an appreciation we must look at particular groups. For example, a lower exchange rate will benefit the domestic tourism industry as foreigners will find it cheaper to spend their vacations in the country. An appreciation will benefit domestic residents travelling abroad. It will more generally benefit domestic importers but hurt domestic import-competing firms and their stakeholders.

A note on monetary policy

We are now in a position to include an additional route through which monetary policy can affect aggregate demand. Easy monetary policy may increase not only consumption expenditures (C) and investment expenditures (I) but will also net exports (NX), another component of aggregate demand. Lower interest rates decrease the attractiveness of saving and the cost of borrowing for

households and firms but also decrease the exchange rate, making exports more competitive and imports less attractive. This route may prove more effective in a deep recession as it is not affected by low levels of domestic confidence.

Conversely, tighter monetary policy to decrease inflationary pressures will not only dampen consumption and investment expenditures but also net exports. The higher interest rates will appreciate the currency, making exports less competitive abroad and imports cheaper domestically. Not only will net exports tend to decrease but production costs may also decrease if domestic firms rely on the now cheaper inputs.

Fixed exchange rates

A fixed exchange rate system is defined as a system in which the exchange rate is set by the government at some desired level (usually against a major currency, say, the US dollar or the euro), and is then maintained at that level through appropriate intervention in the foreign exchange market by the central bank . The UAE dirham (AED), for example, has been fixed for a long time against the US dollar at AED3.67 per US$1. The Danish currency, the kroner, has been fixed against the euro at a "central" rate of 7.46 kroner per €1. "Central" means that the kroner can fluctuate within a disclosed ± 2.25% band around that rate.

How is the exchange rate maintained at the set level? What can and should a central bank do to maintain the rate at the desired level if, for example, there are pressures for it to devalue? If there is pressure for the currency to devalue then there is excess supply of it in the foreign exchange market. Somehow this excess supply must be eliminated. The central bank must therefore increase the demand for the currency. It can do this either by buying the currency itself using its foreign exchange reserves (such as dollars) or by inducing foreign investors to start buying it. How can the central bank induce investors? It can increase interest rates, making deposits denominated in its own currency as well as domestic bonds more attractive. This is shown in Figure 4.5.9.

In Figure 4.5.9 it is assumed that currency A of country A is pegged against, say, the dollar at e*. If demand and supply forces are at D1 and S1 the exchange rate will be at e* so there is no reason for the central bank to intervene.

Assume now that supply for the currency increases to S2, perhaps as a result of accelerating domestic inflation increasing imports. Supply of currency A will shift to S2. At the target exchange rate e* there will now be excess supply for A equal to HF units of A per period. This excess supply exerts pressure on currency A to devalue towards e'.

The exchange rate will be maintained at the desired target level e* only if somehow the central bank managed to increase demand for its currency to D2 to eliminate the excess supply.

How can the central bank do this? One obvious option is for it to enter the foreign exchange market and start buying HF units of A per period using its foreign exchange reserves (for example, dollars). If the central bank starts buying HF units of A per period it is increasing the demand for currency A from D1 to D2.

To defend the exchange rate (meaning to maintain its parity at e*) the central bank can also increase interest rates. This would be the next line of defence as the foreign exchange reserves of any central bank are limited; the central bank cannot go on selling dollars to buy its currency if it has no more dollars left to sell.

The higher interest rates in country A will attract inflows of financial capital because domestic bonds and deposits denominated in currency A will become more attractive. Foreigners will buy currency A in the foreign exchange market in order to buy country A's bonds or make deposits denominated in currency A. This can also increase the demand for A, shifting it to the right from D1 to D2.

Higher interest rates though impose a real cost on country A's economy as growth will slow down and unemployment will increase.

The government may also resort to official borrowing of foreign exchange in an attempt to maintain the currency at e*. However, borrowing to defend the currency cannot continue for long as repayment of the loans imposes

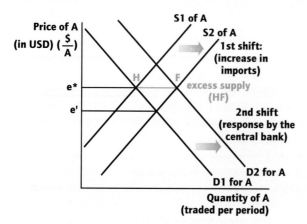

Figure 4.5.9 Fixed exchange rates: how are they maintained?

significant future costs on an economy. Or, the government may try to limit pressure on the currency to devalue by restricting imports into the country so that supply of currency A in the foreign exchange market decreases. Governments can also restrict access to foreign exchange in the country, reducing the supply of its currency in the foreign exchange market. Of course, exchange controls may lead to "black markets".

If, in contrast, there are forces pushing up the currency then the central bank can sell its currency, buying dollars in the foreign exchange market to eliminate the excess demand that is causing pressure for the currency to rise above the target parity. The central bank may also lower domestic interest rates to decrease the attractiveness of domestic bonds and deposits in the country's currency. Note that both options increase the money supply and so they may lead to accelerating inflationary pressures.

Managed exchange rates

Between floating and fixed exchange rate systems we have the most common exchange rate system, managed exchange rates. Within a managed exchange rate system, the authorities try to decrease exchange rate movements and at the same time maintain some flexibility. The exchange rate floats but there is periodic intervention by the central bank whenever the currency starts to move in a direction or at a speed considered undesirable. In some managed float systems, the currency is allowed to float within a targeted but undisclosed to the public band.

To decrease short-term volatility a central bank will typically intervene in the foreign exchange market by buying or selling its currency. If it wishes to slow down a fall in its exchange rate it will start buying its currency whereas if it wishes to slow down an appreciation it will start selling it. Illustrating the former case, a central bank would have to increase the demand for the currency, shifting it closer to D2 for currency A in Figure 4.5.9, so that the exchange rate does not fall much below e*. In the latter case, a central bank would have to shift the supply of the currency so that it does not appreciate as much.

Sometimes a central bank will perform sterilized intervention, which means that it will try to neutralize any changes in the money supply. For example, if a central bank would like to

avoid further weakening of its currency it would start buying it in the foreign exchange market. This, though, would decrease the reserves that commercial banks have. If the central bank wishes to avoid this decrease in reserves, it could perform open market operations and start buying bonds so that bank reserves return to their previous level.

Maintaining disequilibrium exchange rates
Keeping the currency undervalued

Sometimes countries try to maintain the exchange rate of their currency undervalued. This means that they try to maintain it at a level below the free market equilibrium level. Why would policymakers decide on something like this and what are some of the consequences?

An undervalued currency automatically implies cheaper and thus more competitive exports. This is the biggest advantage of such a policy. The increased export penetration and resulting higher export revenues increase aggregate demand and, through the export multiplier, accelerate growth. Undervalued currencies have significantly contributed to the spectacular export-led growth that several developing countries, including China, have achieved.

How could a country keep its currency undervalued against, for example, the US dollar? Its central bank would have to be purchasing US dollars by selling its currency in the foreign exchange market. The supply of its currency would in this way be artificially higher. Alternatively, it must keep interest rates low.

What are the risks? First, the export success from keeping the currency undervalued creates trade frictions with trading partners. One country's export success means that import-competing industries of the trading partner will suffer. In addition, exports of the trading partner will be more expensive and less competitive. The distress caused will increase cries for retaliation and protection. Another risk is that by continuously selling the currency to keep its price low or by maintaining low interest rates there is increased risk of inflation.

Keeping the currency overvalued

Sometimes countries try to maintain the exchange rate of their currency overvalued. This means that they try to maintain it at a level above the free market equilibrium level. Why would policymakers decide on something like this and what are some of the consequences?

Many developing countries have in the past tried to keep their currency overvalued as part of an import-substitution strategy (see section 4.10). The basic idea is that these countries were trying to shift out of agriculture and into manufacturing by substituting domestic production for imports. They erected trade barriers to protect their "infant industries" and at the same time maintained their exchange rate overvalued. This sounds absurd because at a higher exchange rates imports become cheaper. However, the goal was to lower the price of imported machines and other inputs (that is, the price of capital goods and raw materials) that would decrease the production costs of their new

industries. The trade barriers would be used to keep out of the country any goods that could be considered substitute goods in the eyes of domestic buyers, permitting the growth of the domestic infant industries. This was a policy to accelerate industrialization.

How could a country keep its currency overvalued against, for example, the US dollar? Its central bank would have to be purchasing its currency by selling US dollars in the foreign exchange market. The demand for its currency would in this way be artificially higher. Alternatively, it must keep interest rates high.

The downside was that the overvaluation of the currency acted as a tax on exports as exports became more expensive abroad. In the case of traditional primary export commodities (for example, coffee) for which the price was determined in world commodity markets and quoted in dollars, farmers earned less units of domestic currency for each dollar earned from their exports. An overvalued exchange rate would hurt the export sector of the developing country.

Maintaining the currency overvalued may be part of a policy to combat inflationary pressures. Exports that are part of aggregate demand will decrease, "cooling off" the economy. In addition, cheaper imports also help. First, the cost of living of the population is lower (the typical consumer's basket of goods also includes imports). It forces domestic import competing industries to cut their costs increasing their efficiency and keeping their own prices low. Lastly, production costs of domestic firms using imported inputs remain low. With inflation contained, the country can keep interest rates low, which encourages long-term investment and growth.

Fixed versus floating exchange rate systems

HL

When comparing floating with fixed exchange rate systems keep in mind that the advantages of one system can be considered disadvantages of the other.

Advantages of floating (flexible) exchange rates

Policymakers are free to use monetary policy to achieve domestic goals. They can use loose monetary policy to boost the economy as the currency depreciation that follows the lower interest rates will also lead to an increase in net exports, a component of aggregate demand. They can use tight monetary policy to decrease inflationary pressures as the currency appreciation that follows the higher interest rates will also lead to a decrease in net exports and so in aggregate demand.

A trade deficit (when M > X) may be automatically narrowed. A trade deficit implies that more of the currency is supplied than demanded in the foreign exchange market. The excess supply will depreciate the currency. Assuming

that the Marshall-Lerner condition is satisfied (HL, see section 4.6, page 184) then the trade deficit will narrow as exports become cheaper abroad and more competitive, while imports become pricier domestically and less attractive. This is important because there is less need for the government to adopt costly contractionary demand-side policies (see section 3.5, page 114) that will slow down growth and therefore decrease imports but also increase unemployment.

Exchange rate adjustments through time are usually smooth and continuous. This means that currency crises are avoided.

Concerning speculation: there is risk of destabilizing speculation if, for example, the fundamentals of an economy (inflationary pressures and so on) point to a weakening currency. Speculators may then start massively selling the currency, leading to an unnecessarily sharper decrease in its value.

There is less need for the central bank to carry large foreign exchange reserves as there is no need to intervene constantly to maintain the exchange rate at a fixed parity.

Disadvantages of floating (flexible) exchange rates

Since in a floating system the exchange rate goes up and down with any domestic or world economic or political development affecting it unpredictably, there is a lot of uncertainty in the foreign exchange market as to its future path. Exporters and importers, as well as investors, face significant exchange rate risks against which they can only partially protect themselves. As a result, both the volume of international trade in goods and services and the volume of cross-border portfolio investments are negatively affected. Smaller firms and smaller investors, with fewer resources available to protect themselves against such risks, will drop out of the market.

Governments lack the "policy discipline" that a fixed exchange rate system imposes. A country may therefore be more prone to inflation. For example, expansionary policies to accelerate growth could be more easily adopted by a government even if it means that the resulting growth will be inflationary.

Recap

Floating exchange rates—advantages and disadvantages

Advantages

- Policymakers can freely use monetary policy to achieve domestic goals.
- Trade imbalances are in principle automatically corrected through exchange rate adjustments only.
- Exchange rate adjustments are usually smooth and continuous.
- There is less need for the central bank to keep foreign exchange reserves.

Disadvantages

- At times, there is risk of destabilizing speculation.
- Increased uncertainty decreases the volume of trade and cross-border investment flows and it forces smaller firms and investors to drop out.
- The government may be more prone to adopt expansionary policies for short-term gains even if these accelerate inflation.

Advantages of fixed exchange rates

Less uncertainty and exchange rate risk means that firms engaged in international trade can easier predict their export revenues or import bill. Portfolio investors also avoid exchange rate risk that could lower their return from any investment. Fixed exchange rates increase the volume of exports and imports as well as of capital flows.

Since inflation is not compatible with a fixed exchange rate system, governments cannot easily pursue expansionary fiscal policy that may prove inflationary. Fixed exchange rates impose fiscal discipline on governments. Fixing the exchange rate has therefore often been a policy choice for governments determined to curb high inflation and maintain price stability.

In addition, firms are forced to be efficient and to keep their costs and prices down to maintain whatever competitive advantage they have. They cannot hope for a depreciation to regain any competitive advantage in world markets.

Disadvantages of fixed exchange rates

Policymakers are deprived of monetary policy as a tool to affect domestic economic activity. Monetary policy may be used only to ensure that the exchange rate remains fixed.

Policymakers are also deprived of exchange rate policy to deal with domestic policy objectives.

Even the use by policymakers of expansionary fiscal policy is constrained because budget deficits need to be financed somehow. Financing a large budget may lead to either faster growth of the money supply (if the deficit is financed through "printing" money) or higher interest rates because of crowding out (HL). Neither of these possibilities is acceptable under a fixed exchange rate system.

Devaluation or revaluation can prove disruptive as each implies a sudden change in the value of the currency.

To avoid the need to resort to devaluation a trade deficit must be corrected by adopting contractionary fiscal policy to lower the national income and so decrease import absorption. The disadvantages are that this means slower growth, possibly even a recession, as well as higher cyclical unemployment.

The central bank must maintain large foreign exchange reserves to be able to intervene in the foreign exchange market and maintain the exchange rate at the target level. This involves a high opportunity cost as reserves earn either low or no interest.

Recap

Fixed exchange rates—advantages and disadvantages

Advantages

- Less uncertainty and exchange rate risk increases the volume of trade and cross-border investment flows.
- Fiscal discipline is imposed on governments; a fixed exchange rate system may be a policy choice to maintain price stability.
- Firms are forced to be efficient to maintain any competitive advantage they have.

Disadvantages

- Policymakers cannot use monetary policy to achieve domestic goals.
- The government is deprived of an exchange rate policy.
- The use of expansionary fiscal policy is constrained because financing a deficit may affect the money supply or interest rates, neither of which is acceptable.
- Exchange rate adjustments are sudden, so they are potentially disruptive.
- Trade deficits are not automatically corrected, requiring use of painful contractionary fiscal policy.
- The central bank may maintain large foreign exchange reserves, which is costly.

Calculations

1. To convert the cost of good expressed in dollars ($) into pounds (£), just remember that

$$\text{price in £} = \text{price in \$} \times \frac{£}{\$}$$

Notice that the dollars ($) on the right-hand side cancel out so that the result of the multiplication is pounds (£).

2. To convert the cost of good expressed in pounds (£) into dollars ($) just remember that

$$\text{price in \$} = \text{price in £} \times \frac{\$}{£}$$

Notice that the pounds (£) on the right-hand side cancel out so that the result of the multiplication is dollars ($).

3. Calculating a "cross-exchange-rate" is easy.

Assume that you are given the price of the pound (£) both in euros ($\frac{€}{£}$) and in dollars ($\frac{\$}{£}$) then: if you are asked for the dollar price of the euro ($\frac{\$}{€}$) divide the dollar price of the pound $\frac{\$}{£}$ by the euro price of the pound $\frac{€}{£}$:

$$\frac{\frac{\$}{£}}{\frac{€}{£}} = \frac{\$}{£} \times \frac{£}{€} = \frac{\$}{€} \text{ as the pounds (£) cancel out}$$

If you are asked for the euro price of the dollar ($\frac{€}{\$}$) divide the euro price of the pound $\frac{€}{£}$ by the dollar price of the pound $\frac{\$}{£}$:

$$\frac{\frac{€}{£}}{\frac{\$}{£}} = \frac{€}{£} \times \frac{£}{\$} = \frac{€}{\$} \text{ as the pounds (£) cancel out}$$

4.6 Balance of payments

The balance of payments is defined as a record of the value of all transactions of a country with the rest of the world over a period of time, usually a year.

Transactions that lead to an inflow of currency are known as credit items and enter the account with a plus sign. Transactions that lead to an outflow of currency are referred to as debit items and enter the account with a minus sign.

The two types of transaction are shown in the following examples.

- If Raquel, who lives in Mexico City, buys a $250 Italian jacket, this is an outflow of currency from Mexico. For Mexico it is a debit item and enters its balance of payments with a minus sign. For Italy it is an inflow of currency, so it is a credit item and enters Italy's balance of payments with a plus sign.

- If Layla, an American college student, visits Mazatlan in Mexico during her spring break and spends $1200 on her stay, this money is an inflow of currency into Mexico.

It is a credit item for Mexico and enters its balance of payments with a plus sign. For the USA it is an outflow of currency, so it is a debit item and enters the US balance of payments with a minus sign.

- If Mexico's largest steel company acquires for $1.2 billion a Turkish steel manufacturing firm, this is an outflow of currency from Mexico. It is a debit item for Mexico and enters Mexico's balance of payments with a minus sign. For Turkey it is an inflow of currency so it is a credit item and enters Turkey's balance of payments with a plus sign.

- If Arturo, a resident of Mexico City, buys $500,000 worth of Delta Airlines shares listed in the New York Stock Exchange, this an outflow of currency from Mexico. It is a debit item for Mexico and enters Mexico's balance of payments with a minus sign. For the USA's balance of payments it is an inflow, so it is a credit item and enters its balance of payments with a plus sign.

Components of the balance of payments

The balance of payments is divided into three major components, the current account, the capital account and the financial account.

The current account

The current account includes the following components.

The balance of trade in goods

The goods account includes the value of all the goods (physical or tangible merchandise) a country exports or imports; for example, farm products, oil, machines, cars, laptops, airplanes, wine or medical equipment. More generally, it includes imports and exports of raw materials, intermediate products and final products. Exports are credits and are recorded with a plus sign as they lead to an inflow of currency. Imports are debits and are recorded with a minus sign as they lead to an outflow of currency. The difference between the value of exports of goods and imports of goods is referred to as the balance of trade in goods. If it is positive there is a surplus in the balance of trade in goods. If it is negative there is a deficit in the balance of trade in goods.

The balance of trade in services

The services account includes the value of all the services a country exports or imports; for example, insurance, shipping, tourism, education, financial, architectural, legal services and others. Again, exports are credits and are recorded with a plus sign whereas imports are debits and are recorded with a minus sign. When Germans visit India it is an export (a credit and so a plus sign) for India and an import (a debit and so a minus sign) for Germany. When an Italian architect designed the Whitney Museum of American Art in Boston it was an export for Italy and an import for the USA.

The difference between the value of exports and imports of services is referred to as the balance of trade in services. If it is positive there is a surplus in the balance of trade in services. If it is negative there is a deficit in the balance of trade in services.

Often the two accounts are combined to arrive at the balance of trade in goods and services.

Net income from abroad (the primary income account)

This account records differences between income received from abroad (inflows) and income payable abroad (outflows). Primary income includes mostly two types of income.

- It includes profits, interest and dividends from portfolio and direct investments.

- It includes compensation (wages and salaries) of employees who work in a country but only for a short period of time then return home (so they are not considered residents of the country). An example would be the compensation paid by a South Korean university to a British academic delivering a series of lectures in Seoul.

Note that "net income from abroad" is what distinguishes GDP from GNI in macroeconomics.

Net current (unilateral) transfers

This account records gifts that a country makes and gifts that it receives. It includes migrant workers' remittances, international pension flows, donations, transfers related to international cooperation between governments (such as receipts and payments to EU institutions), foreign aid including food aid and emergency aid after natural disasters and so on. If it is positive (negative) it means that the inflows (outflows) of such moneys exceed the outflows (inflows).

Current account balance

The sum of net exports of goods and services, net income and net current transfers over a period of time (a year) is defined as the current account balance. If this is positive, we say that there is a current account surplus. If it is negative, we say that there is a current account deficit.

The capital account

Typically, the capital account is small and usually of minor importance. It includes:

- net capital transfers between countries, such as debt forgiveness, which is counted as a debit for the lender; and the assets (goods and financial assets) of migrants as they enter (credit) or leave (debit) a country

- net purchases and sales of non-financial, non-produced assets, such rights to natural resources (fishing rights, land rights, mineral rights and so on), patents, copyrights, trademarks, franchises, leases and internet domain names.

The financial account

The financial account includes direct investment, portfolio investment as well as changes in the official international reserve assets of the central bank of the country.

Direct investment

Direct investment (often referred to as foreign direct investment or FDI) refers to long-term investment by firms from one country (the source) in productive facilities in another country (the host). The distinctive characteristic of direct investment is the intent of lasting interest.

Direct investment includes the following.

- Building of new facilities (factories, distribution facilities, stores and so) from scratch ("greenfield" investment) is direct investment. The objective is to establish a new presence in the host country and have full control over the operations of the new firm.

- Investing in or taking over an existing foreign company ("brownfield" investment) is also direct investment. The objective is either to gain complete control or to exert significant control over the management decisions of the firm. The IMF typically requires acquiring at least 10% of the foreign company's shares for the investment to qualify as having a lasting interest.

Portfolio and other investment

Portfolio and other investments refer to the acquisition and sale of corporate stocks, government and corporate bonds as well as changes in loans and deposits. For example, when a resident of Egypt buys stocks of Turkish companies, or buys Turkish bonds, then an outflow of money is recorded in the Egyptian financial account and an equal inflow of money in the Turkish one. Buying such assets leads to an outflow of funds—it is a debit item and is recorded with a minus sign. Note that next year when the resident of Egypt receives dividends and interest payments from the investments then that inflow of money (credit) into Egypt will be recorded

in the Egyptian current account as a receipt of investment income under the current account. The equal outflow of money (debit) will be recorded in the Turkish current account as a payment of investment income under its current account.

Changes in official holdings of international reserves

A central bank must hold reserve assets that are generally acceptable by all countries, so they are readily available for use to finance balance of payments needs or to intervene in the foreign exchange market in order to affect the exchange rate.

These reserve assets include:

- foreign currency holdings and deposits (in US dollars, euros, Japanese yen, Chinese renminbi, British pounds, Australian dollars, Canadian dollars and Swiss francs, as these are the eight reserve currencies the IMF recognizes)

- short-term government bonds (such as US Treasury Bills) that can be easily transformed into a reserve currency

- gold

- a few other assets.

Note here that a decrease in official reserves enters the balance of payments with a plus sign whereas an increase in official reserves enters the account with a minus sign. This seems strange until we realize that by accounting convention the official reserves are considered assets residing outside the economy. One way to understand this is to visualize the central bank of a country as a separate entity from the economy holding a foreign exchange savings account.

Interdependence between the accounts

The following necessarily holds true:

$$CA = -FA - KA$$

$$\text{or, } CA + FA + KA = 0$$

where CA is the balance on the current account, FA is the balance on the financial account and KA is the balance on the capital account. The capital account (KA) is very small and therefore insignificant so we will be ignoring it in for the time being, so

$$CA = -FA \quad (1)$$

This is an identity which means that it always and necessarily holds true. It simply states that if a country has a current account deficit so that it is importing (that is, buying) more goods and services from the rest of the world than it is exporting (that is, selling) to the rest of the world, then it must have an equally sized surplus in its financial account. Why? The reason is that it must finance this deficit somehow.

There must be an inflow (plus sign) of dollars from the financial account of equal magnitude. For example, if the deficit in the current account is 489 billion dollars (–489), then the country must have somehow found these 489 billion dollars to pay for the excess of goods and services it imports over what it exports. It must be that

$$-489 = -(+)489 \text{ so that } -489 + 489 = 0$$

If you are having trouble with this, think of a family. Assume that its income from selling its labour services in 2020 was

$25,000 (consider these the "exports" of the family). During the same year the family bought goods and services worth $28,000 (consider these its "imports"). How could the family have spent more than it earned? It must have somehow financed the $3,000 deficit it had. It may have sold some assets (such as a used bicycle) and/or decreased savings and/or borrowed from banks. If we add these "inflows" into the family then its accounts are balanced.

The financial account includes buying and selling of stocks and bonds, deposits and loans as well as direct investments. It also includes changes in official holdings of reserves of the central bank. Let's now separate the changes in official holdings of reserves of the central bank from the financial account to clarify an important point. We can now rewrite relationship (1) above as:

$$CA + FA + \text{official reserve transactions} = 0$$

If we now also include the capital account (KA) the relationship can be written as

$$CA + KA + FA + \text{official reserve transactions} = 0 \quad (2)$$

Items included in the current account, the capital account and the financial account excluding the official reserve transactions by the central bank are referred to as "autonomous" transactions because they are transactions taken for business purposes. Examples are firms importing cars or exporting grain and investors buying or selling bonds or stocks or firms. Changes in official reserve transactions are referred to as "accommodating" transactions.

If the sum of autonomous transactions is negative it is referred to as a balance of payments deficit. If the sum of autonomous transactions is positive it is referred to as a balance of payments surplus.

For the overall balance of payments to balance there must be an equal accommodating transaction with the opposite sign. This transaction is the change in official financing.

An example will help clarify. Assume that a country recorded the following balance of payments values for some year:

$$CA = -470 \text{ billion dollars}$$

$$KA = -5 \text{ billion dollars}$$

$$FA \text{ (excluding official financing)} = +425 \text{ billion dollars.}$$

Further assume that its central bank held 690 billion dollars in official reserves.

This country has a combined current account and capital account deficit totaling $475 billion. This means that $475 billion more flowed out of the country than flowed in. How could that be? This combined current and capital account deficit was financed from the financial account, which recorded a surplus of $425 billion as $425 billion more flowed into the country than flowed out. For example, foreigners bought $425 billion more in bonds, stocks and domestic companies than domestic residents bought foreign bonds, stocks or foreign companies.

However, there are still $50 billion missing. This is where the accommodating transactions come into play, namely the changes in official reserves that the central bank holds. The official reserves of the country were used to finance the balance of payments deficit and force it to balance overall.

The central bank used $50 billion from its reserves to finance this deficit. The official foreign exchange reserves of the central bank decreased by $50 billion and are now equal to $640 billion. This decrease is recorded with a plus sign because this amount "left" the central bank and "entered" the economy. Remember that by accounting convention the official reserves held by the central bank are considered assets residing outside the economy. Note also that if a country has insufficient foreign exchange reserves it will be forced to resort to official borrowing to pay for its financing needs.

Returning now to the identity above (2) it should make sense:

$$CA + KA + FA = \text{Official reserve transactions} = 0$$

or

$$-470 - 5 + (425 + 50) = 0$$

or, $CA + KA + FA = 0$ as official reserves are included in the FA.

Consider now a different example where the inflows of foreign exchange of a country exceed the outflows. Let:

$$CA = +228 \text{ billion dollars}$$

$$KA = -2 \text{ billion dollars}$$

$$FA \text{ (excluding official financing)} = -205 \text{ billion dollars.}$$

Further assume that its central bank again was holding 690 billion dollars in official reserves.

The sum of all autonomous transactions is now +21 billion dollars. What happens to the official foreign exchange reserves of the country? They increase by $21 billion and become $711 billion. This increase is recorded with a minus sign because this amount "left" the economy and "entered" the central bank. Remember that by accounting convention the official reserves held by the central bank are considered assets residing outside the economy. Note that a country with plentiful foreign exchange reserves may officially lend other countries.

Again, referring to the identity above (2):

$$CA + KA + FA = \text{Official reserve transactions} = 0$$

or

$$+228 - 2 + (-205 - 21) = 0$$

or, $+228 - 2 - 226 = 0$ as official reserves are included in the FA.

Errors and omissions

It would be good if every single autonomous transaction was recorded properly by the statistical authorities (customs, banks and other financial institutions) but unfortunately this is never the case. It is never the case because data collection is costly and far from perfect. Many transactions, especially in the financial account (which is the hardest one to compile with accuracy), are simply not recorded and some even have to be estimated. So, typically the sum of all accounts including changes in official reserves do not add up, as they logically should, to zero.

If the sum is not zero but, say, −5 billion dollars, then statisticians include the aptly named errors and omissions entry at the very bottom of the balance of payments equal to +5 billion dollars and therefore artificially force the balance of payments to equal zero. If the sum of all accounts including changes in official reserves was not zero but plus 5 billion dollars, then the errors and omissions entry that statisticians would add would be minus 5 billion dollars to artificially force the balance of payments to equal zero. The balancing item therefore has the same magnitude but the opposite sign of the error.

If the errors and omissions entry in an economy is relatively large, it may point to illicit drugs or arms trade or to residents underreporting their income from their offshore investments or sending their wealth abroad without reporting the transaction to the authorities (part of what is known as capital flight—see section 4.9, page 193).

CURRENT ACCOUNT	
(1)	Net exports of goods
(2)	Net exports of services
(3)	Net income from investments
(4)	Net current transfers
(5)	Balance on current account: (1) + (2) + (3) + (4)
CAPITAL ACCOUNT	
(6)	Net capital transfers
(7)	Net purchases of non-produced, non-financial assets
(8)	Balance on capital account: (6) + (7)
FINANCIAL ACCOUNT	
(9)	Net portfolio investments
(10)	Net FDI
(11)	Changes in official holdings of international reserves
(12)	Balance on financial account: (9) + (10) + (11)
(13)	(Errors and omissions)

Notes

Items (5), (8), (9) and (10) include autonomous transactions. Item (11) is the accommodating transaction. If the sum of (5), (8), (9) and (10) is negative then we say there is a balance of payments deficit. By adding item (11), namely the changes in the official holdings of foreign exchange by the central bank, the balance of payments will balance because the accounting identity below must hold:

$$CA + KA + FA = 0$$
$$or, (5) + (8) + (12) = 0$$

If the above sum does not equal zero, then we must add item (13), errors and omissions (the statistical discrepancy) with the opposite sign, to force the balance of payments to balance.

Table 4.6.1

Relationship between the current account and the exchange rate

We have established that the equilibrium exchange rate is determined by the interaction of the demand and supply of a currency.

What will happen to the exchange rate if, ceteris paribus, a country's exports decrease and/or its imports increase and the current account records a deficit? To answer we will simplify matters and assume that the demand for and the supply of a currency reflect only trade flows (that is, only exports and imports of goods and services and no financial flows).

Let's focus on Australia and the Australian dollar (AUD) with trade flows only between the USA and Australia. In this simplified set-up, shown in Figure 4.6.1, the demand for AUD reflects the value of Australia's exports as Americans need AUD to buy Australia's products. The supply of AUD reflects the value of imports of Australia as Australians need to buy US dollars to import US goods and services and to buy USD they must first sell and offer AUD in the foreign exchange market.

Initially the exchange rate for the Australian dollar (USD per AUD) is at e1 where the demand for AUD (D1) intersects the supply of AUD (S1). At e1, Australia's current account is balanced as the value of exports (X) is equal to the value of imports (M). Specifically, at the exchange rate e1, e1a Australian dollars are demanded by Americans to buy Australian products (Australia's exports) and e1a Australian dollars are also supplied by Australians to buy US products (Australia's imports).

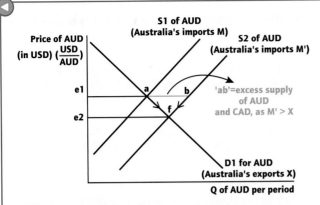

Figure 4.6.1 Impact on the AUD of a current account deficit

Now, if for whatever reason, perhaps because of faster growth, Australia starts importing more goods and services from the USA, the supply of Australian dollars will increase with the supply curve shifting to the right to S2. At the original exchange rate e1, there is now in the foreign exchange market an excess supply of AUD equal to line segment ab. At e1, the value of exports is e1a but now the value of imports is greater at e1b. At e1, imports exceed exports in value by ab. The distance ab is the current account deficit that Australia now registers but also the excess supply of AUD in the foreign exchange market. The AUD, ceteris paribus, will therefore tend to depreciate until it reaches e2. As it depreciates, Australia's current account (its trade in goods and services) deficit will narrow as its exports become more competitive abroad and imports less attractive. At e2 trade balance has again been achieved as the value of exports and the value of imports are both equal to e2f Australian dollars and there is neither excess demand nor excess supply of AUD in the foreign exchange market. Australia's current account deficit has led to a depreciation of the Australian dollar.

Note that a current account deficit and therefore an excess supply of Australian dollars would also result if instead Australia's exports had decreased. The bottom line is that a current account deficit will, ceteris paribus, lead to a fall in the value of the currency.

The above conclusion rests though on the ceteris paribus clause mentioned, namely that the demand for and supply of AUD only reflect trade flows. As explained in section 4.5 (page 164) the demand for and the supply of a currency do not only reflect trade flows but also reflect financial flows (buying and selling of financial and other assets) between countries.

Relationship between the financial account and the exchange rate

What will happen to the exchange rate if, ceteris paribus, inflows into a country's financial account increase and/ or outflows decrease and the financial account (excluding changes in official reserve transactions by central banks) records a surplus? In order to simplify the analysis, assume that the demand and the supply of a currency now only reflect portfolio and direct investment flows between countries.

Figure 4.6.2 maintains focus on the Australian dollar. We assume now that Australia is exhibiting phenomenal non-inflationary growth and that it is believed that this outstanding performance will continue—therefore, investors are eager to invest in the Australian economy. Demand for Australian stocks and bonds is increasing and so are the direct investment flows into its economy.

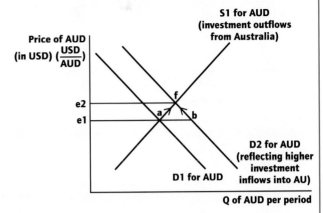

Figure 4.6.2 Impact on the exchange rate of a financial account surplus

The demand for Australian dollars will increase and the demand curve will shift to the right to D2 as investors need to buy more Australian dollars in order to buy more Australian stocks and bonds, to acquire controlling share of more Australian firms or to establish a greater business presence in Australia. At the original exchange rate e1 there is now excess demand for Australian dollars equal to ab, reflecting the surplus in Australia's financial account that results from private American investors investing in Australia more than Australian investors are investing into the US economy. The Australian dollar will tend to appreciate to e2. It follows that if there are more private financial capital flowing into an economy than flowing out of an economy then the currency will, ceteris paribus, tend to appreciate.

This conclusion rests once again on the ceteris paribus clause mentioned. Remember that the demand for and the supply of a currency do not only reflect financial flows (buying and selling of financial and other assets) but also trade flows (exports and imports of goods and services) between countries.

The bottom line

Does the financial account have a stronger effect on the exchange rate than the current account?

Comparing Figures 4.6.1 and 4.6.2 it should be clear that a current account deficit may lead to a depreciation of the currency, but whether it does or not depends on the financial account of the country. It could well be that despite a current account deficit, the currency may be appreciating. For example, for the period 1994–2002 the USA was recording a rising trade deficit but the dollar was appreciating. How could that be? The USA was attracting more than sufficient cross-border financial capital inflows to offset the downward pressure on the dollar from the current account deficit. In terms of Table 4.6.1), the currency may even appreciate even if there is a current account deficit (a negative item 5) if the sum of items (9) and (10) are positive and greater than item (5) in value.

The bottom line is that a current account deficit may lead to a depreciation (and a surplus may lead to an appreciation) of a currency but whether either happens depends on what is going on in the financial account. In general, it is more probable that a currency will depreciate in countries that due to their current account deficit and their overall economic prospects do not inspire confidence in international investors.

A similar issue applies to countries with current account surpluses. If analysed in isolation, a current account surplus will lead to an appreciation of the currency. Why? If exports exceed imports then more of the currency is demanded than supplied. The resulting excess demand will push the currency to appreciate unless residents of the country and perhaps its government (and so the central bank) are buying more and more foreign-owned assets (stocks, bonds, real estate, companies and so on). To buy these assets the central bank will first need to sell the currency in the foreign exchange market, increasing the supply of the currency and potentially staving off its appreciation. For example, China was recording significant current account surpluses, but the yuan was kept from appreciating against the US dollar as there were massive purchases of US Treasury bonds that increased the demand for US dollars.

Implications of a persistent current account deficit

A current account deficit exists if the sum of net exports of goods and services plus net investment income plus net current transfers is negative. This implies that the sum of the debit items exceeds the sum of the credit items so that outflows of currency are greater than inflows of currency, resulting in pressure for the currency to weaken.

Several questions arise. Is a current account deficit a cause for alarm? The answers are not simple. As in most questions in economics, it depends. First, to evaluate whether a current account deficit is a cause for concern we must be able to judge its size. Its dollar size is not a useful measure because economies may differ vastly in size. The same dollar size deficit may pose absolutely no problem for a large in size economy, but it may be a cause of concern for a much smaller economy. We must therefore "scale for size" and we do that by dividing the size of the current account deficit by the GDP of the country. Consider the data for Mexico in Table 4.6.2.

	2016	1992
Current account balance in current USD	–24.311 billion dollars	–24.442 billion dollars
Current account balance as a % of GDP	–2.255%	–6.73%

Table 4.6.2 Current account data for Mexico. Source: data.worldbank.org

The 2016 current account deficit in Mexico was roughly the same as in 1992 (only 131 million dollars smaller) but in 1992 the deficit represented 6.73% of Mexico's GDP whereas in 2016 it represented only 2.26% of the economy. The Mexican economy grew significantly over this 24-year period so that the roughly same current account deficit in dollar terms represented in 2016 a much smaller proportion of the economy. Imagine now comparing the dollar deficits of small and large countries. No valid conclusions could be made.

Given the above, if a current deficit narrows in size is this necessarily a positive development for the economy? Again, it depends. A current account deficit may be the result of a growing economy. During a boom, incomes increase and therefore more imports are absorbed, and a current account deficit may widen. It follows that a smaller deficit may not be a reason to celebrate because it may be the result of a severe recession.

Is a growing current account deficit a cause for concern? Once again, not necessarily. A developing economy attempting to establish certain industries may initially be importing expensive capital equipment and record a sizable current account deficit. If the country is successful in establishing an export-oriented sector, this deficit may become a surplus.

What if a country's exports rely heavily on agricultural products and extreme weather conditions in one year destroy most agricultural output, also wiping out its exports? Would this be a cause of concern? The concern might be limited to considering compensation for the affected farmers in that year, because it would be hoped that the extreme conditions would not be experienced again in the following year.

It follows that a current account deficit should not raise the alarm if it is temporary. Temporary deficits are reversible as is the case of deficits that increase in a boom because they will narrow in a slowdown. Other examples are when deficits are of a transitory nature, such as in the cases of the failure of a particular crop, or a massive labour strike that disrupts the production process of major exporting industries.

Current account deficits are a cause for alarm if they represent a significant proportion of the country's GDP and if they are persistent. A persistent current account deficit is of a long-term nature and often reflects an ailing economy. Chronic inflation, uncompetitive product markets or rigid labour markets are all possible causes of a persistent current account deficit. All of these problems erode the competitiveness of a country's exports as they become more expensive in foreign markets while they increase the attractiveness of imports to domestic buyers.

No matter what the cause of a persistent current account deficit it will need to be financed and it is this financing that may create problems for the economy. Financing requires either an inflow of private financial capital from abroad (selling foreigners financial or real assets such as bonds, stocks or firms) or official borrowing. The implications may prove severe.

The possible adverse implications for various different factors are described below.

The exchange rate

A current account deficit exerts pressure on the exchange rate to depreciate. As long as the economy's growth prospects look promising it will attract inflows of foreign financial capital and the currency may not depreciate. The problem arises if foreign investors lose confidence and start to pull their funds out of the economy. This may lead to a sudden and sizable depreciation of the currency that could prove disruptive as import prices will surge. This will hurt households, especially those with low income, and will increase the risk of cost-push inflation. Note that there are also positive effects from a significant depreciation, such as increased export sales—but the adverse impact is more immediate.

Interest rates

In order to attract private inflows of financial capital and to stave off a depreciation of the currency, the central bank may be forced to increase interest rates. Higher interest rates make domestic bonds and deposits more attractive to foreign financial investors, who will want to buy them. The currency may not depreciate but this choice is costly. By selling bonds to foreigners it is promising them future interest payments as bonds represent debt for the issuer. These interest payments may prove costly as government funds will need to be diverted from domestic purposes. Higher interest rates will also decrease domestic consumption and investment spending, lowering aggregate demand and risking recession.

Foreign ownership of domestic assets

Selling assets requires willing buyers. Willing buyers exist if either the future prospects for the economy look so good that investors buy shares, businesses or real estate expecting to collect profits, or if the selling price of the asset is exceptionally low. In the former case the sale of assets is not considered a problem. In the latter case it may prove a problem as the assets sold to foreigners can be both sizeable and of significance. A country may be forced to sell to foreigners significant natural resources, banks, large industries or state-owned assets such as airports and harbours. Such a development carries the threat of loss of economic sovereignty.

National debt and credit ratings

If the persistent current account deficit forces the government to borrow from abroad this involves future repayment of the capital plus interest. In the future, part of national income must be diverted away from domestic uses towards the repayment of past borrowing. These funds could have been used by the government to finance increased public investments on infrastructure, health or education. Since repayment of any such borrowing from abroad must be made in foreign exchange, it also means that future foreign exchange earnings from exports will need to be diverted away from the purchase of imports of often necessary consumer and capital goods.

Mounting foreign debt may create increasing adverse effects on an economy. Foreigners will be willing to lend only at higher and higher interest rates to compensate for the additional risk they face. Higher interest rates, though, imply surging interest costs, further worsening the country's foreign debt problem.

As the risk of the country defaulting increases (meaning that there is fear that it will not be able to continue repaying its foreign debt), its credit rating by international credit rating agencies, such as Fitch, Moody's and Standard & Poor's, could be downgraded. Such agencies evaluate the creditworthiness of countries and assign a grade to the debt they issue. If it is decided that risk is increasing, the country's bonds will receive a lower grade, which means that investors will only lend to the country at even higher interest rates. This tightens the squeeze on the country as the cost of borrowing continues to rise and the economy will not avoid a recession. If it defaults on its loans, then it is typically required to agree to painful restructuring policies.

Demand management

Persistent current account deficits require adoption of contractionary demand-side macroeconomic policies. Their aim is to narrow the current account deficit by decreasing aggregate demand and national income since lower income levels will decrease spending on imports. These polices will be explained below but, clearly, they are painful for the population especially for lower income households, who will suffer rising unemployment and loss of income.

Growth prospects

The points above suggest that the price paid by an economy for recording persistent current account deficits may be very high. The costs usually extend deep into the future. It may take years for countries to recover from a current account crisis. Growth prospects are compromised for many reasons. Governments are not in a position to fund necessary public investments. It may take time for foreign investors to return and lend to the country or make direct investments. The cost incurred is usually higher for lower income households, which implies that income inequality will have increased. This will further dampen growth prospects, as explained earlier. It is very risky for an economy to consume for a long time beyond its means.

> **Recap**
>
> Persistent current account deficit
>
> A persistent current account deficit may lead to:
>
> - a sudden and severe depreciation of the currency
> - much higher interest rates to attract lenders
> - the sale of domestic assets at reduced prices
> - mounting foreign debt and downgrading by credit agencies
> - painful demand-side policies
> - diminished growth for many years.

Correcting a persistent current account deficit: Methods and their effectiveness

There are three types of policies available to policymakers to deal with a persistent current account deficit: expenditure-reducing policies, expenditure-switching policies and supply-side policies.

Expenditure-reducing policies

These include policies that decrease the level of aggregate demand. They thus include contractionary fiscal policy (decreasing G and/or increasing T) but also tighter monetary policy (increasing interest rates). By decreasing aggregate demand, they reduce the level of national income (Y) therefore decreasing spending on imports (M). Remember that imports are directly related to the level of income. If incomes rise, then spending on imports rises; if incomes decrease then spending on imports decreases. Note that the decrease in aggregate demand will also decrease inflation. This will benefit the export sector as the competitiveness of exports will increase. All in all, shrinking imports and perhaps rising exports will help narrow the current account deficit.

Note though that such an adjustment policy comes at a high cost. Growth will surely slow down or may even turn negative, which means that the economy may suffer a recession. Recessions are painful. Output and incomes decrease, firms contract or shut down and unemployment rises.

Expenditure-switching policies

The aim of this set of policies is to switch spending away from imports towards domestically produced goods and services. To induce such a switch, imports must become more expensive, to make them less attractive, and this can be achieved in two ways: by decreasing the value of the currency or by protection.

In a fixed exchange rate system, the central bank may permit the currency to devalue instead of trying to maintain it artificially at its fixed value. In a managed exchange rate system, the central bank may permit the value of the currency to slide and even keep it undervalued. Decreasing the price of the currency makes imports more expensive domestically. Consumers will switch to relatively cheaper domestic goods and services. Import expenditures will decrease. Note that exports will also become cheaper abroad and more competitive so that export revenues will increase. Both effects will tend to correct the current account deficit.

A potential risk of a rapid depreciation or devaluation is that inflation may accelerate. Import prices will rise, therefore domestic firms that use imported raw materials and/or intermediate products will experience an increase in their production costs. In addition, the cost of living will immediately increase and this may compel workers to demand higher wages, further increasing production costs. Aggregate supply may therefore decrease, leading to cost-push inflationary pressures. In addition, since exports will also increase, aggregate demand will increase and the demand curve will shift to the right, leading potentially to demand-pull inflation.

Alternatively, policymakers could resort to protection. Tariffs and other trade barriers will make imports more expensive in the domestic market, so less attractive. Households and firms will substitute domestic products for imports, decreasing the country's import expenditures.

Unfortunately, such protectionist policies create trade frictions and invite retaliation from affected exporting nations. In addition, they go against WTO membership rules.

If they are implemented then inefficiency also increases as resources are misallocated. The country suffers the costs of protectionism.

Supply-side policies

Policies to help correct a persistent current account deficit also include certain supply-side policies (see also section 3.7). Supply-side policies are of a long-term nature and can help restore an ailing economy's competitiveness, curing a persistent deficit in the current account. Persistent current account deficits may result from uncompetitive product markets characterized by high monopoly power. Excessive regulation of businesses may also be responsible, as regulations will increase production costs. Rigid labour markets dominated by labour unions, high minimum wage laws and high worker protection may also contribute to higher priced, so uncompetitive, goods and services. It follows that market-based supply-side policies that focus on product markets may help restore competitiveness and correct a persistent current account deficit. Such policies are considered most important as they may treat the fundamental cause of the external imbalance.

Unfortunately, supply-side policies have major drawbacks (as explained earlier). Within this framework, the most significant drawback is that they are difficult to implement, and any benefits will appear only after a very long time lag. Although these policies are instrumental and necessary in the long term to achieve and maintain competitiveness, persistent current account deficits must be dealt with immediately.

Recap

Expenditure-reducing, expenditure-switching and supply-side policies

Expenditure-reducing policies are policies that decrease aggregate demand (such as contractionary fiscal and monetary policies) and so national income. They decrease imports. They lead to slower growth, possibly a recession and higher unemployment.

Expenditure-switching policies are policies that switch away from imports towards domestically produced goods. They include lowering the exchange rate and increased protection that make imports more expensive. They may lead to retaliation and inflation.

Supply-side policies include policies to make product markets more competitive and labour markets more flexible so that costs and prices decrease. They are often necessary but only effective in the long term.

The Marshall-Lerner condition and the J-curve effect

Devaluation or a sharp depreciation implies that the foreign price of exports decreases and the domestic price of imports increases. With exports more competitive abroad and imports less attractive domestically we expect that export revenues will increase and import expenditures will decrease. Therefore, a trade deficit will improve.

Such a development crucially rests on the size of the price elasticity of demand (PED) for exports and the PED of imports. The reason relates to the fact that the behaviour of revenues and of expenditures following a change in price depends on PEDs.

The Marshall-Lerner condition states that for devaluation or a sharp depreciation of a currency to improve a current account deficit, the sum of the PED for imports and the PED for exports must be (absolutely) greater than one.

Marshall-Lerner condition: a devaluation (or a sharp depreciation) will improve a trade deficit

$$\text{if } (ped(x) + ped(M)) > 1$$

The proof needs some elementary calculus, but the following may help to explain the condition. If we express the German trade balance in dollars, then a sharp depreciation of the euro will make American Abercrombie & Fitch (A&F) shirts pricier in euros even though their dollar price is constant. Let PED(M) = 0 so that exactly the same quantity of A&F shirts is bought in Germany. With their dollar price the same and the quantity demanded and imported the same, import expenditures expressed in dollars will necessarily remain the same. Germany's trade balance will improve if export revenues (expressed in dollars) increase.

Since the depreciation of the euro made the dollar price of BMW cars in New York lower, Germany's export revenues in dollars will increase if the quantity of BMW cars demanded by Americans increase by proportionally more than the decrease in their New York price so that PED(X) > 1. The sum of the two elasticities would thus exceed one. It follows that if the Marshall-Lerner condition is satisfied then the German trade balance, following a sharp depreciation of the euro, will improve.

The condition is not satisfied in the short term, though, because the PED for exports and the PED for imports are initially low. They are low for many reasons. Firms and especially households may not even be aware of the new prices. A sharp depreciation of the euro will mean that European cars are now cheaper in the USA. Will the average US household immediately realize that European cars are now cheaper and more competitive? Not necessarily, as access to new information is not instantaneous.

Even if it becomes widely known that European cars are now cheaper in the USA, the typical American may need time to switch away from buying American cars if he or she has always bought Fords. Buying habits also need time to be overcome.

Most importantly, commercial contracts between exporting and importing firms are slow to respond to a currency change. Importers may have signed long-term contracts with foreign firms that are difficult to terminate or change. It takes time to change business contracts.

Lastly, in the case of firms importing inputs, it may take time before they run out of inventories and need to place new orders or before they need to replace an imported machine.

The J-curve effect

Since PEDs are low in the short run and so the Marshall-Lerner condition is not immediately satisfied, any improvement in a trade deficit will take time to be realized. In Figure 4.6.3, time is on the horizontal axis and the trade balance in goods and services (X – M) is on the vertical axis, the path through time of the balance of trade following devaluation will trace the letter "J". This is referred to as the J-curve effect.

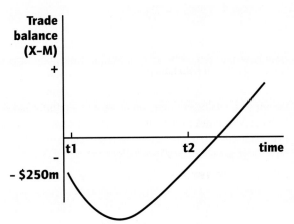

Figure 4.6.3 The J-curve effect

Assume an economy with a trade deficit equal to, say, $250 million deciding to let its currency sharply depreciate (or to devalue if in a fixed exchange rate system). Initially, the deficit becomes larger and larger because the Marshall-Lerner condition in the short term is not satisfied: PEDs for exports and for imports are very low and their sum does not exceed unity. Only after time t2 in Figure 4.6.3 is the condition satisfied and the trade deficit shrinks below the $250 million level.

Note that an inverted J-curve results after a revaluation (appreciation), where the surplus initially becomes bigger and only starts to shrink later.

Implications of a persistent current account surplus

A current account surplus exists if the sum of net exports of goods and services plus net income and net current transfers is positive. It is acceptable, even though not strictly speaking correct, to say that it exists when export revenues from the sale of goods and services over a period of time exceed import expenditures on goods and services.

A current account surplus in general is not considered an issue, especially if the surplus is small or transitory. Typically, it is also not considered an issue if it is a result of an export-oriented growth strategy because its perceived benefits to policymakers and the government outweigh any risks it may involve. There may, though, be certain consequences that need to be explained. These relate to various factors, as described below.

Domestic consumption and investment

Two points need to be clear here.

1. If we focus only on the trade in goods and services balance of the current account, then if it is positive it implies that the value of goods and services exported exceeds the value of goods and services imported.

2. If there is a current account surplus, then there is a combined capital and financial account deficit. Ignoring the capital account, as it is small and insignificant, this means that more financial capital is flowing out of the country that flowing into the country. Domestic residents are buying more foreign bonds, stocks and foreign companies than foreigners are buying domestic bonds, stocks and domestic companies.

Point 1 implies that the country is consuming inside its production possibilities. Consumption bundles that could have been enjoyed are sacrificed. From a static point of view this implies that living standards are lower than they need to be but from a dynamic point of view this argument may be turned on its head. Foreign markets can and have proved to be opportunities for long-run growth and have permitted many countries to enjoy higher levels of income, with millions of people escaping poverty.

Point 2 may be interpreted to imply that fewer domestic investment projects are being financed as financial capital flows out of the country. Empirically this has not been the case as export performers are usually efficient producers with high rates of domestic economic investment. In addition, the returns from these investments (profits, interest and dividends) boost national income.

Exchange rates and export competitiveness

Perhaps the most serious problem associated with a persistent and widening current account surplus is that it puts pressure on the exchange rate to appreciate. This is even more serious if the trade surplus is mostly due to one export (for example, oil or natural gas). The appreciation means that all other exports of the country become less and less competitive in foreign markets and as result suffer a decrease. This is referred to as the Dutch disease. On the other hand, the appreciation puts pressure on firms to cut down on waste and become more efficient.

Remember that if the current account surplus is the result of the country artificially maintaining its currency undervalued so that its exports remain cheap and competitive in foreign markets, then the country runs the risk of inflation.

Inflation

A large and growing current account surplus implies that the net exports (NX) component of aggregate demand is positive and increasing. This increases aggregate demand, shifting the AD curve to the right. The increase in aggregate demand, ceteris paribus, will exert pressure on the average price level, leading to accelerating inflation. Such a conclusion, though, ignores the possibility that policymakers have ensured that domestic economic investment is also increasing so that the productive capacity of the economy is also increasing through time. In this case, the increase in aggregate demand will not lead to inflation as the LRAS curve will have also shifted to the right.

Employment

To the extent that a current account balance in trade surplus increases aggregate demand then the resulting faster growth will increase employment. More workers will be employed in the export sector and also more in the import-competing sector.

The response of trading partners

Large bilateral trade surpluses carry the risk of retaliatory protectionist measures by deficit countries. To the extent that the surplus country relies on foreign demand for its growth, retaliation may pose a serious risk. The deficit country may suddenly adopt highly protectionist policies, blocking out imports, which could halt the growth of the exporting surplus country. The recent wave of US protection on China's exports may be understood as the dissatisfaction of many in the USA with China's export success, especially in areas that have suffered the greatest import penetration.

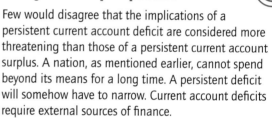

Policymakers' perspective

Few would disagree that the implications of a persistent current account deficit are considered more threatening than those of a persistent current account surplus. A nation, as mentioned earlier, cannot spend beyond its means for a long time. A persistent deficit will somehow have to narrow. Current account deficits require external sources of finance.

However, foreign investors may suddenly decide to withdraw their funds if they feel uncertain about the future prospects of the country. If significant investors do this, the country will face dire consequences. The currency may sharply depreciate, causing import prices to soar. Most countries rely on imported oil. Many rely on imported pharmaceuticals and food. To avert a sharp depreciation, policymakers may be forced to increase interest rates dramatically in order to induce inflows of private foreign capital that will curb the pressure on the currency to depreciate. Higher interest rates also cause distress and, worse still, they may prove ineffective in averting a currency crisis.

It follows that a persistent current account deficit must be dealt with before matters escalate. Expenditure-reducing policies should be adopted early even though they are also costly. A controlled depreciation of the currency may succeed in restoring competitiveness without surging import prices. Targeted protection may also be considered even though this usually proves counterproductive. Policymakers must try to ensure that growth is not inflationary, that markets are not dominated by monopolies, that wage costs are not prohibitively burdensome for firms and, most importantly, that growth is inclusive so that trust is maintained and people will be willing to make short-term sacrifices to reap long-term benefits.

4.7 Sustainable development

The meaning of sustainable development

Sustainable development is a central concept for our age. A wide range of definitions of sustainable development exists. The most commonly used one is that of the Brundtland Commission of the United Nations, which defined sustainable development as "development that meets the needs of the present without compromising the ability of future generations to meet their own needs" (World Commission on Environment and Development 1987a: 43).

Sustainable development has three major aspects: economic development, social progress and environmental protection, and requires a balance between them.

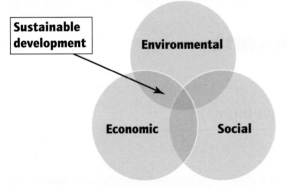

Figure 4.7.1 Aspects of sustainable development

This means that the promotion of human well-being (which involves both economic and social dimensions) does not result in the destruction of the environment.

Sustainable development also requires that the needs and well-being of future generations are to be taken into account, given that human actions today might jeopardize the ability of future generations to meet their needs. For example, failure to maintain an adequate natural resource base could make it impossible for future generations to have sufficient food supplies. Therefore, resources must not be depleted; they must be available from one generation to the next.

Lastly, sustainable development also necessitates that the basic needs of all people living today are met, and that the current inequality at the global scale is reduced. This refers to inequality in the distribution of:

- income and wealth
- basic social goods such as health and education
- material goods such as food and shelter.

As such, the overall goal of sustainable development is the long-term stability of the economy, the society and the environment.

Sustainable Development Goals (SDGs)

The Sustainable Development Goals (SDGs) are 17 global goals set by the United Nations General Assembly in 2015 for the year 2030. The SDGs build on the previous Millennium Development Goals (MDGs) but they go further and aim to promote prosperity while protecting the planet. The SDGs are listed below.

1. No poverty
2. Zero hunger
3. Good health and well-being
4. Quality education
5. Gender equality
6. Clean water and sanitation
7. Affordable and clean energy
8. Decent work and economic growth
9. Industry, innovation and infrastructure
10. Reducing inequality
11. Sustainable cities and communities
12. Responsible consumption and production
13. Climate action
14. Life below water
15. Life on land
16. Peace, justice and strong institutions
17. Partnerships for the goals.

These goals aim to address and incorporate in a balanced way all three dimensions of sustainable development and they are universally applicable, meaning that the rich countries, like the poor, have to learn to live sustainably.

So far, evidence has shown that there has been an acceleration of poverty reduction, disease control, and increased access to schooling and infrastructure in the poorest countries of the world, and especially in Africa, as a result of the Millennium Development Goals. The sustainable development agenda is of course bigger and more difficult to achieve than the Millennium Development Goals, which themselves were not small challenges. Therefore, the Sustainable Development Goals include not only the continuation of the Millennium Development Goals, but also the integration of these goals with several others, including social inclusion and environmental sustainability.

Relationship between sustainability and poverty

Poverty is a major cause of environmental degradation. Poor people often rely entirely on agriculture for their incomes. As farmers cannot afford the contemporary means of production such as fertilizers, machinery or crop protection chemicals they overuse the land, trying to maximize output. When land is continuously used to grow crops, the soil cannot retain nutrients and moisture and so the quality and productivity of the land falls over time.

Moreover, in poor regions there is high population growth, which puts an extra burden on the environment as the growing population tries to maintain its livelihood. Trees may be cut down to provide clearings for agriculture, construction materials, and fuel for cooking and warmth. This may eventually lead to deforestation. Pastureland and fisheries may also become depleted because of overgrazing animals and overfishing.

Due to these activities, in an effort to survive, poor people often destroy their immediate environment. This poses a threat to sustainability, as future generations will be deprived of an adequate natural resource base.

4.8 Measuring development

The multidimensional nature of economic development

Economic development is an aspect of sustainable development. More specifically, economic development is a multidimensional concept. It refers to an improvement in living standards which involves increases in per capita income levels, reductions in poverty, increased access to health care and education, and increased employment opportunities, as well as reduced inequalities of income and wealth.

Economic development can be measured either with the use single or composite indicators.

- Single indicators record the progress made towards a particular dimension of development.
- Composite indicators are summary measures of several dimensions of development.

Single indicators

GDP/GNI per capita at purchasing power parity (PPP)

GDP/GNI per capita at purchasing power parity (PPP) can to some extent provide information on the level of development of a country, as there is a positive correlation between per capita income and well-being. Remember that PPP stands for purchasing power parity dollars. These are dollars of equal purchasing power (that is, they buy the same basket of goods and services that the national currency buys).

The UN and the World Bank keep systematic records of per capita GDP and GNI and classify countries on this basis. For instance, the World Bank uses per capita GNI to place countries into three main categories: high income, middle income and low income. A country is low income if GNI per capita is below $975 per year. In a middle income country GNI per capita is between $976 and $11,905 per year and

in a high income country it is above $11,906. The middle income group, which is quite big, is split between the upper middle income and the lower middle income, with the dividing line at $3,855.

This classification is useful and may provide us with some information on the level of development. For example, few would question that Norway is more developed than Somalia. However, since there several limitations associated with the use of per capita GDP and GNI as measures of well-being, classification based on per capita income can be problematic. Per capita GDP and GNI fail to incorporate income distribution considerations, do not take into account the value of the environmental degradation, fail to include non-marketed subsistence production, conceal useful information on the composition of output and do not include the value of the stream of services flowing from the accumulated social and other capital of an economy (see section 3.1). Consequently, such indicators may be useful as measures of national economic performance but they are not entirely suitable as indicators of economic development.

Health and education indicators

Health-related indicators include:

- health expenditure per capita
- life expectancy at birth (years)
- infant mortality (per 1,000 live births)
- malnutrition prevalence
- maternal mortality ratio (per 100,000 live births)
- improved sanitation facilities (the percentage of the population with access)

- prevalence of HIV (the percentage of the population aged between 15 and 49 years)
- physicians (per 10,000 people) or hospital beds (per 10,000 people).

Education-related indicators include:

- literacy rate (the percentage of the population who know how to read and write)
- mean years of schooling (of people aged 25 years and older)
- pupil–teacher ratio
- school enrolment, primary, secondary and tertiary (the percentage of school age children enrolled in each level).

According to the definition of economic development, health care and education are important parts of the development process. Checking health- and education-related indicators helps to monitor progress in these dimensions.

Economic/social inequality indicators

Economic and social inequality indicators include:

- the Gini coefficient, which is the most widely cited measure of income inequality
- the Robin Hood index, which shows the proportion of all income that would have to be redistributed to achieve a state of perfect equality
- the 20/20 ratio, which compares the ratio of the average income of the richest 20% of the population to the average income of the poorest 20% of the population
- the Social Institutions and Gender Index (SIGI), which is a cross-country measure of discrimination against women in social institutions.

Inequality indicators can be useful in assessing the progress made in terms of reducing inequalities, which is another important dimension of economic development.

Energy indicators

Energy indicators include:

- percentage of traditional fuel energy use
- share of households with access to electricity
- total energy consumption per capita
- the ratio of energy use to GDP.

Trends in overall energy use indicate the general relationship of energy consumption to economic development that shows a positive correlation. These trends therefore provide a rough basis for projecting energy consumption and its environmental impacts with economic growth.

Environmental indicators

Environmental indicators include:

- ecological footprint, which relates to land use and CO_2 emissions
- the Living Planet Index (LPI), an unweighted index developed by the World Wide Fund for Nature (WWF) to indicate changes in the number and diversity of biological species
- the Environmental Sustainability Index (ESI) developed by the World Economic Forum (WEF)
- the OECD's "core set of environmental indicators", which involve climate change, stratospheric ozone depletion, eutrophication, acidification, toxic contamination, urban environmental quality, biodiversity, cultural landscapes, waste, water resources, forest resources, fish resources, soil degradation and material resources.

Environmental indicators can be used to evaluate whether the development process is also sustainable.

Composite indicators

Human Development Index (HDI)

The most widely used composite indicator is the human development index (HDI). It was constructed by the United Nations Development Programme (UNDP) as a comprehensive measure of development. The HDI measures average achievements of a population in terms of health, education and access to goods and services. These three dimensions are measured by the indicators:

- life expectancy at birth
- mean years of schooling and expected years of schooling
- GNI per capita (in US$ PPP).

Each dimension takes a value between 0 and 1, with 0 being the lowest possible value and 1 being the highest. The composite index is the average of the three dimensions, so each country receives an HDI value from 0 to 1 and is then ranked accordingly.

Since 1990, the HDI has been reported annually by the UNDP in its Human Development Report. One interesting aspect of the HDI is that it demonstrates that some countries with modest incomes, such as Costa Rica, Cuba and Sri Lanka may score relatively highly in terms of human development since they have life expectancy and literacy rates comparable with those of advanced economies.

Overall, the HDI was successful in displacing per capita income as a summary measure of development. However, the HDI has some limitations. It remains an average, as it conceals important differences within a country. Women and rural populations as well as the very old and the very young often suffer disproportionately but this is not illustrated through the HDI as it does not consider income distribution or gender inequalities. In addition, it does not include any assessment of environmental changes or impacts. As a result, a country's HDI score may rise as a result of improvements in longevity, education and per capita income even though those improvements might be achieved at the cost of unacceptable natural resource depletion and environmental degradation.

Note that two additional composite indicators were introduced by the UNDP in 2010 capturing multidimensional inequality—the Inequality Adjusted HDI, known as the IHDI—and gender disparities—the Gender Inequality Index.

Inequality Adjusted Human Development Index (IHDI)

The inequality adjusted HDI (IHDI) measures development in the same three dimensions as the HDI, adjusted for inequality in each dimension. The IHDI attempts to capture losses in development that arise from inequality. (If there were no inequality the IHDI and the HDI would be equal.)

Gender Inequality Index (GII)

The Gender Inequality Index (GII) measures inequalities between the genders in three dimensions. Often women and girls are discriminated against in health care, education and in the labour market. The GII captures the loss in development of women due to inequalities in these areas.

The UNDP developed another composite indicator, the Capability Poverty Measure (CPM), which focuses on the capacity of people to lead worthwhile lives.

The Capability Poverty Measure (CPM)

The Capability Poverty Measure (CPM) emphasizes the importance of basic opportunities for personal development and is measured as a lack of these basic opportunities. It is the arithmetic mean of three variables:

- the lack of capability to be nourished and healthy, measured as the proportion of children under 5 years of age who are underweight
- the lack of capability to be educated, measured as the proportion of females aged 15 years and over who are illiterate
- the lack of capability for healthy reproduction, measured as the proportion of births unattended by trained health-care workers.

It is notable that the CPM places a strong emphasis on the lack of women's capabilities, in acknowledgment of the fact that, if women are deprived, then the human development of families and entire societies is adversely affected. In common with the HDI, however, the CPM does not take any account of the environmental dimension.

Another composite indicator that could be used to track development is the **Happy Planet Index (HPI)** that was explained in section 3.1. The Happy Planet Index measures how well nations are doing at achieving long, happy and sustainable lives.

Strengths and limitations of approaches to measuring economic development

In relation to economic development, the range of possible indicators is vast and, in some cases, the suitability of those indicators is questionable. It is not always clear at which scale—global, national, regional or local—those indicators should be applied. At the same time, the availability and reliability of data can also be problematic. Nevertheless, despite such complexities, it is important to have indicators to measure progress—or lack of progress—in promoting development.

Given the vast scope of economic development, the use of a single indicator to assess economic development fully is "an impossible dream". Consequently, an alternative approach has been to produce attempts and use composite indicators.

The use of such indicators provides some opportunities—but also raises some issues. On the positive side, composite indicators may provide clear overviews of trends in development, highlighting where performance and progress have been particularly strong or weak, and they permit comparisons to be made between countries. On the negative side, composite indicators have several important limitations.

- They may contain indicators that are difficult to aggregate, especially where different units of measurement are used.
- A composite indicator, while useful for comparisons between countries, may be of limited use in informing policy.
- Composite indicators may fail to take account of the interconnections between the economic, social and environmental dimensions of development.
- The use of composite indicators may conceal the fact that development involves a wide diversity of issues, each requiring a different indicator, and that those indicators may be moving in different directions.

Consideration of the issues associated with single indicators and composite indicators suggests that none of them is ideal as a measure of economic development. All of the indicators discussed in this section have certain advantages—but all provide selective and partial representations of reality.

Relationship between economic growth and economic development

Economic growth refers to increases in the real GDP of an economy through time. Growth does not necessarily involve development. A country may grow without any development objective being met.

The United Nations Development Programme has described four types of growth that obstruct the development process. They are:

- jobless growth, where employment opportunities for the poor do not expand
- ruthless growth, where income inequality widens
- futureless growth, where the environment is degraded and natural resources depleted
- voiceless growth, where individual empowerment falls behind.

As such, economic growth does not guarantee that economic development will occur. Usually, though, development requires growth. Some economic development may be possible in the absence of growth in the short term, if the policies followed provide access to basic social services for the poor. However, in the long term, the development process necessitates that developing countries are growing.

4.9 Barriers to economic growth and/or economic development

There are a number of factors that can prevent countries from growing and developing.

The poverty cycle or trap

Poverty locks individuals into a vicious poverty cycle or trap, or what Nobel Laureate Gunnar Myrdal called "circular and cumulative causation." The poverty cycle is shown in Figure 4.9.1.

Poor people live on a very low income, which is spent entirely on necessities. This means that, in poor countries, the level of available savings in the economy is very low. As a result, investments in physical capital (machines, equipment and infrastructure) and in human capital (education and health care) cannot be financed so they are also low. Productivity will remain low, so incomes remain low. The country is trapped in a situation where people's poverty leads to more poverty.

It is important to note that the poverty cycle is transmitted across generations as children are caught in the trap with their parents, which limits their possibilities for higher earnings. Therefore, the poverty cycle is a significant barrier to growth and development in the short term but also in the longer term.

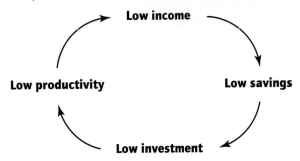

Figure 4.9.1 The poverty cycle or trap

Economic barriers

Rising economic inequality

Globally, the lowest 20% of people receive just 1.5% of the world's income—the scale of global inequality is immense. There are also large income disparities within developing countries. Latin American countries tend to be highly unequal. Several African countries also have among the highest levels of inequality in the world. Inequality is also particularly high in many resource-rich developing countries, notably in the Middle East and sub-Saharan Africa. Table 4.9.1 shows the Gini coefficient based on the most recent World Bank estimates for some of the countries with the highest income inequality in the world.

Country	Gini coefficient
South Africa	0.63
Namibia	0.59
Zambia	0.57
Lesotho	0.54
Brazil	0.53
St. Lucia	0.51
Panama	0.50
Colombia	0.49
Mexico	0.48
Cameroon	0.47

Table 4.9.1 Gini coefficient for selected countries.
Source: https://www.indexmundi.com/facts/indicators/SI.POV.GINI/rankings

High and rising inequality implies that a large part of the population does not have access to education and health services. The economy is deprived of their skills and talents.

The poor have limited or no access to credit. They cannot borrow to invest in their children's education or to start or expand a business.

High and rising inequality also reduces the overall savings in the economy, as it is the middle class that saves the most. The rich spend large amounts on imported luxuries and channel their savings abroad to foreign tax havens. This results in fewer funds and resources available for domestic productive investments and lower demand for domestically produced goods and services.

High inequality also increases the prevalence of corruption which reduces the probability of "doing business". In the presence of corruption, investment can be discouraged because entrepreneurs face higher costs in dealing with "red tape" and regulatory burdens and may even be forced to pay bribes. Lastly, inequality may lead to social unrest and political instability, which increases the risks investors face and discourages both domestic and foreign direct investment (FDI).

Rising economic inequality leads to lower growth rates and so restricts the process of economic development.

Lack of access to infrastructure and appropriate technology

Infrastructure refers to the economy's physical capital such as transportation systems (roads, railways, ports and airports), telecommunications, energy systems (electricity and gas), water supplies, sanitation and sewerage. Infrastructure is a major facilitator of economic activity and contributes to economic development. Infrastructure is typically financed from government funds.

However, in developing countries often governments do not have the required resources to invest in and maintain infrastructure. Many parts of Africa are so poor that the most basic infrastructure such as electrification or a road network in many areas does not even exist or is crumbling. Lack of infrastructure limits growth and development prospects. For instance, inadequate roads and poor road access increase the cost of transportation and limit the access to local markets as well as to education and health facilities.

Closely related to the lack of infrastructure is the lack of access to appropriate technology. Appropriate technology refers to technology that is best suited for a country's factors of production. In general, technologies can be distinguished into capital-intensive, relying mostly on machines, and labour-intensive, relying mostly on workers. Since in most developing countries labour is the relatively abundant factor of production, it follows that appropriate technologies are often labour-intensive. Nevertheless, the lack of such technologies means that there is less employment, less income and more poverty, and therefore less growth and development.

Low levels of human capital—lack of access to health care and education

In developing countries levels of human capital are low, which becomes an impediment to these countries' growth and development. Compared with developed countries, much of the developing world has lagged in its average levels of nutrition, health (as measured, for example, by life expectancy or extent of undernourishment), and education (measured by literacy rates or school enrollment ratios). One of the reasons is that many developing nations are deprived of the resources needed to maintain adequate health and education services. Also, poverty may prevent access to health and education.

This lack of health care and education is responsible for decreased labour productivity, individuals facing fewer employment opportunities, higher risk of spreading diseases, fewer technological innovations (because of fewer skilled individuals) and therefore more poverty. Human capital formation is absolutely necessary to achieve higher labour productivity, long-term growth and improved living standards. Remember that achieving better health and education are themselves development goals.

Dependence on primary sector production

Throughout Africa, the Middle East and Latin America, primary product exports have traditionally accounted for a sizable proportion of individual gross domestic products. In some of the smaller countries, a substantial percentage of the economy's income is derived from the exports of agricultural and other primary products or commodities such as coffee, cotton, cocoa, sugar, palm oil, bauxite and copper. A few countries may even depend on producing and exporting a single primary commodity. Niger, for example, is extremely dependent on the extraction and exportation of uranium.

This primary sector dependence can be a major obstacle to growth and development. One reason is that demand for most primary exports is income inelastic and, as a result,

demand for such products in countries with rising incomes does not grow fast enough to boost growth. Also, the prices of primary goods tend to fluctuate because farm products are affected by weather conditions and other random factors and also have low price elasticity of demand (PED) and price elasticity of supply (PES). As prices fluctuate, so do farmers' incomes, the country's export revenues and levels of employment.

Lack of access to international markets

Developed economies such as the USA, the European Union and Japan provide large agricultural support to their farmers, mainly in the form of subsidies. This results in lower world prices with which developing countries cannot compete and therefore they cannot expand their exports to international markets. This inability to access these markets is a barrier as it leads to lower incomes, lower agricultural investment, lower employment opportunities for farm workers and increased poverty.

This has been the case with US cotton subsidies and the Cotton-4 (C-4) countries (Benin, Burkina Faso, Chad and Mali). Cotton is the primary export crop accounting for the majority of agricultural export earnings in each C-4 country. Cotton is also the dominant source of employment in cotton-producing regions in each of these countries. The US administration has been granting subsidies to the US cotton industry for seven decades, which have contributed to a decline in global cotton prices. Due to the prominent role cotton plays in the economies of C-4 countries, low cotton prices significantly affect the ability of their farmers to obtain sufficient income and to increase production and employment. This means that US cotton subsidies may have obstructed the development of the C-4 countries, which are listed among the world's poorest.

Apart from agricultural support developed economies offer to their farmers, they also impose trade barriers, mainly tariffs, to protect their industries from foreign competition. This further limits the ability of developing countries to access international markets, impeding both growth and development.

Note that one criticism of the World Trade Organization (WTO) relates to this issue. The WTO has been accused of treating the developing world relatively unfavourably. IT is criticized for not doing enough to force the USA and the EU to open up their own agricultural markets to imports. The inability to reach an agreement in agriculture is considered the main reason why the Doha Round of trade negotiations organized by the WTO failed (section 3.4).

Informal economy

The informal economy lies outside the formal one and is where unregistered, unregulated and untaxed economic activities take place. Unregistered activities range from street vendors to tricycle drivers and often become a way for people to survive. In fact, in many developing countries, about half of the employed urban population works in the informal sector.

The workers in this sector are generally unskilled and they lack access to financial capital. As a result, workers' productivity and income tend to be lower than in the formal sector. Another issue is that workers in the informal sector do not enjoy the measure of protection afforded by the formal sector in terms of job security and decent working conditions. As a result, living standards for these workers are low and as long as the informal economy remains unregulated the development prospects are limited. Moreover, the government does not earn any tax revenue from informal sector activities—and lower tax revenues also limit the ability to finance pro-development goals.

Capital flight

Capital flight refers to the rapid outflow of large sums of money out of a country, typically as a result of economic and political instability. A debt crisis can, for example, trigger capital flight as it can induce wealthy nationals seeking safety to send vast amounts of money out of the country. For instance, in 2001 Argentina defaulted on its debt when it owed $100 billion, which led to massive capital flight. Expectations of exchange rate devaluation may also contribute to substantial capital flight, as investors flee from the country before their assets lose too much value. Outflows of the Chinese yuan occurred several times after 2015, when the government devalued the currency. Lastly, political turmoil can also lead to capital flight as better-off residents seek to protect their wealth.

Capital flight can become an impediment to economic growth and in turn to economic development because it involves a loss of financial capital that could have been invested within the country. Moreover, since these funds are no longer subject to tax, governments lose tax revenue that could have been used to support the financing of development goals. For instance, in the case of Africa, high levels of capital flight deprive governments of the ability to mobilize domestic resources and this has a material impact on economic development. Estimates from the OECD show that each year Africa loses up to $50 billion through capital flight.

Indebtedness

High levels of indebtedness characterize many developing countries as their governments have had a past history of overspending and over-borrowing.

High debt levels require large repayments to service the debt. This implies that governments have fewer funds available to invest in health care, education and infrastructure, which are all necessary for economic growth and development. More specifically, according to the World Bank since 2013, median government debt in developing countries has risen by about 20% of GDP. As a result, in most of these countries debt payments are absorbing an increasing proportion of government revenues that could have been used to finance pro-development projects.

At the same time, high levels of debt imply that any export revenue earned which could have been used to finance the importation of say, pharmaceuticals or machine-parts must be diverted to creditors for the servicing of the debt. Hence, indebtedness also obstructs developing nations from using foreign exchange to attain necessary imports.

Geography—including being landlocked

The geographic location of many developing countries may act as barrier to their growth and development. In fact, according to Jeffrey Sachs of Columbia University, physical geography is the fourth most important contributor to poverty.

Many of the poorest developing countries around the world are landlocked. In Asia, for example, Afghanistan, Nepal, Bhutan and Laos are all landlocked countries. In Africa, roughly one-third of the countries are landlocked. Economic growth and development depend heavily on international trade, which is significantly more difficult and costly for landlocked countries. Being on the coast, near ports or near major rivers allows for a higher degree of international trade. It allows exports to reach world markets at low costs, and also enables the economy to obtain imported inputs at low costs. This can boost productivity and provide opportunities for economic growth and development.

Even if not landlocked, countries may have the problem of being in mountainous regions, such as Bolivia. This makes it difficult for them to engage in farming and low cost manufacturing. Also, some developing countries are in geographic locations that are exposed to natural disasters such as cyclones, storms, floods and droughts. This applies to a number of small island economies, for instance the Philippines and Haiti.

Such examples show that geography can play an important role in the process of economic development. Nevertheless, "geography is not destiny"; countries can come up with meaningful alternatives when underlying geographical conditions are difficult.

Tropical climates and endemic diseases

There are obviously climate differences from country to country but almost all developing countries have tropical and subtropical climates. This is considered to be a factor that has prevented many of them from growing and developing. Climate has a huge effect on crop productivity, water scarcity or availability, and even labour productivity. Tropical climates tend to be "less gentle" in terms of the factors already mentioned and may therefore limit growth and development prospects.

In addition, climate plays an important role for endemic diseases. Places that are warm all year round, such as tropical Africa, generally have very high year-round malaria transmission. Besides malaria, schistosomiasis is also prevalent in tropical and subtropical areas, especially in poor communities without access to safe drinking water and adequate sanitation. It is estimated that at least 90% of those requiring treatment for schistosomiasis live in Africa. Since development depends on a healthy population, regions beset by a heavy disease burden are held back.

A great concern going forward is that global warming is projected to have its greatest negative impact on Africa and South Asia. Rising temperatures will increase the occurrence of droughts, heat waves, potential crop failures and disease incidence in these areas, which may further impede their growth and development prospects in the near future.

Recap
Economic barriers to growth and/or development

- **High and rising economic inequality** deters access to health care, education and credit, reduces savings in the economy and can increase corruption while fuelling social and political instability. As such, productivity and investment spending remain low, leading to lower growth rates and restricting the development process.

- **Lack of access to infrastructure** increases the cost of transportation and limits the access to local markets as well as to education and health facilities.

- **Lack of appropriate technology** means that there is less employment, less income and more poverty. These factors limit economic growth and development.

- **Low levels of human capital—lack of access to health care and education** is responsible for decreased labour productivity, individuals facing fewer employment opportunities, higher risk of spreading diseases, fewer technological innovations and therefore more poverty. This acts as a barrier to economic growth and development.

- **Dependence on primary sector production** is an obstacle to growth and development, because of the low income elasticity of demand that prevents demand for primary products to grow fast enough to generate growth. Also, primary product prices are highly volatile, leading to fluctuations in farmers' incomes, the country's export revenues and levels of employment.

- **Lack of access to international markets** is a result of the agricultural support developed economies offer to their farmers and of the trade barriers developed countries impose. Restricting the ability of developing countries' exports to reach international markets leads to lower incomes, lower agricultural investment, lower employment opportunities for farm workers and increased poverty. All of these factors impede growth and development.

- An **informal economy** will have a negative effect on economic growth and development. In the informal sector worker productivity and incomes are low and there is decreased job security and poor working conditions. This means that living standards for workers in the informal economy are low. Also, tax revenues are lower and this limits the ability to finance pro-development goals.

- **Capital flight** is barrier to economic growth and in turn to economic development because it involves a loss of financial capital and a loss of tax revenue that could have been invested within the country.

- **Indebtedness** requires large debt repayments and so the government has fewer funds available to invest in health care education and infrastructure, which are all necessary for economic growth and development. Also, there is less foreign exchange to finance the purchase of necessary imports.

- **Geography, including being landlocked**, is often an economic barrier. Economic growth and development depend heavily on international trade, which is significantly more difficult and costly for landlocked countries. Also, countries in mountainous regions or exposed to natural disasters may also face issues in terms of growth and development.

- **Tropical climates and endemic diseases** affect the economy. A feature of a tropical climate is warm weather all year round, which negatively affects crop productivity, water availability and labour productivity while favouring the spread of endemic diseases such as malaria. These factors lead to slower growth and impede economic development.

Political and social barriers

Weak institutional framework

There are many economic, legal and social institutions that influence economic growth and development. However, in developing countries the institutional framework is rather weak and this can impede the process of growth and development.

Inadequate legal system

In developing countries, legal systems are often not capable of applying and enforcing laws equitably and efficiently, and laws often are not subject to predictable interpretation. This creates uncertainty, which is closely related to the rapidly increasing number of pending court cases and corruption that can all hurt economic growth and, in turn, economic development. Quite often legal institutions in developing countries may be a product of elite interests, or may be open to capture by such interests. As a result, these institutions serve to increase the power and wealth of a few at the expense of the majority of the community, leaving the poor suffering the harshest consequences.

Ineffective taxation structures

Tax revenues are needed by governments to make investments in health care, education, infrastructure and in other areas important for economic growth and development. However, tax revenues in developing countries are not simply low because of low incomes. The tax system itself is often ineffective in collecting tax revenues due to complicated procedures, tax exemptions for the wealthy with political influence and corrupt tax authorities. At the same time, the existence of a large informal sector may also restrict the amount of tax revenues governments can raise since the transactions taking place are not recorded.

Lack of property rights and land rights

Property rights involve laws that ensure legal rights to ownership and transfer of ownership from one owner to another. In developing countries, property rights are usually not well defined and enforced. This leads to lower investment as there is risk of loss of the investment, which can then limit growth.

Peruvian economist Hernando de Soto considers the lack of property rights the most significant barrier to economic growth and economic development. According to relevant research about 5.3 billion people in the world do not have well-defined property rights and so their assets become "dead capital" which cannot be used to generate income or growth. For example, entrepreneurs in poor nations lacking secure property rights have no ability to leverage their home as an asset to create more business opportunities. As a result, the poor remain trapped, hurting individuals and broader economic development.

Related to property rights are land rights. In many developing countries, the majority of land is under customary tenure: the rights, rules and responsibilities to possess, occupy and use it are based on community customs. However, customary-held land rarely enjoys adequate protection under national laws. This has often led to land being appropriated, grabbed and sold by governments, private firms and powerful individuals at the expense of poorer individuals. In many cases this happens in rural areas where these individuals' livelihoods are much more dependent on land and agriculture. The result is that poverty in rural areas persists, hindering the development process.

Inadequate banking system

Banking services and access to credit are very important to economic growth and development, as they allow for investments in human, physical and natural capital. Yet the commercial banking system in many developing countries is not properly functioning, as it does not accommodate poor and small-scale producers, farmers and traders. It is therefore a major restraint on growth and development. This relates to lack of property and land rights explained above. When ownership of assets is not well-defined and secured the assets cannot be used as collateral, so loans cannot be issued. This leaves the poor without access to credit and therefore unable to finance investment that could have boosted economic growth and development.

Note that most developing countries were once colonies of Europe or otherwise dominated by European or other foreign powers, and institutions created during the colonial period often had negative effects on development that in many cases have persisted to the present day. Colonial era institutions often favoured extractors of wealth rather than creators of wealth, harming development then and now. According to Daron Acemoglu and James Robinson, nations with extractive political and economic institutions are likely to be poor, whereas those with inclusive institutions are likely to be rich. That is to say that "institutions matter" and colonial institutions, in particular, have played a significant role in shaping the economic development of colonized countries. For example, Spanish colonialists put Latin America on a path of extractive and unproductive institutions that still exist and still impede the development process across Latin American countries.

Gender inequality

In many developing countries there is gender inequality. Gender inequality refers to limited access for women to social and economic opportunities compared with men. Being excluded because of their gender, women have less access to education, formal-sector employment, social security and government employment programmes, which keeps them excluded. As a result, they are more likely to be poor and malnourished, and less likely to receive medical services, clean water, sanitation and other benefits.

This has significant consequences for growth and development. In the long term, the low status of women is likely to translate into slower rates of economic growth. This is because the educational attainment and future financial status of children are much more likely to reflect those of the mother than those of the father. So, the benefits of current investments in human capital are more likely to be passed on to future generations if women are successfully integrated into the growth process. According to Lawrence Summers, educating girls yields a higher rate of return than any other investment available in developing countries.

Poor governance and prevalent corruption

High levels of corruption hold back growth and development because the country is suffering from poor governance. Extreme poor governance and corruption can certainly stop and even reverse the process of economic growth and development.

One major reason is that corruption disproportionately affects the poor. The rich may spend large amounts on bribes and other pay-offs to corrupt governments, but for the poor such payments will be a much larger proportion of their income. A small-scale business may pay a higher percentage of its sales revenue in bribes than a large firm. In addition, "government for sale means government for the highest bidder". When corruption is prevalent, the poor find fewer services in their communities and only have access to poor education and health facilities. This makes it more difficult to accumulate the means to escape from poverty.

Policies containing potential strategies for economic growth and development may be damaged by inefficiency or incompetence (individually or in combination). The potential strategy may not be fully or adequately implemented.

> ### Recap
> #### Political and social barriers to growth and/or development
> Barriers include:
> - a weak institutional framework, in terms of:
>   - an inadequate legal system
>   - ineffective taxation structures
>   - lack of property rights and land rights
>   - an ineffective banking system
> - gender inequality
> - poor governance and the prevalence of corruption.

Policymakers' perspective

The mix and severity of the barriers to growth and development described above largely frame the development constraints and policy priorities of each developing nation. They all reflect common problems shared in varying degrees by most developing countries. Behind these common barriers however, there are very substantial differences among developing countries. Some nations are large, others small; some resource-rich, others resource-barren; some are subsistence economies, others are modern manufactured-good exporters; some are private-sector oriented, others to a large degree are run by the government. It is important to appreciate and take into account these differences when deciding development policy. According to Jeffrey Sachs, economists, like medical clinicians, need to learn the art of "differential diagnosis". This implies that instead of unthinkingly relying on standardized policy options, policymakers should focus on the key underlying causes of economic distress and use appropriate measures that are well tailored to each country's specific conditions.

4.10 Economic growth and/or economic development strategies

There are several strategies that can help developing countries overcome the barriers holding them back and promote their growth and development.

Trade strategies

Developing countries can base their growth and development on trade strategies.

Import substitution

Import substitution (also known as import substitution industrialization) is a strategy where a country begins to manufacture simple consumer goods, such as textiles or shoes, aiming to substitute domestically produced goods for imports and therefore promote its domestic industry. Import substitution requires trade barriers such as tariffs and quotas to prevent the entry of imports and to protect the newly established industries. These barriers stay in place until the firms grow sufficiently in size and acquire the necessary know-how to lower unit costs. Trade barriers are reduced when the firms are able to compete with imports and survive within the domestic markets. At the same time, the exchange rate is kept overvalued so that prices of necessary imported manufacturing inputs are low.

Import substitution has been practised by a number of developing countries in Latin America, Asia and Africa in an attempt to create a manufacturing sector so that reliance on the primary sector is reduced. Ultimately, as seen in the case of industries in South Korea and Taiwan, domestic firms may be able not only to produce for the domestic market but also to export their manufactured goods to the rest of the world (see "Export promotion" below).

However, import substitution may be associated with inefficiency because trade protection reduces competition. Secure behind protective trade barriers, many industries remain inefficient and costly to operate. In some cases, this has led to production of goods that are low in quality but high in cost and price.

The overvalued exchange rate affects primary exports, hurting local farmers because for each dollar of exports they earn fewer units of the domestic currency. This may increase poverty for some parts of the population. Import substitution has in practice often worsened the distribution of income by favouring the urban industrial sector while discriminating against the rural sector and lower income groups.

The newly established industries may use capital-intensive production methods, limiting employment opportunities and leading to jobless growth. This growth is usually not followed by development.

Export promotion

Export promotion is a trade strategy where a country attempts to achieve economic growth by expanding its exports. Japan was the first country to have adopted this strategy and was followed by South Korea, Taiwan, Hong Kong and Singapore (known as the East Asian Tigers) and other countries including, of course, China.

Export promotion has been a success story for many countries. The export revenues earned alleviated problems with the balance of payments. For example, the export growth Taiwan and South Korea enjoyed contributed over 80% of both nations' foreign exchange earnings. With higher export earnings there is less danger of an economy running into foreign exchange and foreign debt problems. Rising export revenue increases aggregate demand, fuelling growth in output and incomes.

In addition, firms are forced to learn more about manufacturing their products more efficiently. International competition provides the stimulus.

Note that the government's role is very important for export promotion to be a successful growth and development strategy. It can help exporting firms with state subsidies, investment grants and tax exemptions while making large investments in key areas such as education that improves the skills of the workforce, in research and development that can lead to innovation, and in transport and communications infrastructure that can assist production. Therefore, through varying degrees of state intervention, economies can slowly shift their production to manufactured goods, diversify and become more insulated from industry-specific risks.

However, strong dependence on exports makes the economy vulnerable. If trading partners go into a recession, the exporting economies will be adversely affected. The trade barriers imposed by developed economies may hurt exports and export revenue. Developed economies have imposed extensive trade barriers, and their rates of protection are often higher against exports from developing countries exports than against those of high income countries. Income distribution may worsen as the rural sector may be neglected while those involved in the exporting sector will enjoy a larger share of national income.

Lastly, focusing on export promotion as a growth process may lead policymakers to postpone the creation of a social safety net that would include state pensions and health insurance. This is because the growth process does not rely on the ability of the population to spend on domestic goods and services.

Economic integration

Regional integration among developing countries may prove beneficial as a trading bloc increases the size of the potential market for each exporting firm. The expanded market size can also provide the opportunity for lower unit costs for developing countries' industries. Integration helps to avoid the obstacles of the protectionist barriers of developed countries. In addition, integration can decrease the level of dependence on developed countries' markets while providing member countries with greater political and bargaining power in negotiations with developed economies.

Integration can also be viewed as a mechanism to encourage a division of labour among a group of countries, each of which is too small to benefit from such a division by itself.

Examples of economic integration among developing countries include the Latin America Free Trade Association (LAFTA); MERCOSUR, a customs union among Argentina, Brazil, Uruguay, and Paraguay; and the Asia-Pacific Economic Cooperation (APEC), a group of 21 nations that border the Pacific Ocean.

Many attempts to form trading blocs among developing countries have encountered the following problems. There have been significant organizational and administrative problems. Political rivalry between and within countries and lack of commitment have also prevented progress.

One of the operational problems for firms is transport costs. These are especially high, since road and other necessary infrastructure is often poor.

In addition, the structure of production and of trade in developing countries lacks a sufficient complementary nature, as their economies tend to exhibit high similarity. This restricts mutually beneficial trading.

Recap

Trade strategies		
Import substitution is the creation of an industrial base to substitute domestically produced manufactured goods for imports.	**Export promotion** is when a country attempts to achieve economic growth by expanding its exports.	**Economic integration** is regional integration among developing countries through preferential trading agreements.
• A manufacturing sector is created, reducing reliance on the primary sector.	• Export growth increases export revenue and foreign exchange earnings. • Foreign competition increases efficiency in production. • Export growth changes the structure of the economy.	• The size of the potential market is increased. • The protectionist barriers of developed countries are avoided. • Dependence on developed countries' markets decreases. • Integration provides member countries with greater political and bargaining power. • Division of labour is encouraged.
Disadvantages of trade strategies		
Import substitution • It reduces competition, leading to inefficiency. • It hurts primary sector exports, increasing poverty among the rural population. • Inequality may widen. • The increased use of capital-intensive production technology can lead to jobless growth.	**Export promotion** • Dependence on exports makes the economy vulnerable as it is subject to any shock its trading partners may undergo. • The trade barriers of developed economies still need to be successfully overcome. • Distribution of income may worsen as the exporting sector enjoys a greater share of national income. • Policy focus may shift away from creating a social safety net.	**Economic integration** • There are organizational and administrative problems. • Political rivalry and lack of commitment prevent progress. • Transport costs are high due to poor infrastructure. • Similarities in the structure of some countries' economies may restrict mutually beneficial trade.

Diversification

One of the major problems that many developing countries face is their over-dependence on a narrow range of agricultural products. Diversification involves broadening the range of goods and services developing countries are able to produce. This allows such economies to benefit from worldwide economic growth as manufactured products and services have higher income elasticity of demand. Also, they will no longer be subject to price volatility, which will stabilize incomes and export earnings.

At the same time diversification may create new jobs. It can lead to the improvement of skills and technologies in order to support the broader range of production.

Nevertheless, diversification may not guarantee that developing countries' exports will no longer be subject to trade protectionism. Also, some of the benefits of specialization in the form of efficiency may be lost.

Market-based policies

The idea behind market-based supply-side policies is that markets are the most effective mechanism for growth and in turn for development. Since the late 1980s, a number of prominent institutions including the IMF and the World Bank have supported a set of free-market policies to encourage growth. This set of policies is often referred to as the Washington Consensus and includes the following.

- **Trade liberalization:** this refers to the reduction, or complete removal of protectionist measures that prevent free trade.
- **Privatization:** this refers to the transfer or sale of state owned sets (typically firms but also airports, harbours and so on) to the private sector (see section 3.7, page 132).
- **Deregulation:** this refers to the process of dismantling or relaxing inappropriate rules, restrictions and laws in the operation of firms or markets (see section 3.7, page 132).

Trade liberalization can allow developing countries to expand their exports in international markets and enjoy greater export revenue. Together with all the other benefits of free trade (see section 4.1) trade liberalization can allow for greater economic growth, creating new jobs and encouraging rural development, which can significantly reduce poverty levels. However, trade liberalization on its own may not be enough. Developing countries lack skilled labour, technology and are focused on the primary sector. This means that even with greater access to global markets they will still export a narrow range of products and will therefore have low export shares in world trade.

Market-based policies, such as privatization and deregulation, increase efficiency and contribute to economic growth. More specifically, the profit motive forces privatized firms to cut costs and decrease inefficiencies. Deregulation decreases production costs and so it leads to higher levels of output. In both cases there is faster economic growth. Labour market reforms are also part of market-based policies and aim to increase labour market flexibility (see section 3.7, page 132). As a result, labour costs decrease and firms' profitability, together with employment, increase. Higher profits may then increase investment and accelerate growth.

However, market-oriented supply-side policies can only be effective in the long term. They are not capable of dealing with short-term problems. Privatization often has led, at least in the short term, to increased unemployment. It can lead to monopoly pricing, which is something developing countries cannot afford. Deregulation may not always be successful, especially in cases where special interest groups have exerted political pressure to ensure that they enjoy preferential treatment.

Lastly, labour market related policies increase income inequality, which is particularly damaging for developing countries where income inequality is often already high.

In the case of developing countries the goal is to devise regulations that improve the functioning of markets. Environmental or health and safety regulations, which aim to promote social objectives when free markets fail to deliver, could be helpful in the process of economic development.

Recap

Market-based supply side policies

The market-based supply-side policies that aim to generate and accelerate economic growth are:

- trade liberalization
- privatization
- deregulation.

Disadvantages

Trade liberalization	Privatization	Deregulation
Developing countries lack skills, technology and are focused on the primary sector→ they will still export a narrow range of products → they have low export shares in world trade.	The results of privatization can be unemployment and monopoly pricing, which may hinder the development process.	This policy may not always be successful, especially in cases where special interest groups manage to get preferential treatment.

Interventionist policies

Interventionist policies that aim to reduce income inequality and make growth inclusive will encourage development. Poverty reduction depends not only on income growth but also on how income is distributed: poverty is reduced and development is achieved if there is growth accompanied by narrowing income inequality. Redistribution policies can help in that direction.

Redistribution policies

Redistribution policies include tax policies, transfer payments and minimum wages.

High and rising inequality is one major factor that prevents growth and development. Therefore, implementing policies to redistribute income can be of particular importance. To do this, governments can use progressive income taxes and transfer payments. By taxing individuals with higher incomes more heavily than those with lower incomes and spending more on transfer payments, national income may be redistributed. This will reduce inequality, allowing for more growth and development. In addition, the introduction of a minimum wage can support the incomes of low skilled workers and in turn further help in narrowing inequality.

Yet, many developing countries have ineffective taxation systems, which limits the amount of tax revenue that can be raised. In addition, governments usually run on very low budgets, which does not leave much room for government spending. These factors may therefore limit the effectiveness of the measures outlined above. It is also important to note that in the case of transfer payments there is risk that the beneficiaries become overly dependent on them, unless they are effectively designed as conditional cash transfers (see section 3.3). Regarding the introduction of a minimum wage, in some cases this has created unemployment. Still, if the minimum wage is not remarkably high then unemployment may not necessarily increase.

Perhaps a more promising but long-term route to a more equitable distribution of income is to improve the quality and access to education and health care. Schools, health-care centres, better sanitation and clean water supplies will all contribute to an increase in human capital, which will increase the income earning capacity of the poor leading to higher incomes, growth and development. Nevertheless, the government's lack of resources may still be an issue.

Provision of merit goods

The government can subsidize or directly provide services such as health care, education and infrastructure.

Health and education programmes

Health and education are vital drivers of growth and development. Better health and education increase labour productivity. Since higher productivity is the key to long-term growth, it can also lead to development. In addition, improved health and education allow individuals to have more, better and higher paid employment opportunities, improving living standards.

There are also external benefits to health or education. A healthy person is not only less contagious but can also benefit the community through more active and productive participation. Moreover, educated people provide benefits to people around them, as they contribute more to the generation of new ideas that benefit the community.

Something that adds further to the importance of health and education is that they are interdependent. Greater health improves education because health is a critical factor in school attendance. Also, healthier individuals are more able to use education productively at any point in life. At the same time, better and more education improves health, because basic skills such as personal hygiene and sanitation are often learned at school. In addition, education is needed for the formation and training of health personnel. There is also considerable evidence that the better the education of the mother, the better the health of her children.

The points made above show that provision of health and education can be of substantial importance in growth and development. Note that it is imperative that governments seek to make health and education services accessible as early in life as possible. This relates to the idea that a person's capabilities, health and productivity at any stage of life depend on the choices made at earlier stages. For example, the mother's health in pregnancy, a healthy childbirth, an infant's good health and proper nutrition for a child are vital for a productive and prosperous life as an adult. Similarly, in the case of education—given that a child's cognitive development begins at an early age—the formal education process should begin even before the start of primary school.

Infrastructure

Infrastructure includes energy, transport, telecommunications, clean water and sanitation.

Infrastructure increases productivity and lowers the costs of production. For instance, transportation systems allow more output to be transported and production costs to be lowered, irrigation contributes to higher levels of agricultural output while reliable energy systems allow for increased worker productivity through the introduction of simple electrically powered machines and equipment. At the same time, access to clean water and sanitation have major effects on the health of a population, preventing illnesses and premature deaths. Therefore, the provision of infrastructure is also crucial for growth and development.

Still, it should be noted that health and education as well as infrastructure are largely dependent on the government, which can be an issue when the government lacks funds that would allow for subsidies or direct provision. For instance, many governments in developing countries have their investment plans at the ready; they plan for improvements in health and education, building of roads, ports, and power grids, access of the poor to safe water and sanitation—but they lack the financial resources to carry out those plans. In addition, poor governance and prevalent corruption may impede investments in human capital and infrastructure.

Recap
Provision of merit goods

Health care and education	Infrastructure
• Increased labour productivity → economic growth → development	• Lower costs of production → higher productivity → economic growth → economic development
• Better and higher-paid employment → improved living standards	• Access to clean water and sanitation prevents diseases → reducing public health risks.
• External benefits	
• Interdependence: greater health improves education while greater education improves health.	

Problems	
• Developing countries' governments may be deprived of the funds necessary to subsidize or directly provide health care, education and infrastructure	
• Poor governance and corruption may also prohibit public expenditure on these merit goods.	

Inward foreign direct investment (FDI)

Multinational corporations (MNCs) such as Apple, Tata Group, Kia Motors, HSBC, Siemens and Unilever are able to establish their presence in more than one country through foreign direct investment (FDI). FDI refers to long-term investment by firms from one country in productive facilities in another country. This includes investing in new facilities and acquiring a controlling percentage of the shares of existing local companies.

Inward FDI would mean attracting more MNCs in developing countries. MNCs have good reasons to be willing to expand their operations in developing nations. They gain access to more markets and so they can expand their sales. They can lower costs of production, as labour costs are usually lower in developing countries. If they are involved in extractive activities, MNCs can benefit from the rich natural endowments of oil, bauxite, copper or other metals and minerals that can be found in developing countries.

In order to attract FDI certain conditions must exist or be created within the developing country. Some of the "pull factors" for FDI are:

• economic and political stability
• large and growing markets
• public policy with favourable tax treatment and ease of profit repatriation
• low labour costs
• high levels of human capital and labour productivity
• infrastructure such as roads and ports or telecommunications
• membership in free trade areas or trading blocs to avoid tariffs
• clearly defined property rights and a functioning legal system.

How does FDI help growth and development?

FDI can increase employment opportunities in the developing country as MNCs may hire local workers in their production facilities. At the same time, the local workforce may receive training, which leads to skill creation and so it improves human capital. Moreover, FDI can bring along organizational and managerial know-how, as well as new production technologies, which can all be learned and adopted by the local workforce and local businesses. This contributes to further improvements in human capital and also to technological improvements. FDI inflows are a source of foreign exchange, which may be used to finance much needed imports and a trade deficit. If the government of the developing country taxes MNCs then tax revenues will increase. This provides the government with funds to spend in other areas that will assist growth and the development process. Lastly, the inflows of FDI funds into the developing country can increase savings, increasing the amount of investment.

Therefore, FDI can help improve technology and human capital, add to tax revenues and increase the level of investment. All of this leads to higher economic growth and to increased possibilities for pursuing development objectives.

However, this is only the positive side of FDI. The skills of the local workforce may not improve if workers are used to fill only the positions of low skill and no training is provided. The technology brought may be capital intensive and thereby inappropriate, not creating employment positions. MNCs may hurt local firms by eliminating competition and by importing intermediate products instead of buying them from domestic suppliers.

The tax contribution of multinational corporations may be considerably less than it should be as a result of favourable tax allowances. Also, MNCs may use their economic power to influence government policies in directions unfavourable to the development process, such as the weakening of labour protection laws or environmental protection laws.

Lastly, in many cases the operation of MNCs has caused environmental damages in the developing country. This is both against development and against sustainability.

These facts suggest that although growth may come about through FDI the development prospects of the country may not necessarily improve.

Recap

Inward FDI

Advantages include:

- increased employment opportunities
- training of the local workforce, leading to improved human capital
- transfer of organizational and managerial know-how and new production technologies
- providing a source of foreign exchange
- higher tax revenues that can be used to fund spending in other areas
- higher savings, leading to more investment.

Disadvantages include:

- lack of training if the local workforce is employed only in low skill positions
- capital-intensive technology that does not create employment
- elimination of competition
- tax contribution that is not significant
- forced relaxation of labour and environmental protection laws
- environmental damage.

Foreign aid

Foreign aid refers to the transfer of funds in the form of loans or grants, or to the transfer of goods and services in the form of gifts to developing countries. Aid is non-commercial, as the transfers do not involve buying and selling transactions. Note that in order for loans to be considered part of foreign aid, they must be offered in concessionary terms (that is, at lower than market interest rates and with longer repayment periods).

- When aid comes from the governments of donor countries it is referred to as Official Development Assistance (ODA) and can be bilateral or multilateral.

  - Bilateral aid involves one donor country; aid flows from one advanced economy to the developing country.

  - Multilateral aid involves an international organization such as the United Nations (UN), the World Bank or the IMF; aid flows through the organization to the developing nation.

- Aid may also come from non-governmental organizations (NGOs). NGOs are organizations pursuing objectives for the public interest. Their aim is to prove services to the public, directly or indirectly (see below).

Aid is usually distinguished into humanitarian aid and development aid offered through ODA and NGOs.

- Humanitarian aid aims to save lives and ensure access to basic necessities such as food, water, shelter and health care. For instance, humanitarian aid may be provided in emergency situations resulting either from violent conflicts or from natural disasters such as floods, earthquakes and tsunamis.

- Development aid aims to help developing countries achieve their growth and development objectives and can take the form of:

  - project aid, where the funds must be used to finance the construction of a particular project (such as a dam, a road or a hospital)

  - programme aid, where the funds are used to support sectors of the economy, such as health care or education

  - tied aid, where the funds must be used to buy imports from the donor country.

Why do donors give aid?

There are three main motives for providing aid to developing countries.

- Humanitarian motives are the moral or ethical reasons for providing aid. For instance, given that the consequences of the Covid-19 pandemic are particularly severe in countries in where the health-care system is comparatively weak, Germany made available 450 million euro in aid for humanitarian projects to fight Covid-19.

- Political motives or strategic reasons may exist, in that aid has been used in an effort to build closer political and strategic relations with other countries. Donor countries have also used aid programmes as a bargaining tool for international negotiations.

- Economic motives, such as to develop markets and dispose of surpluses, may exist. Aid has often been directed to promote a country's exports of manufactured goods and imports of raw materials. China's post-2000 astonishing growth of aid in Sub-Saharan Africa and elsewhere is considered to be driven by such a motive.

Why do recipient countries accept aid?

The major reason why developing nations have usually been eager to accept aid is typically economic. Developing countries have often tended to accept the proposition that aid is a crucial and essential ingredient in the development process. It supplements scarce domestic resources, it helps transform the economy structurally, and it contributes to economic growth. The economic rationale for aid is therefore partly based on accepting the donor's perceptions of what poor countries require to promote economic development.

Evaluating the impact of foreign aid

The issue of the effects of foreign aid is a highly debated topic. On one side are those who argue that aid is necessary and has indeed promoted growth and development in many developing countries. Jeffrey Sachs, in particular, argues that massive infusions of aid are needed to break the poverty cycle and considers aid a powerful determinant of long-term growth. Poor countries are poor because they are hot, infertile, infested with malaria and many are landlocked, making it hard to increase productivity without help to deal with such endemic problems. Neither free markets nor democracy, in Sachs' opinion, will do very much for them.

On the other side are critics who argue that aid does not promote faster growth but may, in fact, retard it. They say that aid substitutes for, rather than supplements, domestic savings and investment and worsens the balance of payments deficits as a result of rising debt repayment obligations (when aid takes the form of loans, even if at reduced interest rates). William Easterly, for example, argues that aid does more harm than good. It is often wasted instead of being spent productively. It may prevent people from devising their own solutions to the specific problems they face. In addition, critics believe that aid often corrupts or is granted to corrupt autocrats and undermines local institutions. It is typically fragmented among too many donor countries and is thinly spread over too many sectors with a lot of overlapping and confusion.

Some aid programmes help more than others. It is not easy to determine which ones are effective in promoting development goals and which ones are ineffective. Recently, Esther Duflo, Abhijit Banerjee of MIT and Michael Kremer of Harvard University introduced randomized control trials (RCT) to help determine whether a particular form of aid is or is not effective, just as pharmaceutical corporations try to determine the effectiveness of a new drug or vaccine. These three economists shared the 2019 Nobel Prize for Economics. According to the Nobel Prize committee, RCTs, by carefully designing such experiments, help to obtain reliable answers about the best ways to fight poverty.

Positive effects

- Aid is linked with higher growth rates.
- Aid can help developing countries escape the poverty trap.
- Aid is effective when it is narrowly targeted to specific pro-development projects and objectives, such as the prevention and elimination of certain diseases.
- Aid is effective when it is reinforced by appropriate domestic policies and institutions in a non-corrupt government environment.
- Aid is effective when it is not tied to buying products from donor countries.

Negative effects

- Aid can lead to dependency, as it creates the need for more and more aid.
- Aid may be abruptly terminated if a donor's budget proprieties change.
- Aid can be ineffective when it is given to countries with corrupt governments.
- Aid can be ineffective when it induces countries to postpone improvements of macroeconomic conditions.
- Aid can be ineffective when the technologies transferred and the advice given are inappropriate.

The role of NGOs

One of the fastest-growing and most significant forces in the field of aid is that provided through NGOs. They represent specific local and international interest groups with concerns as diverse as providing emergency relief, protecting child health, promoting women's rights, alleviating poverty, protecting the environment, increasing food production and providing rural credit to small farmers and local businesses. Some familiar NGOs include Oxfam, Doctors Without Borders, the World Wildlife Fund, Project HOPE and Amnesty International.

NGOs have two important advantages. First, they face fewer political constraints and most NGOs are able to work much more effectively at the local level with the people they are trying to assist than massive bilateral and multilateral aid programmes can. Second, by working directly with local people, many NGOs are better able to avoid the suspicion and cynicism on the part of the mostly poor people they serve that their help is insincere or likely to be short-lived. It is estimated that NGOs in developing countries are positively affecting the lives of some 250 million people.

Debt relief

High indebtedness is another setback for developing nations. Remember that high debt levels require large debt repayments that do not allow enough funds for spending in other areas. Debt relief involves cancelling a portion of debts. This means that the amount that must be repaid is reduced, which releases some funds that can finance growth and development strategies.

This is why the Heavily Indebted Poor Countries Initiative (HIPCI) and Multilateral Debt Relief Initiative (MDRI) were designed and launched. The goal of the HIPCI was to ensure deep, broad and fast debt relief and through this to contribute towards growth, poverty reduction and debt sustainability in the poorest, most heavily indebted countries. The goal of the MDRI was to provide additional support to HIPCs. To date, 37 countries—31 of them in Africa—have debt relief for which they were eligible through the HIPCI and the MDRI.

Multilateral development assistance

Multilateral assistance involves an international organization. The most well-known organizations of such assistance are the World Bank and the IMF.

The World Bank is a development assistance organization that extends long-term loans to developing countries for the purpose of promoting economic development and structural change.

The IMF is a multilateral financial institution that oversees the global financial system, stabilizes exchange rates and helps countries in financial crises by extending loans. Lately, IMF lending has become almost exclusively focused on the developing world.

Both the World Bank and the IMF assist developing countries through the loans they extend. The loans offered are conditional and require agreeing to adopt particular policies (known as structural adjustment policies). Such policies usually involve deficit reduction, privatization, deregulation, improved tax collection and labour market reforms.

However, such loans deprive the borrowing country of control over its domestic affairs and may have long-term negative effects on economic development. For instance, in some cases, IMF and World Bank officials have asked impoverished nations to cut budgets, and even to privatize health services as part of the conditions for lending. Yet, such measures may prevent human or physical capital improvements and therefore act against development objectives.

Social enterprise

Social enterprise refers to for-profit businesses engaged in socially beneficial activities. Social enterprise is a groundbreaking response to the funding problems that many non-profit organizations are facing. Developing countries can greatly benefit from social enterprise, as it can provide aspects of aid that are not addressed through conventional routes. This can be achieved through innovation. For example, Phandeeyar is an innovation laboratory that is pioneering the use of technology to accelerate change and development in Myanmar. Phandeeyar invests in local start-ups, trains new entrepreneurs and builds the pool of tech talent. Another example is the Buffalo Bicycle Company; it builds bicycles specifically for the southern African terrain in order to assist local people with the transport challenges they are facing. The progress made by these types of enterprise has increased recognition that social entrepreneurship can benefit the developing world.

Institutional change

Improved access to banking

The importance of access to banking lies in the simple fact that, typically, if you cannot borrow you cannot make any investment in physical, natural or human capital. It follows that a functional banking system is vital in breaking the poverty cycle. Yet, the banking system in many developing countries does not accommodate poor and small-scale producers, farmers and traders (see page 195).

Microfinance

Microfinance has been heralded as a solution to the banking problems many individuals in developing countries face.

Microfinance focuses on making available very small loans to the very poor, helping them to start a small business, expand an existing one, or meet an emergency arising from disease or bad weather. The scheme was initiated by Muhammad Yunus, who created the Grameen Bank several decades ago. Microfinance can help developing nations as it can have a positive impact on poverty reduction and it can allow for improvements in health, nutrition and primary school attendance. Many microfinance institutions lend almost exclusively to women, which has helped women in their empowerment; (see below for other aspects of women's empowerment). Women's participation in microfinance programmes gives them greater bargaining power and enables them to take part in family decision-making. However, microfinance has recently come under attack, as most borrowers do not appear to be climbing out of poverty while some are getting trapped in a spiral of debt, according to studies and analysts.

Mobile banking

Access to banking has also increased in developing countries due to mobile banking. Mobile banking is a useful tool in countries where there are few banks but where most of the people have a mobile phone. In Latin America, for example, only 35% of people have bank accounts but 90% have mobile phones. Mobile banking is simple and low cost. All that is needed is a mobile phone and a banking SIM card, no smartphone or special app is required. Money can be sent and received by text message. In this way, more people get access to formal financial services, allowing for financial inclusion. According to Jay Rosengard, adjunct lecturer in Public Policy at the Harvard Kennedy School, financial inclusion improves the livelihood of individual families and encourages local and national economic growth. In fact, Rosengard's research in Kenya showed that thanks to mobile banking, the share of Kenyans with access to a financial account jumped from 42% in 2011 to 75% in 2014. This mobile banking revolution has also created greater financial stability for Kenyan families, as they were able to handle major reductions in their income—such as a bad harvest, a job loss or a failing business—without a devastating effect on their living standards.

Increasing women's empowerment

Reducing gender inequality can significantly improve development. Not only do deprived girls and women benefit, but also the growth and development process accelerates.

The most important way to empower women is through educating girls. An educated mother will enjoy higher earning ability outside the home for each extra year of schooling. She will have fewer children, increasing the income available per child, which can result in even higher long-term productivity and output gains. Her children will be healthier and she will make sure that they are also educated, creating a virtuous circle. Educating women decreases mortality in children, decreasing the costs of health-care intervention. Lastly, better and more educated women can lead to higher women's participation in the labour force as well as in politics, allowing them to influence policy. Educating girls is considered by many as the most influential investment for accelerating the development process. Over the years, at the primary education level, the enrollment gap between boys and girls has nearly closed and in some parts of the world girls' enrollments rates have overtaken those of boys at the secondary and tertiary levels.

To close the remaining gender gap, legal reform should be deployed. For example, given that in some countries gender barriers are legal, reform can allow women to receive public services, to own and run businesses and to inherit property. This will reduce gender disparities, as women will gain a more active role in their communities.

As for female representation in politics, some societies now require a certain proportion of a party's representation list to be occupied by women. When women enter parliament and government there can be a very powerful effect on changing ideas, norms and policies. Government financial support for maternity leave and childcare can also play a large facilitating role to help women in the labour force.

Lastly, given that a large number of women around the world face violence better law enforcement, laws, and public leadership are absolutely necessary.

Reducing corruption

Indicators of corruption regularly show that the incidence of corruption is far higher in developing countries than in developed countries. Improvements in governance, in general, and reduction of corruption, in particular, could be means to accelerate the process of development.

To tackle corruption, countries can:

- eliminate inefficient regulations
- make public expenditures more transparent
- promote competition in order to avoid too much power concentrated in large monopolies
- improve pay and incentives for public servants

- reduce immunity from prosecution of executive and legislative figures
- provide judicial independence.

Still, with many forms of corruption and many differences across nations and communities, there is no single best way to fight corruption.

Property rights and land rights

As people without property rights cannot use their resources to create wealth, their assets become "dead capital". If property titles are provided, the capital will no longer be "dead". The poor will be able to use their small assets in order to borrow money and start businesses, unlocking the entrepreneurial potential of billions of people. This will enable them to generate income, reducing inequality while allowing for growth and development. According to research estimates, providing the world's poor with property titles would unlock $9.3 trillion in assets, a substantial amount for poverty reduction.

In addition, strengthening the legal framework for customary land-rights holders is also crucial for the development process. Strong, properly enforced land rights allow for the legal recognition and protection of their holders and can in turn boost growth, reduce poverty and strengthen human capital. For instance, World Bank Group efforts have enabled one million hectares of indigenous land in Nicaragua—over 30% of the country's territory—to be demarcated, titled and registered, a process that has benefited some of the country's most vulnerable groups.

Nevertheless, land titling may not always work as expected. Once land rights are issued then the rich may capture them as they can pay more to acquire them. Also, the poor may end up losing their land because they may not be able to repay a loan or may be forced to sell it if they experience a crop failure or a poor harvest.

Recap

Institutional change	
Improved access to banking	Access to banking allows for borrowing which allows for investment in physical, natural or human capital. This can be achieved through microfinance or mobile banking.
Increasing women's empowerment	Empowering women can accelerate the development process. This can be achieved through educating girls and through legal reforms to ensure more active participation of women in various domains including business and politics.
Reducing corruption	Tackling corruption allows for greater economic growth and development, which can be achieved by increasing transparency and improving regulations.
Property rights	Secure property rights will ensure that the poor will be able to generate income, which will reduce inequality while allowing for growth and development.
Land rights	Strong, properly enforced land rights can boost growth, reduce poverty, strengthen human capital and so promote economic development. However, land titling does have flaws and may result in the poor ending up without land rights.

Government intervention versus market-oriented approaches

One of the biggest debates in the area of economic growth and development is whether developing countries should adopt a more interventionist rather than market-based approach or vice versa.

Adopting a market-based approach is based on the idea that market powers always lead to the best possible outcome. Indeed, free markets can lead to allocative efficiency as the market mechanism typically directs resources in their best possible use. The market also provides the necessary incentives, such as higher incomes and profit, that encourage economic activity and generate growth. Still, the role of government in economic development is absolutely crucial.

The government is vital for financing the building of infrastructure and is also essential for human capital formation, which are both necessary for any economy to develop. If health care and education are left to the market they are underprovided—remember they are merit goods. Public financing is therefore essential to ensure that the country has the necessary infrastructure to function effectively and that the poor have access to merit goods.

However, good governance is not common in many developing countries. As a result, the available infrastructure, as well as the educational and health-care services offered, are often inadequate or poor. Yet, when it comes to reducing poverty a market approach is highly problematic. Markets are basically designed to "ignore" the poor, as their incomes are low, so they cannot "vote with their dollars". The government is therefore needed to ensure economic opportunity for all. The government is also needed to regulate key sectors of the economy. The banking sector is one of them. Unregulated banking systems tend to experience crises.

Nevertheless, corrupt governments may encourage or allow illegality, which neither helps in regulating markets nor in creating equal opportunities. Overall, national governments have played an important role in the successful development experiences of the countries in East Asia. In other parts of the world, however, the government often appears to have been more of an obstacle.

A market approach is preferable when there is government failure while good governance is needed when there is market failure. That is to say, that the roles of the market and the government are complementary.

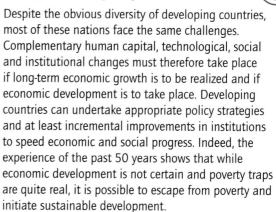

Policymakers' perspective

Despite the obvious diversity of developing countries, most of these nations face the same challenges. Complementary human capital, technological, social and institutional changes must therefore take place if long-term economic growth is to be realized and if economic development is to take place. Developing countries can undertake appropriate policy strategies and at least incremental improvements in institutions to speed economic and social progress. Indeed, the experience of the past 50 years shows that while economic development is not certain and poverty traps are quite real, it is possible to escape from poverty and initiate sustainable development.